Multicultural Perspectives in Music Education

Multicultural Perspectives in Music Education

Edited by
William M. Anderson and Patricia Shehan Campbell

MENC
MENC
MENC
MUSIC EDUCATORS NATIONAL CONFERENCE

This book is dedicated to the memory of Selwyn Ahyoung.

Cover: *Second photograph from top*, by Christopher Waterman,
University of Washington, Seattle;
other photographs, courtesy of Kent State University, Kent, Ohio.

CONTENTS

CONTRIBUTORS

William M. Anderson, editor, is a professor of music education, director of the Center for the Study of World Musics, and associate dean of the Graduate College at Kent State University. He is author or coauthor of three books and has been a consultant for three series of school music books. He is currently chairman of the editorial committee for the *Music Educators Journal*.

Patricia Shehan Campbell, editor, is an associate professor of music at the University of Washington. She has conducted clinics on multicultural music education, music and movement, and early childhood and elementary general music techniques. Campbell's research on music learning and preference has appeared in several books and in numerous scholarly journals.

Selwyn E. Ahyoung was a native of Trinidad who, at the time of his death in 1988, was completing his doctoral degree in music education/ethnomusicology at The Florida State University. Ahyoung had received many honors, was very active in the Society for Ethnomusicology, was the first teacher of F.S.U.'s Steel Band, and was a promising young scholar.

Han Kuo-Huang is a professor of music in the School of Music, Northern Illinois University. He teaches courses on the music of China and the music of Southeast Asia, a survey of world music, research in ethnomusicology, and the playing of Indonesian *gamelan* and Chinese instruments. His publications have appeared in many music journals, and he gives numerous lectures, demonstrations, and workshops.

Barbara Reeder Lundquist is a professor of music education and systematic musicology and chair of the music education division at the University of Washington. She has served as a public-school teacher and music supervisor and as a consultant and examiner in curriculum development and music education. She has presented clinics on multicultural music education and has published articles in many scholarly journals.

Ellen McCullough-Brabson teaches music education at the University of New Mexico as an associate professor of music. She has presented numerous multicultural music workshops, and has published articles on topics including Appalachian music and the dulcimer. McCullough-Brabson plays the viola with the New Mexico Symphony Orchestra.

Dale A. Olsen received his Ph.D. in ethnomusicology from the University of California at Los Angeles, and is currently a professor of ethnomusicology at The Florida State University in Tallahassee. He has conducted research in South America, and was a Fulbright scholar in Peru. He performs on numerous musical instruments from the Andes and has produced many publications about Latin American music.

George Sawa studied Middle Eastern zither and music theory at the Higher Institute for Arabic Music in Alexandria, Egypt. He completed his doctorate on the performance practice of medieval Arabic music at the University of Toronto, and has concertized and lectured widely. Sawa currently teaches and researches contemporary and medieval Arabic music.

James A. Standifer is a researcher, lecturer, and consultant on multicultural music education, curriculum, and urban school music education. Standifer has published articles in scholarly journals, has coauthored several books, and has served as an adviser to educational television. He teaches at the University of Michigan, where he is a professor in the School of Music and director of the Oral History archive of the African-American music collections.

Ricardo D. Trimillos is professor in ethnomusicology at the University of Hawaii. He has developed curricular materials for world music and for music theory. His research focuses on traditional learning, transculturation, ethnic identity, and the geocultural areas of Japan, insular Southeast Asia, and Hawaii. A consultant on arts and public policy, he performs music for *koto, gagaku*, and *kabuki*.

PREFACE

The content of music programs in American schools has historically been associated with the art and traditional musics of western Europe. Despite the presence of native American Indians long before (as well as during) the formative years of the republic, the arrival of Africans beginning in the eighteenth century, and the waves of immigrants from Asia, Latin America, and Europe that have come to this country since the 1840s, the K-12 music curriculum has seldom reflected the ethnic diversity of American society. Rather, the schools have been a bastion for teaching European choral and instrumental music, and students of every color and creed have always been (and remain) more likely to learn music that is Germanic rather than Japanese, French rather than Filipino, and Irish rather than either native American or Asian Indian.

Our colonial heritage was linked to Western civilization by the nature of those Europeans who first settled the eastern seaboard, and our pervading sociopolitical system is an extension of Anglo-Saxon and Germanic traditions, but American society has emerged as a unique blend of cultures from every part of the world. To believe that we can blindly continue to maintain a narrow focus on the customs and values of a single culture in the social sciences and the arts is to ignore the realities of our multicultural society. Moreover, in this international age, we must seek to understand the perspectives of people from every part of the globe. Cultures and countries are increasingly interdependent in economic and political matters. Our survival as a world community may depend on our ability to understand the similarities that bind and the differences that distinguish us as subsets of the human species.

The Music Educators National Conference maintains the slogan "Music for *every* child—every child *for* music" as the core of its professional philosophy Embedded in this slogan is the knowledge that school music must be more broadly defined to encompass the ethnic diversity of American schools and society. Beginning with Karl W. Gherkens's recommendation in 1924 that music instruction be available to all children, a gradual awakening of interest in music of other cultures has been evident: At that time, music educators began to make isolated attempts to feature a variety of the world's musics in school programs and textbooks.

The Tanglewood Symposium paid tribute to the importance of musics of various ethnic and racial groups, triggering the first substantial movement of music educators in the direction of multicultural music education. By the 1970s,

MENC established a Minority Concerns Commission, followed by a Multicultural Awareness Commission, with the intention of raising the level of consciousness and promoting the use of traditional musics of many cultures in the curriculum. In the past two decades, the growing interest among music educators in world musics was evident in workshops at national conferences and in special issues of the *Music Educators Journal* (such as those of October 1972, and May 1983).

The Society for Ethnomusicology began to develop ways to infuse world musics into collegiate, secondary, and elementary school programs. Beginning with philosophical statements that provided a rationale for world musics, the Society established an Education Committee to review appropriate curricular materials and to provide workshops for educators at their national conferences. These efforts lessened the gap between research in the field and the dissemination of world musics to the general public.

Teaching resources, however, were not developed fast enough for those who were philosophically convinced of the merits of multicultural teaching in music. Teachers were largely left to their own imaginative devices, to their own extended efforts to design lessons from Folkways recordings, and to summers spent reading scholarly writings on the music traditions of unfamiliar cultures. The commitment to providing students with global perspectives in music involved a considerable time expenditure for those few teachers who translated, interpreted, and finally applied the results of independent research to their classrooms.

The principal aim of this book is to provide a pragmatic approach to the integration of world music traditions in general music classes, particularly at the upper elementary, middle school, and high school levels. By the time they reach the intermediate grades, students have developed an understanding of fundamental music concepts. They also possess a knowledge of people and places beyond their family and immediate community through their study of geography, history, and foreign languages. These students have the intellectual capability and sufficient aural and performance experiences to attain greater musical and multicultural understanding by means of the lessons in this book.

Teachers can use *Multicultural Perspectives in Music Education* at the upper elementary and secondary levels, and suitable adaptations of the lessons can be made at the collegiate level. Many occasions are appropriate for providing information on the world's musics through listening and performance experiences, including general studies courses designed for the nonmajor, music literature and history classes, and music education methods courses. Regardless of the grade level, the incorporation of world musics in general music classes will serve a dual purpose: to reinforce the knowledge of music elements through their use and interpretation in various musical styles, and to develop a greater understanding of people in other cultures.

The contributions of music educators and ethnomusicologists come together in this volume, ensuring that music examples are both representative and realistic for use in teaching in the general music classroom. We would like to thank the principal contributors for their work, MENC Director of Communications Mary Ann Cameron and the publications committee who supported this project from its inception, and the MENC editorial staff, especially Jenifer Wood and Michael Blakeslee, for their helpful comments.

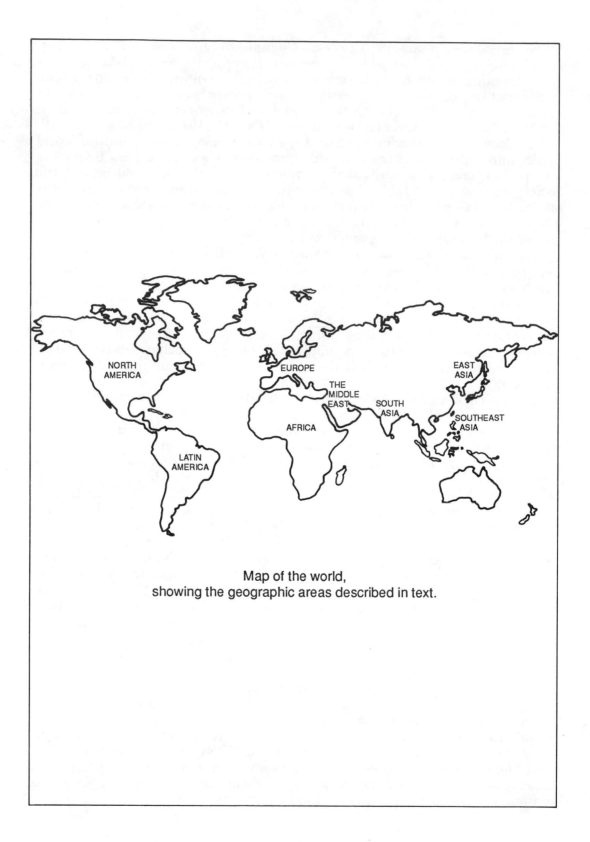

Map of the world,
showing the geographic areas described in text.

1

TEACHING MUSIC FROM A MULTICULTURAL PERSPECTIVE

by William M. Anderson and Patricia Shehan Campbell

A multicultural approach to learning centers around organizing educational experiences for students that encourage and develop understanding and sensitivity to peoples from a broad spectrum of ethnic backgrounds. If students are to learn from a multicultural perspective, teachers need to develop an educational philosophy that recognizes the inherent worth of endeavors by different cultural groups. Multicultural education develops the understanding that there are many different but equally valid forms of musical and artistic expression and encourages students to develop a broad perspective based on understanding, tolerance, and respect for a variety of opinions and approaches.

Multicultural music education reflects the ethnic diversity of the world—and of the United States in particular—through representative songs and instrumental selections, dances, and guided listening. Educators also should encourage interdisciplinary study of ethnic cultures through art, literature, drama, and social studies. Performances by choral and instrumental ensembles and dramatic

1

presentations, puppet plays, and folk dances are some of the experiences that enliven classroom study. The challenge in multicultural music education is to provide such avenues of exploration so students can gain a better understanding of the world and of their American heritage.

Rationale

A multicultural approach to music learning in American schools is important for many reasons. The United States has an extremely diverse population. People from more than one hundred world cultures now reside in the United States, and some ethnic groups now number in the tens of thousands or millions.

Major changes in the patterns of immigration to this country have occurred in the nearly four centuries since the founding of Jamestown in 1607, when native American Indian tribes were the only diverse cultural groups. The largest number of immigrants has come from European countries, first from north-western Europe and then from southeastern Europe. Substantial numbers of peoples from Africa also arrived during the eighteenth and nineteenth centuries. Today nearly 40 percent of legal immigrants come from Asia, and another 40 percent are from Mexico, Central and South America, and the Caribbean.[1]

The United States now has a population of approximately 240 million, which includes about 50 million blacks, Hispanics, and Asians. Many geographical areas throughout the country now have large ethnic populations, some of which have been increasing at dramatic rates in recent years. Cleveland identifies itself as a "city of nations," and this description is surely appropriate for metropolitan regions such as New York, Washington, D.C., Chicago, Miami, and Los Angeles. In the Los Angeles area alone there was an influx of more than 2 million immigrants during the 1970s. Demographers predict that by 2010, California will be the first state, with the exception of Hawaii, "to have a population whose majority is made up of minorities."[2]

At one time it was fashionable to speak of America's cultural diversity in terms of a "melting pot," with each ethnic group absorbed into some part of a national American community, but the acceptance of this myth is clearly waning. The civil rights movements of the 1950s and 1960s stimulated ethnic revitalization: Groups that had previously denied their cultures now proclaim their unique identities. Thus, today the United States is best described as a country composed of a mosaic of various ethnic communities that contribute to the national culture as they maintain distinct identities.

The dynamics of cultural diversity are reflected at all levels in American schools. Students come from many different ethnic groups. Some of America's major school systems, like those in Chicago, Los Angeles, and New York, now offer instruction in a dozen different languages. The superintendent of the Milwaukee Public Schools remarked that in a visit to one school, the pupils displayed a sign that said "welcome in 27 different languages, because those languages were represented at that one school."[3]

Ernest Boyer, president of the Carnegie Foundation for the Advancement of Teaching, stated that "what is coming toward the educational system is a group of children who will be . . . more ethnically and linguistically diverse" than ever before.[4] A 1984 American Broadcasting Company television documentary corroborated this view, stating that by the year 2000, one out of three schoolchildren in the United States will either be black or Hispanic and that in fifty-three major cities the majority of students will be nonwhite.[5]

Because of this multicultural diversity, curricula in all subject areas are being designed to encourage the broadest world perspectives. In some curricular areas administrators have attempted to design educational programs that help students understand the cultural diversity of their own country and of the world. The intent of these programs is to help students develop an international point of view that will prepare them to live in a global environment.

In music, a multicultural approach to education is clearly in keeping with perhaps the most significant trend of the past forty years: the growing understanding of music as a world phenomenon. The research of many distinguished ethnomusicologists and historical musicologists has shown that the world contains a number of highly sophisticated musical traditions that are based on different but equally logical principles. Many who have studied a variety of these musical traditions have begun to realize that the often-used concept of "music, the international language" has little validity in the present world. With highly sophisticated musical traditions based on different conceptual frameworks, one must learn the operative principles of any tradition in order to understand it.

In the past, as a result of emphasizing selected aspects of Western European and American classical and folk music, American teachers have often led students to believe there was only one major musical system in the world, the Euro-American system. By stressing the importance and perhaps "superiority" of that system, educators have taught by implication the relative unimportance, if not the actual inferiority, of other musical systems. Today's scholars have clearly demonstrated that educational institutions at all levels need to ensure that music curricula contain balanced programs that are representative of the world and also of the multicultural nature of the United States itself.

Many teachers are aware of the need to present a broad spectrum of music to their students. The Music Educators National Conference has given priority attention to the multicultural aspect of music education: Numerous sessions on various musical traditions have been presented at national, regional, and state conventions. Furthermore, a number of other national and international organizations, including the Society for Ethnomusicology and the International Society for Music Education, have strongly endorsed the study of world musics at all levels of instruction. To support the increased interest in a multicultural approach to music education, many book, record, and film companies (domestic and international) are now producing large quantities of materials on world musics. Several series of music textbooks for elementary and secondary schools also have enabled teachers to introduce study of world musics. Clearly, the concept of studying music from a multicultural perspective is becoming an integral part of music instruction at all educational levels.

Although many people have encouraged an investigation of world musics for intercultural and interracial understanding, multicultural music study can also provide a number of strictly musical contributions. First, students are introduced to a great variety of musical sounds from all over the world. Their palette of musical experiences is expanded as they come to realize the astounding variety of sonic events worldwide. An early exposure to a large array of musical sounds

3

is important in helping students become receptive to all types of musical expression.

Second, students begin to understand that many areas of the world have music as sophisticated as their own. Until recently, peoples of both non-Western and Western cultures thought that Western classical music was "superior" to other musics. Today composers, performers, and teachers are coming to realize that many equally sophisticated music cultures are found throughout the globe and that Western classical music is one of the many varied styles.

Third, students can discover many different but equally valid ways to construct music. For many students this may be one of the most important gains derived from a study of music in its multicultural manifestations. They discover that musics from other cultures often have principles that differ significantly from those principles contained in music of their own culture and that one should learn the distinctive, inherent logic of each type. What would be an unacceptable practice in Western music may be perfectly acceptable in music from another area of the world. Also, the terminology used to describe Western music often is not appropriate for describing another musical tradition, so more global-oriented nomenclature is needed.

Fourth, by studying a variety of world musics, students develop greater musical flexibility, termed by some as "polymusicality." They increase their ability to perform, listen intelligently, and appreciate many types of music. Research has shown that when students gain a positive attitude toward one "foreign" music and are able to perform and listen intelligently to that music, they become more flexible in their attitudes toward other unfamiliar musics. Through involvement with other musics, students develop a number of vocal and instrumental techniques. Their capacity for learning different musics grows, and they are able to study and perform new musics with increased understanding and ease. Furthermore, with this flexibility, they are much less prone to judge a new music (whether Western or non-Western) without first trying to understand it. In addition, by studying the function of such elements as melody, rhythm, texture, timbre, and form in producing various musics, students begin to reappraise Western music and often come to view it in a completely different manner. When students study a variety of musics, they become more aware of aspects of their own music that they have previously taken for granted.

Instructional approaches

Teaching music from a multicultural or global perspective can be done in a variety of ways. Music specialists, working in conjunction with classroom teachers, can develop curricula for the study of many of the world's musics. These curricula could contain performance, improvisation and composition, movement, and focused listening designed to enhance students' musical understanding. Such a design could also include related disciplines: literature and theater, the visual arts, social studies, geography, and history. Teachers should develop curricula in which the study of the musics of various peoples is placed in the broadest possible cultural context.

Upper elementary, middle school, and secondary school students are at a pivotal point in the development of skills, knowledge, and attitudes toward music. They possess the coordination and strength needed for performing

4

vocally or on instruments. They can think in abstract, critical, and analytical ways. They are often intrigued by the new and unfamiliar and may be fascinated by a comparison of "new" to "known" phenomena.

These students have the potential to examine musics and cultures beyond their immediate surroundings. They do not easily change their preference for their own music, but they may explore with enthusiasm various global musics when they become an active part of the learning process. Through guided performance and listening, students can eventually understand that music is not just an American or European phenomenon.

In addition, students can learn that many musical styles of the world are represented in the United States. This nation of immigrants provides ample opportunities for discovering the music, the arts, the cuisine, and various customs of the world. Students who have experience with a variety of what now constitute "American musics" may gain a new understanding of the cultural plurality of their own country. The study of this plurality has become an important curricular theme at both upper elementary and junior high or middle school levels nationwide.

Since global musical experiences can foster understanding among the peoples of the world and in the United States and since studying music of more than one culture helps students develop musical flexibility, students should experience many musical styles as part of their formal education. The following are some of the approaches for teaching these styles.

Music concepts. A curriculum based on multicultural musical experiences can focus on the study of the fundamental concepts of music: melody, rhythm, texture, timbre, dynamics, and form. Many teachers use these six concepts as a framework around which to organize a broad spectrum of musical experiences. Units developed around this framework help both teachers and students organize musical information into meaningful and lifelong learning experiences. Furthermore, an understanding of how each distinct musical tradition organizes events in terms of general concepts provides students with a structure for perceiving similarities and contrasts among various world music cultures. Such a conceptual framework also helps students develop a perception and understanding of their own multicultural musical environment in the United States.

As students study the fundamental concepts of melody, rhythm, texture, timbre, dynamics, and form, teachers may wish to post a "Multicultural Musical Concepts Chart" and have students fill in appropriate information as they study various musical selections from different cultures.

Such a framework is important in helping students understand how a distinctive treatment of a musical concept leads to a particular musical style. It also allows students to focus on similarities and contrasts among different musics. The perception of similarities is important in helping students understand the fundamental processes found in musics around the world, and the perception of contrasts helps demonstrate the many different ways of organizing musical sounds. Focusing on similarities and contrasts often provides students with an understanding of the musical phenomena in their own surroundings that they have previously taken for granted.

Performance. Multicultural music study can be approached through various

5

experiences in singing, playing instruments, moving to music, and guided listening. Whenever possible, attention should be directed toward an experiential approach to learning. Through performance, students become actively involved in discovering how musics of various cultures are constructed. The pedagogical principles of Europeans Emile Jaques-Dalcroze, Zoltan Kodály, and Carl Orff provide teachers with excellent models for designing multicultural musical experiences.

From the earliest years in elementary school, children can learn to sing songs that represent numerous cultures, perhaps starting with those most familiar in the United States. These songs should be taught as authentically as possible. Children can learn to sing many songs in the original languages. They enjoy learning to pronounce new words, and they may best identify with the culture and people by using a song's original language. Teachers should avoid using harmonic piano accompaniments when they do not resemble the practice of the original cultures.

In addition to singing, students can also learn to play authentic musical instruments from many music cultures. Native instruments from many areas of the world are now available in the United States and can be used effectively in schools. For example, schools can purchase African *mbira* ("thumb pianos"), *shekere* (rattles), and *gankogui* (iron bells) in this country, and these instruments can be effective in teaching students their African musical heritage.

In school systems that do not have access to authentic musical instruments from various cultures, teachers can frequently create instruments that simulate the sight and sounds of real instruments. By coordinating performance on handmade instruments with pictures (slides, filmstrips, films, or videotapes) of the original instruments, teachers can provide effective and valid presentations of different musical cultures.

In many areas of the United States people from other areas of the world perform their own native musics. This is particularly true in urban areas and in college and university communities, where there are distinguished performers from many diverse cultures. Such persons provide an important resource for teachers and schools, and many are willing to instruct and perform.

Along with singing and playing instruments, students can experience various musical traditions by moving to music. Movement activities should center around developing an understanding of basic concepts such as rhythm and form. Students should move to the beat, meter, and changes of tempo in music. They can also learn to "feel" the form in a work of music by devising movement activities to illustrate different sections. Students will gain exposure to different musics by learning the folk dances of these traditions. Because of the close relationship between motor activity and mental activity, movement is likely to facilitate and enhance conceptual learning. In music learning, the mind and body function together, and the sensory feedback from movement is connected to higher mental processes. Children create natural and spontaneous rhythms when they listen to music; these movements provide the impetus for expressive movement and patterned folk dance.

Guided listening. After experiencing the fundamental structural principles of other musics through active participation, students are ready to listen perceptively to recorded performances of world musics. Listening to examples of many

6

different musical cultures is an important element of any instructional program. A large number of recordings from most areas of the world are now available in the United States, and many excellent examples of world musics also appear on films and videotapes. In addition, a number of ethnic performing artists live in the United States, and others come to visit this country each year. Thus, teachers now can have actual performances in their classrooms. Such presentations are especially effective in helping children identify with the cultures from which the music is derived.

Integrated learning. Developing a cultural context is an important part of any multicultural music program. Although students can explore other musics without investigating the cultures themselves, the most effective approach coordinates a study of the people and their music. Students enjoy learning about different peoples from both their own and other countries by studying their customs, crafts, painting, sculpture, architecture, literature, dance, and music. Through an interrelated study of many aspects of a culture, students develop new and important understandings of other peoples, and they begin to realize the integral place of music and the arts in other cultures.

Concept and content

This book includes information and suggestions for teaching students their musical heritages. It is designed as a practical, experience-oriented guide for helping students develop a broad understanding of musics in their world and an appreciation of their multicultural musical heritage in the United States. It focuses on helping students discover some of the inherently different but equally valid ways in which various cultural groups organize musical events. Finally, the book is designed to help students learn and appreciate the exciting world of music.

NOTES
1. "Patterns in Our Social Fabric Are Changing," *Education Week* 5, no. 34, 14 May 1986, 16.
2. "Patterns in Our Social Fabric Are Changing," 16.
3. Quoted in "Patterns in Our Social Fabric Are Changing," 16.
4. Quoted in "Patterns in Our Social Fabric Are Changing," 16.
5. ABC News, "To Save Our Schools, To Save Our Children," 4 September 1984.

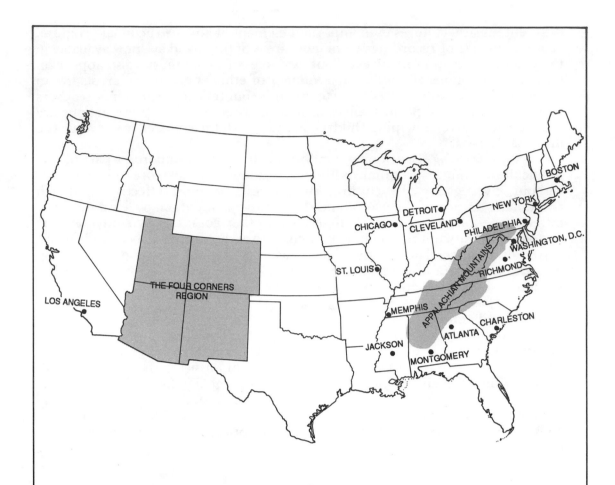

The continental United States, showing cities and areas
important to the musics of the Southern Appalachian Mountains,
the Native Americans of the Southwest, and African Americans.

CHAPTER TWO

2

NORTH AMERICA

by Ellen McCullough-Brabson, Patricia Shehan Campbell, and James Standifer

The United States and Canada stretch across the continent of North America, from the Atlantic to the Pacific oceans and from the Arctic Circle to Mexico and the Caribbean. The cities, states, and provinces of the continent are populated with a cross section of people that include Native Americans, early settlers from Western European countries, and later arrivals from every region of the world. American society has been compared to a mosaic of cultures that fit into the New World culture conglomerate while still retaining individual characteristics of their old world traditions.

Such a multicultural society is difficult to represent thoroughly, so the descriptions of North American music in this book will be confined to three cultures: Native Americans, Anglo-Americans, and African Americans. These cultures were selected partly because of their long history of settlement on the continent and also because these peoples typify three important cultures that are identified with the United States, and with Canada.

9

Europeans from non–English-speaking countries, Asians, and Latins have had their strongest impact on American society relatively recently (in the last century) and thus have not developed music traditions that are easily distinguishable from their old-world practices. Bulgarian-American music, for example, still sounds much as it would in the Rhodope mountains of that Balkan country, although immigrants from that country began arriving in America about 1900. The music of earlier Americans, which originated in northern Asia, the British Isles, and Africa, has developed on this continent over a longer time; generations of Americans have shaped a style uniquely expressive of their experiences together in a new land. African-American music exemplifies this uniqueness: It differs substantially from the music of West Africa.

Even these three North American subcultures are represented here by samples rather than through a comprehensive discussion of the diverse groups that exist within each subculture. The music practices of Native American groups such as the Seminoles of Florida, the Iroquois of New York and New England, the Sioux of the Dakotas, the Innuit of Alaska and the Canadian Northwest, and the Navajos of the Southwest are all linked by some similarities, but there are obvious differences as well. The functions assigned to music, the instruments, language, and treatment of musical elements varies from one group to the next. The focus on the Native Americans of the southwestern United States was chosen partly because they make up the majority of the population of that area and partly because many Native Americans in the Southwest retain their native life-styles both on and off the great reservations found in Arizona and New Mexico. The indigenous ceremonial music, mythology, and artistic expressions are therefore more likely to be preserved.

The selection of particular ethnic groups for inclusion in this chapter does not, therefore, present a complete picture of musical life on the continent, but rather offers a taste of three long-standing subcultures. The music of other North American subcultures can be partially understood by studying the practices of their mother countries in the other chapters of this book.

ANGLO-AMERICANS OF THE SOUTHERN APPALACHIANS

Have you ever heard of a dulcimer, a gee-haw-whimmydiddle, or a flipper-dinger? Have you churned butter, brewed sassafras tea, or listened to a "Jack" tale? These traditions (and many others) are indicative of the culture and the customs of the peoples of the Southern Appalachian Mountains.

The Southern Appalachian Mountains extend through parts of Virginia, West Virginia, North Carolina, South Carolina, Tennessee, Alabama, Georgia, and Kentucky. This extensive region is part of the oldest mountain range on the North American continent. This area, often called "the everlasting hills," is known for its beautiful terrain, bluegrass and country music, coal mining, and (in some sections) acute poverty.

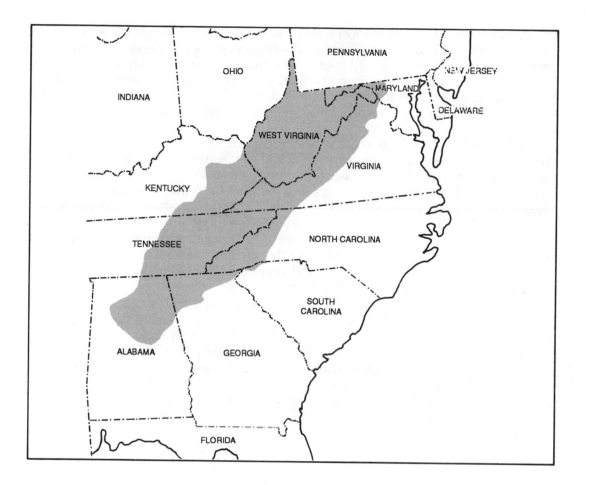

Appalachia is often thought of in terms of physical geography only; however, many people who live in this area have a strong sense of cultural identity and refer to themselves as *Appalǎchians*, pronouncing the word with a short "a" (as in add) rather than with the long "a" of the academically preferred pronunciation: *Appalāchian*. The difference may seem insignificant, but the residents of this area value their regional pronunciation as they try to define accurately and authentically their importance in the cultural makeup of the United States. Their ethnic composition is a mixture of Scotch-Irish, English, Welsh, German, French, African, American, and Cherokee, as well as other European nationalities. Regrettably, this rich culture is sometimes labeled with a negative stereotype, "hillbilly," propagated by the mass media.

In the history of the Southern Appalachian Mountains, music has been an integral part of its culture. In the early seventeenth century, immigrants from parts of the British Isles (England, Scotland, and Wales) began to arrive in America and settle in this area, bringing their music with them. Many of the

11

immigrants were illiterate laborers, servants, and farmers, however, so the music was not written down; it was passed orally from generation to generation. In the seclusion of the Southern Appalachian Mountains, the pioneers kept much of their music intact for many years. In fact, many of the people now living in the Southern Appalachians are direct descendents of the first English settlers and continue to pass on their musical heritage in the same manner as their ancestors did.

Cecil Sharp, an English scholar and musician, discovered this reservoir of Anglo-American music when he first visited the Southern Appalachian Mountains in 1916 in search of British folk songs. He found many songs from the British Isles that were still being sung by the mountain people, seemingly untouched by the passage of three centuries. Sharp was amazed at the isolation of the area. He wrote, "There are but few roads—most of them little better than mountain tracks—and practically no railroad. Indeed, so remote and shut off from outside influence were, until recently, these sequestered mountain valleys that the inhabitants have for a hundred years or more been completely isolated from all traffic with the rest of the world."[1]

Sharp, with his assistant Maud Karpeles, collected 1,612 songs in forty-eight weeks of travel through the rugged Appalachian terrain during the years 1916–1918. Sharp wrote down the melodies and Karpeles copied the texts, and in 1932 Sharp published a two-volume set, *English Folk Songs from the Southern Appalachians*, containing 968 of these tunes. Because the purely oral transmission of these songs had led inevitably to some changes in interpretation by individual performers or local communities, there were many variants in tunes and texts.

The modern world, through such industries as coal mining, has since intruded into Southern Appalachia. Nonetheless, the old songs continue to be sung and passed on. Traditional Southern Appalachian Mountain music is still being performed today and is a significant part of the cultural heritage of the United States. It has formed the basis for many contemporary styles of music, such as country and bluegrass. Like a patchwork quilt from the same region, Appalachian music blends a wide spectrum of color, texture, and personal expression. It is a vibrant component of the musical heritage of the United States, a musically valid and interesting art form, and it offers an intriguing study of human feeling expressed through sound. It provides a natural springboard for the examination of other American music.

The music and traditions of the Southern Appalachian Mountains are essential ingredients of the heritage of the United States and are, therefore, a meaningful part of a complete multicultural curriculum. Cecil Sharp supported this idea when he said, "remembering that the primary purpose of education is to place the children of the present generation in possession of the cultural achievements of the past so that they may enter as quickly as possible into their racial inheritance, what better form of music or of literature can we give them than the folk songs and folk ballads of the race to which they belong, or of the nation whose language they speak?"[2]

Form

Ballads, songs, and play-party games are frequently used forms for the traditional vocal music from the Southern Appalachian Mountains. There is much use of repetition in each of these song types. A ballad is a song that tells a story. Appalachian ballads are traditionally performed by a solo, unaccompanied voice, even in the rather common case of a text that contains dialogue. No matter what the theme of the ballad, it is delivered in a detached, objective manner. Cecil Sharp commented on this unique style of Appalachian ballad singing: "During the performance the eyes are closed, the head upraised, and a rigid countenance maintained until the song is finished. A short pause follows the conclusion, and then the singer relaxes his attitude and repeats in his ordinary voice the last line of the song, or its title."[3]

Ballads are traditionally performed at home for family and friends and sometimes at public events. The focus is on the song, not the singer, and the singers are never conscious of the audience. Although delivered in an objective manner, the singing of the ballads is a very personal experience. No two singers would ever sing the same song in exactly the same way. Sometimes the same tune is sung with different texts.

Ballads have been written about a wide variety of topics: romance, humor, tragedy, happiness, religion, the supernatural, heroes, and historical events. An example of a ballad that may have been based on a historical event is "Wraggle-Taggle Gypsies." This ballad tells the story of a woman who is enticed to leave her husband, riches, and home to run away with the gypsies. Her husband is outraged and searches for her. There are various endings to this story, but, in one instance, there is a battle where many are killed. This ballad may have been written about a real event that occurred in the seventeenth century, when a gypsy named Johnny Faa was killed in England when he defied many laws of the land.

An example of a humorous ballad is "The Farmer's Curst Wife." It is the story of a man who gives his wife to the devil. When she creates so many problems for the devil, however, he quickly gives her back to the farmer.

"Barbara Allen" is a ballad about love and tragedy. The heroine rejects a man who deeply loves her. He dies of a broken heart, and soon after, Barbara dies of sorrow. The ballad lyrics traditionally end by describing an image of a rose growing from the lover's grave and a thorn from Barbara's: The roses and thorns entwine as they reach upward.

The functions of the ballads varied. Because a large proportion of the population was illiterate, ballads were a source of entertainment. In addition, some ballads were used to illustrate and transmit the ideals of socially acceptable behavior: A person in a ballad who did not behave correctly was punished in some manner.

Francis James Child, an American scholar, grouped British ballads in a collection of 305 "genuine" songs (of popular origin) and gave each one a number. The texts (but not the music) of these ballads, collectively known as the "Child ballads," are contained in Child's five-volume work, *The English and Scottish Popular Ballads* (see Bibliography). Although the title for a ballad may vary in different localities, it can always be identified by a Child number.

There were also ballads native to America that covered a wide range of topics. According to one source, "These tales of murder and other crimes, true and false lovers, disasters, tragedies, and other adventures in the lives of sailors, lumberjacks, cowboys, solders, and even common citizens are the New World's contribution to oral-tradition balladry."[4] An example of a ballad based on an identifiable event is "Lily Schull," about the 1903 murder of a woman in Tennessee by her jealous boyfriend, Finley Preston.

In addition to the ballads, there are other styles of Anglo-American vocal literature. Cecil Sharp collected many types of music that contained only a fragment of a story or no story at all. He classified these as "songs" and described them as more emotional and passionate than a ballad. They portrayed a personal experience, rather than an objective narration of an event, and used texts shorter than those of ballads. Love is a popular theme of the songs, and the texts are often sung in the first person. Song melodies are built along more elaborate lines than are ballad tunes, and they are often sung as unaccompanied solos.

Another category of vocal music is the play-party game. Although these games may be thought of as children's songs, they actually provided recreational and social activities for young rural adults. Because dancing was once considered socially unacceptable, the euphemism "playing games" was frequently substituted for the word "dancing." Movements to the games, often very simple, were insignificant; the primary function of the dance was the selection of partners. Jealousy was not uncommon.

Melody

The melodies of the traditional ballads and songs from the Southern Appalachian Mountains are rich and varied. Some are complex, haunting, and beautiful; others are simple. Many are built on brief melodic fragments with ranges that may extend to an octave or more. Pentatonic and modal scales are frequently used, and melodies usually end on the tonic.

When Cecil Sharp studied the Anglo-American songs, he discovered much use of the pentatonic (five-note) scale. Sharp suggested that the use of this scale can be attributed to the influence and popularity of pentatonic melodies used in the northern parts of England and Scotland. All modal forms of the common pentatonic scale (which is formed by the black keys on the piano) are used in this music; that is, any one of the five notes of the scale may serve as the tonic. Examples of traditional Appalachian pentatonic songs are "What'll I Do with the Baby-O," "Skin and Bones," and "The Mocking Bird." (See Patricia Brown's *The Mountain Dulcimer*, listed in the Bibliography, for printed versions of these songs.) Another good example of a pentatonic tune is "Sourwood Mountain," reproduced in this chapter as figure 5.

Modal melodies are based on the diatonic modes. Each mode is known by a Greek name and is defined by its characteristic half- and whole-step patterns. The most prominent modes used in the traditional ballads and songs are Ionian (the "white note" scale starting on C), Dorian (that starting on D), Mixolydian (that starting on G), and Aeolian (that starting on A). The Ionian mode, also known as major, is the most frequently used mode in Anglo-American folk tunes. "Go, Tell Aunt Rhody," figure 1 in this chapter, is an example. "Skin and Bones" may be played in the Dorian mode as well as in Aeolian and Phrygian (see Patricia Brown's *The Mountain Dulcimer* for a printed version of this song). The Mixolydian mode is used for "Old Joe Clarke," and the Aeolian or minor mode is the basis for the "Wraggle-Taggle Gypsies" (see *Exploring Music* by Eunice Boardman, Beth Hardis, and Barbara Andress, listed in the Bibliogra-

14

phy, for this example). The Phrygian (E), Lydian (F), and Locrian (B) modes are rarely found in Appalachian music.

Appalachian music is usually based on a four-phrase melodic structure, although some irregular phrase lengths do occur. Melodies usually vary from one phrase to the next.

Rhythm

The rhythm of traditional Appalachian ballads and songs depends on the lyrics. Texts are usually balanced, four-line stanzas that rhyme at the ends of lines two and four, although this pattern may be altered by repeating the last line. Lines with four and three stressed syllables often alternate. Some refrain lines are composed of nonsense syllables.

Appalachian music commonly uses both duple and triple meters, but the meter may change frequently to accommodate the text or the singer. Sometimes the singer will sustain a note of the melody (usually a weaker accent), which sometimes disguises the rhythm. This breaks up the monotonous regularity of the phrase and creates the effect of improvisation.

Texture

Monophonic texture is usually used when performing traditional Appalachian music. Ballads and songs are commonly sung by a solo, unaccompanied voice; fiddle tunes are also played without accompaniment. A dulcimer is used occasionally to harmonize by providing a countermelody and drone or occasionally by producing a chordal accompaniment. Polyphonic and homophonic textures are more common in contemporary performances of Appalachian music. In these performances the dulcimer may play a countermelody instead of a harmonic accompaniment. The singer and the dulcimer accompaniment may exchange melody and countermelody. The song "Go, Tell Aunt Rhody" (figure 1) illustrates this type of accompaniment.

Appalachian music also can be homophonic, using chordal accompaniments on the guitar, banjo, dulcimer, or a combination of these instruments.

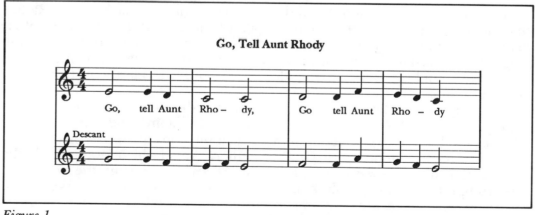

Figure 1.

Preserving the oral traditional of Southern Appalachian Mountain music is essential; thus, the expressive use of dynamics and interpretation of a selection are not written down but are left to the discretion of the individual performer. Because most traditional music is unaccompanied, the dynamic range is typically piano or mezzo forte. Instrumental music that accompanies dancing is louder.

Timbre

A discussion of Southern Appalachian Mountain music would be incomplete without the mention of some of the instruments that are commonly used. The mountain dulcimer, fiddle, banjo, and limberjack are colorful instruments that contribute richly to the musical whole.

The Appalachian or mountain dulcimer is one of the earliest American folk instruments still in use. Although the origin of the dulcimer remains a mystery, it was played in the Southern Appalachian Mountains as early as the eighteenth century. The word "dulcimer" is derived from the Latin *dulcis* (sweet) and *melos* (sound). Dulcimers can be constructed in a variety of forms, but the most familiar design is that of an elongated violin. It is a fretted instrument with either three or four strings. On a three-string dulcimer, the first treble string is used to play the melody and the second treble and bass strings are used to play drones. The frets are arranged to yield a diatonic scale, making it possible to play in all seven diatonic modes by emphasizing a different pitch center.

To play the dulcimer, the performer holds the instrument across his or her lap and plucks the strings with a quill or pick held in the right hand, while the left hand stops the strings to change the pitches. Sometimes a "noter" (a small dowel) is used to play the melody. The noter is used to slide from fret to fret without leaving the string, which produces a whistling sound. Occasionally, snake rattles are placed inside the body of the instrument to make the strings sing out more and to strengthen the sound.

When the settlers arrived in America from the British Isles, they brought the violin with them. It was a favorite instrument, used to accompany communal social dancing, and was commonly called the fiddle. Until the twentieth century, fiddle playing was usually unaccompanied. Most music for the fiddle was handed down through an oral tradition for at least two centuries; more recently, written transcriptions have become available. Many of the Appalachian fiddlers were musically illiterate, and they did not follow traditional playing style. Rather than holding the violin in the manner of a classical violinist, fiddle players often held the instrument against the chest and grasped the bow some distance up the frog. In some instances, steel strings were used on the fiddle to provide a more percussive sound, or rattlesnake rattles were also put inside the instrument to create the same effect.

Many tunes were played that an Appalachian audience would have associated with specific texts. "Old Joe Clarke," "Sourwood Mountain," and "Eliza Jane" are a few examples that can be found in many compilations of Appalachian music.

The banjo was commonly used in the Southern Appalachian Mountains in the nineteenth century. It was modeled after an African instrument, the *halam*, and was brought to America by black slaves. Since there were so few blacks living in this region, however, the banjo was probably introduced by traveling minstrel shows or by whites who learned it from blacks living on plantations. The common banjo has frets and five strings and is plucked with either the fingers or a pick.

The limberjack is a rhythm instrument native to the Southern Appalachian Mountains. It is usually constructed in the shape of a small man with a stick stuck into his back (see figure 7). When played, it is suspended over a board. The performer sits on one end of the board and hits the free end. As the board moves up and down, the limberjack goes "flying" in all directions. The motions of the limberjack imitate the movement and sounds of Appalachian clog dancing (basically a flat-footed walk with embellishments).

L E S S O N   O N E

1

■ OBJECTIVES:

Students will:
1. Listen to and sing "Mister Frog Went A-Courtin' " and accompany the song on a dulcimer.
2. Identify the characteristics of a ballad.
3. Listen to two recordings of "Mister Frog Went A-Courtin' " and describe similarities and differences in the performances.
4. Draw selected scenes from the ballad and create their own picture book for the song.
5. Locate the Southern Appalachian Mountains on a map of the United States.

Materials:
1. A picture book of "Mister Frog Went A-Courtin' " (You may want to make one, or you can use *Froggie Went A-Courting* by Chris Conover, listed in the Bibliography).
2. A map of the United States
3. Crayons
4. Paper
5. Dulcimer, if available. (If this is not available, sing the song as an unaccompanied melody.)
6. Recordings:
   Old Mother Hippletoe: Rural and Urban Children's Songs, New World Records 291 ("Mister Frog Went A-Courtin' ")

17

Brave Boys: New England Traditions in Folk Music, New World Records 239 ("A Frog He Would A-Wooing Go")
7. Film:
Frog Went A-Courtin' (see Filmography)

■ PROCEDURES:
1. Introduce a ballad as a song that tells a story. Explain why and how many ballads were preserved in the Southern Appalachian Mountains. Locate this area on a map of the United States.
2. Sing the song "Mister Frog Went A-Courtin' " for the students, without accompaniment (see figure 2). Ask them to join in on the "um-hm."
3. Tell the history of the song. "Mister Frog Went A-Courtin' " is an Anglo-American children's song that has existed for more than four hundred years. It was passed on from one generation to the next by oral tradition rather than by music notation. This accounts for the many variations of tune and text: in the case of this song, there are more than two hundred variants. In some accounts of the story, the mouse and the frog live happily ever after rather than being swallowed. The different endings probably reflect the society in which they were sung. When there were good times for the common people, the song had a happy ending. When the times were bad, however, the ending was sad. Another variation of the song suggests that Miss Mouse represented Queen Elizabeth I of England and that Mister Frog was le Duc d'Alençon, the French ambassador to the English court, who wanted to marry her. The song was used as a social protest against the marriage.
4. Use a homemade or printed storybook of "Mister Frog Went A-Courtin' " to illustrate the lyrics. Teach the song to the students.
5. If a dulcimer is available, tune it to the Ionian mode (the strings of the dulcimer should be tuned to D_3, A_3, and A_3), and have a student accompany the song by playing the open strings to the beat.
6. Have the students listen to the two recorded versions of "Mister Frog Went A-Courtin'." Discuss similarities and differences (for example, rhythm, lyrics, melody, and texture).
7. Have the students draw selected scenes from the song and create their own storybook. A mural could also be drawn on a large piece of paper.

Supplemental activities:
1. Show a film of "Mister Frog Went A-Courtin' " (see "Materials"). Sing along with the film.
2. Write new verses to the song.
3. Stage a mini-drama of the song with solos and chorus.
4. Make puppets and use them to dramatize the song.
5. Discuss oral tradition and play the "gossip game." One person creates a simple story (about three sentences) and whispers it to the next person, who whispers it to the next, and so on. This continues until everyone has heard the story. The last person speaks the story out loud. The last version will probably be quite different from the first. This activity will show how a song can also undergo radical changes as it is transmitted orally over time.

18

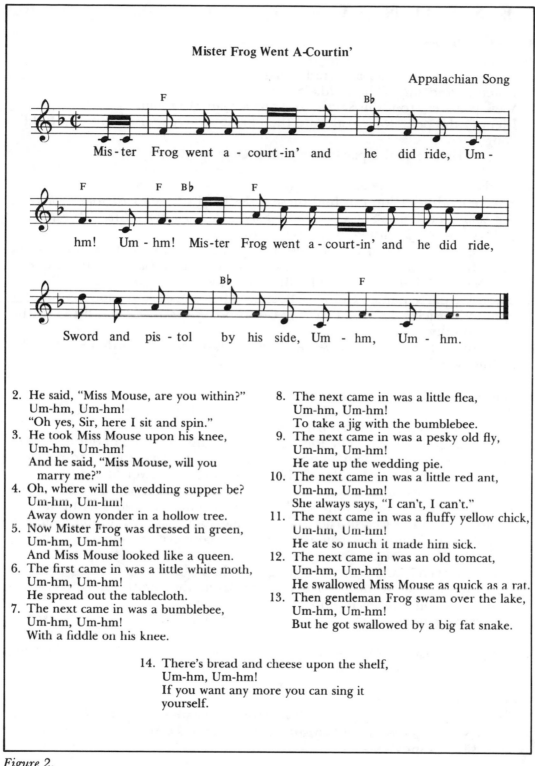

Mister Frog Went A-Courtin'

Appalachian Song

Mis-ter Frog went a-court-in' and he did ride, Um-hm! Um-hm! Mis-ter Frog went a-court-in' and he did ride, Sword and pis-tol by his side, Um-hm, Um-hm.

2. He said, "Miss Mouse, are you within?"
Um-hm, Um-hm!
"Oh yes, Sir, here I sit and spin."

3. He took Miss Mouse upon his knee,
Um-hm, Um-hm!
And he said, "Miss Mouse, will you
marry me?"

4. Oh, where will the wedding supper be?
Um-hm, Um-hm!
Away down yonder in a hollow tree.

5. Now Mister Frog was dressed in green,
Um-hm, Um-hm!
And Miss Mouse looked like a queen.

6. The first came in was a little white moth,
Um-hm, Um-hm!
He spread out the tablecloth.

7. The next came in was a bumblebee,
Um-hm, Um-hm!
With a fiddle on his knee.

8. The next came in was a little flea,
Um-hm, Um-hm!
To take a jig with the bumblebee.

9. The next came in was a pesky old fly,
Um-hm, Um-hm!
He ate up the wedding pie.

10. The next came in was a little red ant,
Um-hm, Um-hm!
She always says, "I can't, I can't."

11. The next came in was a fluffy yellow chick,
Um-hm, Um-hm!
He ate so much it made him sick.

12. The next came in was an old tomcat,
Um-hm, Um-hm!
He swallowed Miss Mouse as quick as a rat.

13. Then gentleman Frog swam over the lake,
Um-hm, Um-hm!
But he got swallowed by a big fat snake.

14. There's bread and cheese upon the shelf,
Um-hm, Um-hm!
If you want any more you can sing it
yourself.

Figure 2.

19

LESSON TWO

■ OBJECTIVES:
Students will:
1. Answer contemporary and traditional riddles.
2. Listen to and sing "The Riddle Song."
3. View pictures from the Southern Appalachian Mountains.
4. Identify the pentatonic scale and the phrase structure used in "The Riddle Song."
5. Sing and move to the play-party game "Goin' to Boston."

Materials:
1. Selected riddles (You can find these in Richard Chase's *American Folk Tales and Songs* and James Still's *Way Down Yonder on Troublesome Creek: Appalachian Riddles and Rusties*, listed in the Bibliography).
2. Twelve pictures from the Southern Appalachian Mountains (You can get these from *Where Time Stood Still: A Portrait of Appalachia*, by Bruce Roberts and Nancy Roberts, listed in the Bibliography).
3. The play-party game "Goin' to Boston" (The music and motions for this appear in Richard Chase's *Singing Games and Playparty Games*, listed in the Bibliography.)
4. Recording: *Edna Ritchie, Viper, Kentucky*, Folk-Legacy Records FSA-3 ("The Riddle Song")

■ PROCEDURES:
1. Ask the class a variety of riddles. Explain that these are an old tradition in many cultures including Appalachia.
2. Sing, unaccompanied, "The Riddle Song" (see figure 3). Point out that there are four statements, four questions, and four answers. Riddle songs were once very popular in the British Isles. The correct answer to a riddle could mean a great fortune, a "yes" to a marriage proposal, or a life saved. In the United States, ballads with riddles were neither as widespread nor as complex as in the British Isles. "The Riddle Song," as sung in the Southern Appalachian Mountains, contains a melodic sequence in its first two phrases and is built on a pentatonic scale.
3. Have the class listen to the recording of "The Riddle Song." As the students are listening, show the twelve pictures from the Southern Appalachian Mountains (one for each phrase).
4. Teach the students "The Riddle Song." Study the pentatonic scale used in the song. Have the students identify the number of phrases.
5. Sing and illustrate the play-party game "Goin' to Boston." Teach the song and motions to the students.

Supplemental activities:
1. Learn other play-party games. Several of these games are printed in Richard Chase's *Singing Games and Playparty Games* and his *Old Songs and Singing Games* (see Bibliography).

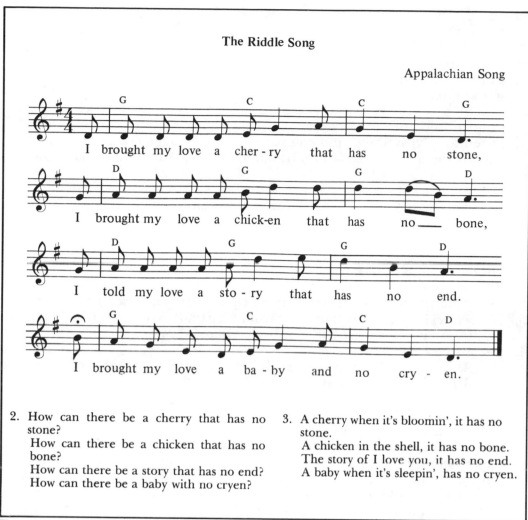

The Riddle Song

Appalachian Song

I brought my love a cher-ry that has no stone,

I brought my love a chick-en that has no bone,

I told my love a sto-ry that has no end.

I brought my love a ba-by and no cry-en.

2. How can there be a cherry that has no stone?
   How can there be a chicken that has no bone?
   How can there be a story that has no end?
   How can there be a baby with no cryen?

3. A cherry when it's bloomin', it has no stone.
   A chicken in the shell, it has no bone.
   The story of I love you, it has no end.
   A baby when it's sleepin', has no cryen.

Figure 3.

2. Read about the Ritchie family in *Singing Family of the Cumberlands* (see Bibliography).
3. Listen to other dulcimer recordings such as *The Appalachian Dulcimer by Jean Ritchie: An Instruction Record*, Folkways FI 8352; *Edna Ritchie, Viper, Kentucky*, Folk-Legacy Records FSA-3; and *Larkin's Dulcimer Book*, Ivory Palaces Cassette IPC 7007 (see Discography).
4. Make a dulcimer and learn how to play it. You can get information on dulcimer kits from Backyard Music, P.O. Box 9047, New Haven, Connecticut 06532.
5. Create an accompaniment for "The Riddle Song" using Orff instruments.

L E S S O N   T H R E E

■ OBJECTIVES:

Students will:

1. Listen to the story "Sody Sallyraytus" and play a "bear's roar" instrument for sound effects.
2. Listen to and sing the "Wraggle-Taggle Gypsies" and watch a puppet dramatization of the story.
3. Listen to "Gypsy Davy" and compare it with "Wraggle-Taggle Gypsies."
4. Discuss the importance of oral tradition in the Southern Appalachians.
5. Identify a Child ballad.
6. Use a limberjack to accompany a recording of "Sourwood Mountain."
7. Move to the beat of "Sourwood Mountain" and imitate the motions of the limberjack.

Materials:

1. Finger puppets that represent one male and two female gypsies, the lady and lord of the manor, and a servant
2. "Sody Sallyraytus" in Richard Chase's *Grandfather Tales* (see Bibliography)
3. Limberjacks (You can obtain these from William R. Saling, Upper Sarahsville Studio, Route One, Box 308, Caldwall, Ohio 43724.)
4. Recordings:
   Folk Music of the United States: Anglo-American Ballads, Library of Congress, AFS-L1 and AFS-L12 or AFS-L21

■ PROCEDURES:

1. Tell the tale "Sody Sallyraytus." Ask a selected student to play the "bear's roar" instrument for sound effects. You can construct one from an empty paper oatmeal container. Punch a hole in the closed end, insert a four-foot-long piece of string through the hole, and tie the string around a used matchstick to hold it. The matchstick should be held against the inside of the box. Wet a piece of cloth, grasp the string with the wet cloth, and run your hand along the string. It will make a sound like a bear's roar.
2. Sing "Wraggle-Taggle Gypsies" (see figure 4). If you are teaching younger students, act out the story with finger puppets. You need six characters: three gypsies (one male, two female), the lady, the lord of the manor, and the servant.
3. Teach the song "Wraggle-Taggle Gypsies" to the students.
4. Listen to "Gypsy Davy" on *Folk Music of the United States: Anglo-American Ballads*, AFS-L1. Discuss the way this tune and text is varied from "Wraggle-Taggle Gypsies," and examine the term "oral tradition." Discuss characteristics of ballads (as explained in the beginning of this chapter), and explain why "Wraggle-Taggle Gypsies" is a Child ballad.
5. Introduce the limberjack, a rhythm instrument from the Southern Appalachian Mountains. After showing students how to play the limberjack, have a student play it as an accompaniment to the recording of "Sourwood Mountain" as the students sing along. (See figure 5; it is recorded on *Anglo-American Songs and Ballads*, AFS-L12 or AFS-L21. Record number L12 is a

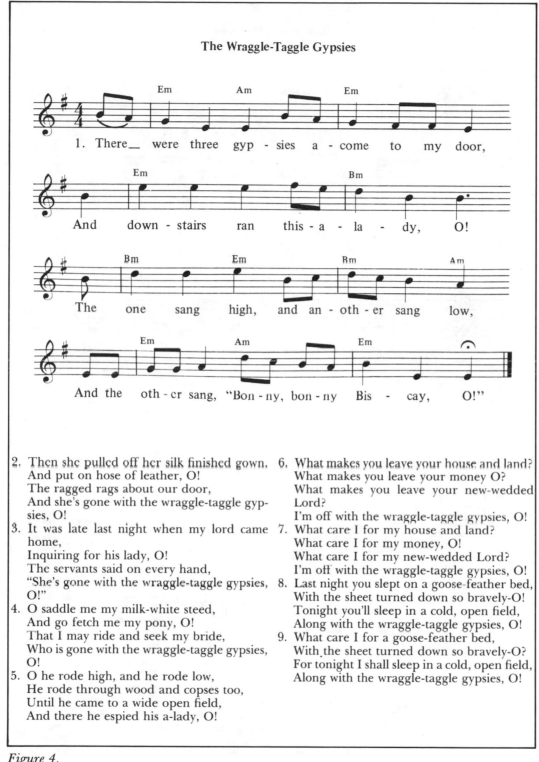

The Wraggle-Taggle Gypsies

1. There_ were three gyp - sies a - come to my door,
And down - stairs ran this - a - la - dy, O!
The one sang high, and an - oth - er sang low,
And the oth - er sang, "Bon - ny, bon - ny Bis - cay, O!"

2. Then she pulled off her silk finished gown,
And put on hose of leather, O!
The ragged rags about our door,
And she's gone with the wraggle-taggle gyp-sies, O!

3. It was late last night when my lord came home,
Inquiring for his lady, O!
The servants said on every hand,
"She's gone with the wraggle-taggle gypsies, O!"

4. O saddle me my milk-white steed,
And go fetch me my pony, O!
That I may ride and seek my bride,
Who is gone with the wraggle-taggle gypsies, O!

5. O he rode high, and he rode low,
He rode through wood and copses too,
Until he came to a wide open field,
And there he espied his a-lady, O!

6. What makes you leave your house and land?
What makes you leave your money O?
What makes you leave your new-wedded Lord?
I'm off with the wraggle-taggle gypsies, O!

7. What care I for my house and land?
What care I for my money, O!
What care I for my new-wedded Lord?
I'm off with the wraggle-taggle gypsies, O!

8. Last night you slept on a goose-feather bed,
With the sheet turned down so bravely-O!
Tonight you'll sleep in a cold, open field,
Along with the wraggle-taggle gypsies, O!

9. What care I for a goose-feather bed,
With the sheet turned down so bravely-O?
For tonight I shall sleep in a cold, open field,
Along with the wraggle-taggle gypsies, O!

Figure 4.

Sourwood Mountain

Appalachian Song

Solo
1. Chick - en crowin' on Sour - wood Moun - tain,

Chorus
Hey de - ing dang did - dle al - ly day.

Solo
So man - y pret - ty girls, I can't count 'em,

Chorus
Hey de - ing dang did - dle al - ly day.

Solo
My true love, she lives in Letch - er,

Chorus
Hey de - ing dang did - dle al - ly day.

Solo
She won't come and I won't fetch her,

Chorus
Hey de - ing dang did - dle al - ly day.

2. My true love's a blue-eyed daisy,
   Hey de-ing dang diddle ally day.
   If I don't get her, I'll go crazy,
   Hey de-ing dang diddle ally day.

3. Big dog bark and little one bite you,
   Hey de-ing dang diddle ally day.
   Big girl court and little one slight you,
   Hey de-ing dang diddle ally day.

Figure 5.

field recording sung by I. G. Greer of Thomasville, North Carolina, to a dulcimer accompaniment by Mrs. I. G. Greer; record number L21 is played on the banjo by Rufus Crisp.)

The limberjack can dance to the solo part of the song and the students can sing the chorus. Have different groups sing the solo and the chorus. Explain that this type of singing is termed "call and response."

6. Have the students imitate the movements of the limberjack, as described in the introduction to this section, by moving to the beat of "Sourwood Mountain." You can lead by swinging your arms, hands, or elbows, or by lifting your knees.

Supplemental activities:

1. Have the students make their own limberjacks. A good description of the materials needed and the methods of making a limberjack can be found in *Foxfire 6*, edited by Eliot Wigginton (see Bibliography).
2. Read other stories from the Southern Appalachian Mountains. You can find these in *American Folk Tales and Songs* or *Jack Tales*, both by Richard Chase (see Bibliography).
3. Learn a simple dance to "Sourwood Mountain." See the textbook *Music* by Elizabeth Crook, Bennett Reimer, and David S. Walker, listed in the Bibliography, for the music and dance steps.
4. Have the students make their own finger puppets for the "Wraggle-Taggle Gypsies."

L E S S O N   F O U R

4

■ **OBJECTIVES:**
Students will:
1. Observe a clogging demonstration.
2. Identify characteristics of clogging.
3. Dance the clogging step.

Materials:
1. *Clog Dance in the Appalachians*, by Jerry Duke (see Bibliography)
2. Recording: *Appalachian Clog Dancing and Big Circle Mountain Square Dancing*, Educational Activities AR 53

■ PROCEDURES:

1. Give a brief history of clogging. Clogging originated as a combination of foot movements and was brought to America by the early settlers. Many regional styles of clog dancing evolved and are popular in the United States today.

2. After learning the clogging steps from *Clog Dance in the Appalachians*, demonstrate how to clog. A good method for learning to clog is to pretend that you have just stepped, with the tip of each shoe, on two wads of gum. Try to get the gum off the left shoe first: Raising your heel slightly, shuffle the ball of your foot with a quick forward-and-backward motion, moving a few inches in front of your body. Keep the ball of your foot in constant contact with the floor so that it makes two distinct sounds as you move it forward and backward for the "shuffle." Then step in place with your left foot. These two movements are called the "shuffle-step" and are performed in the following rhythm:

Another variation, the "shuffle-step-step-step," is performed in the following rhythm (L represents the left foot, R the right):

3. Teach the students these simple clogging steps as they stand in place. Ask them to emphasize the rhythm of the dance with the sounds of their feet striking and shuffling along the floor. The explanations describing the clog step on *Clog Dance in the Appalachians* are clear and precise.

4. If possible, invite dancers from the community to give a clogging demonstration.

26

L E S S O N   F I V E

■ **OBJECTIVES:**

Students will:

1. Listen to "Old Joe Clarke" and identify Mixolydian mode in the verse and chorus of the song.
2. Sing "Old Joe Clarke" and create new verses.
3. Accompany "Old Joe Clarke" with a limberjack. A source for these instruments is listed in lesson three.
4. Clog to "Old Joe Clarke."

Materials:

1. Limberjacks
2. Recording: *Going Down the Valley: Vocal and Instrumental Styles in Folk Music from the South.* New World Records 236 ("Old Joe Clarke")

■ **PROCEDURES:**

1. Have the students listen to the recording of "Old Joe Clarke" (see figure 6) and identify the mode of the tune as Mixolydian.
2. Teach the students "Old Joe Clarke." Once the song has been mastered, create new verses. Discuss the humor of the lyrics and the use of exaggeration techniques.
3. Listen to another version of the song; a good source is the recording that accompanies the Boardman and Andress publication, *The Music Book* (see Bibliography). Ask the students to compare and contrast the two recordings, paying special attention to the melodies. How is variety created in each one?
4. Accompany "Old Joe Clarke" with a limberjack (see figure 7). For variety, have the students play the limberjack only on the verse or the chorus.
5. Clog to a recording of "Old Joe Clarke."

Supplemental activities:

1. Listen to other recordings of traditional Appalachian instrumental music on *The Appalachian Dulcimer by Jean Ritchie* (Folkways FI 8352) and *Brave Boys: New England Traditions in Folk Music* (New World Records 239). Ask the students to identify the instruments on each recording.
2. Listen to the fiddle in bluegrass music. Some good recordings are *Hills and Home: Thirty Years of Bluegrass* (New World Records 225) and *The Great Bill Monroe and His Bluegrass Boys* (Harmony HS 11335).
3. Invite a fiddler from the community to visit your class and perform for the students.

Old Joe Clark

Verses

1. Old Joe Clarke he had a house,
Fif - teen stor - ies high, And ev - 'ry stor - y
in that house Was filled with chick - en pie.

Chorus

Fare ye well, Old Joe Clarke, Fare ye well, I say.
Fare ye well, Old Joe Clarke, I'm a - goin' a - way.

2. Old Joe Clarke he had a mule,
[It's name]* was Morgan Brown,
And ev'ry tooth in that mule's head
Was sixteen inches 'round.
3. Old Joe had a yellow cat,
[She'd nei]ther sing nor pray,
(She) stuck her head [in the] [butter]milk jar
To work her sins a-way.

4. I went down to Old Joe's house,
[Never] been there before,
(and) He slept on a feather bed
And I slept on the floor.
5. Sixteen horses in my team,
The leaders they are blind,
And every time the sun goes down
There's a pretty girl on my mind.

6. Eighteen miles of mountain road
And fifteen miles of sand,
If I ever travel this road again,
I'll be a married man.

*Sing the two syllables that are enclosed in brackets on one note.

Figure 6.

Figure 7. Two limberjacks

L E S S O N   S I X

■ **OBJECTIVES:**

Students will:

1. Sing "Every Night When the Sun Goes Down" in a call and response fashion.
2. Listen to two or more of the following songs: "Barbara Allen," "The Devil's Nine Questions," "House Carpenter," "The Farmer's Curst Wife," and "Gypsy Davy." Complete worksheets for each song.
3. Identify and discuss characteristics of traditional Anglo-American ballads.

Materials:

1. Listening worksheets
2. Recording: *Folk Music of the United States: Anglo-American Ballads*, Library of Congress AFS-L1

■ PROCEDURES:

1. Sing the song "Every Night When the Sun Goes Down" (see figure 8). The teacher should sing the lead, and the students should echo the response. A dulcimer can be used to play the echo.
2. Listen to recordings of "Barbara Allen," "The Devil's Nine Questions," "House Carpenter," "The Farmer's Curst Wife," and "Gypsy Davy" on *Folk Music of the United States*. Ask the students to complete worksheets for each song, or copy the worksheet format on the board.

Listening worksheet:

A. Circle the correct answer:

1. accompanied	unaccompanied
2. woman's voice	man's voice
3. refrain line, nonsense syllables	no refrain line, no nonsense syllables
4. strict meter	flexible meter
5. rhyming scheme (phrases 1 and 3)	rhyming scheme (phrases 2 and 4)

B. Give a brief summary of the story line.

3. Identify and discuss characteristics of traditional Anglo-American ballads as explained in the beginning of this chapter. Remember to refer to the presence of these musical characteristics in traditional Southern Appalachian Mountain music.

Supplemental activities:

1. Listen to other recordings of traditional vocal music of the Southern Appalachian Mountains. You can find good examples on *British Traditional Ballads in the Southern Mountains* (Folkways 8352) and *Edna Ritchie, Viper, Kentucky* (Folk-Legacy FSA-3).
2. Identify contemporary songs that are ballads (for example, "The Wreck of the Edmund Fitzgerald" (Reprise, 1976, by Gordon Lightfoot). Ask the class to compare and contrast other contemporary ballads with traditional Anglo-American ballads.

Integrating music with other studies

Social studies

1. Lead the class in a discussion about the coal mining industry and how it has affected the land and the people who live in the Southern Appalachian Mountains.

2. Listen to several protest songs about the coal mining industry: "Black Waters," words and music by Jean Ritchie, Geordie Music Publishing, 1971, and "West Virginia Mine Disaster," words and music by Jean Ritchie, Geordie Music Publishing, 1971. These songs are recorded on *Clear Waters Remembered* (Sire/London Records, 539 West Twenty-Fifth Street, New York 10001).

3. Investigate traditional customs and crafts of the Southern Appalachian Mountains. A good source is *The Foxfire Book* edited by Eliot Wigginton (see Bibliography).

Ev'ry Night When the Sun Goes Down

Appalachian Song

Figure 8.

4. Interview an older person in the community who can share something about his or her musical past. This is an example of oral history.

5. Examine stereotypes. Discuss the following statements and draw conclusions from them. Are stereotypes fair representations?
   a. Fat people are jolly.
   b. Wolves are bad animals.
   c. Teenagers are always drunken drivers.[5]

6. Read *Grandfather Tales* and *Jack Tales* by Richard Chase (see Bibliography), and discuss the role of storytelling in a society.

Geography

1. Locate the Southern Appalachian Mountains on a map of the United States. Compare the topography and location of the Southern Appalachian Mountains with the entire Appalachian range.

2. Examine photographs of the land and people of the Southern Appalachian Mountains. You can find these photographs in *Where Time Stood Still: A Portrait of Appalachia*, by Bruce Roberts and Nancy Roberts (see Bibliography).

3. Compare and contrast the terrain of the Southern Appalachians with the type of environment in which you live.

4. Read poems that describe the geography of the area. You can find examples in *A Jesse Stuart Reader: Stories and Poems Selected and Introduced by Jesse Stuart* (see Bibliography).

5. Read *The Dollmaker* by Harriette Arnow (see Bibliography), and discuss the differences, as illustrated in the book, between living in rural Appalachia and post–World War II Detroit.

6. Discuss how geography played a role in the traditional ballad lyrics, and explain how geography influenced the preservation of the ballad. How does the isolation of an area affect the music? Does it produce more melancholy, soulful tunes? You can find this information in Cecil Sharp's *English Folk Songs from the Southern Appalachians* (see Bibliography).

History

1. Examine the history of the Southern Appalachian Mountains as told through music. Follow the growth of Anglo-American music as it influenced bluegrass and country music. See the *New Grove Dictionary of American Music*, especially the article titled "Country Music," and the *Music Educators Journal* article by Peggy Langrell, "Appalachian Folk Music: From Foothills to Footlights" (see Bibliography), for information.

2. Historical figures have played a role in Appalachian ballads, as discussed in lesson one. What contemporary songs have been written about recent figures and events?

Visual and performing arts

1. Draw a mural representing the story line of a ballad.
2. Select a ballad and present it as a drama.
3. Create a picture book illustrating the story line of a ballad.
4. Listen to a movement from any recording of *Appalachian Spring* by Aaron Copland, and create a dance to a portion of it.

NATIVE AMERICANS OF THE SOUTHWEST

From Alaska and the northern reaches of Canada to the tip of South America, Native Americans are found in traditional settings and in modern conglomerate communities. The Indians of the southwestern United States are known throughout North America for their efforts to maintain traditional customs while still contributing to the contemporary society that has largely enveloped them. This instructional unit emphasizes the traditions of several cultures of southwestern Native American groups.

New Mexico and Arizona and the southern portions of Colorado, Utah, and Nevada are home to many Native Americans. Groups including the Navajo, Hopi, Zuni, Apache, Pima, Acoma, Papago, Ute, and the Tewa-speaking peoples live in this area. The "four corners" region (see map) is especially rich in the variety of Native Americans who reside there. The desert, high plateau lands, forests, and mountains of the region provide natural resources for their traditional economy and customs as well as inspiration for their stories, songs, visual arts, and architecture.

The history of the southwestern Native Americans began about nine thousand years ago when the Anasazi ("those who had gone before") first inhabited the region. These people were nomads who lived by hunting and by gathering edible seeds. Archaeologists suggest that they used stone tools and often lived in caves cut into the sides of mountains. As their culture developed, they banded together in large clans and built stable communities and developed agricultural societies.

Native Americans began the cultivation of corn (maize) five thousand years ago, and it is still a great staple of the diet of their descendants. They attached great importance to the weather and developed ceremonies to honor the earth, rain, wind, and fire. In some societies, rain making became a prominent ritual; many communities paid homage to deities such as the Sun Father and the Earth Mother.

By 700 A.D., Native Americans had developed bows and arrows for hunting and were making pottery; these were artistic as well as functional endeavors. Shortly after 1150 A.D., they began to develop the now famous architectural style known as "pueblo," which has come to typify southwestern Native American culture (somewhat inaccurately, as other styles were and are used). Built of adobe (bricks of sun-dried mud) and stone, these several-story complexes housed several hundred people. Today the pueblos still stand as reminders of the artistic abilities of the earliest inhabitants of the United States.

During this same period, nearly one thousand years ago, music, dance, art, and ceremonial life developed as an integral part of daily life in these cultures. This holistic ideal is consistent with the contemporary philosophy of the Native Americans who continue traditional practices; they tend to synthesize aspects of an event rather than to analyze them as separate components. Even after the arrival of the Spanish explorers in the sixteenth century and the extensive attempts to blend the Indians into a transplanted European culture, Native

33

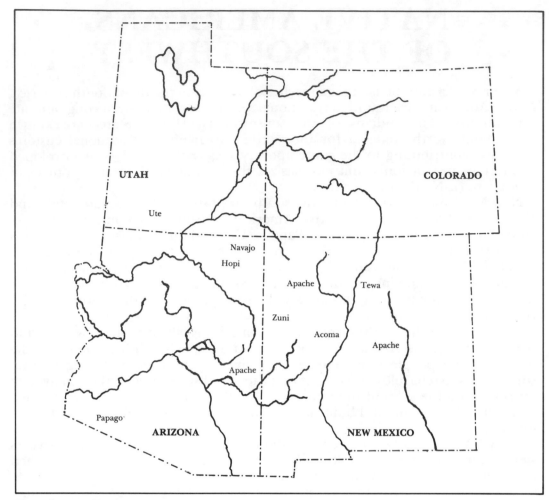

Four Corners Region

Americans held on to traditions that were formulated over many millennia. They lived in harmony with nature and showed the value that they placed on the natural elements in their expressive arts.

There are currently more than two hundred tribes in North America who speak at least one hundred distinct languages. The cultural attitudes of the Pueblo groups of the Southwest differ from other Native American groups such as the Comanche and Sioux of the plains: The plains Indians pride themselves on their individualism, but the Pueblos contribute extensively to their agricultural community. They value cooperation, and they respect the amenities of life in the modern world without losing touch with their ancient customs.

Music is strongly embedded within the traditional practices of Native Americans, and it exists in an inclusive setting, which is different from many other music traditions in the world. Music is a significant part of storytelling, dance, ceremony, hunting, fishing, and food preparation, and it is closely integrated in

34

the daily and occasional ceremonial life experiences. Musical instruments are often symbols of the natural and supernatural worlds: Many consist of animal parts, such as rattles made from deer hooves or musical horns fashioned from a cow's horns. Music is so central to the Native Americans, so embedded in their culture, that many Native American languages have no words to express the concept of music as separate from other facets of life.

In most traditional Native American societies, people view music as a personal, god-given, or magical power. They believe that when certain songs and chants are performed, the melody, words, and vocables (syllables with special extra-linguistic meaning) communicate to the deities and to other members of the group in ways that words cannot. Petitions to the powers of the earth, of wind, of rain, and of the sky are produced through music, just as the wisdom of the gods is transmitted to individuals by supernatural visions in the form of personal songs.

Today, Native American culture has merged with the contemporary world beyond the pueblo and the wigwam. In the Southwest, members of groups such as the Navajo and Hopi are sometimes difficult to distinguish from the mainstream of American culture. Although certain ceremonies preserve ancient traditions, greater numbers of Native Americans live like other contemporary Americans do as they drive their flat-bed trucks, wear their blue jeans, and tune in to country and western music. There are still, however, older Native Americans who linger in their traditional customs and young people who return to seek their roots. One result of maintaining this heritage has been that Native American music has become a significant means of transmission for traditional thought and practice.

General characteristics

The music of Native Americans is rich and varied. For most North American groups, the voice is the principal medium for musical expression. In traditional communities there are few who claim an inability to sing. A good voice is not considered when a leading singer is chosen. Instead, the performer's teacher and the extent of the individual's training, his or her reputation based on past performances, a flexibility in adapting to new performance and social settings, and the strength and endurance of the singer's voice are the criteria when selecting principal singers. Women are likely to have a different repertoire from that of men: In many communities, men occupy most of the ceremonial roles and women perform "domestic" music such as social dance songs and songs for children.

Rattles and drums often provide the only accompaniment to the traditional songs of Native Americans, particularly those from the Southwest. These rattles and drums are unique for each group and are constructed from locally available resources. These groups continue to use the voice, the drum, and the rattle, maintaining the close union with nature that is their heritage; they have recognized that adaptation of European stringed and wind instruments would place them at a distance from their environment. The Navajos use a drum-rattle instrument, made from rawhide and filled with pebbles or dried beans. The instrument is played by both shaking and beating motions. Dancing bells are often worn around the neck, waist, wrist, knee, or ankle; they sound as the

35

performer dances. Among the most ancient instruments are "bullroarers," slats of wood with holes cut into them. These are swung around through the air and produce whistles and unearthly sounds believed to be the voices of the spirits.

The music of Native Americans of the Southwest, and to a lesser extent of other North American groups, usually has the following characteristics:

1. Largely vocal rather than instrumental
2. Melodic rather than harmonic
3. Performed solo or by groups in unison
4. Constructed of phrases that begin on high pitches and descend an octave or more
5. Set primarily in duple meter
6. Used to communicate a specific message through words or meaningful vocables such as *he, ne, yo,* or *heyo*
7. Used in ceremonial rituals
8. Often accompanied by dance
9. Accompanied by percussion instruments, especially the drum and the rattle

There are, of course, exceptions to these general statements. A more detailed discussion of these characteristics can be found in David McAllester's *Indian Music in the Southwest* (see Bibliography).

L E S S O N   O N E

■ OBJECTIVES:

Students will:

1. Note the use of descending pitches through the use of hand gestures at the end of the song.
2. Recognize the importance of the vocal medium in Native American music by singing without instrumental accompaniment.

■ PROCEDURES:

1. Have the students keep a steady pulse by patting their laps while the teacher sings the song "Mos', Mos'!" (see figure 9).
2. At the end of the song (the part with the vocables "nya, nya. . .") lead the students in following the descending pitch with hand movements from high to low.
3. Teach the song by rote, the traditional teaching process among Native Americans.
4. Discuss the origin of the song. This transcription of "Mos, Mos!" (Cat, Cat!) was made from the version that was sung by Bonner McAllester in the summer of 1955, when she was six years old. She was playing with some Navajo children near Tse Bonito, New Mexico, and her anthropologist

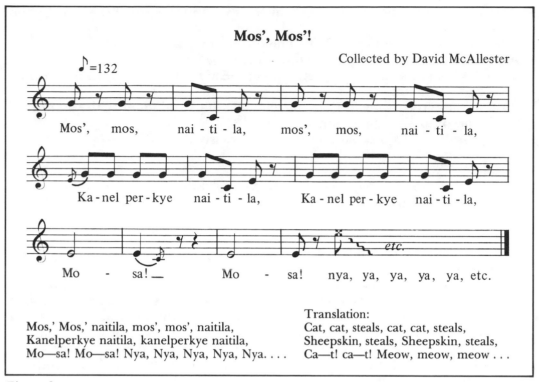

Mos', Mos'!

Collected by David McAllester

♪=132

Mos', mos, nai - ti - la, mos', mos, nai - ti - la,

Ka - nel per - kye nai - ti - la, Ka - nel per - kye nai - ti - la,

Mo - sa! __ Mo - sa! nya, ya, ya, ya, ya, etc.

Mos,' Mos,' naitila, mos', mos', naitila,
Kanelperkye naitila, kanelperkye naitila,
Mo—sa! Mo—sa! Nya, Nya, Nya, Nya, Nya. . . .

Translation:
Cat, cat, steals, cat, cat, steals,
Sheepskin, steals, Sheepskin, steals,
Ca—t! ca—t! Meow, meow, meow . . .

Figure 9.

father, David McAllester, began taping the songs the children were teaching each other. In this case, she was teaching a Hopi song to the Navajos (which she learned from her father, who learned it in 1938 at Moen Kopi, a Hopi town in Arizona).

The word *mos* means "cat," and it was widely adopted by the Native Americans of the Southwest from the Spanish word *musa*—which may have come from their association with the Aztecs. *Naitila* means "he is hiding it." *Kanelperkye* is "sheepskin," and *nya, nya, nya* is from the "cat language" meaning "meow."

L E S S O N   T W O

2

■ **OBJECTIVES:**
Students will:
1. Listen to "Shi Naasha."
2. Locate the Navajo nation on a map of the United States.

3. Discuss the meaning of the song "Shi Naasha" and the use of the song by the Navajo people.
4. Identify the descending melodic line of the song.
5. Sing "Shi Naasha" without accompaniment.
6. Sing "Shi Naasha" as one student plays a steady drum beat, with no accents, as accompaniment.
7. Listen to the recording of the song "Shi Naasha," and identify the accordion as the accompanying instrument.
8. Perform the Navajo social dance to "Shi Naasha."

Materials:
1. Recording: *Music of the Sioux and the Navajo*, Ethnic Folkways Library, RE 4401 ("Shi Naasha")
2. Hand drum
3. Map of the United States

■ **PROCEDURES:**
1. Sing the song "Shi Naasha" (see figure 10) with a drum accompaniment to the beat of the song. The text is pronounced as follows: "Shee nahshah, shee nahshah, shee nahshah, lah dee hozhoenee ayee yah hayee neeya/ Ahahlah ahahlahgoe nahshah, ahahlahgoe nahshah." For correct pronunciation of the Navajo words, listen several times to the Folkways recording of the song.
2. Identify where the Navajo nation lives in the United States. Ask the students to locate this area on the map.
3. Tell the history of the song. "Shi Naasha" (Song of Happiness), was composed as the Navajo (also known as the People or the Dine) were on their way back to their homeland after being incarcerated at Fort Sumner, New Mexico, from 1864 to 1868. A great Navajo leader, Barboncito, pleaded with the government to end the captivity, concluding his pleas with the now famous words, "I hope to God you will not ask me to go to any other country except my own."[6] As the Navajo left Fort Sumner, "Shi Naasha" was composed.
4. Translate the Navajo words of "Shi Naasha." Sing the song again, and have the students listen for the descending melodic line. The individual words of the text can be translated as follows:

    shí—I; me
    naashá—I walk; I am walking
    ladéé—from there; from somewhere around
    hózhóńi—beautiful
    ahála'—sadly
    ahála'go—about to do it; about to happen
    kéyah—earth; home area; reservation

5. Teach the song "Shi Naasha" to the class. The traditional accompaniment to the song is a steady quarter-note drum beat. Select a student to play this part.
6. Listen to the recording of "Shi Naasha." Point out that the accordion is used

Figure 10.

as the accompanying instrument, which shows European-American influence.

7. Sing the song "Shí Naasha," and demonstrate the Navajo round dance, a social dance that is usually performed by men, although women sometimes form a circle of their own and dance inside the men's circle. It is usually danced on the third day of an "Enemy Way Sing." The "Enemy Way" is an ancient war ceremony for the purification and protection of warriors. For example, after World War II many of the Navajo servicemen, known as the "code talkers," participated in an Enemy Way Sing before they returned to their families. Perform a simplified version of the Navajo round dance by having the dancers hold hands in a circle. They should move clockwise with a sidestep, stepping with a downward bounce onto their right feet on the strong beat, followed by a step with the left foot. The rhythm is short-long, with the accent on the right foot as it leads the left foot around the circle.

For more information regarding the Navajo round dance, see David McAllester's *Enemy Way Music* (see Bibliography).

Supplemental activities:
1. Make a Navajo water drum. Directions for this activity can be found in *Simple Folk Instruments to Make and Play* by Ilene Hunter and Marilyn Judson (see Bibliography).
2. Discuss the importance of oral tradition in the Navajo culture.
3. Listen and examine other Navajo songs. A good source is *Navajo Music for Classroom Enrichment* by Dollie Yazzie (see Bibliography).

3   L E S S O N   T H R E E

■ OBJECTIVES:
Students will:
1. Listen to three dance songs of southwestern Native American groups.
2. Discuss the purposes and functions of the songs.
3. Identify instruments, rhythms, forms, and pitches of the songs.
4. Perform some rhythms that are characteristic of Pueblo music.
5. Compose a song based on the characteristics of Native American music of the Southwest.

Materials:
1. Recordings:
    Turtle Dance Songs of San Juan Pueblo, Indian House 1101-C
    Sounds of Indian America: Plains and Southwest, Indian House 9501-C
2. Drum, rattle

■ PROCEDURES:
1. Listen to "Turtle Dance Song" (side one, number one of *Turtle Dance Songs of San Juan Pueblo*). Explain that the people of San Juan Pueblo in northern New Mexico perform the turtle dance each year on December 26 to pray for good crops and protection and to thank the deities for the past year's blessings. The significance of the ceremony's name may derive from the turtle's protective shell. The turtle dancers wear black *mantas* (capes) and dance in a line in each of the pueblo's two plazas. The translation, found in the notes that accompany the tape, clarifies that the song is sung in the morning when "the mist of the sun" is "coming in to the mist of the lake." The text illustrates an important gender factor among the Tewa-speaking Indians: The boys sing, while the girls echo their voices.
2. Have the class listen to "Turtle Dance Song" several times, asking them each time to focus on one of these elements with the following questions:
    ● What instruments are featured? (voice, rattle, drum)
    ● What pitches are sounded? (B-flat, C [the tonal center], E-flat, and G: Ask the class to sing the pitches.)
    ● What kind of scale is this? (tetratonic)

- What instruments are featured? (voice, rattle, drum)
- What is the texture of the example? (monophonic or unison)
- What is the meter? (duple)
- What four-beat rhythms do you hear? (See figure 11: Ask the students to tap the rhythms or play them on rattles and drums.)
- What is the form of the song? (binary: AABBA)

3. Assign one student to maintain a steady beat on drum and one to maintain it on rattles. Ask the remaining students to imitate you on each of the rhythms of "Turtle Dance Song." Ask the class which rhythms are syncopated or have irregular accents, and indicate that Native American music often uses extremely complex rhythms.

4. Arrange for the class to listen to the "Hopi Buffalo Dance" (side A, band one of *Sounds of Indian America*). Explain that the dance is performed in November to pray for an increase in game animals and for prosperity for all Hopis. The dance is performed by two women who choose, as partners, men who are traditionally uncles or cousins. The women prepare food to give to their dance partners, and the men offer gifts to the women who choose them. The dance is performed throughout the day, so that all members of the community have the opportunity to participate.

5. Allow the students to listen to the "Hopi Buffalo Dance" several times, so that they can answer one question after each presentation:
- What instruments are featured? (voice, rattle, drums)
- What pitches are sung? (C, E [the tonal center], F, and G: Ask the students to sing them.)
- What kind of scale is this? (tetratonic)
- What is the meter of the example? (duple)
- What is the texture? (Monophonic; a leader calls directions while a chorus sings in unison.)
- How is the dance song organized? (In two parts: a slow section separated by a pause from a fast one.)

6. Have the class listen to the "Navajo Feather Dance" (side A, band six of *Sounds of Indian America*). Describe the context of the song and dance, which is performed in the winter for a person whose illness is attributed to contact with bears. Two or more dancers move back and forth from a fire, waving wands decorated with feathers and ribbons. As the song continues, an eagle feather is mysteriously raised from a basket near the center of the dance area and begins to dance (apparently by itself). The song is thought to restore the ill person to health and to communion with nature.

7. Lead the class through several playings of "Navajo Feather Dance." Point out the similarities of the song's music characteristics to those of "Hopi Buffalo Dance" and "Turtle Dance Song": tetratonic scale (sing the pitches C, D, E-flat, G), duple meter, voice, rattle, and drum.

8. Review the scales of the three dance songs both orally (through imitation) and by notating them on the staff. Apply several of the rhythms in figure 11 to the pitch sets presented in these scales, composing or improvising brief melodic phrases.

9. Divide the class into groups. Ask the groups to prepare eight-measure songs that use only one pitch set and no more than four rhythm patterns selected

41

Figure 11. Rhythms from "Turtle Dance Song"

from those presented in this lesson. As an added challenge, suggest that they add words based on a nature theme.

Supplementary activities: Explore the contemporary Native American music style illustrated by *Proud Earth* (see Discography). The literary theme of the text is still the spiritual aspects of nature (in a Christian context), but the music style is a mixture of piano, guitar, and violins in an Anglo-American folk-hymn style.

4 LESSON FOUR

■ OBJECTIVES:
Students will:
1. Watch the movie *Discovering American Indian Music.*
2. Discuss the variety of Native American music in the film.
3. Make a drum or rattle.
4. Use homemade instruments to accompany a Native American song.

Materials:
1. Film: *Discovering American Indian Music* (see Filmography)
2. Materials for making a Navajo drum rattle and dancing bells

■ **PROCEDURES:**
1. Watch the movie *Discovering American Indian Music*.
2. Examine and discuss the variety of music found in native American cultures.
3. Ask students to make either a drum rattle or a set of dancing bells to simulate the sounds of Native American music.

    a. The following is a list of materials and instructions for constructing a Navajo drum rattle:[7]

Materials
(1) One long, strong, thin branch freshly cut from a tree for each drum rattle, about 12″–16″ long and ¼″ in diameter

(2) Twine

(3) Two 6″ squares of lightweight cotton cloth

(4) White glue

(5) Two bowls or plastic margarine containers, 3″–6″ in diameter

(6) Waxed paper

(7) Dried beans or pebbles

(8) One 36″ shoestring

(9) One paper punch or cloth punch

Instructions
(1) Bend one end of the branch into a loop, 4″ in diameter. Tie the loop with twine to hold it in place (see figure 12). If necessary, soften the branch by soaking it in water or by whittling it until it is thin and supple.

(2) Cut the cloth into two 6″ circles.

(3) Soak the cloth in a solution of three parts white glue and one part water. Place waxed paper over bowls (see figure 13). As it dries, the cloth will harden into the shape of the bowls.

(4) Place one cloth circle on each side of branch loop. Trim off any excess cloth. Punch holes around the edge of the cloth ½″ apart (see figure 14).

(5) Lace the shoestring in and out of holes punched in the cloth (see figure 15). Note: Before you complete the lacing, place about twelve beans or pebbles inside the rattle drum.

(6) Play the drum rattle by striking the cloth side. The instrument combines the sounds of both a rattle and a drum.

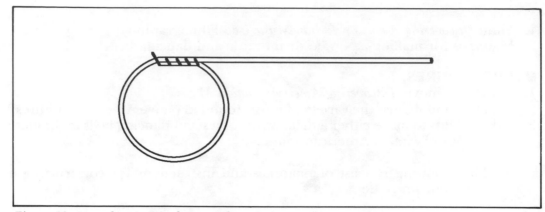

Figure 12. Loop for Navajo drum rattle.

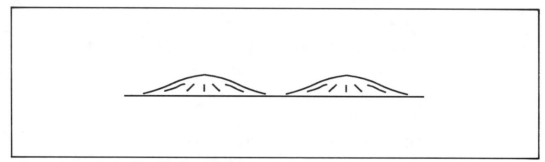

Figure 13. Bowls for Navajo drum rattle.

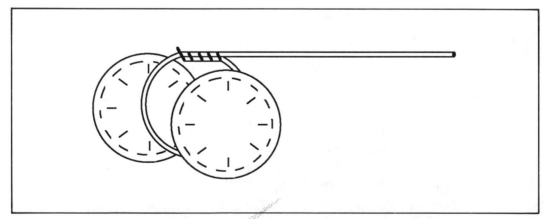

Figure 14. Assembly of Navajo drum rattle.

44

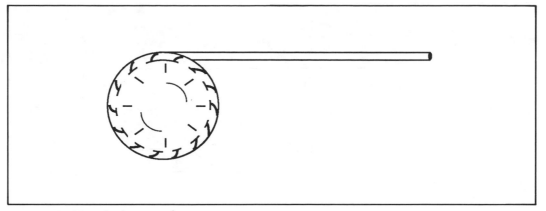

Figure 15. Navajo drum rattle.

b. The following is a list of materials and instructions for constructing dancing bells:

Materials

(1) Five jingle bells

(2) One strip of felt, 2″ × 6″

(3) One 12″ shoestring

(4) Scissors or knife

Instructions

(1) Cut twelve slits in the felt, one at each end and five more closely grouped pairs (see figure 16).

(2) Using the shoestring, lace the bells to the felt through the five pairs of slits. Lace each end of the shoestring through the end slits. Leave enough shoestring hanging from each end for tying the strip around an arm or leg.

(3) Decorate the felt with feathers by gluing feathers under bells. The students can also draw Native American pictures on the felt strips.

(4) Step a steady walking rhythm and wear the dancing bells for accompaniment.

45

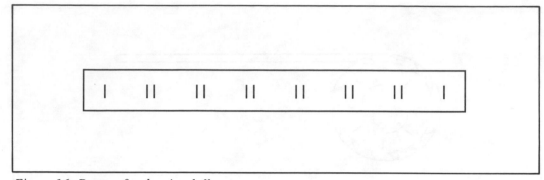

Figure 16. Pattern for dancing bells.

Supplemental activities:
1. Use the homemade instruments to accompany a Native American song such as "Shi Naasha."
2. Examine Native American arts and crafts and decorate the drum and rattles. You can find information about appropriate decorations in *Myths and Legends of the Indians of the Southwest* by Bertha Dutton and Caroline Olin (see Bibliography).
3. Read *Simple Folk Instruments to Make and Play* by Ilene Hunter and Marilyn Judson (see Bibliography) for suggestions on how to make other folk instruments.

Integrating music with other studies

Social studies
1. Study Navajo art and culture. A good source is *Navajo Art, History and Culture*, by Stephen Wallace, Regina Lynch, and Marvin Yellowhair (see Bibliography).

2. Read current newspapers and magazines to discover the current issues involving the Native Americans of the Southwest, their land, and their economy.

3. Read several Navajo "coyote tales," and discuss how they were and are used. Coyote tales are stories with a moral that were told in many Native American cultures for entertainment and for teaching right and wrong. Tradition dictates that Navajo coyote tales should only be told between the first frost of winter and the first thunder of spring. Ask students if there are any traditions like this in their own cultures.

4. Make Navajo fry bread or Indian corn pudding. Recipes can be found in *Many Friends Cooking* by Terry Cooper and Marilyn Ratner (see Bibliography).

5. Examine the similarities and differences between Native American groups in the Southwest. For information, read McAllester's *Indian Music in the Southwest* (see Bibliography).

Geography

1. Locate the southwestern Native American tribes on a map of the United States. One source of this information is the map, *Indians of North America*, distributed by the National Geographic Society (see Bibliography).

2. Read *The Goat in the Rug* by Martin Link and Charles L. Blood (see Bibliography). Discuss how geography can influence the arts and crafts of a culture.

3. Examine photographs of the land and Native American people of the Southwest. The National Geographic Society's publication, *The World of the American Indian,* is a good source for these photographs (see Bibliography).

History

1. Study the history of Native American groups. One source is *Navajo Art, History and Culture*, by Stephen Wallace, Regina Lynch, and Marvin Yellowhair (see Bibliography).

2. Research the Navajo "code talkers" and their importance in World War II. *Navajo Code Talkers*, by Doris A. Paul, is a good source for this information (see Bibliography).

Visual and performing arts

1. Write a "coyote tale." For models, read *Coyote and . . .* by Joe Hayes (see Bibliography).

2. Examine the music of Native Americans who live in your area. For information, you can contact any office of the Bureau of Indian Affairs, an office of the U.S. Department of the Interior.

Literature

1. Explore some of the myths of Native Americans from the Southwest, such as the Hopi *Kátsimas*, the Zuni Salt Mother, the Acoma Spirit Rainmakers, the Navajo Creation Story, and the Apache Mountain Spirits. A good source is Bertha Dutton and Caroline Olin, *Myths and Legends of the Indians of the Southwest* (see Bibliography).

2. Read some of the legends told by Native American children of Arizona and printed in Byrd Baylor's *And It Is Still that Way* (see Bibliography). Explain about the importance of storytelling and the heritage of oral transmission in Native American cultures. Describe the extensive use of nature topics, especially the stories of coyotes, rattlesnakes, bears, rabbits, deer, dogs, and birds. Ask students to tell stories of their own traditions that they learned orally from their families.

3. If your students are ages ten to thirteen, suggest that they read *Racing the Sun* by Paul Pitts (see Bibliography) as a class project, and discuss the traditional and contemporary life-styles of Native Americans portrayed in the book.

4. Read aloud to the class excerpts from *The Way to Rainy Mountain* by N. Scott Mamaday (see Bibliography). The author describes Kiowa myths, recalling his grandmother's traditions. (The Kiowas of northwest New Mexico are less sedentary than are the southwestern Native Americans discussed in this chapter, and they are more similar to the plains tribes in their nomadic wanderings.)

AFRICAN AMERICANS

The music of African Americans, rich in variety and yet representing a unique tradition, has had considerable influence on contemporary music. It is not inappropriate to speak of the melody, rhythm, texture, form, and timbre of African-American music in the ways in which we describe American music in general. There are, however, significant differences in the elements and structure of this music that are largely derived from the contributions of the African heritage of African Americans. This heritage has indelibly shaped African Americans' musical behavior and has produced a unique American music.

African-American music is set apart from other American musics because of the African-American history of slavery and the countless strictures imposed by that system. This period caused the people to develop new ways to express their reactions to what was going on in their lives. African forms of music were once prohibited among slaves, so the slaves were encouraged to practice a new music that blended the sounds of their homeland with the styles practiced by their colonial masters.

An especially important concept of African-American music is its rhythm. The African influence in African-American music is shown in the rhythmic hand clapping, "hot" rhythms, and the use of strong metric and polymetric effects. To truly experience and understand the nuances of the music, both the listener and performer must become involved in the music's rhythm. By singing, providing body percussion sounds, and moving and dancing, the essence of African-American music begins to emerge.

It is difficult to listen to music of African Americans without wanting to move in response to its infectious rhythms. Dance, movement, and music-related activities such as hand clapping, feet stamping, and the chanting of speech patterns (known as rapping) are important for a clear understanding of African-American music. This kinetic sense permeates all African-American folk music traditions, and it is an integral part of customs associated with work, worship, and entertainment.

As in African culture, African-American music allows ample opportunity for improvisation. Much reciprocity exists between dance and music, because the music will often shape a dance and, in turn, a dance will often shape the music. In the church, for example, religious fervor will often determine the movements of the worshipers, just as their movements will often influence the power and dynamics of the service.

In the African tradition, dance- and music-related movements are often functional. They are done for specific reasons: perhaps to honor a birth or celebrate a successful hunt or harvest. In the African-American culture these functions are replaced by more contemporary ones of a social or religious nature. Black dance, for example, often mixes the sacred with the profane. Dance is a part of the practices of certain fundamentalist religious groups, and dance movements are created by youngsters on the playground and elsewhere in response to contemporary popular music. The older layer of dance movements and the musical characteristics of those movements, however, remain alive.

48

An awareness of African-American musics in its various forms is critical to understanding and appreciating the development of African-American culture in the last few centuries. An active and physical involvement in these traditions will provide dividends unavailable through any other approach.

All sorts of tastes in music exist among African Americans. As is true with other Americans, they have various kinds of music activity that they enjoy, support, are involved with, or merely tolerate. Furthermore, there is as much difference between the tastes of different socioeconomic levels as there is among different age groups within the total African-American population.

For at least the last two centuries there have been two dominant musical traditions in America: the musical traditions or aesthetic of white people of the Western world and the musical traditions of black people transplanted to the New World. The major arts institutions in America were founded on a European approach to the arts, in which the primary concerns are more reflective than immediate. The traditional music performed in American concert halls and the exhibitions displayed in American museums often celebrate the creative talents of European creators. African-American arts traditions more often than not focus on immediacy and a "nowness" of this time and this country.

African-American music, at least that most closely associated with folk music traditions, is seldom divorced from everyday life. Generally, performing groups are large and often broken up into sections (for example, a percussion section, a melodic instrument and choral section, and dancers, with physical movement by all those involved). The audience and onlookers constitute a significant and complementary part of the music performance. They are not passive receivers but active participants who involve themselves as singers, handclappers, or voluntary dancers. In short, the musical behavior of African Americans is similar to that of their African ancestors: It is an extension of the activity of their daily lives. It may also, however, be similar to that of their European ancestors. This is especially true of their behavior in concert audiences: The tradition of this behavior is ostensibly passive, more reflective than immediate, more interpretive than creative.

Before Negro slavery was abolished in the United States and for a short time thereafter, communal gatherings such as the "praise meetings" that took place in slave quarters were the only organized forms of musical expression. Although that has changed, these gatherings continue to function as the wellspring of African-American musical behavior. Throughout African-American history, the church and praise meetings have been the environments in which most of the musical behaviors of African-American people were born and nurtured. Religious expression and African-American musical behavior almost from the start were one and the same; both manifested themselves in the experience of singing and in the behavior of being "hit by the spirit." This behavior consisted of shouting, dancing, arm-waving, screaming and hollering, swaying back and forth, moaning, fainting, and so on. It began in African musical behavior and existed in clandestine slave gatherings. As African-Americans were converted to Protestant sects such as the Baptist and Methodist churches, these behaviors were integrated into the worship services.

This behavior and this music results from a fusion of the African and

49

American experiences. It is generally agreed that the hymns of Dr. Watts and the a cappella moaning style typical of these hymn arrangements (for example, the hymns "Amazing Grace" and "Must Jesus Bear the Cross Alone") are evidence of this fusion. These hymns were highly favored by the slaves and were probably the first hymns sung by them in the New World. These rugged eighteenth-century English hymns were altered by the African Americans, and a style of song emerged that has various names: surge-singing, lining-out, long meter, or "Dr. Watts style." In this style, a leader recites a line of text, followed by the congregation singing the same line of text in a slow, deliberate style. This manner of presentation permits intricate embellishment and improvisations on the basic tune by both leader and congregation as well as much sliding among the basic tones.

These hymns motivate the participants to "get happy." Thus, the style of singing, the text, and the emerging sounds have produced unique musical behaviors that truly represent African Americans. These musical behaviors include making a melodic idea and then reshaping that idea melodically or rhythmically, making the music reflect a feeling or mood by "bending" the tones so that they imitate sounds of man or nature. Alternately, performers will sometimes take a vocal sound and recreate it to sound instrumental (or vice versa).

African-American music in this sense is inextricably tied to a belief that the concern of the aesthetic being is to reflect or emulate reality. But African-American music is also an escape from involvement in the complexities of reality. It is important to understand that African-American music and deeply felt responses to it are the accomplishment and, most significant, the *operation* of creating. The *process* is immensely more important than the result. One African-American music scholar, Jimmy Stewart, put it succinctly when he said:

What results there from (the operation of creating) is merely momentary residue of that operation—a perishable object and nothing more, and anything else you might imbue it with (which white aesthetic purports to do) is nothing else but mummification. The point is—and this is the crux of our opposing conception of being—that the imperishability of creation is not in what is created, is not in the art product, is not in the "thing" as it exists as an object, but in the procedure of its becoming what it is.[8]

Finally, there is the question of perceptual experience among cultures. It is erroneous to assume, because the African-American and European-American cultures are so integrally related in experiences and are interchanged so easily by individuals because of their use of similar musical elements, processes, and structures, that similar connotations or associations are evoked in musical encounters within each culture. Similar concepts may be characterized different-ly in different cultures or even within a single culture; not because association is inconstant, but because the concept is viewed in different ways. Also, each individual ethnic group and even each individual is apt to bring to that experience different "cultural baggage" —that is, different cultural backgrounds and experiences.

The African-American existence "between the traditions" of the European-American and the African cultures permits the establishment of a kind of sonic flexibility in the mind and ear. This, in turn, makes possible more efficient

50

moves to other, more specific music styles and behavior such as blues, ragtime, rhythm and blues, and jazz. Using tonal memory has always been crucial to the musical behavior among black people, and they have used it in highly successful ways in their attempts to accommodate the scales, modes, harmonic progressions, and other distinctive elements of the two dominant musical traditions of America. These elements do not remain constant from culture to culture. What does remain constant is the way the mind, operating in the context of a culturally established grammar, selects, organizes, evaluates, and perhaps reinterprets the musical materials presented to it.

One may generalize that some of the selection and use of elements of music by African Americans are due, in large part, to the long historical consequence of the way slavery was practiced in America and the ensuing introduction of the slaves into the enslaving society. These selections of elements, the forms such environmental factors have engendered (including almost all the well-known forms of African-American music), and the seemingly uninhibited responses to the dynamic processes of these musics may be directly traceable to the general mode of musical behavior among Africans: a highly active, improvisatory, and provocative involvement in musical activities and a refusal to differentiate these activities from the realities of everyday life.

General characteristics

African-American music has its roots in Africa, especially West Africa. The early history of Africa is replete with slave trade activity. Countless Africans were captured and shipped to America (among other places). Those blacks who survived the long, arduous voyage were the ancestors of present-day African Americans.

Music, music-related behaviors, and other life patterns were the only cultural baggage the Africans brought with them. But in the slave camps, these traditions were often practiced under fearful and tragic circumstances. Musicologist Eileen Southern said:

A . . . common practice was to force slaves to sing and under the most tragic circumstances. On the slave ships loaded with human cargo, captured Africans were frequently made to dance and sing during their "airings" on deck, the reluctant ones among them being stimulated by the sting of the whip. In the slave pens of the States, slaves were often forced to sing and dance prior to being put up for sale on the auction block.[9]

These and similar circumstances inspired countless African-American musicians to create music that is currently treasured the world over. There were, however, times of play and entertainment in the slave camps, and many equally creative recreational styles of African-American music developed during this time.

Some of the most obvious characteristics of African-American song can be loosely categorized in six topic areas. First, African-American music has been directly influenced by the tonal languages of West Africa in its deliberate and direct use of various pitch inflections and gestures to communicate a wide range of emotions and experiences. Second, African-American musicians commonly use African vocal techniques in which the musician functions as a storyteller and communicator either verbally (as exemplified by contemporary "rap") or with vocables and instrumental sounds ("scat," using the voice to imitate instrumental sounds). Third, musicians use instrumental sounds to imitate the human voice or in reciprocal imitation with singers; and fourth, these musicians often use African scales or melodic resources such as the tonal alterations and patterns of blues scales. A fifth African musical characteristic prevalent in the music of African Americans is polyrhythmic layering of rhythmic patterns and the preponderance of syncopation. Finally, African-American musicians characteristically use improvisation as an important means of truly individualizing the total musical experience.

There are many vocal and instrumental performance traditions among African Americans. African-American musicians perform in a variety of styles and produce sounds that are oriented toward the Western classical tradition. Other traditions exist, such as those in the Caribbean or Brazil, that show a significant African influence. Few African influences are found in other forms of American folk music traditions. This gives African-American traditional music a unique place in American music—indeed, in world music.

When listening to African-American music and observing the ways in which it is performed by African Americans, one can easily see that the slave in early American history was successful in adapting many of the major European musical characteristics in a process of assimilation that continues to the present day. These European characteristics include tonal language practices: the tendency toward regularity of pitch in the diatonic scale and aspects of the European melodic ideal, such as correctness of pitch, purity of tone, and the emphasis on the finality of melodies that have easily grasped melodic and structural devices. The most important characteristic may be the European "sound phenomenon": the method of creating and making music. The slaves were plunged into a musical environment that negated their musical history, but, as eminently musical people, they adapted to this environment. Their solution was to use what was appropriate for their music ideal and to adapt those aspects of European music that did not. Although forbidden to use their own unique way of making music, they made similar changes in the process of music making as well. The result is African-American music.

Melody

The use of "blue notes" is a common melodic trait that probably results from the blending of African and European cultures. The term blue note refers to altering the third and seventh degrees of the scale by slurring, sliding, swooping, groaning, moaning, and shaking. The blue tonality is the result of a partially flatted third or seventh. This may be an attempt to produce a tone foreign to the Western tonal system and possibly unique to the African tonal system as well as an avenue for the use, in a Western harmonic context, of the expressive characteristics of the tonal languages of Africa.

Pentatonic scales provide the pitches for many folk songs and children's songs. African Americans frequently use gapped scales as well, in which the melody in an otherwise major scale may be lacking the fourth or seventh degree; this may result in a hexatonic (six-pitch) scale. The intervallic structure of African-American melodies varies, with frequent use of seconds, thirds, fourths, fifths, and sixths.

52

Melodic ornamentation is a common stylistic device; syllabic song has little place in African-American music. The more melismatic songs often use turns and the sliding and bending of pitches.

Rhythm

The distinctive features of African-American rhythm are the syncopation, accents, and the anticipated beats that "beat the barline" by sounding slightly in advance of the regular pulse, the percussive style of performance practice that maintains the rhythmic pulse, the layering of several rhythmic patterns simultaneously, and the continuous rhythms. These ostinatos often exist in several layers that form a resultant sound that is quite different from the individual parts. The energy of the music is caught up in its rhythm, and in its pulse.

Texture

In traditional African-American music, a type of polyphony frequently results from the concurrent singing of the melody and the different rhythms of the hand-clapping that serves as accompaniment. The interplay between voices and instruments also provides interesting examples of counterpoint. Some vocal styles, including gospel, are set for a lead voice and a homophonic four-part ensemble. The texture of jazz as performed by African Americans ranges from heterophonic to polyphonic to melody with block-chord homophonic accompaniments.

Form

Perhaps the best known formal structure of African-American music is the African-derived call-and-response form. The interplay between a solo and group, vocally or instrumentally, often parallels question-and-answer structure. The lead musician is allowed, however, to use his or her voice to produce the unique and characteristic sounds that integrate speech, recitation, chant, and song and that are so prized in African-American culture. Slurs, slides, and even shrill hollers are sometimes featured, and the responding group may even chant a refrain instead of singing. In call-and-response form, the leader's part will often overlap with the response part, producing an overlay of beginnings and endings with the group. This is especially true in the lining-out form of religious song, which is still performed today in certain denominations such as the African Methodist Episcopal Church and the black Baptist Church.

Vocal interjections are often used in African-American vocal music, particularly in religious songs, for example, "Oh Lord!" "Sing it children!" or "Hallelujah!" Interjections can be melodic or rhythmic, and they occur spontaneously as the spirit or the impact of the music's content moves the individual.

Timbre

African-American musicians have found a wide range of sound qualities in their voices and in their adaptation of European instruments. Their unique vocal techniques include nasal sounds, falsetto, shouting, and guttural tones (such as moaning and groaning, raspy tones, and a throaty quality). These techniques are considerably different from the norm of European folk and art musics.

The creative essence of African-American music is its spontaneous variation. This music is thus an avenue to a very important goal of music education: the nurturing of creative musical expression. Teachers can help reinforce uniqueness of African-American musical style by guiding students to sing a selected song as it is notated and to improvise on it. In doing so, the salient characteristics of the African-American musical style may emerge through (1) the addition of melodic ornamentation, including slurs, slides, and bends; (2) accompaniment with hand-clapping patterns; (3) the use of vocal interjections; and (4) improvisations. Through performance will come an understanding of the elements that constitute the music of African Americans.

1 L E S S O N   O N E

■ OBJECTIVES:

Students will:

1. Experiment with the way the speaking voice can be "stretched" toward singing through sustained speech and vocal inflections.
2. Discuss the function of shouts, hollers, and cries in communication across distances.
3. Listen to hollers as produced by African-American workers in rural areas.
4. Trace the melodic contour of the holler by drawing in the air and mapping on the blackboard.

Materials:

1. Recordings:
   Negro Blues and Hollers, Library of Congress AFS-L59 (side A, band one)
   Negro Folk Music of Alabama, vol. 1, Folkways FE 4417 ("Hey Rufus" greeting call)
   Negro Work Songs and Calls, Library of Congress AAFS-L8 ("Arwhoolie" cornfield holler)
   The World of Popular Music: Afro-American Album XLII, Follett BS 12192 ("Complaint Call" holler)
2. Blackboard
3. Paper
4. Markers

■ PROCEDURES:

1. As a class, select a phrase or sentence and repeat it together several times, listening for the rhythm and the pitch inflections of the words. Use a colloquial phrase such as "It's time to go home," "Will you please put that down?" or "I finished all my homework." Ask individual students to sound

54

the phrase in different inflections: Then have the class repeat it. Students should listen for fast and slow and high- and low-pitched syllables.

2. Discuss how song can develop as an extension of speech. Ask the students to name jump-rope chants that became songs. Suggest that a call in a baseball, basketball, or soccer game can sound musical in its melody and rhythm. Also discuss the calls of street vendors in the city and the singing way that they advertise their food, drink, and newspapers. You can find examples of these calls in Eleanor Fulton and Pat Smith's *Let's Slice the Ice: A Collection of Black Children's Ring Games and Chants* (see Bibliography), or in the recording of the "Crab Man" and "Strawberries" calls on side three, band eight of Gershwin's *Porgy and Bess* (see Discography).

3. Play a recording of a "holler," the sustained, musical call of African-American field workers used in the eighteenth, nineteenth, and early twentieth centuries. (Any of the selections listed in the "Materials" for this lesson is acceptable). Listen to the tonal language and the pitched speech that are used in the examples. Although this type of call was in actual use until recently (one example was recorded as sung by an unidentified singer at Clarksdale, Mississippi, as late as 1941), the holler is a remnant of an important tradition from the time of slavery.

4. Listen to the beginning of the recording that you have chosen several times, tracing the contour of the melody in the air with the fingers. Note the rise and fall of the melody and the typical rise at the end of the phrase. Ask several students to map the melody on the board while they listen; check the map while listening to the melody once again.

5. Divide the class into small groups in which they can proceed to shape a speech phrase to a song phrase, with the students in each group trading phrases continuously and rhythmically. The activity should culminate with their performance of a model phrase, arrived at by group consensus.

6. Listen to other examples of calls and hollers from Alabama on *Negro Folk Music of Alabama*. Explain that the melismatic singing, the ornamentation in glides, swoops and bends, and the free rhythms are the foundation for the classic African-American genre known as the blues.

L E S S O N   T W O

2

■ **OBJECTIVES:**
Students will:

1. Listen to examples of contemporary African-American work songs or prison songs.
2. Study the call-and-response form through listening and performance.
3. Observe the use of a pentatonic scale that includes a minor seventh above the tonic as the basis of the melody.

55

Materials:
1. Recordings:
   Negro Prison Songs, Tradition 1020 ("Long John" and "Michael, Row the Boat Ashore")
   The World of Popular Music: Afro-American, Album XLII, Follett BS 12192

■ **PROCEDURES:**
1. Discuss how singing, humming, or whistling can make a task seem easier. Which musical element can be associated most closely with work? (rhythm)

Long John

2. And I heard a little boy
   Didn't see no one.
   It was long lost John
   He said he was long gone.

3. Like a turkey through the corn
   With his long clothes on.
   Had a heel in front
   And a heel behind.

Figure 17.

Explore with the class some of the rhythms we produce while writing, erasing a chalkboard, or sweeping the floor. Lead the class in marking the pulse, tapping lightly as one student performs a task.

2. Explain that the work song, a dying tradition, was once prevalent among African Americans, It can still be heard in the southern prisons as the prisoners labor. Listen to several examples of prison songs from *Negro Prison Songs* or to "Raise 'Em up Higher," a Texas State Prison song recorded on *The World of Popular Music: Afro-American*. Note that the words are derived from some experience other than work and that the singers use the call-and-response form.

3. Learn the song "Long John" (see figure 17; recorded on *Negro Prison Songs*). Ask the students to repeat the words and melody after you; they will discover that the call-and-response form can feature a response that is a preestablished phrase sung by a group or an imitation of the leader. Observe the melody's use of the pentatonic scale F, (G), A, C, D with the addition of E-flat—a lowered seventh (compared to the diatonic major scale).

4. One work song from the mid-nineteenth century is "Michael, Row the Boat Ashore" (on *Negro Prison Songs*; see figure 18). It exemplifies both the call-

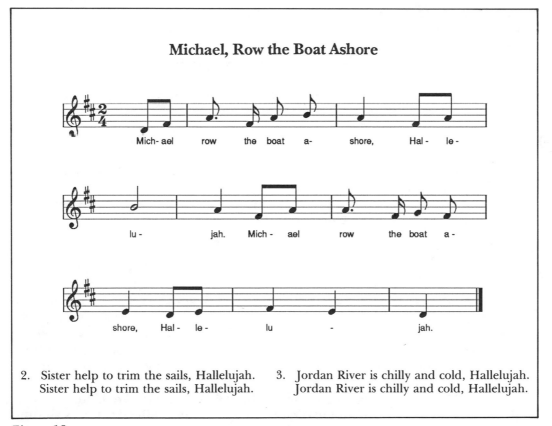

Michael, Row the Boat Ashore

Mich-ael row the boat a-shore, Hal - le -

lu - jah. Mich - ael row the boat a -

shore, Hal - le - lu - jah.

2. Sister help to trim the sails, Hallelujah.
   Sister help to trim the sails, Hallelujah.

3. Jordan River is chilly and cold, Hallelujah.
   Jordan River is chilly and cold, Hallelujah.

Figure 18.

and-response form and the use of words that take the minds of workers off their labors. Students may learn it in the way in which it was traditionally transmitted—orally, without notation.

3 L E S S O N   T H R E E

■ OBJECTIVES:

Students will:
1. Develop an understanding of the blues genre by reading and discussing blues texts about loneliness and hardship.
2. Recognize how hollers and work songs are antecedents to the blues.
3. Listen to examples of the blues, pointing out its characteristic vocal and instrumental styles.
4. Learn to sing a blues song.
5. Learn an instrumental accompaniment to emphasize the formal and harmonic structure of the blues.
6. Trace the older blues form to the rhythm and blues genre of the 1950s and 1960s.

Materials:
1. Recordings:
    The Rural Blues: A Study of Vocal and Instrumental Resources, RBF RP5
    Mean Old Bed Bug Blues, Columbia G30818
    The World of Popular Music: Afro-American, Album XLII, Follett BS 12192
    Chuck Berry's Golden Hits, Mercury 8262561

■ PROCEDURES:

1. Discuss the meaning of the phrase, "I've got the blues." What do you feel when you feel blue? (Lonely or depressed.) Read the following blues song verse: "You'll never miss your water till your well runs dry./ You'll never miss your water till your well runs dry./ I never missed my baby till she said goodbye." What is the sentiment of the verse? Note the AAB form of the verse.
2. Listen to "Milk Cow Blues" (side two, band one on *The Rural Blues*), and listen for the falsetto and the tonal inflections of speech in the vocal quality that the singer has chosen for this song.
3. Listen to "Warm Up" (side three, band three of *The Rural Blues*), and explain the bottleneck guitar technique (determining pitches on the strings by sliding a bottle's neck over a section of the fingerboard rather than pressing the

58

strings on the frets). This technique imitates the sound of African-American vocal slides and slurs. Discuss the use of a solo voice with instrumental accompaniment and occasional vocal interjections, moans, and spoken commentary as characteristic of the blues. Point out the aspects of the holler and the work song, especially the flatted third and seventh scale tones, and the use of the flatted third and syncopation. Discuss other components of the blues, such as the use of solo voice with instrumental accompaniment, call-and-response between voice and instruments, and the use of occasional interjections, moans, and spoken commentary.

4. Listen to "Mean Old Bed Bug Blues" by Bessie Smith. You can find it on the *Mean Old Bed Bug Blues* or on *The World of Popular Music: Afro-American.* Use the listening chart in figure 19 to demonstrate the AAB form and the interchange between the voice and instruments, or call-and-response technique, which is frequently encountered in African-American music and in related music. There are three vocal phrases: The first two have the same text and melody, and the last has a new text and melodic phrase. The vocal phrase (the call) is answered each time by an instrumental phrase (the response), which comments on the vocal phrase. Each chorus, therefore, contains three call-and-response units.

    Make certain that the students know where the first beats fall in each measure (shown by check marks on the transcription). Try calling each number before the entrance of the corresponding material (or have a student volunteer call them). Direct the students' attention to events that demonstrate the music's stylistic elements as the events occur. If you ask them to follow the music printed in the transcription, they will notice that some of the pitches will be a bit flatter and some of the rhythms a bit freer than the notation indicates. Each blues singer may give a slightly different rendition of any given melody on different occasions; the transcription given here is a close approximation of the performance by Bessie Smith on the recordings listed in "Materials."

5. Teach "Mean Old Bed Bug Blues" to the students. Discuss how the singer is sad and lonely now that her husband has been sent to prison. Note the AAB form of the text and music. Sing the third degree of the scale as a lowered pitch, just as it is sung on the recording.

6. If your students play guitar, have them learn a guitar accompaniment to the blues. The chords shown in figure 19 can be used to give a solid harmonic structure to any twelve-bar blues: If you study other blues compositions and the students perceive differences in detail, these differences can themselves be a subject for class discussion.

7. Although acoustic blues is still performed, as well as the more urban style of electric blues, a more contemporary style has developed with rhythm and blues. The roots of rock (and soul) music are found in rhythm and blues, or "R and B" style. This "blues with a big beat" is best demonstrated with the 1950s music of Chuck Berry, Fats Domino, and Ray Charles, whose recordings are available in large record stores and libraries. Listen for the blues form and harmonic structure in "Rhythm and Blues," or "R and B" selections such as Chuck Berry's "Maybelline" and "Johnny B. Goode," available on *Chuck Berry's Golden Hits.*

Mean Old Bed Bug Blues

Transcribed by
J. Standifer

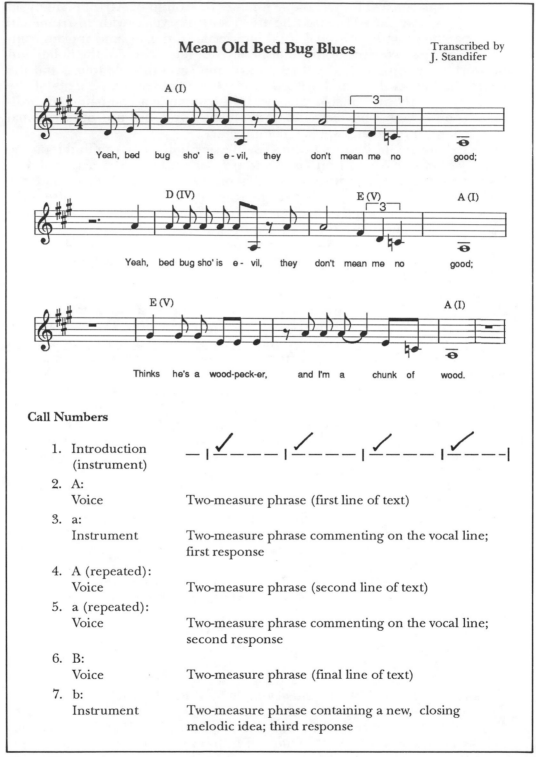

Yeah, bed bug sho' is e - vil, they don't mean me no good;

Yeah, bed bug sho' is e - vil, they don't mean me no good;

Thinks he's a wood-peck-er, and I'm a chunk of wood.

Call Numbers

1. Introduction
   (instrument)

2. A:
   Voice   Two-measure phrase (first line of text)

3. a:
   Instrument   Two-measure phrase commenting on the vocal line;
                         first response

4. A (repeated):
   Voice   Two-measure phrase (second line of text)

5. a (repeated):
   Voice   Two-measure phrase commenting on the vocal line;
                         second response

6. B:
   Voice   Two-measure phrase (final line of text)

7. b:
   Instrument   Two-measure phrase containing a new, closing
                         melodic idea; third response

Figure 19.

L E S S O N   F O U R

4

■ **OBJECTIVES:**

Students will:
1. Listen to examples of ragtime music.
2. Recognize the use of syncopated melodies against steady accompaniment patterns by tapping and chanting.
3. Understand ragtime form by listening to excerpts from each section separately before listening to an entire selection.

Materials:
1. Recordings:
   Piano Rags by Scott Joplin, Nonesuch H-712 48
   The Complete Works of Scott Joplin, Audiophile AP 71–72
   The World of Popular Music: Afro-American, Album XLII, Follett BS 12192
   Heliotrope Bouquet Piano Rags (1900–1970), Nonesuch H 71257
2. Film: *Scott Joplin*, Pyramid, 15 minutes, color, 1977
3. Piano

■ **PROCEDURES:**

1. Explain that ragtime music was developed by itinerant African-American pianists, such as Scott Joplin, who traveled in the Midwest from 1890 to 1920, playing a music based on a mixture of formal European and informal African-American folk traditions. Emphasize that ragtime music was fully composed before it was performed, unlike the oral traditions of work songs and blues.
2. Show the film *Scott Joplin*.
3. Listen to a ragtime selection such as "The Entertainer" or "Maple Leaf Rag" on one of the recordings listed under "Materials" for this lesson. Focus on the even left-hand chords by tapping a steady beat while listening. Listen also to the right-hand melody for the following syncopated rhythm:
4. Have the class say the chant in figure 20 to demonstrate the characteristic syncopation of ragtime melodies. Have students pat the rhythm of the chant

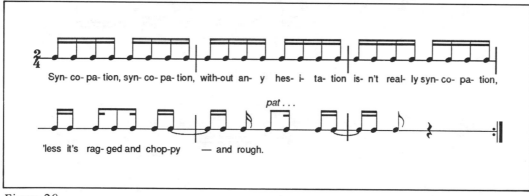

Figure 20

on their laps. Divide the class and have one group clap and chant the words
"rag time" to steady eighth notes.

5. Play the themes of the "Maple Leaf Rag" on the piano (see figure 21).
   Sections A, B, C, and D should be repeated until the students are familiar
   with their sounds. Explain that the most common ragtime form is
   AABBACCDD. Write that scheme on the blackboard, and play the record-
   ing, asking students to raise their hands every time they hear a new section.
   Point to the letters of the sections as they occur.

6. Have the students listen to "Pegasus" by James Scott (1886–1936), a classic
   rag written in 1919. This composition is recorded on *Heliotrope Bouquet Piano
   Rags* and on *The World of Popular Music: Afro-American*. As they listen, have
   them follow each section of the piece and write down the form (Introduc-

Figure 21. Themes from "Maple Leaf Rag"

tion / A / B / C / Bridge / B). Notice that the bridge section features a return of the introductory material.

L E S S O N   F I V E

■ **OBJECTIVES:**
Students will:
1. Sing a spiritual.
2. Listen to spirituals and gospel songs, and recognize their religious and vocal significance in African-American culture.

Materials:
Recordings:
The Fisk Jubilee Singers, Folkways FP-72
The World of Popular Music: Afro-American, Album XLII, Follett BS 12192
Walking in Space, A & M Records SP 3023

■ **PROCEDURES:**
1. Describe the origin of the spiritual as a religious song genre in which slaves expressed their hope for a better life after death. Although they were sung during the period of slavery, spirituals gained in popularity during religious camp meetings. The Western world took note of the spiritual when the Fisk Jubilee Singers of Fisk University of Nashville, Tennessee, performed these songs around the country and in Europe from the 1870s to the end of the nineteenth century.
2. Sing "There's a Great Camp Meeting" (see figure 22). Call attention to the call-and-response setting that alternates a leader and the chorus and to the syncopations in the melody. After listening to "There's a Great Camp Meeting," have students listen to African-American composer Thomas Kerr's composition for piano, "Easter Monday Swagger," which is based on the spiritual. Kerr's work is recorded on *The World of Popular Music: Afro-American*.
3. Listen to *The Fisk Jubilee Singers*, "There's a Great Camp Meeting" (side two, band two) and "Rocking Jerusalem" (side one, band three). Compare the distinctly different musical and textual contents of spirituals with those of the blues examples studied in lesson three.
4. Define the gospel song, a religious form that originated early in the twentieth century. (Gospel songs use a biblical text: Music based on a secular text can be called "rhythm and blues.") Listen to "O Happy Day" on Quincy Jones's *Walking in Space* or any other gospel song that students may wish to share with the class. When distinguishing gospel music from spirituals, point out the following differences: (a) The music is composed, unlike folk music, which is not written down; (b) it requires instrumental accompaniment rather than a cappella performance; (c) it uses highly ornamented, often improvised

63

Figure 22

melodies rather than a straightforward rendition of the printed notation; and (d) the text is about contemporary moral issues, not biblical stories. Both spirituals and gospel songs are religious and vocal in nature, but can be readily identified by these traits.

L E S S O N   S I X

6

■ OBJECTIVES:

Students will:

1. Identify Dixieland jazz music and distinguish it from other styles of jazz.
2. Demonstrate an understanding of syncopation by performing it, and listen for examples of syncopation in a recorded selection of Dixieland.
3. Demonstrate an understanding of improvisation by performing it, and listen for examples of improvisation in a recording of Dixieland jazz.

Materials:

1. Recording:
   The Smithsonian Collection of Classic Jazz, P6 11891
   ("Red Onion Jazz Babies")
2. A map of the United States

■ PROCEDURES:

1. Discuss the following concepts of Dixieland jazz:
   a. Dixieland is a type of jazz from the area known as Dixie: the southern region of the United States that includes Alabama, Georgia, Mississippi, and Louisiana. Find these states on the map.
   b. Dixieland, the earliest type of jazz, developed around 1900 from the rhythmic music of the African slaves (influenced by the instrumental music of the European settlers) in New Orleans.
   c. The street bands of African Americans are probably the source for Dixieland music. African-American musicians often took folk songs, hymns, and spirituals and "jazzed them up" for weddings, funerals, parades, and processions.
2. Lead the class in singing "Down by the Riverside," learning the song by ear as African-American singers would have learned it (see figure 23). Note that although many jazz musicians could read music, they learned their music largely by ear.
3. Syncopation is an important component of jazz and Dixieland music. Have the students clap on beats one and two (two beats per measure) as they sing "Down by the Riverside." Add syncopation by clapping on the off-beats (1 *and* 2 *and*). Ask the class to stamp their feet *on* the beats, and to clap *off* the beats. Sing the song with the syncopated hand-claps. The relationship between melody and its syncopated accompaniment is a fundamental principle of Dixieland jazz.

65

Down by the Riverside

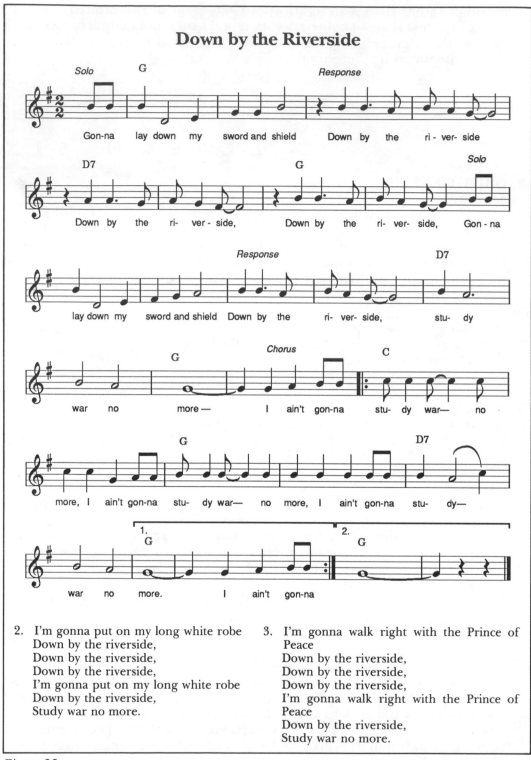

2. I'm gonna put on my long white robe
Down by the riverside,
Down by the riverside,
Down by the riverside,
I'm gonna put on my long white robe
Down by the riverside,
Study war no more.

3. I'm gonna walk right with the Prince of
Peace
Down by the riverside,
Down by the riverside,
Down by the riverside,
I'm gonna walk right with the Prince of
Peace
Down by the riverside,
Study war no more.

Figure 23.

66

4. Improvisation is basic to all jazz, and Dixieland is no exception. Lead the class in singing "Down by the Riverside" again, but this time assign the solo part in each verse to a small group of students. This will underscore the relationship of Dixieland jazz to many other African-American music genres through the use of call-and-response. Encourage students to create new solo texts that can be improvised. Eventually, suggest that students take some liberty with the melody and shape it to their own expressive needs.
5. Listen to "Red Onion Jazz Babies," performed by Louis Armstrong on cornet, Sidney Bechet on soprano saxophone, and others in 1924. The instruments constitute a typical Dixieland jazz ensemble: cornet, saxophone, trombone, piano, and banjo. Clap the steady beats of the duple meter while listening, first on the beat and later on the offbeats. Listen to the interplay of solo instruments and the full instrumental ensemble, noting the improvised solo sections.

Integrating music with other studies

1. Explore poetry and literature for a fuller understanding of the African-American experience. Read excerpts from the poetry of Langston Hughes and Paul Dunbar and the short stories and novels of James Baldwin (including *Go Tell It on the Mountain*) and Richard Wright's *Native Son*. Also introduce the class to James Baldwin's "Notes of a Native Son," which provides much useful information for interpreting Wright's book (see Bibliography).

2. For examples of African-American folktales presented in a local dialect, read the Uncle Remus stories by Joel Chandler Harris (see Harris's *Uncle Remus, His Songs and His Sayings*, listed in the Bibliography). These tales are set in the context of the culture of the people of the Georgia Sea Islands, who even in the twentieth century retain many traditions from the period of slavery. The songs of Bessie Jones, collected in *Step It Down* by Jones and Beth Lomax Hawes (see Bibliography), are further examples of this regional culture.

3. The visual arts of African Americans are exemplified by the patchwork quilts and basketry of the rural people of the southern United States. Search for examples of these traditions in the collected volumes of American folk art such as Stephanie Miller's *Creative Patchwork* or Robin Franklin and Tasha Lebow Wolf's *"Remember the Ladies": A Handbook of Women in American History* (see Bibliography). Show your class the videotape, *A Gift of Hearts and Hands* (see Filmography) or the book that accompanies it, *Hearts and Hands: The Influence of Women and Quilts on American Society*, by Elaine Hedges and Julie Silva.

4. On a map, trace the migration of African peoples in the eighteenth and nineteenth centuries from the west coast countries of Dahomey, Nigeria, Ghana, and the Ivory Coast to the seaports of Charleston, South Carolina, and throughout the south; to Atlanta, Georgia; Richmond, Virginia; Montgomery, Alabama; and Jackson, Mississippi. Trace the northern migration during the years following the Civil War: up the Mississippi river to Memphis, Tennessee; St. Louis, Missouri; and Chicago. Point out cities with large African-American communities, including those previously noted as well as Detroit, Cleveland, Washington, D.C., New York, Philadelphia, Boston, and Los Angeles. Suggest the historical significance of the industrial revolution, which provided jobs for African Americans in the factories of urban areas.

SOUTHERN APPALACHIAN MOUNTAINS

BIBLIOGRAPHY

Armstrong, Randall. "The Adaptable Appalachian Dulcimer." *Music Educators Journal* 66, no. 6, February 1980, 39–41. This article provides information about the dulcimer and how to play it.

Arnow, Harriette. *The Dollmaker*. New York: Macmillan, 1954. This is a touching story about an Appalachian woman and her family who move to Detroit.

Bennett, George E. *Appalachian Books and Media for Public and College Libraries*. Morgantown: West Virginia University Library, 1975. This annotated bibliography includes picture books, folklore and music, films, videotapes, phonograph recordings, and periodicals.

Boardman, Eunice, and Barbara Andress. *The Music Book*. New York: Holt, Rinehart and Winston, 1981. This book contains lessons with selected Appalachian songs.

Boardman, Eunice, Beth Landis, and Barbara Andress. *Exploring Music*. New York: Holt, Rinehart and Winston, 1975. The lessons in selected grade levels of this textbook contain Appalachian songs.

Botkin, B. A. *The American Play-Party Song*. New York: Frederick Ungar, 1963. This book contains many detailed discussions of play-party games.

Brown, Patricia. *The Mountain Dulcimer*. Woods Hole, MA: N.p., 1979. This is an excellent resource and visual aides for learning how to play the dulcimer.

Brown, Tom. "Sugar in the Gourd: Preserving Appalachian Traditions." *Music Educators Journal* 70, no. 3, November 1983, 52–55. The author describes an innovative project to help keep the Appalachian musical heritage alive.

Bryant, Larkin. *Larkin's Dulcimer Book*. Memphis, TN: Ivory Palaces Music Publishing, 1982. This book presents a logical, easy method for playing the dulcimer. An excellent audiotape accompanies the book.

Campbell, Olive, and Cecil J. Sharp. *English Folk Songs from the Southern Appalachians*. New York: Putnam, 1917. This is a collection of ballads and songs from the Southern Appalachian Mountains.

Chase, Richard. *American Folk Tales and Songs*. New York: Dover Publications, 1971. This is a compilation of folk tales, songs, and riddles.

Chase, Richard. *Grandfather Tales*. Boston: Houghton Mifflin, 1948. This collection of stories indigenous to the Southern Appalachian Mountains includes "Sody Sallyraytus."

Chase, Richard. *Jack Tales*. Boston: Houghton Mifflin, 1943. This book contains traditional stories from Appalachia about a boy named Jack.

Chase, Richard. *Old Songs and Singing Games*. New York: Dover Publications, 1972. This is an excellent collection of songs, ballads, carols, folk hymns, rounds, singing games, play-party games, and country dances from the Southern Appalachian Mountains.

Chase, Richard. *Singing Games and Playparty Games*. New York: Dover Publications, 1967. This is a book of folk games, children's singing games, and boy's singing games.

Child, Francis James. *The English and Scottish Popular Ballads*. New York: Dover Publications, 1965. This is a collection of the Child ballads.

Conover, Chris. *Froggie Went A-Courting*. New York: Farrar, Straus and Giraux, 1986. This book contains both the music for the ballad and charming illustrations of it.

Cooperative Recreation Service. *Songs of All Times*. Burnsville, NC: World Around Songs, 1957. This publication contains representative songs and ballads from the Southern Appalachian Mountains.

Crook, Elizabeth, Bennett Reimer, and David S. Walker. *Music*. Morristown, NJ: Silver Burdett, 1981. The lessons in selected grade levels in this textbook contain Appalachian songs.

Duke, Jerry. *Clog Dance in the Appalachians*. San Francisco: Duke Publishing, 1984. This book gives a history of clogging and a variety of clogging styles.

Hamm, Charles. *Music in the New World*. New York: Norton, 1983. A discussion of Anglo-American music is included in this book.

Hitchcock, H. Wiley, and Stanley Sadie, eds. *The New Grove Dictionary of American Music*. New York: Macmillan, 1986. This reference work is a good source of information on many aspects of American music.

Karpeles, Maud, ed. *Eighty English Folk Songs from the Southern Appalachians.* Cambridge, MA: The MIT Press, 1968. An interesting introduction to this collection provides information about how Karpeles and Cecil Sharp collected these folk songs.

Landeck, Beatrice, Elizabeth Crook, and Harold C. Youngberg. *Making Music Your Own.* Morristown, NJ: Silver Burdett, 1971. Selected grade levels in this textbook contain a variety of Appalachian songs.

Langrell, Peggy. "Appalachian Folk Music: From Foothills to Footlights." *Music Educators Journal* 72, no. 7, March 1986, 37–39. The author describes the roots of traditional Appalachian music and its influence on country music.

Langstaff, John. *Frog Went A-Courtin'.* New York: Harcourt Brace, 1955. This is a colorful picture book of this old Anglo-American ballad.

Lomax, Alan. *American Ballads and Folk Songs.* New York: Macmillan, 1964. This collection contains a wide variety of traditional tunes and texts.

Marsh, Mary Val, Carroll Rinehart, and Edith Savage. *The Spectrum of Music with Related Arts.* New York: Macmillan, 1980. Selected grade levels in this book contain a variety of Appalachian songs.

Nettl, Bruno. *Folk Music in the United States: An Introduction.* Detroit: Wayne State University Press, 1976. This is a discussion of Southern Appalachian Mountain music.

Ritchie, Jean. *The Dulcimer Book.* New York: Oak Publications, 1974. The author presents a history of the dulcimer and clear, simple instructions on how to play it.

Ritchie, Jean. *Singing Family of the Cumberlands.* New York: Oxford University Press, 1955. This book includes interesting vignettes from the life of the Ritchie family as seen through the eyes of Jean Ritchie.

Roberts, Bruce, and Nancy Roberts. *Where Time Stood Still: A Portrait of Appalachia.* New York: Crowell-Collier Press, 1970. This publication contains excellent pictures of the region and its people.

Seeger, Charles. "The Appalachian Dulcimer." *Journal of American Folklore* 72, January–March 1958, 40–51. This is a discussion of the history and construction of the dulcimer.

Seeger, Ruth. *American Folk Songs for Children.* Garden City, NY: Doubleday, 1948. This is an excellent resource with songs and notes on how to teach them.

Sharp, Cecil J. *English Folk Song: Some Conclusions.* 4th ed. Belmont, CA: Wadsworth Publishing, 1965. The author discusses musical characteristics of English folk songs and Southern Appalachian Mountain music in this book.

Sharp, Cecil J. *English Folk Songs from the Southern Appalachians.* London: Oxford University Press, 1952. This is a classic and timeless collection of ballads and songs from the Southern Appalachian Mountains.

Still, James. *Way Down Yonder on Troublesome Creek: Appalachian Riddles and Rusties.* New York: Putnam, 1974. This is a collection of Appalachian sayings and riddles.

Stuart, Jesse. *A Jesse Stuart Reader: Stories and Poems Selected and Introduced by Jesse Stuart.* New York: McGraw, 1963. This book contains a variety of literature by an Appalachian author.

Wigginton, Eliot, ed. *The Foxfire Book.* New York: Anchor Books, Doubleday, 1972. Written by high school students from Appalachia, this book contains a wealth of information about traditional Appalachian customs and ways of doing things.

Wigginton, Eliot, ed. *Foxfire 6.* New York: Doubleday, 1980. This book includes a description of the process of making a limberjack.

DISCOGRAPHY

Anglo-American Ballads. Folkways 2037. This record contains excellent representative recordings.

Appalachian Clog Dancing and Big Circle Mountain Square Dancing. Educational Activities AR 53. This is a demonstration record by Glenn Bannerman with clear instructions on how to clog.

The Appalachian Dulcimer by Jean Ritchie: An Instruction Record. Folkways FI 8352. This record provides excellent playing instructions and models of dulcimer playing.

Brave Boys: New England Traditions in Folk Music. New World Records 239. This record features Gail Stoddard Storm singing "A Frog He Would A-Wooing Go."

British Traditional Ballads in the Southern Mountains. Vol. 1. Folkways 8352. Selected Child ballads are featured in this recording by Jean Ritchie.

Child Ballads Traditional in the United States (I) and (II). Library of Congress, AAFS L57, AAFA L58. This is an excellent resource for traditional ballads sung by untrained singers, edited by Bertrand H. Bronson. "The Two Sisters," "Lord Bateman," and "The Devil and the Farmer's Wife" are included.

Children's Songs and Games from the Southern Mountains. Folkways FC 7054. Features Appalachian music for children as sung by Jean Ritchie.

Edna Ritchie, Viper, Kentucky. Folk-Legacy Records FSA-3. This record includes "The Riddle Song."

Folk Music of the United States: Anglo-American Ballads. Library of Congress, AFS-L1, AFS-L12, and AFS-L21. This contains an excellent variety of traditional ballads and singers, edited by Alan Lomax.

Going Down the Valley: Vocal and Instrumental Styles in Folk Music from the South. New World Records 236. This recording includes "Old Joe Clarke."

The Great Bill Monroe and His Bluegrass Boys. Harmony HS 11335. This is a recording of classic bluegrass music at its best.

Hills and Home: Thirty Years of Bluegrass. New World Records 225. This is a representative sample of bluegrass music.

I'm On My Journey Home: Vocal Styles and Resources in Folk Music. New World Records 223. I.N. Marlor sings "Barbara Allen" on this recording.

Larkin's Dulcimer Book. Ivory Palaces Cassette IPC 7007. This is a good introduction to the dulcimer.

Oh, My Little Darling: Folk Song Types. New World Records 245. Several Anglo-American ballads are featured on this recording.

Old Mother Hippletoe: Rural and Urban Children's Songs. New World Records 291. This recording features Almeda Riddle singing "Mister Frog Went A-Courtin'."

Richard Chase Tells Three "Jack" Tales from the Southern Appalachians. Folk-Legacy FTA-6. Three stories are told on this record, taped before a live audience of children.

FILMOGRAPHY

End of an Old Song. Produced by John Cohen. Macmillan Films, 34 MacQuesten Parkway South, Mt. Vernon, NY 10550. 16mm, 26 minutes, black-and-white. This film features mountain songs from North Carolina.

Fine Time at Our House: A Film on Old-Time Mountain Music. Produced by Lois Tupper and Boston University, 1972. Available from Lois Ann Tupper, 60 Chilton Street, Cambridge, MA 02138. 16mm, 30 minutes, color. This film presents mountain people who sing and play their music as they go about their daily lives.

Frog Went A-Courtin'. Produced and distributed by Weston Woods Studios, 389 Newtown Turnpike, Weston, CT, 06883. 16mm. 12 minutes, color. This is a sing-along performance by John Langstaff.

Froggie Went A-Courtin'. Produced and distributed by Barr Films, 3490 East Foothill Boulevard, Pasadena, CA 91107. 16mm, 6 minutes, color. This is a dramatization of the ballad.

A Froggie Went A Courtin'. Produced and distributed by Lucerne Films, 37 Ground Pine Road, Morris Plains, NJ 07950. 16mm, 4 minutes, color. This is an animated version of the song.

Music Makers of the Blue Ridge. Produced by David Hoffman, National Educational Television, 1966. Available from NET Film Service, Indiana University Audio-Visual Center, Bloomington 47401. 16mm, 45 minutes, black-and-white. This film features folk music and folk dances.

Music of Many Mountains. M-12a, Mountain Music; M-12b, Tommy Jarrell; M-12c, Taylor and Stella Kimble; M-12d, Mountain Music. These videotapes are available from Broadside T.V. and Videomaker, 204 East Watauga, Johnson City, TN 37601.

Tomorrow's People. Produced by Appalachian Educational Media Project, P.O. Box 743, Whitesburg, KY 41853. 16mm, 25 minutes, sound. The music of Appalachia is presented without narration in this film.

NATIVE AMERICANS OF THE SOUTHWEST

BIBLIOGRAPHY

Baylor, Byrd. *And It Is Still that Way*. Santa Fe, NM: Trails West, 1988. This is a collection of legends as told to the author by Navajo, Hopi, Papago, Pima, Apache, Quechan, and Cocopah children. It includes stories of the coyote and other animals, heroes, magic, and creation.

Burnett, Millie. *Dance down the Rain, Sing up the Corn: American Indian Chants and Games for Children*. San Francisco: R and E Research Associates, 1975. This is a collection of children's game songs from southwestern Native American groups.

Cooper, Terry, and Marilyn Ratner. *Many Friends Cooking*. New York: Philomel Books in cooperation with the United States Committee for UNICEF, 1980. Includes recipes for making Navajo fry bread and Indian corn pudding.

Dutton, Bertha, and Caroline Olin. *Myths and Legends of the Indians of the Southwest*. Vol. 1, *Hopi, Acoma, Tewa and Zuni*; vol. 2, *Navajo, Pima, and Apache*. Santa Barbara, CA: Bellerophon, 1979. These books contain many line drawings of costumes, traditional designs, deities, and ritual events. They also present traditional stories and convey the values of these southwestern peoples.

Frisbie, Charlotte J., and David P. McAllester. *Navajo Blessingway Singer: Frank Mitchell 1881–1967*. Tuscon: University of Arizona Press, 1978. This fascinating story of the life of a Navajo ceremonial singer includes his comments on the value and function of Navajo songs and the way in which these songs are learned.

Hayes, Joe. *Coyote and. . . .* Santa Fe, NM: Mariposa Publishing, 1983. This is a good source for models of Navajo coyote tales.

Herndon, Marcia. *Native American Music*. Darby, PA: Norwood Editions, 1980. This book provides an anthropological view of the function of music in traditional and contemporary Native American societies.

Hunter, Ilene, and Marilyn Judson. *Simple Folk Instruments to Make and Play*. New York: Simon and Schuster, 1977. This book contains directions for constructing a drum rattle and a water drum.

Kurath, Gertrude P., and Antonio Garcia. *Music and Dance of the Tewa Pueblos*. Santa Fe: Museum of New Mexico Press, 1980. This book contains a description of important songs, dances, and ceremonies of Pueblo peoples from northern New Mexico. It is written from the perspectives of a Tewa-speaking Native American and a dance ethnologist.

Link, Martin, and Charles L. Blood. *The Goat in the Rug*. New York: Parents' Magazine Press, 1976. This book shows how geography can influence the arts and crafts of a culture.

Mamaday, N. Scott. *The Way to Rainy Mountain*. Albuquerque: University of New Mexico Press, 1969. This award-winning collection of poetic images (for adults) provides the insight of a twentieth-century Kiowa from northeastern New Mexico and the earlier traditions of his grandmother.

McAllester, David P. *Enemy Way Music*, Vol. 41, no. 5 of the *Papers of the Peabody Museum of Archaeology and Ethnology*. Cambridge, MA: Harvard University Press, 1954. This is a scholarly account of the music and culture of the Navajo people.

McAllester, David P. *Indian Music in the Southwest*. Colorado Springs: The Taylor Museum of the Colorado Springs Fine Arts Center, 1961. This is a good source for information about similarities and differences among southwestern Native American groups.

McAllester, David P. "North American/Native American." In *Worlds of Music*, edited by Jeff Todd Titon, 12–63. New York: Schirmer Books, 1984. This chapter contains a description of several Native American song styles, including those of the Sioux, Zuni, Iroquois, and Navajo, with an emphasis on their cultural contexts and functions. Transcriptions are included, and a tape of ten selections (including "Proud Earth") accompanies the chapter.

McAllester, David P. *Peyote Music*. No. 13 of *Viking Fund Publications in Anthropology*. New York: Viking Fund, 1949. This is a landmark study of the Navajo people; their beliefs; and the music, dance, and rituals that are inspired by them.

National Geographic Society. *The World of the American Indian*. Washington, DC: National Geographic Society, 1974. This is a good source of photographs of the land and Native American people of the Southwest.

71

National Geographic Society. *Indians of North America.* Washington, DC: National Geographic Society, 1974. This map shows the location of southwestern Native American tribes.

Nettl, Bruno. *Folk and Traditional Music of the Western Continents.* Englewood Cliffs, NJ: Prentice-Hall, 1974. The chapter on Native American music includes descriptions of the principal tribes of North America.

Nettl, Bruno. *Folk Music in the United States.* Detroit: Wayne State University Press, 1976. This book includes a chapter on the general characteristics of Native American music.

Paul, Doris A. *Navajo Code Talkers.* Philadelphia: Dorrance, 1973. This book reveals the importance of the Navajo code talkers in World War II.

Pitts, Paul. *Racing the Sun.* New York: Avon Books, 1988. This novel is suitable for young readers, ages ten to thirteen. It illustrates the plight of a Native American boy who, through the presence of his grandfather as a roommate, discovers an ancient heritage that he can proudly preserve.

Wallace, Stephen, Regina Lynch, and Marvin Yellowhair. *Navajo Art, History and Culture.* Rough Rock, AZ: Navajo Curriculum Center/Rough Rock Demonstration School, 1984. This book contains a review of the arts and a history of Navajo culture.

Witherspoon, Gary. *Language and Art in the Navajo Universe.* Ann Arbor: University of Michigan Press, 1977. This book addresses the nature of language and art as expressions of Navajo thought.

Yazzie, Dollie. *Navajo Music for Classroom Enrichment.* Rev. ed. Rough Rock, AZ: Navajo Curriculum Center, 1976. This is a collection, accompanied by a cassette tape, of Navajo songs from the Rough Rock Demonstration School, Chinlo, Arizona.

DISCOGRAPHY

Cloud Dance Songs of San Juan Pueblo. Indian House 1102, 1972.

Folk Music of the United States from the Archive of Folk Song, Apache. Library of Congress AAFS L42.

Folk Music of the United States from the Archive of Folk Song, Indian Songs of Today. Library of Congress AFS L36.

Folk Music of the United States from the Archive of Folk Song, Navajo. Library of Congress AFS L41.

Folk Music of the United States from the Archive of Folk Song, Pueblo: Taos, San Ildefonso, Zuni, Hopi. Library of Congress AAFS L43.

Hopi Katcina Songs and Six Other Songs by Hopi Chanters. Ethnic Folkways Library FE 4394, 1964. Historical documentary collection recorded under the supervision of Jesse Walter Fewkes in Arizona, 1924.

Indian Music of the Southwest. Folkways FW 8850. Recorded by Laura Bolton in 1959.

Music of the American Indians of the Southwest. Ethnic Folkways Library FE 4420. Recorded by Willard Rhodes in 1951.

Music of the Sioux and the Navajo. Ethnic Folkways Library RE 4401. This recording contains the Navajo song "Shi Naasha" and a six-page pamphlet on the meaning and function of the songs.

Navajo Sway Songs. Indian House IH 1501, 1968.

Pueblo Indian Songs from San Juan. Canyon ARP 6065, 1969.

Pueblo Songs of the Southwest. Indian House 9502. This record contains songs from Pueblo Native American groups, including the Hopi, Zuni, and Tewa-speaking groups.

Note:

The following are addresses for recordings of Native American Music:

Canyon Records, 4143 North Sixteenth Street, Phoenix, AZ 85016.

Indian House, Box 472, Taos, NM 87571

Library of Congress, Music Division, Recording Library, Washington, DC 20540

The Smithsonian Institution, Constitution Avenue between Twelfth and Fourteenth Streets NW, Washington, DC 20560 (Distributor of Folkways recordings)

Proud Earth. Salt City Records SC-60. Chief Dan George, Arliene Nofchissey Williams, and Rich Brosseau perform on this record of songs that fuse Native American traditions with Christian values.

Sounds of Indian America: Plains and Southwest. Indian House 9501-C. This collection, recorded at the Gallup Intertribal Ceremonial in 1969, includes the "Navajo Feather Dance," the "Hopi Buffalo Dance," and dance music of the Ute, Zuni, Qechan, Kiowa, and Crow.

Traditional Apache Song. Canyon ARP 6071. Recorded in 1970 by Philip Canyon.

Turtle Dance Songs of San Juan Pueblo. Indian House 1101-C. Four songs of the December 26 Turtle Dance ceremony of northern New Mexico are heard on this recording.

FILMOGRAPHY

Discovering American Indian Music. 16mm, color. Santa Monica, CA: Bailey Film Associates. This film is an examination of several kinds of Native American music. Filmed mostly on location, it features Native American instruments, singing, dancing, and costumes.

The New Mexico State Library Audio/Visual Department has 16mm films and videocassettes available on Native American dances. For more information, call the library 505-827-3800.

AFRICAN AMERICANS

BIBLIOGRAPHY

Baldwin, James. *Notes of a Native Son.* New York: Dial, 1963. This is an excellent source that can be used in the study of Richard Wright's *Native Son.*

Berendt, Joachim-Ernst. *Jazz: A Photo History.* Translated by William Odom. New York: Schirmer Books, 1979. This striking visual history of jazz features stories and photographs of New Orleans, spirituals and gospels, blues, jazz performers, big bands, bebop, cool, and jazz in Europe and Japan. It includes an excellent discography.

Brooks, Tilford. *America's Black Musical Heritage.* Englewood Cliffs, NJ: Prentice-Hall, 1984. This comprehensive, indexed volume on African-American music covers forms before 1900, the development of jazz, and African-American composers.

Davis, Nathan. *Writings in Jazz.* 3d ed. Scottsdale, AZ: Gorsuch Scarisbrick, 1985. This book covers jazz, blues, religious styles, minstrelsy, and the musics of Chicago, Kansas City, and other landmark cities in the history of African-American music. It contains good discussions of jazz-rock fusion and women in jazz, a bibliography, a discography, and list of examples for suggested listening, with all recordings categorized according to music style.

Feather, Leonard. *The New Edition of The Encyclopedia of Jazz.* New York: Bonanza Books, 1960. This reference work includes most major jazz performers and their works and gives comprehensive answers to most questions about this subject area.

Fox, Sidney, Barbara Reeder Lundquist, and James Standifer, comps. *The World of Popular Music: Afro-American.* Chicago: Follett, 1975. The songs discussed here include "Oh Happy Day," "Rockin' Jerusalem," "Great Camp Meeting," and other recordings used in this chapter. Available from Follett Publishing Company, Department DM, 1010 West Washington Boulevard, Chicago 60607. Also see the recordings that accompany this book, listed in the Discography.

Franklin, Robin, and Tasha Lebow Wolf. *"Remember the Ladies": A Handbook of Women in American History.* Ann Arbor: The University of Michigan School of Education's Program for Educational Opportunity, 1980. This source includes information about women of the colonial period, the revolutionary era, the early nineteenth century, pioneer and Native American women, women during the Civil War era, women in the years from 1880 to 1920, and women during the period from 1920 to the present. It also includes a reading list with details about resources on women's contributions to the artistic developments of American society.

Fulton, Eleanor, and Pat Smith. *Let's Slice the Ice: A Collection of Black Children's Ring Games and Chants.* St. Louis: Magnamusic Baton, 1978. This collection contains several interesting examples of games and chants. See especially "This Away Valerie" (pp. 22–23), "Who Stole the Cookie from the Cookie Jar?" (p. 52), and "Bluebells and Cockle Shells" (p. 37).

Harris, Joel Chandler. *Uncle Remus, His Songs and His Sayings.* New York: Penguin, 1982. This source contains the legends, songs, and sayings of Uncle Remus, using the text of the first edition (1880) of Harris's attempt to record traditional stories of his time.

Hughes, Langston. *Ask Your Mama: Twelve Moods for Jazz.* New York: Knopf, 1969.

Hughes, Langston. *Selected Poems of Langston Hughes.* New York: Knopf, 1959.

Hughes, Langston, and Anna Bontemps, eds. *The Poetry of the Negro—1746–1949.* Garden City, NY: Doubleday, 1945.

Jones, Bessie, and Beth Lomax Hawes. *Step It Down.* New York: Harper & Row, 1952. This book includes children's songs and games from the Georgia Sea Islands.

Levine, Toby, and James Standifer. *Jumpstreet Humanities Project: Learning Package: Curriculum Materials for Secondary School Teachers and Students in Music, Language Arts, History, and the Humanities.* Washington, DC: Greater Washington Education Telecommunications Association, 1981. See especially the multicultural unit on music, dance, and poetry on pages 155–72.

Miller, Stephanie, comp. *Creative Patchwork.* Edited by Liz Goodman and Susan Joiner. New York: Crescent Books, 1973.

Morgenstern, Dan. *Jazz People.* Englewood Cliffs, NJ: Prentice-Hall, 1976. This book contains excellent photos and some scholarly text.

Neff, Robert, and Anthony Connor. *Blues.* Boston: David R. Godine, 1975. Blues musicians talk about themselves and their art in this book.

Oakley, Giles. *The Devil's Music.* New York: Harcourt Brace Jovanovich, 1976. This historically sound primer on the development of the blues includes an annotated bibliography and discography and numerous photographs.

Southern, Eileen. *The Music of Black Americans: A History.* New York: Norton, 1971. This is a well-documented history of all aspects of African-American music from the African past to the mid-twentieth century.

Standifer, James A., V. Butcher, and Toby Levine. *From Jumpstreet: A Story of Black Music.* Ann Arbor: University of Michigan School of Education's Program for Educational Opportunity, 1980. A secondary school teaching guide designed to be used with the television series *From Jumpstreet* (see Filmography for more information), this publication contains a complete lesson guide for each of the series' programs, focusing on blues, gospel, dance, jazz, soul, concert music, and other forms. Bibliographies, discographies, and photographs are provided.

Stearns, Marshall W. *Jazz Dance: The Story of American Vernacular Dance.* New York: Macmillan, 1968. Stearns discusses a wide variety of dances in America and their historical place in our music culture.

Tirro, Frank. *Jazz: A History.* New York: Norton, 1977. This well-balanced and well-illustrated history of African-American music styles and their development contains excellent music examples, an annotated bibliography, and a discography.

Work, John Wesley. *Folk Songs of the American Negro.* New York: Negro Universities Press, 1915. Reprint. Westport, CT: Greenwood Press, 1969. The author directed of the Fisk Jubilee Singers, who introduced this folk music to the world. The book includes examples of prominent spirituals, work songs, blues, hollers, and other African-American songs. It includes excellent discussions of each of the song types with definitive materials about the origins of these musics gleaned from Work's research in the area of African-American music and its practice at Fisk University's music program and with the Fisk Jubilee singers. The volume also contains an excellent bibliography and index of song titles.

Wright, Richard. *Native Son.* New York: Harper & Row, 1940. In the Afterword of this book John Reilly states: "This novel has become a classic; it is dramatic, unsentimental, and uncompromisingly realistic. The main character, Bigger Thomas, is a character to shock everyone: the liberal who believes himself a friend of the Negro cause is disappointed . . . while many Negroes recognize that oppression makes Bigger their brother."

DISCOGRAPHY

Chuck Berry's Golden Hits. Mercury 8262561.

The Complete Works of Scott Joplin. Audiophile AP 71–72. This is the most important complete collection of Joplin's ragtime works.

Deep South Country Blues. Flyright Label, Album 102. This record contains examples of blues from the 1920s and 1930s.

Eubie Blake Blues and Rags: His Earliest Piano Rolls, 1917–1921. Biograph BLP 10110, Vol. 1. This is an excellent source of the late Eubie Blake's compositions as they were originally recorded on piano rolls. Its selections include "Charleston Rag." The record is available from Biograph Records, P.O. Box 109, Canaan, NY 12029.

The Fisk Jubilee Singers, Directed by John W. Work. Folkways FP-72. This record includes performances of "There's a Great Camp Meeting" and "Rockin' Jerusalem."

Heliotrope Bouquet Piano Rags (1900–1970). Nonesuch H 71257. This record includes piano rags from the early years of the form up to more recent examples.

Mean Old Bed Bug Blues. Columbia G30818. This recording contains examples of thirty-three of Bessie Smith's best known blues performances of songs such as "You've Been a Good Old Wagon," "Yellow Dog Blues," and "Saint Louis Blues."

Music Down Home: An Introduction to Negro Music, USA. 4 vols. Folkways FA 2691 A, B, C, D, 1965. This record contains a broad sample of work songs, blues, spirituals, and related folk musics of African Americans. Excellent notes and complete texts to all songs are included.

Negro Blues and Hollers. Library of Congress AFS-L59. This record is a collection of field hollers and rural blues from the southern United States.

Negro Folk Music of Alabama, vol. 1. Folkways FE 4417. This record includes Alabama field hollers, work songs, and blues.

Negro Prison Songs. Tradition 1020. This is a recording of songs from southern United States penitentiaries sung by African Americans.

Negro Work Songs and Calls. Library of Congress AAFS-L8.

Piano Rags by Scott Joplin. Nonesuch H-712 48. This is an assortment of Joplin's ragtime piano works, including "Maple Leaf Rag."

Porgy and Bess. London OSA 13116. This is a production of Gershwin's opera with some material cut from the original score. It includes, however, the best known arias and interesting performances of "Strawberry Woman" and "Crab Man." The record includes a booklet that provides the text of all the scenes that are included in this release and photographs of the cast and sets of the original 1935 production.

The Rural Blues: A Study of Vocal and Instrumental Resources. RBF RP5. This recording includes selections for unaccompanied voice and voice with acoustic instruments.

Scott Joplin—1966: Classic Solos Played by the King of Ragtime Writers and Others from Rare Piano Rolls. Biograph BLP-10060. This recording was made from piano rolls labeled "Played by Scott Joplin himself!" Available from Biograph, P.O. Box 109, Canaan, NY 12029.

The Smithsonian Collection of Classic Jazz. P6 11891. Distributed by Norton, 500 Fifth Avenue, New York 10036. This set of six records contains samplings of the jazz styles by the greatest performers, including Jelly Roll Morton, Louis Armstrong, Duke Ellington, and John Coltrane.

Step It Down. Rounder Records 8004. This record includes children's songs and games from the Georgia Sea Islands. It is designed to accompany the publication by Bessie Jones and Beth Lomax Hawes, *Step It Down* (see Bibliography).

The Story of the Blues. 2 vols. Compiled by Paul Oliver. CBS 6618, 66232. Volume 1 covers blues from the 1920s, 1930s, World War II, and the postwar years. Volume 2 features guitarists, women blues musicians, pianists, and ensembles.

Walking in Space. A & M Records SP 3023. Side one of this album is a tribute to the Broadway musical *Hair*. Side two includes the gospel tune "Oh Happy Day," written by Edwin Hawkins, in a primarily instrumental version of the tune played by excellent jazz performers.

The World of Popular Music: Afro-American. Album XLII, Code 4608, Follett BS 12192. This record includes "Oh Happy Day," "Rockin' Jerusalem," and "There's a Great Camp Meeting," instrumental compositions such as Thomas Kerr's "Easter Monday Swagger" (based on "There's a Great Camp Meeting"), and many other interesting and useful selections. It also includes student and teacher books (with explicit lessons that use the recorded examples) and a poster. This is a very useful resource for any class devoted to African-American music and history.

The World of Popular Music: Jazz. Album XL, Code 4628, Follett BS 23539. This recording includes examples that demonstrate African-American styles, blues, ragtime, spirituals, Dixieland, swing, bop, and cool jazz.

FILMOGRAPHY

The Black Experience as Expressed Through Music. Four VHS videotapes, 60 minutes each tape. Los Angeles: Los Angeles Public Schools, Music Division, 1978. This series consists of programs on gospel, spirituals, jazz, and ragtime. (There are two 30-minute programs on each tape.) One program includes an interview with Eubie Blake, who performs many of his own compositions and talks about his career. For information, contact Betty Cox, Beem Foundation, 3864 Grayburn Avenue, Los Angeles 90008, 212-291-7252.

Forever Free: The Story of Blind Tom Bethune. VHS, 30 minutes. A teleplay by Kathleen McGhee-Anderson, 1987. This program relates the life story of the blind African-American piano genius, Blind Tom Bethune. For more information, contact Betty Cox, Beem Foundation, 3864 Grayburn Avenue, Los Angeles 90008, 212-291-7252.

From Jumpstreet: A Story of Black Music. Washington, DC: Greater Washington Educational Telecommunications Association, 1981. (Telephone 703-998-2851.) This series of thirteen 30-minute television programs was hosted by writer and playwright Oscar Brown, Jr., and produced for secondary school audiences by WETA-TV. Brown explores the black musical tradition from its African sources to its present place in American music. The program's locations were chosen from a variety of areas in which black music flourishes. It was written primarily for the secondary school level, but it has much information that is relevant to other educational levels. It also has very inclusive, up-to-date bibliographies and discographies. National Public Radio has made available a ten-part audiotape series of *From Jumpstreet*. For more information, call 202-822-2670. Preview videocassettes (¾″ only) are available from GPN, P.O. Box 80669, Lincoln, NE 68501, 800-228-4630.

A Gift of Hearts and Hands. Videotape, 1 hour, color. This is a PBS program about the influence of black and white women on American society through the art of quilting. It includes many news clips and still photographs that match the quilt patterns shown, bringing home the meaning of each quilting pattern as it relates to historical events such as women's suffrage, the fight for freedom and emancipation by courageous African-American women like Harriet Tubman, and the underground railroad. A book, *Hearts and Hands: The Influence of Women and Quilts on American Society*, by Elaine Hedges and Julie Silva, accompanies the videotape. For more information, write The American Experience #112, Hearts and Hands, Box 322, Boston 02134.

Scott Joplin. Pyramid, 15 minutes, color, 1977. This film gives a brief introduction to the life and works of the most famous of all ragtime composers.

Videotaped Interviews with Prominent Black Musicians and Others Associated with the Development of Black Music in the U.S. VHS. Ann Arbor: The University of Michigan Afroamerican Music Collections, Oral History Section, the N. C. Standifer Archive. This series consists of more than 250 videotaped interviews with prominent musicians, including Count [William] Basie, Eubie Blake, Anne Brown, William Dawson, Todd Duncan, Katherine Dunham, John Hammond, Alberta Hunter, Andy Kirk, William Grant Still, and Marylou Williams. For more information, call The University of Michigan School of Music, Afroamerican Music Collection, at 313-764-5429 or The University of Michigan Center for African and Afroamerican Studies at 313-764-5513.

NOTES

1. Cecil J. Sharp, *English Folk Songs from the Southern Appalachians* (London: Oxford University Press, 1983) 1: xxii.
2. Sharp, *English Folk Songs* 1: 2.
3. Sharp, *English Folk Song: Some Conclusions*, 4th rev. ed. (Belmont, CA: Wadsworth, 1965), 134.
4. Charles Hamm, *Music in the New World* (New York: Norton, 1983), 60.

5. Pamela L. Tiedt and Iris M. Tiedt, *Multicultural Teaching: A Handbook of Activities, Information, and Resources* (Boston: Allyn & Bacon, 1979), 54–57.
6. Stephen Wallace, Regina Lynch, and Marvin Yellowhair, *Navajo Art, History and Culture* (Rough Rock, AZ: Navajo Curriculum Center/Rough Rock Demonstration School, 1984), 21.
7. Adapted from Ilene Hunter and Marilyn Judson, *Simple Folk Instruments to Make and Play* (New York: Simon and Schuster, 1977), 54–56.
8. Jimmy Stewart, "Introduction to Black Aesthetics in Music," in *The Black Aesthetic*, ed. Addison Gayle Jr. (Garden City, NY: Doubleday, 1971), 84.
9. Eileen Southern, from a presentation at the University of Michigan School of Music Musicology Conference, November 1984.

**MAJOR COUNTRIES
OF LATIN AMERICA**

Including North America, Central America,
South America, and the Caribbean

Map and photographs for Chapter 3 by Dale Olsen

3

LATIN AMERICA AND THE CARRIBEAN

by Dale A. Olsen and Selwyn Ahyoung

Latin America is a vast area that stretches from the northern border of Mexico in North America, through Central America, to Cape Horn at the southern tip of South America. Many of the inhabitants of the neighboring Caribbean basin are of northern European or African descent, so the term "Caribbean" (a geographic term) is often used separately from Latin America. In our context, however, the term "Latin America" will include the Caribbean area. There are so many countries included in this vast region that not all of them can be included in this chapter.

Latin Americans are not all of one race or ethnic group. They can be separated into five large groups as follows: (1) The descendants of the original Native Americans, commonly called Indians, who inhabited this region before the arrival of Columbus; (2) peoples of African descent, mainly from Western and Central Africa; (3) peoples of European descent, mainly Spanish and Portuguese, but also French, Dutch, Italian, British, and others; (4) peoples of Asian descent, mainly Chinese, Japanese, Indians, and Javanese; and (5) peoples who are mixtures of any of these groups.

Latin America's geography and culture are tremendously varied. Although it is impossible to make sweeping statements that describe the music and way of life of the many peoples living in Latin America, it can be said that contemporary

79

Latin American music and culture is the direct result of certain shared historical influences.

In the late fifteenth century, for example, Europeans invaded the region now called Latin America and maintained control of it for about four hundred years. In some places, such as the Caribbean islands, most of the Native Americans did not survive the European domination, but in certain parts of Central and South America some Native American cultures survived by retreating into the dense jungle interiors or the vast mountain reaches. The Europeans also brought in large numbers of African slaves to work on the islands and the coastal areas of Latin America, and after the slaves obtained their freedom they were replaced by hired workers from other far-off lands. In Guyana, Jamaica, and Trinidad the Europeans brought in Asian Indian and Chinese laborers, and in Brazil and Peru many Japanese were imported as laborers. Many of these workers never returned to their native lands after their contracts ran out.

Contemporary Latin America is the product of the influences of several cultures. Many of these diverse groups handed down and maintained their customs, beliefs, and culture patterns for generations. Not only do these cultures contain original traits from their past, but the fact that they came together in similar geographical regions under similar historical circumstances caused many of them to interact, mix, blend, and create new and unique cultural patterns. It is more accurate to describe Latin America as an area comprising many cultures, rather than just one.

It was only in Latin America that the musics and cultures of the Aztecs, Mayas, and Incas blended with the musics and cultures of the Spanish. No other geographic region has provided us with such a mixture of African music with Spanish or Portuguese music. Moreover, the steel band of Trinidad bears a resemblance to some African percussion ensembles, but it was born in a new environment using a new set of instruments: oil drums. These examples help illustrate how Latin American musics have a flavor all their own.

The Native American peoples of Latin America, as in North America, probably began arriving in the Western Hemisphere from northern Asia about fifty thousand years ago. During the last Ice Age a land bridge connected Alaska with Russia, allowing ancient hunters to follow game across the Bering Strait. These hunters brought their music with them; melodies were probably sung or played on bone flutes by the shamans (medicine men) to magically lure game animals. The descendants of these native peoples spread throughout the Americas, touching nearly every inhabitable corner of Mexico, Central, and South America. In the few areas, such as the Amazon forest, where Native Americans were not heavily influenced by the African and European newcomers to the Western Hemisphere, their music exists much as it did thousands of years ago.

The traditional musics of the Native Americans are used for curing illnesses; causing rain; making the land, animals, and people fertile; enhancing the harvest; hunting and making war; and praising the gods. Much of their music is purely vocal; when instruments are used, they are traditionally made from natural substances such as bone, clay, bamboo, hollowed sticks, and shells, as well as silver and gold.

80

African slaves were brought to Latin America from Western and central Africa by the first Spanish and Portuguese conquerors and colonists. They worked mainly in sugarcane fields and gold mines as replacements for the enslaved Native Americans who had died of disease. The slave owners believed they had completely converted their African slaves to Christianity, and although the slaves were treated harshly, the Africans were often allowed to live together and perform music after working hours. Many of them also continued to worship their African gods and performed their music for worship at the same time that they worshipped the Catholic saints. Today, in many regions of South America, especially in Brazil and in the Caribbean (especially Cuba, Haiti, and Trinidad), the African and European religions fused to become new syncretic religions that continue to be important to the descendants of the African slaves. Also among the important attributes of this Afro-Latin American culture are various types of musics and dances for entertainment, as well as work songs.

The primary Euro-American influence in Latin America is that of the Spanish and the Portuguese, although British influence is prevalent in portions of the Caribbean. Near the beginning of European exploration of the Western Hemisphere, Pope Alexander VI in 1494 designated an imaginary line, known as the Line of Demarcation, decreeing that everything west of the line belonged to Spain and everything east belonged to Portugal. This led to the formation of Spanish (Hispanic) America and the Portuguese-speaking country of Brazil. These European conquerors, settlers, and religious men brought their music, along with the other aspects of their culture.

In some parts of South America, European music has remained somewhat intact since the colonial period and is still found in certain regions of Chile, Argentina, Colombia, and Brazil. In other regions, Catholic missionaries taught European music directly to the Native Americans and to some of the African slaves, yet in other areas European music was learned by listening to the settlers. Thus, a tremendous and complex mix of musics began in Latin America from the time of the earliest European migrations.

The Asian presence in Latin America is the result of events in the late nineteenth and early twentieth centuries, when East Indians, Javanese, Chinese, and Japanese were brought to British, Dutch, Spanish, and Portuguese lands after African slaves had been granted their freedom. Although their presence in many regions of Latin America is substantial (there are more than one million Japanese and their descendants in Brazil alone), their musics have not blended extensively with the Native, African, and European musics. Rather, the isolated settings for their musics provide examples of traditional Asian culture that are often rare in their countries of origin.

By far the largest number of Latin Americans belong to a mixed culture of one type or another. Many Latin American countries have terms for their people of mixed heritage, such as *mestizo* (mixed, basically Native American and Spanish), *mulato* (African and European), and *zambo* (African and native American). Some countries have no designation for their racial and cultural mixing, since they are almost completely mixed, whereas in Brazil the terms *branco* (white) and *negro* (black) are social rather than color distinctions.

As the races have often mixed in Latin America, so have their musical characteristics. This musical mixing is obvious in the festivals that exist in all Latin American and Caribbean countries. Most of these festivals, such as the carnival in Trinidad and Brazil, are joyful celebrations in which people of all social classes participate for several days. The people who perform as festival musicians or dancers earn great prestige; they often spend most of their year and much of their money in preparation for the festival events and competitions.

Native Americans

The principal Native American ethnic or cultural groups in Latin America share many distinctive musical characteristics in their use of melody, rhythm, texture, timbre, dynamics, and form. Native Americans commonly use descending melodic lines that combine short musical motives. The choice of cadential intervals varies from culture to culture: Minor thirds are used by some ancient cultures in Venezuela, Colombia, Chile, and the Andes; major thirds are used by many Andean groups; major seconds were used by Cariban groups in Venezuela; and microtones (intervals smaller than those used in Western music) were probably used by ancient cultures in Peru, Colombia, and Mexico. Melodic range also varies among cultures: Some groups use one-note recitation; some use ranges of a minor third; and others expand to a perfect fourth or fifth. Scales may be of various types, including microtonal (with intervals smaller than those found in Western music), bitonic (two-toned), tritonic (three-toned), tetratonic (four-toned), and pentatonic (five-toned).

Native American cultures often use specific melodies and rhythmic styles for specific functions. Religious songs may include slow-paced, free rhythms, and dances and lullabies may contain measured rhythms. Most Native American dances are set in duple meter. The Andean dance form known as the *wayno* can be interpreted as being in an additive meter based on $\frac{1}{4}$ (or as $\frac{2}{4}$ with an occasional $\frac{3}{4}$ measure).

Native American musicians also associate specific tone colors with specific purposes. Often, for example, they use a "masked" vocal tone when a song is used to communicate with supernatural powers. In instrumental music, they often emphasize a "buzzing" timbre, using drums equipped with snares and the buzzing sound of native clarinets. Both flutes and human whistling are used to produce a contrasting "whistle" sound.

Many native cultures of Latin America use monophonic textures that are often accompanied by a rhythm instrument such as a rattle or drum. Some perform, however, multipart music in freestyle rounds or canons as well as with parallel melodies. Some cultures sing certain special songs mentally when addressing the supernatural, never singing them aloud. Songs used for curing illnesses or other supernatural songs may be sung very softly, and many cultures follow a dynamic of decreasing volume as melodies descend.

The song text determines the form as well as the dynamics of most religious vocal music. This through-composed music often sounds repetitious to Euro-Americans because the detailed and lengthy texts have to be sung precisely. Native American musicians, on the other hand, often model their dance music in strophic forms, using repetitions necessary for the dance itself.

82

Afro–Latin Americans

The Afro-American subcultures of Latin America have their own distinctive organization of the elements of music. Although they often use scale forms common both to Europe and Africa (including major, minor, modal, and pentatonic scales), they almost always use African-derived call-and-response patterns that alternate between a high-pitched solo singer and an equally high-pitched choral response. This responsorial technique produces the most common vocal texture; many performances include the additional textures of hand clapping and other sounds that accompany dancing such as yells, shouts of encouragement, foot stomping, and talking. The element of call-and-response also provides the singers with a basic strophic form in which the text of the call changes constantly because of improvisation and the choral response repeats predetermined phrases.

In drum ensembles only one drum improvises while the others maintain steady rhythmic patterns or ostinatos. Afro–Latin American musicians most often base their music on duple meters with a very fast pulse or rhythmic density (number of notes per minute). As in traditional African drumming, percussion ensembles display a complex layering of rhythms such as two against three or three against four, creating a wealth of syncopations and cross rhythms.

Afro–Latin American vocal music is often deep-chested, raspy, or gravelly: The instrumental music typically uses resonant drums and sympathetic buzzes produced by attachments to instruments or sounds rich in overtones such as the steel drums of Trinidad. Drummers and groups of singers typically play at high volume levels, and idiophonic ensembles such as the steel band use dynamic nuance as a part of their stylistic language.

Euro–Latin Americans

Euro–Latin American music throughout Latin America shows varying degrees of European characteristics. In certain isolated coastal or highland regions of South America, such as the Colombian Pacific coast and southern Chile, musicians use modal melodies of European Renaissance origin. The most common scale forms, however, are the diatonic major or minor scales, and the "Andalusian cadence" (the chord progression A minor, G, F, and E) is found throughout heavily Hispanic areas such as parts of Venezuela or Colombia, showing the influence of Moorish music on Spain. Euro-Americans generally prefer stepwise, lyrical melodies.

These descendents of the first Europeans in the New World also use some rhythmic practices imported from their homelands. They use dual meter, for example, in two different ways: the $\frac{6}{8}$ against $\frac{3}{4}$ hemiola, called "colonial rhythm" (commonly found in the Spanish *jota*, the Chilean *cueca*, the Peruvian *marinera*, the Argentine *zamba*, the Venezuelan *joropo*); and an alternation between $\frac{6}{8}$ and $\frac{3}{4}$, called *sesquiáltera*, found in Chile, Puerto Rico, Cuba, and immortalized by Leonard Bernstein in the *West Side Story* song "I Like to Be in America." They also use somewhat simpler duple meters in lullabies and dances and triple meters for waltzes.

The texture of Euro–Latin American music ranges from unaccompanied vocal solos, including lullabies, work songs, *desafío* or challenge songs, and

83

ballads; to vocal solos, accompanied by a stringed instrument such as guitar, harp, or other lutes or guitar-like instruments; to vocal duets in parallel thirds, accompanied by European-derived instruments; to ensembles of European-derived musical instruments, such as harp, guitar, and violins. Singers of some cattle songs have a Spanish *cante jondo* style of singing, using deep chest tones and solo guitar music that features alternating plucking (*punteado*) and strumming (*rasqueado*) styles.

Musicians in this culture group commonly use volume to intensify the mood of the music and also use dynamics expressively in ballads. Both vocal and instrumental musicians use strophic forms with a binary structure, which consists of even or uneven measures of two alternating sections that repeat with slight variations.

Mixed American

Latin America contains a great diversity of mixed races, mixed cultures, and mixed musical styles and forms. Many of the musical characteristics of the Native Americans, Afro–Latin Americans, and Euro–Latin Americans can be found in a rich variety of combinations throughout the area.

L E S S O N   O N E

■ OBJECTIVES:

Students will:

1. Explain what a panpipe is and what cultures use them in their music.
2. Identify the principle of interlocking parts as exemplified in Peruvian and Bolivian panpipes (the *siku*).
3. Define the term *syncopation,* and identify syncopated passages in the music.
4. Explain why Peruvian and Bolivian panpipe music is important as a surviving tradition.

Materials:

1. Recordings:
   Kingdom of the Sun, Peru's Inca Heritage, Nonesuch H-72029
   Mountain Music of Peru, Folkways FE 4539
   Instruments and Music of Bolivia, Folkways FM 4012
2. Pictures of the Andes of Peru and Bolivia from *National Geographic* (vol. 144, no. 6, December 1973; vol. 161, no. 3, March 1982; vol. 162, no. 1, July 1982) or other sources

■ PROCEDURES:

1. Show or display pictures of the Andes of Peru and Bolivia. Discuss the cultures of the Peruvian and Bolivian Andes, and explain that the regions of southern highland Peru and most of highland Bolivia lie at very high elevations, where the air is thin, temperatures are often very cold, and wood is scarce. The llama is the chief beast of burden. The two Native American languages spoken there are Quechua and Aymara, and these are the names given to the people as well. The great Quechua-speaking civilization of the Incas captured many other civilizations in its military conquests. Today, music is used by both cultures for religious and festive dancing. The most important instruments are flutes (including panpipes) and drums (see figure 1). The Spanish conquered the Native Americans in the 1500s, and today many of the people are mixed bloods or *mestizos*.

2. Play a recorded example of Peruvian or Bolivian panpipe music to demonstrate the principle of interlocking musical parts, a technique in which two musicians (or multiples of two) play alternate notes of a single melody on a pair of panpipes. These two players consist of the *ira* (leader) and the *arka*

Figure 1. Peruvian sikuri *(panpipes), played by Aconcagua, an Andean music ensemble from Florida State University, Tallahassee.*

85

(follower). The interlocking musical parts can be clearly heard on *Kingdom of the Sun* (side one, band four, and side two, band two) and *Mountain Music of Peru* (side four, band five). Discuss the listening example, and have the class generate a definition for the term "interlocking parts."

3. Discuss the term *syncopation*. The basic "short-long-short" Andean syncopation is very common in *siku* panpipe music and is found in the song "Waka Waka," transcribed on page 88, and in the listening examples in the "Materials" section. Teach it aurally with the syllables "dot-da-dot" while patting in a steady duple pulse. Have the students sing "dot-da-dot" while the teacher claps a steady rhythm; then have the students both sing and clap.

4. Discuss the importance of *siku* music by pointing out that the present panpipe traditions in Peru and Bolivia are continuations of ancient traditions: panpipes constructed from cane, silver, gold, and clay have been found in 3,000-year-old desert tombs. Explain that panpipe traditions are also found in Ecuador, the Amazon forest, Africa, Europe (Romania), Melanesia, and ancient China. Point out these places on a world map and list the countries on the chalkboard. Discuss how panpipes are made by the Native Americans from their local materials (cane or bamboo and string), and explain how we can make them from modern materials: polyvinyl chloride (PVC) plastic tubing and glue.

5. Andean *siku* panpipes can be constructed from a twelve-foot length of ½″ diameter PVC plastic tubing according to the following instructions:

   a. Measure for and mark out lines on a 36-inch, ⅜″ diameter dowel (see figure 2).

   b. Measure the PVC tubing according to the dimensions shown, and cut it with a saw (using a miter box, if possible). Sand the blowing edges inside and outside until smooth.

   c. Using medium sandpaper, remove the printing on the PVC tubes; this will slightly roughen the edges of the tubes to be glued, making the glue hold better.

   d. Insert a cork into the bottom of each properly measured PVC tube. Old wine corks that are tapered are easy to insert; new corks must be compressed many times in a vise for them to be pliable enough to be inserted. Measure the internal length of each tube from the open end to the cork, and compare with the proper mark on the dowel. Cut off the excess cork (the cut-off portion of the cork can be your next plug).

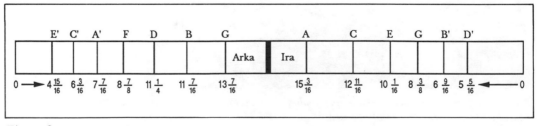

Figure 2

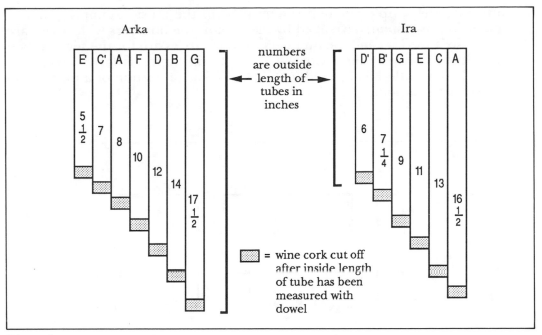

Figure 3

e. Place the tubes into two sets (as shown in figure 3) on a flat surface covered with waxed paper, and place a one-quarter-inch wide bead of PVC glue (see "Caution") along the sanded edge of each tube that is to be joined. Glue and join the tubes one by one; then let the glue dry according to the manufacturer's instructions, or for approximately two hours.

CAUTION: the PVC cement vapors are toxic.
Use the glue outdoors ONLY.

6. Using a marking pen, write numbers on each tube. Beginning with the longest tube of each half at your right, draw at the top of the tubes the numbers 1–6 on the half with six tubes (the *ira*) and 1–7 on the half with the seven tubes (the *arka*) from right to left, or longest tube to shortest tube. Next, on the *ira* half of the instrument only, draw a circle around each number.

7. With the longest tubes to your right, practice playing each half of the panpipe by blowing as you would across a bottle, using the attack "tu" or "pu." Give each note a forceful attack with support from the diaphragm. Sustaining notes is not a part of the *siku* tradition, and the notes of a melody are commonly shared between two players, so you should not become dizzy or short of breath when performing the panpipes. The sound will be loud and breathy.

8. Introduce the simple notation system used in the music examples for this lesson. In this system, developed by the author, the numbers with circles are for the six-tubed *ira* and the numbers without circles are for the seven-tubed *arka*. Study and play the following examples in figure 4: (a) the scale, (b) "Mary had a Little Lamb," and (c) "Waka Waka" (a portion of a piece from the Aymara tradition):

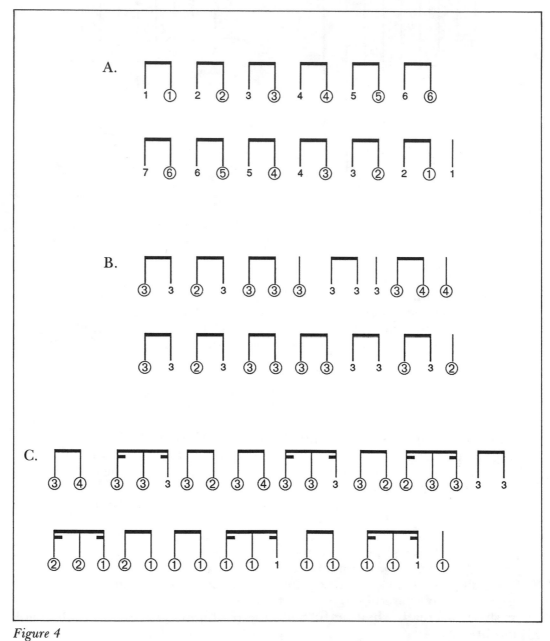

Figure 4

2

■ **OBJECTIVES:**

Students will:

1. Imitate rhythmic patterns created by the teacher or taken from the drum performance on Lyrichord record LLST 7315 (see "Materials"), side one, band two, using percussion instruments or by striking the body.
2. Study and perform some of the layered and interlocking rhythms of the drum ensembles of Brazil, Haiti, Cuba, Surinam, and Venezuela, using classroom percussion instruments.
3. Combine three different rhythmic ostinatos written in TUBS (Time Unit Box System) notation to produce a composite ensemble pattern.
4. Improvise patterns in a small-group setting.

Materials:

1. Recordings:

    Afro-Brazilian Religious Songs: Cantigas de Candomblé/Candomble Songs from Salvador, Bahia, Brazil, Lyrichord LLST 7315

    Amazonia, Cult Music of Northern Brazil, Lyrichord LLST 7300 (optional)

    Refer also to *Sounds of the World: Music of Latin America: Mexico, Ecuador, Brazil* (Reston, VA: Music Educators National Conference, 1987)

2. Classroom drums, preferably bongos or congas
3. *Claves,* triangles, sticks, tins, bottles, spoons, or other available percussion instruments
4. Question and answer sheets (optional)

■ **PROCEDURES:**

1. The teacher should play line A of figure 5 (the quarter-note pulse) on a drum. Have the class imitate it, using their bodies as instruments by tapping, clapping, clicking, or stamping.

Figure 5

89

2. Play line B of figure 5 on a triangle. Ask the students to imitate it using bottles and spoons while saying the vocable "mm" on the rests.
3. Play line C of figure 5 on the *claves*, and instruct the students to imitate it using sticks. Students again say "mm" on the rests.
4. Divide the class into three sections, assigning one section line A, the second section line B, and the third section line C. Begin with one section, and then add the other sections to form a layered texture.
5. After the composite rhythm is successfully achieved, discuss the activity by asking students the following questions:
   a. Did we all perform the same rhythmic pattern after we divided the class?
   b. Did our different patterns fit together?
   c. How did we put them together?
6. *Drum ensemble.* In Afro–Latin America, the drum ensemble is important to both secular and religious festivals (see figures 6 and 7). Using a three-drum ensemble is common. One drummer provides a *time-line* with a simple ostinato that may vary only slightly; another answers with interlocking phrase patterns influenced by the other drummers; the third drummer usually improvises by bringing cross rhythms, syncopations, irregular phrase lengths, and rhythmic excitement to the performance. Certain rhythms are usually associated with specific occasions.

Figure 6. A large mina *drum. The man on the right uses* laures *(sticks) to strike the body of the* mina, *from Northeastern Venezuela.*

Figure 7. A curbata *drum from Northeast Venezuela.*

Discuss the terms *time-line, ostinato, rhythmic layering, interlocking rhythms,* and *composite pattern.* Ask the class what parts of the world have drum ensembles that use these principles.

a. *Time-line:* a steady rhythmic pattern that is repeated throughout a performance. It serves as a foundation or organizing principle for the entire rhythmic structure. It is usually played by idiophones such as the *claves* or cow-bell and is sometimes played in a drum ensemble as a rhythmic ostinato. Sometimes more than one percussion instrument may be used to play the time-line.

b. *Ostinato:* a repeated rhythmic pattern that may be changed slightly during the performance but never loses its basic form.

c. *Rhythmic layering:* the principle of creating a dense texture in which more than one rhythmic pattern occurs simultaneously. If the parts enter at different points, the layering effect becomes more evident.

d. *Interlocking rhythms:* Rhythms that fit together as they progress through time. If the drums or instruments have various pitches or textures, the interlocking effect is easier to detect.

91

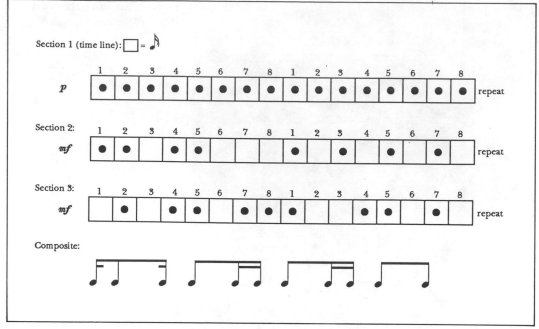

Figure 8

e. *Composite pattern*: the total rhythmic phrase that emerges as the drummers play ostinatos and improvised patterns together.

7. Play a recording of an Afro–Latin American drum ensemble performance ("Oshossi" from *Afro–Brazilian Religious Songs: Cantigas de Candomble/Candomblé Songs from Salvador, Bahia*, side one, band two). List student's answers to the following questions on the board as they listen:

   a. Is there more than one drum playing?

   b. Do you hear a steady pattern that you could imitate?

   c. Does the steady pattern ever change?

   d. What else do you hear? Do you hear voices, clapping, other instruments, or a foreign language?

   e. Can you tell what instrument or instruments play the time-line?

   f. Can you guess what kind of occasion this music is being played for?

   g. Can you guess what country this music comes from?

8. Show the students the example of TUBS notation in figure 8, and explain how to read it. Explain that the notation gives them three different rhythmic ostinatos that they must put together to produce a composite pattern. Lead students in counting eight-beat "measures" slowly. Students should play their percussion instruments when specified by the boxes marked with dots; when the parts are secure, increase the tempo.

9. Divide the class into three sections. Section one establishes the *time-line* using sticks or *claves*, section two plays the second rhythmic layer using sticks and tin cans, and section three plays the third rhythmic layer using bottles and spoons. The rhythms should be precise and the ostinatos regular.

92

10. If possible, select one student from each group, and encourage them to perform the composite pattern as a solo group using three drums. As an alternative, play the record again and have the class perform improvised patterns or ostinatos along with the drum ensemble on the recording.
11. Introduce the idea of improvisation by having students experiment with hitting the drum in various ways, such as with sticks, hands, or fingers, in the middle of the membrane, on the edge, or on the side, and incorporate these new techniques for given measures at prescribed times.

L E S S O N   T H R E E

3

■ OBJECTIVES:
Students will:
1. Define the terms *marimba, ostinato,* and *call-and-response.*
2. Identify the sound of an African-derived ensemble from Colombia or Ecuador that includes the marimba, drums, and a rattle.
3. Identify the stylistic characteristic of parallel thirds in a marimba melody.
4. Identify the call-and-response technique and sing a song using that principle.
5. Explain how music functions as an aspect of Afro–Latin American daily life, especially for entertainment and religious celebrations; perform an *arrulo* and simulate a *currulao.*

Materials:
1. Recordings:
   In Praise of Oxalá and Other Gods, Black Music of South America, Nonesuch H-72036
   Afro–Hispanic Music from Western Colombia and Ecuador, Folkways Records FE 4376
2. A picture of a marimba or a marimba ensemble
3. If possible, a Western marimba or any type of xylophone

■ PROCEDURES:
1. Discuss the region of the Pacific lowlands or littoral of Colombia and Ecuador: It is a tropical rain forest between the Andes mountains and the Pacific Ocean. The region stretches from the border of Colombia with Panama into Ecuador, and much of the area can only be reached by boat. African slaves were brought into the region to work in gold mines, and after the gold was gone, the whites left and the blacks stayed. Today there are about 5,000 blacks living in the area. Buenaventura, Colombia, the only town of any size, has drawn some of the inhabitants from the rain forest, but others continue living in the jungle, where they grow bananas and catch fish. The majority of the population is very poor.

93

2. Explain how music functions as an aspect of daily life, for both entertainment and for religious celebrations. (Refer to the contexts and words of the songs given on the record jacket.) Mention that Afro–Latin Americans use songs to emphasize social relationships and to worship Catholic saints.

   a. Discuss the secular song and dance festival called *currulao* (marimba dance), which is often performed on weekends by the blacks of the Pacific lowlands of Colombia and Ecuador. The typical song text of a *currulao* is sung by a man about his imagined freedom to leave his wife whenever he wishes, while a woman may boastfully sing about her ability to keep her husband. Listen to the *currulao* from *In Praise of Oxalá and Other Gods* (side two, band five), and note the driving, forceful rhythm of this energetic dance, which simulates a contest between a man and a woman. This song uses a marimba ostinato, probably because the context is secular and therefore more African and perhaps because the example comes from a small, isolated village where African elements have been retained.

   b. Discuss the religious songs performed to honor a saint on a special day, which are commonplace among blacks in this area. These songs, known as *arrullos*, are usually sung by women, using the call-and-response technique and are accompanied by marimba, drums, and rattles. Read the information and the text from "San Antonio" (side one, band one of *In Praise of Oxalá and Other Gods*), and play the example.

3. Show a picture of a marimba to the class (see figure 9). If possible, bring a marimba to class and demonstrate how to play it and its scale (playing only the diatonic keys on a chromatic instrument). Define the marimba as an African-derived struck idiophone consisting of many slabs of hard wood placed in descending order from right to left. An Orff diatonic marimba works very well in this context.

4. Play an example of Colombian marimba music, using the records listed for this lesson. Point out the sound of the marimba, the drums, and the rattle.

5. Demonstrate the principles of ostinato and parallel thirds on a marimba, piano, or xylophone, and ask students to identify examples. Either improvise your examples or perform them from (a) the secular song and (b) the marimba melody from a religious song in the following example:

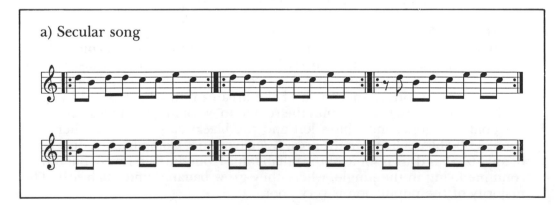

a) Secular song

b) Religious song

With
Call

With
Response

6. Demonstrate the call-and-response technique and discuss this technique with the students. Show how to sing responsorially by using the religious song "San Antonio" (from *In Praise of Oxalá and other Gods,* side one, band one), as a guide; the words are in Spanish and English on the record's back cover. Learn the song by ear or use the following excerpt:

Call   Response

Ri - o   ri   ri - o   ra —   San An -ton -io ya se va

7. Play the marimba melody of the religious song "San Antonio" on the marimba or piano while the students sing the vocal call-and-response of the song.
8. Using phrases from "San Antonio," have students demonstrate the call-and-response technique by individually singing a call while the rest of the class sings a response.

Figure 9. Suspended in a marimba house, this marimba is played by two men with four mallets.

9. Have the students write a brief report about the musical and cultural characteristics of both secular and religious music making among the blacks of the Pacific lowlands of Colombia and Ecuador.
10. Have the students create their own tunes and perform them on xylophones, Orff instruments, or marimbas.

L E S S O N   F O U R

■ OBJECTIVES:

Students will:
1. Describe the background and social context of calypso and steel band music from Trinidad and Tobago.
2. Describe the instruments in a steel band.
3. Perform two rhythmic accompaniment patterns characteristic of the calypso.
4. Sing and play a simple tune that illustrates the calypso style, and create a text based on the tune.
5. Construct a miniature or full-size steel band instrument (this is a long-range project).

Materials:
1. Recordings:
   The Steel Drums of Kim Loy Wong, Folkways FI 8367 and FS 3834
   Calypso Travels, Lord Invader & His Calypso Group, Folkways FW 8733
   The Real Calypso 1927–46, RBF Records RBF #13
   Sparrow, The Greatest, Charlie's records JAF1007
2. *Claves*, sticks, hand drums, or other unpitched percussion instruments; Orff xylophones and metallophones or other melodic instruments
3. Pictures of the Trinidad carnival, a calypsonian, a steel band, or a Caribbean setting [Examples can be found in "Trinidad and Tobago," in *Isles of the Caribbean* (Washington, DC: National Geographic Society, 1980), 10–41.]

■ PROCEDURES:

1. Show or display Trinidad or Caribbean pictures.
2. Discuss Trinidad, its location, and mention that it is an island that contains a rich heritage of traditions. Trinidad, the home of the steel band, lies close to Venezuela in the Caribbean and was discovered by Columbus in 1498. The culture of Trinidad has been influenced by the Spanish, French, British, West Africans, and East Indians. The British ruled for a period beginning in 1797, and Trinidad became independent in 1962.
3. Study the music styles calypso and *soca* as well as the steel band.
   a. Calypso is a very popular type of song in the Caribbean islands, especially in Trinidad, where this art form developed. Calypso has a long history

96

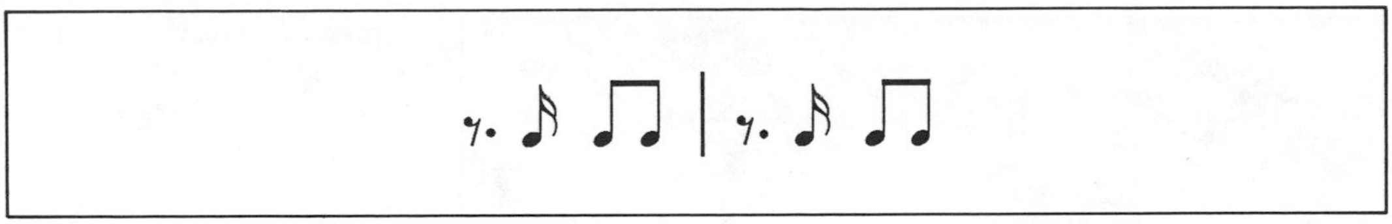

Figure 10

that dates back as far as African slave songs: One of the earliest forms of calypso was the *lavway*, made up of a call-and-response. Modern forms of calypso contain more lines of text, which may be silly, serious, or humorous, and describe news, world events, and village happenings. Many of the texts are political, containing protest themes and social commentary, and may contain double or hidden meanings in their texts as well. Calypsos are composed particularly for the carnival season but are also sung all year round. The melodies, as well as the accompaniments played by brass, pop, or steel bands, have syncopated, dance-like beats, and the tunes include several verses and catchy refrains. Professional calypsonians carefully stage their performances; they wear dazzling outfits and dramatize their songs. There is usually a backup chorus that sings the refrain lines in harmony.

Soca is a new form of calypso that evolved during the 1970s. It is influenced by the East Indian musical rhythms of Trinidad and United States soul music and is called soul calypso or *soca* for short. Its beat is slightly different from the traditional calypso beat. Figure 10 shows a typical bass line rhythmic pattern.

b. The steel band is an instrumental ensemble that specializes in calypso, reggae, and pop music, but it can also play classical and religious music. The instruments used in the band, called "pans," are made from fifty-five-gallon oil drums. Although pans were first created in Trinidad in the 1940s, their percussive ancestors may be traced to Africa, and they have since spread to all parts of the world. Many American high schools, colleges, and universities now have steel band ensembles, and groups can also be heard in major cities where Caribbean blacks have migrated, such as New York, London, and Toronto (see figure 11). Every steel band needs a good arranger and a good tuner, for its overall sound depends on how well the pans are made and maintained, and the making of pans is a complex process requiring skill and patience. The oil drums have to be cut into different sizes since pans come in different ranges and have to be grooved, tempered, and tuned. The spaces on the top surface of the pans, separated by grooves, are tuned to produce different pitches: Generally, the larger the note surface, the lower the pitch; the larger the pan, the lower its range. Pans are played with sticks of varying lengths, covered at one end with some type of rubber tubing. A small band consisting of eight players may be made up of the following instruments (pans are listed in table 1 in descending order of their ranges, from the highest to the lowest):

97

Figure 11. Selwyn Ahyoung (left) and Dale A. Olsen (right) with steel drums.

Table 1

Name of instruments	Number of pans
Single lead or high tenor or ping pong	1
Double tenor	2
Double second	2
Double or triple guitar	2 or 3
Cello	3
Tenor bass	4
Six bass	6

Note: In addition, a steel band often uses conga drum, trap set, scraper, and cow bell.

In Trinidad, traditional steel bands may contain as many as 150 players, whose instruments are placed on stands in gaily decorated, mobile metal frames. These bands have become famous for their fantastic and elaborate calypso arrangements created for carnival street dancing and the Panorama, an annual steel band competition. Players used to hang instruments around their necks and carry them through the streets.

4. Play a recording of a modern calypso. Have the class listen for the words and for any repeated accompanying rhythmic patterns.
5. Sing the tune "Ambakaila," an old *lavway* melody.

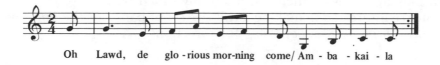

Oh Lawd, de glo-rious mor-ning come/ Am - ba - kai - la

The text is: "O Lawd de glorious morning come/Ambakaila." The song was sung about the "glorious morning" of the stick fight that usually occurred on the first day of Carnival. *Ambakaila* is a corruption of the term *en bataille la,* meaning "in battle." "De glorious morning" was the morning of the stick fight which usually occurred on the first day of Carnival, or the Monday before Shrove Tuesday. *Ambakaila* is an old *lavway* melody. At first, students should sing only the response "Ambakaila," but they may gradually join in on the call as well. Clap the basic accompaniment pattern of the calypso, and have the students follow in rote imitation as they continue to sing the tune and accompany themselves on percussion instruments. Ask the class to practice the following two rhythmic accompaniment patterns of the calypso and use them for "Ambakaila."

6. Pass out transcriptions of "Ambakaila," and have some students play the tune on melody instruments.
7. Have students improvise other words for the call-and-response format of "Ambakaila," such as "Oh Lord, my pocket got a hole/in de center."
8. Have students play "Ambakaila" and harmonize the tune using the tonic, subdominant, and dominant seventh chords.
9. Students can be led through the construction of a miniature set of pans. Use a wooden mallet or small ball peen hammer to depress the surfaces of old 13 oz. to 32 oz. tin cans into concave shapes. Carefully experiment with tuning the cans to selected pitches. (This will not be an easy task.)
   Students can create pans tuned to the scales of C major and to C-sharp or D-flat major. Tune the pans by using a pitch pipe, a tuning fork, another instrument, or a stroboscope. The two major scales will combine to form a one-octave chromatic set (with a few pitches duplicated). Label the pans,

arrange them chromatically in a box or trough, and attach a strap to the box so that it can be carried around the neck. You can even try tuning more tins to extend the range of the set higher and lower. Use larger cans for the lower notes; some may have a pitch that naturally fits the set. Use pencils (with erasers) and sticks to play the tuned tin cans, and let students experiment with playing tunes on their chromatically tuned pans.

10. If you are interested in making a full-size set of pans, see the Folkways album *The Steel Drums of Kim Loy Wong* for directions.

5

L E S S O N   F I V E

■ OBJECTIVES:

Students will:

1. Identify the sound of Euro-Latin American music from Chile and Argentina that features the guitar, the most important Spanish-derived instrument.
2. Identify the two Spanish-derived guitar techniques, the *rasqueado* (strumming) style and the *punteado* (picking) style.
3. Identify the three European-derived meters known as *ritmo colonial* (colonial rhythm, or bimeter), *sesquiáltera* (alternating meter), and European triple meter (waltz time).
4. Perform three notated examples in small ensembles with guitars and recorders or flutes as a long-term or follow-up project.

Materials:

1. Recordings:
   Traditional Chilean Songs, Folkways FW 8748
   Songs of Chile, Folkways FW 8817
   Argentina: The Guitar of the Pampas, Lyrichord LLST 7235
   Refer also to *Sounds of the World: Music of Latin America: Mexico, Ecuador, Brazil* (Reston, VA: Music Educators National Conference, 1987)
2. Musical instruments (optional):
   Guitar (the parts to be played call for strumming only)
   Flute or recorder (to be played using Western notation)

■ PROCEDURES:

1. Show Chile and Argentina on a map, and discuss the two countries, emphasizing that they lie at the southern tip of South America and that their cultures show the strongest European influence of all the Latin American countries. Chile and the much larger Argentina are separated by the Andes mountains. Both countries are famed for their cowboys, known as *gauchos* in the Argentine *pampas* or plains and as *huasos* in the central valley of Chile. These South American cowboys are highly regarded for their singing and guitar playing.
2. Play two of the recorded examples for this lesson. Initially, point out the times when the guitar is strummed (*rasqueado* style) and picked (*punteado*

100

("Colonial Rhythm")
"Adios" (Goodbye)

Figure 12a

style). In the second selection, have students indicate the style of playing

3. Discuss the three most important European-derived meters or rhythms, which are "colonial rhythm" (bimeter), the Spanish *sesquiáltera* (alternating meter), and triple meter (waltz time).

4. Play recordings that illustrate colonial rhythm. Some good examples are "Tonada," on *Argentina: The Guitar of the Pampas* (side one, band eight), "Dos Puntas tiene el camino," on *Songs of Chile* (side one, band five), and "Los Gallos," on *Traditional Chilean Songs* (side one, band five). As you play the recordings, clap a quarter-note pulse in three for $\frac{3}{4}$ time, then follow with a dotted-quarter-note pulse in two for $\frac{6}{8}$ time to show that the two meters are related. Explain that at times the melody is strictly in $\frac{3}{4}$ time while the guitar accompaniment is strictly in $\frac{6}{8}$ and that the music as a whole can be heard in either meter. Divide the class into two sections, and have one section clap $\frac{3}{4}$ and the other $\frac{6}{8}$ simultaneously.

5. Play the recordings that illustrate *sesquiáltera*, using "Si Yo Volviera a Quererte" on *Traditional Chilean Songs* (side one, band one) and "Despedimiento del Angelito" (side one, band seven of the same recording). Clap in three for $\frac{3}{4}$ for the measures that stress three, and clap in two for $\frac{6}{8}$ for the measures that stress two. Emphasize that this is an alternation rather than

101

(Sesquiáltera)
"Dices que me quieres, macho"
("Tell Me You Love Me, 'Tiger' ")

Figure 12b

superimposition and that it often involves the guitar part as well as the melody.

6. Play the recorded waltz example, "La Golondrina," on *Traditional Chilean songs* (side 2, band 4). Clap in three.

7. Play and discuss selected examples of songs that employ colonial rhythm, *sesquiáltera,* or waltz time rhythms and *punteado* or *rasqueado* performance techniques.

8. If time permits, teach the following three songs in figures 12a, 12b, and 12c.

102

(Waltz) "Vals Chilote" ("Waltz from Chiloe")

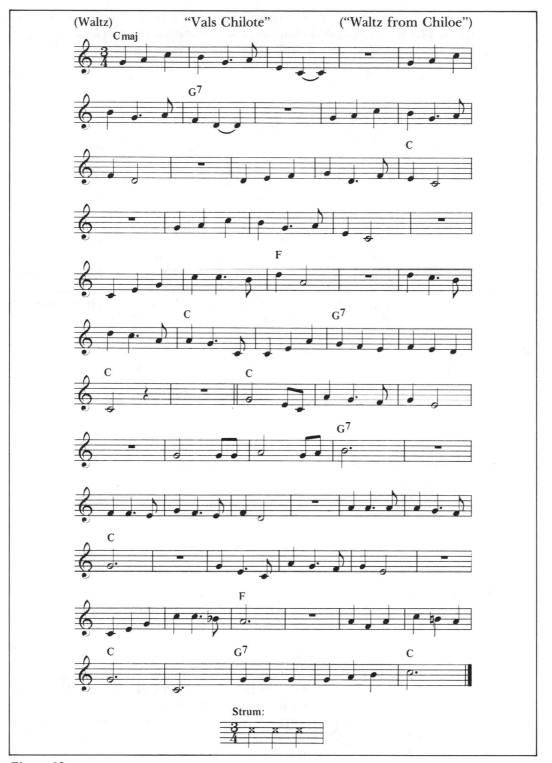

Strum:

Figure 12c

If your students can read Western notation, have them perform in small ensembles. The melody, chord changes, and strumming patterns are indicated in the transcriptions; perform the examples several times so the students understand the European-derived meters.

6

L E S S O N   S I X

■ **OBJECTIVES:**
Students will:
1. Identify pan-Andean music and the following musical instruments that form a typical pan-Andean ensemble: *siku, kena,* guitar, *charango, bombo.*
2. Play music of the pan-Andean tradition using the *siku* constructed in lesson one, a Western flute or recorder to substitute for the Andean *kena* flute, and guitars. The students will learn how European harmony combines with Native American–derived instruments.

Materials:
1. Recordings:
   Pukaj Wayra . . . Music from Bolivia, Lyrichord LLST 7361
   Urubamba, Columbia KCC 32896
   Inti-Illimani 3: Canto de Pueblos Andinos, Monitor MFS 787
   La Flûte Indienne, Olympic Atlas Series 6160
   Refer also to *Sounds of the World: Music of Latin America: Mexico, Ecuador, Brazil* (Reston, VA: Music Educators National Conference, 1987)
2. Optional musical instruments:
   A set of *siku* panpipes, as constructed in lesson one
   Guitar
   Charango or *ukulele*
   Bombo or bass drum
   An Andean *kena* flute or a Western flute or recorder

■ **PROCEDURES:**
1. Present a cultural and historical perspective: Pan-Andean music came about as a result of the racial and cultural mixing of the people of the Andes. Some of the musical instruments from the Andes of Ecuador, Peru, Bolivia, northern Argentina, and Northern Chile have been joined with Spanish instruments such as the guitar and other guitar-like instruments. These combined instruments have formed a musical idiom that reveals the mixed cultural heritages of the Andean people. Today many pan-Andean ensembles from Chile and other countries are living and performing outside of their native lands. Some of the best known groups are Quilapayun (Paris), Angel Parra (Mexico), and Grupo Aymara (New York).
2. Play several selections from the recordings listed, choosing examples that use

all the instruments rather than just guitar. Point out the following musical instruments and discuss their musical characteristics with the students. (You should be able to recognize the instruments after repeated listenings to the recordings.)

a. The *siku* has a breathy quality and is played with the interlocking note technique discussed in lesson one.

b. The *kena* is a vertical, end-blown flute with a ductless, notched mouthpiece. Like the *siku*, these flutes have been found in ancient graves in the coastal regions of Peru and were made from human, llama, or pelican bones and clay, gold, silver, and cane. Today the *kena* is played alone by llama herdsmen (men and boys), by men in *kena* ensembles, and in ensembles with guitars, *charangos*, violins, mandolins, and harps. The *kena*, made with only six finger holes and one thumb hole, was often traditionally played to sound the notes of a pentatonic scale, but in modern pan-Andean music the musicians play in the natural minor and major, and they even play some chromatic notes by using cross fingerings and partially covering the finger holes. The *kena* is played using a fast vibrato mostly in the high register; this style is favored in Andean Native American music. Sometimes the tunings do not correspond to European tuning—the instrument is not out-of-tune, but is just tuned to correspond to Andean cultural traditions. *Kena* players use many ornaments similar to mordents in European music, and sometimes they slide (glissando) from one note to the other.

c. The *charango* is a stringed instrument based on the guitars and guitar-like instruments brought by the Spaniards to the new world (see figures 13 and 14). Because wood is scarce in the high Andes mountains, the Native Americans of Peru and Bolivia constructed these small guitars using armadillo shells as resonators. Today it is illegal to kill armadillos in Bolivia, so the *charango* is often made entirely from wood. A typical *charango* has ten metal or nylon strings, arranged into five double courses (a double course consists of two strings, placed side by side that are tuned to the same pitch and played together). Some varieties may use triple courses and substitute geared metal tuners for the traditional straight, wooden, violin-type pegs.

   Charango players use both the *rasqueado* and *punteado* playing styles, sounding the strings with their fingernails. The instrument is tuned to be played in a very high range, and in Chile the instrument is often called *chillador*, which means "screamer"; players must use fast strums and play melodies in the characteristic range of the instrument (an octave or two above the guitar).

d. The *bombo* is a large, double-headed bass drum. It usually resembles a European Renaissance drum in shape and also is similar to those depicted in paintings about the American Revolution. The term may also be used to describe drums of Native American origin that are similar to Western marching band bass drums. The *bombo* is usually played with only one padded stick when accompanying *siku* orchestras and two padded sticks when accompanying a modern pan-Andean ensemble (one is used to strike the wooden body or the rim of the drum).

105

Figure 13. Andean charangos. *The middle* charango *is from Bolivia; the other two are from Peru.*

    e. The guitar player usually strums but can also pick; often a guitar or a *guitarrón* (large guitar) will play bass notes and fast runs. The instrument used is always a nylon-stringed Spanish guitar.

3. After listening to several examples, discuss the structure of the pan-Andean ensemble. Explain that this ensemble is organized according to the different sounds of the instruments and according to how the instruments are played. For example, high-pitched instruments play the melody and a parallel melody a third lower, low-pitched instruments such as the guitars play harmony, and the *charango* plays either accompaniments in the middle register or jumps to the top register when it plays the melody.

4. An optional project for this lesson could be the following:

Figure 14. Back view of charangos: *left*, charango *with box resonator; middle, with wood resonator; and right, with armadillo shell for a resonator.*

a. Construct a *kena* flute from PVC tubing, tuned in A minor, according to the following diagram and instructions:

Cut a 15½'' section of ¾'' PVC tubing. Using a rat-tail file, make a notched mouthpiece on one end; drill five ⅜'' holes in the front and a ¼'' hole in the back of the *kena*, and smooth the edges of the finger holes with a knife, sandpaper, or a file. Instead of drilling, you can make the finger holes by burning through the tubing with a soldering gun or a heated metal nail or rod. The holes can be then filed to the necessary roundness and size (see figure 15).

b. Learn to play the *kena*. Blow the *kena* as you would a Western flute (except that the *kena* is end-blown) by focusing the airstream against the

107

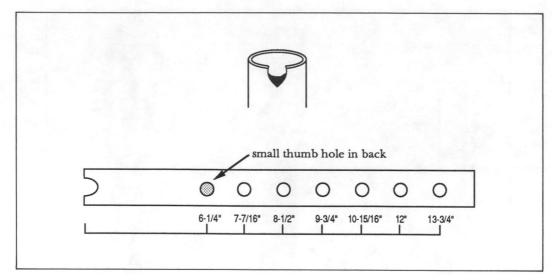

Figure 15

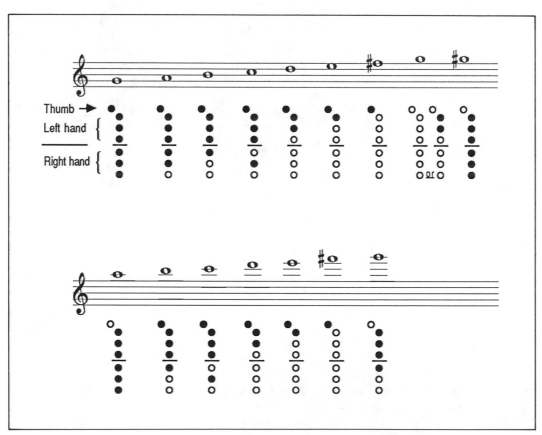

Figure 16

108

Figure 16 (continued)

sharp edge of the notch. Learn the notes according to the fingering chart in figure 16, and notice that the notes basically correspond to a transposed alto recorder or a clarinet in the lower register. Learn "Mary Had a Little Lamb" on the *kena* in both the lower and upper octaves.

5. Organize a pan-Andean music ensemble using a *siku*, a *kena* (a flute or a recorder may be substituted), a *charango* (you may use treble ukulele), a guitar, and a *bombo* (you may substitute bass drum). Professional ensembles usually use only one instrument for each part, but students may double any of the parts if more instruments are available. Learn the piece in figure 17, which is in the style of the Andean music of southern Peru and northern

Figure 17

(Siku Part)

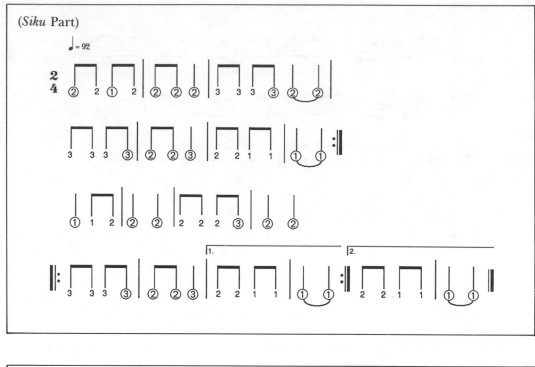

(Guitar and Charango Part)

A

or

(Bombo Part)

B

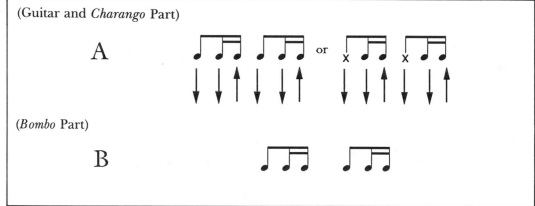

Figure 17 (continued)

Bolivia, titled "Maria" (based on the theme of "Mary Had a Little Lamb"). In the *kena* part, ornaments like mordents are indicated above their corresponding notes. The *siku* part, written in parallel thirds below the *kena* part, is given in Olsen notation, and the guitar and *charango* parts should be played with the *wayno* strum as shown: The X-shaped note heads indicate stopping the strings with the palm of the hand immediately after strumming them with the fingernails.

110

L E S S O N   S E V E N

■ **OBJECTIVES:**

Students will:

1. Identify the instruments and the sound of a big band *salsa* orchestra.
2. Identify the African-derived characteristics of *salsa* music and perform one of them.
3. Identify the musical characteristics of *salsa* music that are Spanish-derived.

Materials:

1. Recordings:

   SAR All Stars, recorded live in Club Ochentas, vol. 1, SAR SLP 1021, Series 0798

   El Baguiné de Angelitos Negros, written, arranged, and produced by Willie Colon, FANIA JM 00506, Series 0698. (FANIA records are distributed by FANIA Records, 888 Seventh Avenue, New York 10019.)

■ **PROCEDURES:**

1. Discuss the origin of *salsa* in Cuba in the 1940s, and discuss how it spread to the rest of the Spanish-speaking Caribbean (especially San Juan in Puerto Rico) and to Miami and New York City: These three centers are known collectively as the "salsa triangle." *Salsa* is an Afro–Cuban music that developed in the nightclubs of Havana, Cuba, and was influenced by American jazz from the swing era (see figure 18). The term *salsa*, which means "hot sauce," was applied because the music was rhythmically spicy, energetic, and appropriate for dancing. Afro–Cuban drumming was and still is an important part of *salsa*, with such drums as the *congas,* bongos, and *timbales* dominating. *Salsa* has its greatest appeal among people from the Spanish Caribbean or those with Caribbean roots.
2. Perform a call-and-response pattern, and have the students sing the response.
3. Play a short excerpt chosen from the suggested recordings of *salsa* music that contains call-and-response patterns and ostinatos.
4. Teach the following African elements:
   a. The metronomic pulse, which is provided by the *claves* in a rhythmic pattern or ostinato that repeats every two measures. (It is often played by the *claves*, which are two 1½" hardwood dowels that are struck together, making a loud, sharp, and resonant sound.)
   b. Layered texture, consisting of rhythmic and melodic ostinatos
   c. Instrumental improvisation
   d. The use of African-derived drums in the ensemble
   e. The use of call-and-response texture
   f. The *montuno* improvised vocal section, which includes African-styled praise texts about women, personages, events, or places
   g. Use of the music for dancing, with a great deal of audience participation by handclapping, singing along, and yells of excitement
5. Teach the following Spanish elements of *salsa:*

111

Figure 18. The Salsa Florida orchestra, Florida State University, Tallahassee. From left to right: bottom row—electric bass, Puerto Rican cuatro, lead singer, cow bell, flute soloist; middle row—congo drums, timbales; top row—two trombones, baritone saxophone, alto saxaphone, two trumpets. Not pictured: piano and claves.

    a. Singers use the Spanish language, often to tell a story about a place or person, much like the ballad in American music.
    b. The music is constructed with Western harmony.
    c. Certain Western instruments are used as part of the ensemble.
    d. The music uses traditional formal structures, such as ABA.

6. Play the recording *SAR All Stars* (side one, band one), and include an introduction to the major instruments in a *salsa* ensemble. The instruments are presented on the recording in the following order:

piano = piano
bajo = bass
congas = conga drums
bongos = bongo drums
güiro = rasp or scraper
tres = guitar with six strings in three double courses (*tres* means three and refers to the courses) (two players)
violín = violin (two players)
trombón = trombone
trompeta = trumpet (three players)
flauta = flute

a. Help the students discover that the first instrument (the piano) plays an ostinato and continues to play it throughout the introduction; the bass and the percussion instruments also play ostinatos throughout the introduction.

b. Ask the class to determine what else is happening musically during the introduction and what its purpose might be. Explain that the melody instruments improvise solos during the introduction in order to feature their sound and skills of the performers; however, after the *tres* and the violin players give their short solos, those two instruments continue by playing ostinatos along with the bass and percussion.

c. Continue playing the recording, using this "discovery and discussion" process. Explain the following to the students:

   (1) When the singer enters, he and a male chorus sing in a call-and-response manner while the instruments play ostinatos.

   (2) The vocal part is followed by brass instruments playing several ostinatos together, layered one on top of the other.

   (3) The ostinatos are followed by the first real improvised solo on the flute. When the improvisation begins, this is called the *montuno* section. The last half of the flute solo is accompanied by layered brass ostinatos.

   (4) This style continues until the end of the performance, with different instruments taking solos, including the singer (this time also improvising during the *montuno* section), and with chorus response.

7. Play side two of the record *El Baquiné de Angelitos Negros*: a *salsa* ballet. Ask the class to help you list on the chalkboard the *salsa* characteristics that they hear, categorizing them as Spanish or African.

Integrating music with other studies

Musical events in Latin America are seldom isolated phenomena. These events nearly always relate to a particular aspect of culture such as ritual, celebration, devotion, entertainment, or work; classes should not, therefore, study any aspect of culture without thinking about the music that may accompany it and form an integral part of it. All of the musical styles discussed in the lessons in this chapter have their own cultural contexts; it is unlikely that the music would be performed outside of that context, or that the context would take place without music. Students might develop an awareness of the cultural background of musical traditions in social science classes such as history, geography, psychology, and sociology. Include a discussion of the following facts about these cultural contexts in the lessons of this chapter, in other lessons dealing with the music of other cultures, or in one lesson that emphasizes music as it relates to culture in general.

Siku panpipe music of Peru is performed during festive celebrations on feast days and other religious holidays.

Afro–Latin American drumming exists in various contexts, including secular, social ones and religious festivals of the Catholic calendar or rituals of African derivation.

113

The Colombian *marimba* is also performed for both secular and religious occasions such as the social *currulao* dance and the festival of Saint Anthony.

Calypsos of Trinidad and Tobago and elsewhere in the Caribbean are often songs of derision and ridicule that regulate social behavior. In addition, they provide joyful rhythms during the annual carnival fête, which provides a release before the solemn celebration of Lent.

The European-derived musics of many Latin American countries function as entertainment or for dancing. In the lonely life of the farmer, rancher, or cowherd, such as the *vaquero* of Venezuela, the *gaucho* of Argentina, and the *huaso* of Chile, music serves to break the solitude.

Pan-Andean music reflects the cultural past and heritages of many of its music makers and listeners. Much pan-Andean music functions as a vehicle for protest against racial, social, and political oppression.

One of the happy musics in Latin America is *salsa*. It inspires even the most inhibited people to dance and have a good time, and the texts speak about happy times and merrymaking. Certain musics developed as they did because of the geographies and histories of certain areas. Search for examples of this concept, such as these that follow:

1. Afro–Latin American musics developed along the hot, humid coastal regions of Latin America and the Caribbean. These were the areas where slaves worked on sugar, cotton, and coffee plantations, and they were also areas that were topographically similar to the African homelands of the slaves. In these areas people of African descent had natural materials with which to construct instrument types similar to African drums and marimbas similar to African marimbas.

2. In cattle-grazing regions that are similar to cattle-grazing regions in Spain and Portugal, many South American cowboys sing songs similar to those sung in the Old World.

3. Geography also determines what materials are available for musical instrument construction. The *charango* of Bolivia and Peru, for example, was made from an armadillo shell because of the scarcity of wood in the high elevations of the Andes mountains.

4. History affects musical development. The Bush Negroes of Surinam have retained a greater amount of African music and culture than any other African-derived culture in the Americas because of an event in history: When the area known today as Surinam was traded by the British for the present Manhattan Island, which was owned by the Dutch, many slaves took advantage of the political confusion and escaped from the plantations into the jungles to establish their own African-type villages and to preserve their culture.

5. More recently, the steel band tradition of Trinidad and Tobago was made possible by the discarded oil drums left on Caribbean beaches during World War II.

In the area of visual arts there are two ways that Latin American music can be studied:

1. The instruments themselves are often works of art and have earned places in museums. The beautiful ceramic instruments of the pre-Columbian cultures of Peru, Ecuador, Colombia, Costa Rica, Panama, and Mexico, for example, are

114

highly valued as art objects. Modern musical instruments are also often constructed and designed with visual beauty in mind.

2. Musical instruments and musical events are often depicted in sculptures and in painting. Much can be learned about the musical contexts of ancient Latin American cultures from this "music iconography" on ceramic pots, such as those found in Peru and Mexico. Modern painting can also be an important source for seeing the contexts of music. Many paintings in Haiti and Brazil, for example, are important sources that illustrate the roles of musical instruments in daily life.

Students can also be brought to understand the relationship of folk music to art music. Music from the oral traditions of Latin America (folk, ritual, and indigenous music) has often provided composers in the European art tradition with sources for musical inspiration. In Brazil, Heitor Villa-Lobos is the best known composer who has been inspired by the folk music of his native land; in Mexico, Carlos Chávez has been similarly inspired, as has been the Argentine composer Alberto Ginastera. Indeed, each Latin American country seems to have its Aaron Copland who has been inspired by the folklore of his or her native land. The interest in this so-called folk music is so great, and musicians of such caliber have given their attention to its composition and performance, that it has become art music in the best and truest sense of the word.

BIBLIOGRAPHY

Béhague, Gerard. "Brazil." In *The New Grove Dictionary of Music and Musicians*, vol. 3. New York: Macmillan, 1980. A comprehensive discussion of the folk and popular music of Brazil.

Béhague, Gerard. "Latin American Folk Music." In *Folk and Traditional Music of the Western Continents* (2d ed.), edited by Bruno Nettl. Englewood Cliffs, NJ: Prentice Hall, 1973.

Bergman, Billy. *Hot Sauces, Latin and Caribbean Pop.* New York: Quill, a division of William Morrow, 1983. A short, well-written book including articles on "Reggae" (Bergman), "Reggae After Marley" (Schwartz), "Soca" (Bergman), and "Salsa and Latin Jazz" (Leymarie).

Isles of the Caribbean. Washington, DC: National Geographic Society, 1980. Special Publications Division. A popular introduction to the Caribbean with several pages about and excellent pictures of Trinidad's carnival.

Olsen, Dale A. "Folk Music of South America—A Musical Mosaic." In *Musics of Many Cultures: An Introduction*, edited by Elizabeth May. Berkeley: University of California Press, 1980. A survey of Spanish and Portuguese-derived, African derived, Native American derived, and nationalistically determined folk music of South America.

Olsen, Dale A. "Symbol and Function in South American Indian Music." In *Musics of Many Cultures: An Introduction*, edited by Elizabeth May. Berkeley: University of California Press, 1980. A survey of the music of Native South Americans.

Olsen, Dale A., Daniel Sheehy, and Charles A. Perrone. *Sounds of the World—Music of Latin America: Mexico, Ecuador, Brazil.* Reston, VA: Music Educators National Conference, 1986.

Perrone, Charles A., and Enlyton de Sá Rego. *MPB: Contemporary Brazilian Popular Music.* Albuquerque, NM: Latin American Institute, 1985.

Roberts, John Storm. *Black Music of Two Worlds.* New York: Morrow Books, 1972. An easily readable book that provides an introduction to the music of Africa and discussions about the black musics of North America, Central America, South America, and the Caribbean.

Roberts, John Storm. *The Latin Tinge: The Impact of Latin American Music on the United States.* 2d ed. Tivoli, NY: Original Music, 1985. An informative book that focuses on Latin American and Caribbean popular musics in the United States.

Sadie, Stanley, ed. *The New Grove Dictionary of Music and Musicians.* 20 vols. New York: Macmillan, 1980. This extensive publication contains informative articles on the music of many Latin American countries.

Stevenson, Robert. *Music in Aztec and Inca Territory.* Berkeley: University of California Press, 1968. Portions of this book give historiographic details about the music of the Andes.

DISCOGRAPHY

African and Afro–American Drums. Ethnic Folkways Library FE 4502. Although somewhat outdated, this is still a good survey of African-derived drumming in the Americas.

Afro–Brazilian Religious Songs: Cantigas de Candomblé/Candomble Songs from Salvador, Bahia. Lyrichord LLST 7315. Contains songs and drumming examples pertaining to Afro–Brazilian religious ceremony.

Afro–Hispanic Music from Western Colombia and Ecuador. Ethnic Folkways Library FE 4376. A very important recording. Music collected and text written by Norman Whitten, one of the foremost authorities on African-derived music from the west coast of Colombia.

Amazonia. Cult Music of Northern Brazil. Lyrichord LL6T 7300. Contains good examples of songs and drumming pertaining to Afro–Brazilian religious ceremony.

Argentina: The Guitar of the Pampas. Lyrichord LLST 7253. This album contains concert music for guitar, composed by Abel Fleury in a folk style and performed by Roberto Lara, a leading South American guitarist.

El Baguiné de Angelitos Negros. FANIA JM 00506, Series 0698. This is a recording of the first *salsa* ballet, written, arranged, and produced by Willie Colon for big band; documentation about the ballet is included. Distributed by FANIA Records, 888 Seventh Avenue, New York 10019.

Batucada Number 3, the Exciting Rhythm of the Wild Brazilian Carnival. Philips 6482 002. Excellent recording featuring *samba* rhythms and percussion improvisations, with individual examples of *samba* instruments.

Black Orpheus (movie sound track). Fontana 67520. Has excellent examples of *samba* music and other popular musics from Brazil.

Calypso Travels. Folkways Records FW 8733. An outdated recording, but still important because it features Lord Invader and his Calypso Group; many song texts are included.

The Columbia World Library of Folk and Primitive Music: Venezuela. Vol. 9, Columbia Masterworks SL-212. Collected by Alan Lomax, this old album contains important examples of Venezuelan traditional musics of many types.

Fiestas of Peru, Music of the High Andes. Nonesuch Explorer Series H-72045. This contains *mestizo* music from Peru, including music of carnivals and festivals, featuring brass bands and traditional ensembles.

Historic Recordings of Mexican Music, Volume 1: The Earliest Mariachi Recordings 1906–1936. Folklyric Records 9051.

Historic Recordings of Mexican Music, Volume 2: Mariachi Coculense de Cirilo Marmolejo 1933–36. Folklyric Records 9052. Volumes 1 and 2, which include informative record notes, are distributed by Down Home Music, 10341 San Pablo Avenue, El Cerrito, CA 94530.

In Praise of Oxalá and Other Gods, Black Music of South America. Nonesuch Explorer Series H-72036. The best anthology of African-derived music of South America, with examples from Colombia, Ecuador, and Brazil (including *candomblé* and *capoeira*).

Instruments and Music of Bolivia. Ethnic Folkways Library FM 4012. Contains many examples of panpipe orchestras from Bolivia.

Inti-Illimani 3: Canto de Pueblos Andinos. Monitor Records MFS 787. An accessible and inexpensive recording by one of Chile's greatest pan-Andean ensembles.

An Island Carnival—Music of the West Indies. Nonesuch 72091. This record is well recorded and documented, but the title is a complete misnomer; it has nothing to do with Carnival in the Caribbean. It contains, however, many examples of small groups performing secular and sacred music, including village bands, bamboo bands, cocoa-lute bands, and Hindu epic songs.

Kingdom of the Sun, Peru's Inca Heritage. Nonesuch Explorer Series H-72029. Good examples of *mestizo* music from Peru, including panpipe music.

Mountain Music of Peru. Folkways FE 4539. This two-record set is the best collection of Peruvian highland music on an American label, including panpipes and flutes of diverse types, guitars, *charangos*, and more, with informative notes.

Music from the Land of Macchu Picchu. Lyrichord LLST 7294. Contains diverse musics from Peru, including black traditions for comparison with Brazil and the Caribbean.

Music of Mexico: Sones Jarachos. Arhollie 3008. Includes texts, translations, and informative notes. Distributed by Down Home Music, 10341 San Pablo Avenue, El Cerrito, CA 94530.

Music of the Incas: "Ayllu Sulca." Lyrichord LLST 7348. This record contains excellent examples of ensemble music from Ayacucho, Peru, performed by Antonio Sulca on the harp, with his family ensemble playing violins, mandolins, and *kenas.*

The Piñata Party Presents Music of Peru. Folkways Records FW 8749. This music shows some recent roots of pan-Andean music; also included are Peruvian Harp duets.

Pukaj Wayra . . . Music from Bolivia. Lyrichord LLST 7361. A good recording by a Bolivian pan-Andean ensemble.

SAR All Stars, Vol. 1. SAR Records SLP 1021, Series 0798. Recorded live in Club Ochentas in New York City, this is one of the best albums of all-star big band style *salsa.* SAR records are distributed by A. G. Records, 639 Tenth Avenue, New York 10036, 212-581-2468.

Songs and Dances of Brazil. Folkways FW 6953. A survey of some of the lyrical musical forms of Brazilian popular music of several decades ago.

Songs of Chile. Folkways FW 8817. Traditional Chilean folksongs, with guitar accompaniment, sung by two Chilean girls; contains good examples of Spanish-derived music.

Sparrow, The Greatest. Charlie's JAF 1007. This album contains recent calypsos by one of Trinidad's most famous singers. Available from Original Music, R.D. 1, Box 190, Lasher Road, Tivoli, New York 12583.

The Steel Drums of Kim Loy Wong. Folkways Records FI 8367 and FS 3834. This is an outdated recording with inferior sound quality, but it still provides an important documentation of steel band, especially when accompanied by Pete Seeger's booklet by the same name.

Traditional Chilean Songs. Folkways Records FW 8748. Sung by Chilean folksinger Rolando Alarcón with guitar accompaniment, this is a good album for Spanish-derived music; it includes song texts in Spanish and English.

Urubamba. Columbia Records KCC 32896. An excellent album of pan-Andean music produced by Paul Simon with the same group that performed "El Condor Pasa" for Simon and Garfunkel's album *Bridge over Troubled Waters.*

Viracocha, Legendary Music of the Andes. Lyrichord LLST 7264. The selections on this record contain three harp performances from Cuzco, Peru, and music by other Peruvian ensembles during festivals.

**Major Countries
of Europe**
Including neighboring
North African countries

CHAPTER FOUR

4

EUROPE

by Patricia Shehan Campbell

What comes to mind when you think of Europe? Do your images include the Eiffel Tower in Paris, St. Peter's Cathedral in Rome, and London's Big Ben clock tower? Do you envision boats on the Rhine or Danube rivers, the breathtaking Alps of Switzerland, the Côte d'Azur of southern France, the islands of Greece, and the fjords of Norway? Do you harbor thoughts of European sidewalk cafes, galleries of great art, the music of concert halls and opera houses, and exquisite cuisine? This is classic Europe as seen on first tours and in travel brochures, but consider these scenes as well: shepherds and their flocks against the backdrop of rocky hills; village women en route to the central market for fresh vegetables, fruits, and grains; three-day wedding feasts and their great spreads of food, drink, and dancing; massive churches with onion-shaped towers rather than spires and steeples; and farms where sickles, scythes, and motorized combines work together. Such are the images of the "other Europe," the more ancient European cultural stratum still found in the rural areas and in the countries along the eastern border.

Europe is a conglomerate of many images and of many nations and is a land of great diversity. Viewed as a whole, Europe is perceived as the foundation of Western civilization. The now widespread Western traditions of governance, education, and the arts first developed in Europe, and European contributions to world progress continue today. Over the centuries, Greece, Italy, Spain, France, Germany, and other nations have emerged as world leaders in the arts, the humanities, and the sciences.

119

The continent of Europe is approximately the same size as the United States, including Alaska. It is outranked in size by all other continents except Australia, but it embraces a great diversity of climates, natural resources, and densities of population. Europe extends from the icy Arctic Circle in northern Scandinavia to the temperate climate of the Mediterranean countries of Spain, Italy, and Greece. The British Isles are its farthest western countries (beyond which is the Atlantic Ocean), and its eastern borders are flanked by the Asian continent (including the Soviet Union) and areas of the Black and Caspian seas. Europe is in close proximity to major cultural regions including North Africa and the Middle East. Despite a one-time policy of isolationism, cultural exchanges among countries have allowed for fascinating new cultural manifestations.

European peoples vary in ethnic composition, language, and religion. For its size, Europe is the most polyglot area in the world. Celtic, Romance, Teutonic, Baltic, Slavonic, Hellenic, Turkic, and Finno-Ugric are some of the broad language classifications, which can be further distinguished by country or region. The Romance languages, for example, include Italian, French, Spanish, Portuguese, and Romanian, as well as Walloon (Belgium), Catalan and Galician (Spain), and Ladin (Italy). Another language group is Slavic, which can be classified into three groups according to regions in Eastern Europe; for example, South Slavic alone is divided into six language groups. Is it any surprise that language has fostered national consciousness and political divisions throughout the continent?

Although there are similarities among European peoples, the cultural regions are distinctive in many ways. Some divide the continent along political boundaries, but the physical characteristics of the land itself may provide clearer borders between cultural regions. The British Isles share elements of the Germanic countries of continental Europe, but England, Scotland, Ireland, and Wales developed customs different from those of the mainland because of their somewhat remote island status. Three of the four Scandinavian countries, Norway, Sweden, and Finland, are separated from the continent by the Baltic Sea; their Nordic cultures are more similar to one another than to the rest of Europe.

The Mediterranean countries of Spain, Italy, and Greece share a more moderate climate than that of Central Europe, and their cultural influences include North Africa and the Middle East. The Germanic countries of Austria, parts of Switzerland, Germany itself, and the Netherlands are united by language and location in the western portion of Europe, and the Alpine regions of the first three countries contribute similar customs beyond their political borders. Eastern European countries, including Poland, Czechoslovakia, Romania, Hungary, Bulgaria, European Russia, and the kingdoms of Yugoslavia remained agrarian societies well into the twentieth century; the rustic peasant life of this region still exists in many communities. The Romantic-Atlantic countries of France, Portugal, and Belgium, which complete the list of major European countries, are akin in location (all are coastal countries on the Atlantic) and language (from the Romance family).

The splendors of Europe are at hand, whether through the romance of transcontinental travel, staring out the windows of the great railway cars that link the cities and the villages, or through the more immediately accessible avenues of knowledge: the literature and the fine arts. Study of these cultural contributions is likely to lead to a deep understanding of Europe's people, and such study may just as surely transport the learner to this historical land of so many of our forefathers. In particular, a view of the music and the dance of these countries offers insight into both the diversity and the similarities among the people of Europe.

Characteristics of European musics

As languages differ among ethnic groups, so do music styles. European folk music can be divided into two genres: songs and dance music. Although some may view the traditional music of Europe as a single unit with common elements maintained across the continent, each region, country, and community has its own style, songs, and dances. Since all music consists of fundamental sonic elements (melody, rhythm, texture, form, and timbre), these are the elements evaluated when reviewing the styles of Europe as a whole and those of the six distinctive regions studied in this chapter: the British Isles, Scandinavia, Germanic Western Europe, the Atlantic Romantic countries, the Mediterranean, and Eastern Europe.

Traditional line dance of Romania

121

Ethnic heritage celebration in midwestern United States; (Macedonian)

European traditional music has many unifying elements. Although we immediately hear differences between the musics of Sweden and Italy, they resemble each other far more than either one resembles Chinese or Native American music. What is so characteristic about European folk music?

Song structure is one important element of European music. Across the continent, the use of strophic form is widespread: Melodies are sung more than once with different words for each repetition. The verse-by-verse and verse-chorus organization of songs reinforces the view of Europe as a distinct musical unit. Meter is another facet common to European traditional music. Most songs and dance music are metric, so that there is a regular and consistent recurrence in the accent patterns. Duple and triple meters (and even irregular meters such as $\frac{5}{8}$ and $\frac{7}{8}$) feature the repetition of accents in a cyclic manner. In songs, this meter is usually linked to the poetry. Music with no obvious metric pattern is rare in Europe.

Certain song genres are found in many parts of Europe. These include the narrative song, love songs, ceremonial songs, seasonal songs, and dance music. Song stories called ballads and their lengthier cousin, the epic, are prominent throughout the continent. Clearly, then, European music can be efficiently classified as songs and dance music.

There are instruments that are associated with the music of the various European countries, but several are so predominant throughout the continent

122

that they can be referred to as "pan-European" instruments. There are perhaps three such instruments: the fiddle, the accordion, and the bagpipe. Although they vary in construction, size, and shape, their tone quality and principles for sound production do not. Other common European instruments include flutes, drums of various types, plucked lutes, and zithers. Certain instruments that are less widespread, including the Swiss *alphorn,* the double-reeds of the Mediterranean countries, and the Irish tin whistle, provide a means of distinguishing the music of a country or region.

The British Isles

Folk music in the British Isles of England, Scotland, Wales, and Ireland is somewhat related to the art music of western Europe, even though the British Isles are geographically separate from the continent. Folk songs, ballads, and dance tunes, like so many madrigals and art songs, are commonly organized into four-phrase melodies or four-line stanzas in duple or triple meters. Folk music of the British Isles has retained its modal structure to a greater extent than has folk music on the continent. The vocal melodies range from strictly syllabic English ballads to the Irish-Gaelic lyrical and melismatic songs of love and war. In fact, Irish music is essentially melodic, relying on ornamentation rather than harmony for its effects. Traditional instruments of the British Isles include fiddles, bagpipes, flutes, and harps. The following elements characterize music and songs in the British Isles:

Melody: Based in C, A, D, and G modes (Ionian, Aeolian, Dorian, and Mixolydian); syllabic vocal music in Britain, more decorative and ornamental music in Ireland

Rhythm: Duple and triple meter; jigs in $\frac{6}{8}$, $\frac{9}{8}$ ("slip jig"), and $\frac{12}{8}$; reels and slow hornpipes in duple meter

Texture: Homophonic song (melody and chords) in Britain; heterophonic music in Ireland, in which several pitched instruments may play simultaneous variations on the melody

Form: Many two-part binary folk songs (AB)

Genres: Jigs, reels, ballads, and love songs

Timbre: Fiddle, flute, tin whistle, Scottish highland bagpipe, smaller *uilleann* "elbow" bagpipe of Ireland, Irish *bodhran* (flat drum), Celtic harp, and concertina

Scandinavia

Denmark, Sweden, Norway, and Finland are referred to jointly as Scandinavia. The first three countries share common linguistic elements, and the last three sit side-by-side, extending from the Arctic Circle into the Baltic Sea. Scandinavian folk music has been influenced by the cultivated traditions of Germany, and the villages maintain traits of an ancient musical tradition. The parallel fifths, or organum, of medieval church practice appear in the folk music of nearby Iceland. Only Albania shows similar early forms, probably because both areas were isolated from Europe's cultural mainstream for centuries. Modal folk tunes and major-minor melodies are prevalent. Stringed instruments, including the standard fiddle and the Norwegian *hardanger fiddle,* the Swedish *nykelharpa,* the Finnish psaltery called *kantele,* and Scandinavian dulcimers, are

123

frequently played to accompany songs and dances. Typical Scandinavian songs display the following elements:

Melody: Based in major, or mixing major and minor modes; arpeggios and triad-like figures

Rhythm: Duple and triple meter (including dances such as the *vals, hambo,* and *polska*); meter obscured by overlapping measures in much instrumental music

Texture: Homophonic (chordal) or polyphonic (independent and interwoven melodic lines)

Form: AB (binary) and ABA (ternary) forms

Genres: Dance music and love songs

Timbre: Fiddle (usually played in pairs or larger ensembles), *hardanger fiddle* (Norway), *kantele* psaltery (Finland), dulcimer, *nyckelharpa,* and flute

Germanic Western Europe

The rich folk music traditions in the Germanic countries of western Europe faded rapidly by the nineteenth century, when other forms, such as church and school songs, easy art and community songs, and popular hits and ballroom dances, grew in popularity. Music making had once been nurtured, but the industrialization of this region created a void of social functions including seasonal agrarian customs, and gatherings for spinning, cornhusking, and other communal activities. Of the remaining folk songs of Germany, Austria, Switzerland, and the Netherlands, the most common consist of arpeggiated melodies set in major keys and in duple or triple time.

Strophic forms, a simple syllabic style, and elementary harmonic sequences characterize the music. In the alpine regions there is a distinctive song style called *jodler,* whose melodies contain wide-ranging leaps and are cast in a major key. Germanic peoples who still use folkloric styles live in the mountainous regions of the area and share instruments like the *alphorn,* the accordion, the wooden hammered dulcimer, and the zither. Folk music of the Germanic countries generally follow these guidelines:

Melody: Songs mostly in major keys; triads and sixths used frequently in melodies

Rhythm: Duple and triple meter, with an emphasis on triple time in southern Germany (Bavaria), Switzerland, and Austria

Texture: Homophonic, melody with chordal accompaniment; polyphonic song tradition

Form: Variety, with emphasis on AB (binary) and ABA (ternary)

Genres: Ballad, love song, *jodler*

Timbre: Alphorn (Switzerland), accordion, wooden hammered dulcimer, zither, occasional brass band, or *rommel pot* (Dutch friction drum)

Romantic-Atlantic Europe

France, Portugal, and Belgium are "Romantic-Atlantic" countries, because they are coastal countries on the Atlantic and because their people speak languages of the Romance family. Of course, there are other countries that border the Atlantic Ocean, and there are other Romance-language nations; these three countries, however, share both geographic and linguistic elements. Folk songs in these countries are largely monodic and sung as solos. Chants and

124

Bulgarian tapan drummer   *Norwegian lur performer*

rounds are associated with the Carnival days preceding Lent, "begging songs" with Christmas, and egg-rolling songs with Eastertide. There are songs whose rhythms and incantations arise directly from work such as wood-carving, shepherding, and spinning. Typical instrumental sonorities in this region include the drone of bagpipes, the grinding timbres of the hurdy-gurdies, and the noisy strains of village wind bands. Belgium also shares in the Germanic tradition, just as Portuguese music frequently sounds Spanish in flavor.

Melody: Mostly major melodies, both diatonic and pentatonic; often conjunct (stepwise)

Rhythm: Duple meter predominant; $\frac{6}{8}$ in Brittany (France) and northern Portugal

Texture: Homophonic (melody and chordal accompaniment)

Form: AB (binary) and ABA (ternary) forms

Genres: Seasonal and love songs

Timbre: Bagpipe, hurdy-gurdy, pipe and drum, and concertina

Mediterranean Europe

North Africans and Middle Easterners have contributed to the music and culture of the Mediterranean countries of Europe—Spain, Italy, and Greece. Although these countries each make unique contributions to the world's music, there are elements that are similar among them. The florid melodies are unmistakably Mediterranean, as is the somewhat nasalized vocal timbre of the singers. Much of the music is metered, but there is also considerable use of the

125

free and flexible rhythms associated with declamatory speech. When musicians play in ensemble, they frequently create simultaneous variations of the melody, particularly in Greece and in the southern portions of Spain and Italy. The world-famous genre of Spanish flamenco dance music exemplifies the passionate music of the Mediterranean. Among the instruments common in these countries are guitars or other types of plucked lutes (Greek *oud* and *bouzouki*), double-reeds, and percussion instruments such as castenets, spoons, tambourines, and rattles. Typical Mediterranean music makes use of these elements:

Melody: Frequent use of minor melodies, largely melismatic and decorative; augmented seconds

Rhythm: Occasionally free of meter; some use of irregular, yet isometric patterns including sevens and fives ($\frac{5}{8}$, $\frac{7}{8}$, $\frac{11}{8}$)

Texture: Heterophonic; polyphonic and chordal in northern Italy and Spain

Form: Through-composed, AB (binary) form

Genres: Love songs and dance music (in Spain, *flamenco*; in Italy, *tarantella*; in Greece, *tsamiko*)

Timbre: Lutes (guitar, Greek *oud, bouzouki*), double-reeds, bagpipes, percussion (especially idiophones)

Eastern Europe

Eastern Europe encompasses a large geographic area and numerous countries. From north to south, they are Poland, Czechoslovakia, Hungary, Romania, Bulgaria, and Yugoslavia; European Russia is farther east. Eastern Europe is much less influenced by art music than is the rest of Europe, and traditional music is prevalent. Bulgaria, Yugoslavia, and Romania, known collectively as the Balkans, share certain style traits with the Mediterranean countries: melismatic singing, heterophonic texture, and irregular or free meter. The pentatonic melodies used by Hungarians are evidence of an ancient layer of musical culture in which pitches are transposed up or down a fifth. Parts of Poland and Czechoslovakia show Germanic influences in the music's major tonalities, duple and triple meters, and use of anacruses. The farther east one moves, the more one will hear folk songs in older church modes, asymetrical meters, and performances in the great polyphonic tradition. The following are elements common to Eastern European styles:

Melody: Major, minor and modal; syllabic in northern and melismatic in southern areas; gypsy scale (augmented seconds of the Balkans)

Rhythm: Duple and triple in northern areas, asymetrical and nonmetric music in the Balkans, little use of anacrusis

Texture: Heterophony or melody and drone in the Balkans, rich polyphony in the north

Form: Through-composed common in the Balkans; also AB (binary) and ABA (ternary) throughout the region

Genres: Epics, wedding song cycles, love songs, dance music (Hungarian *czardas*, Polish *polka*, Bulgarian *rachenitsa*, and Romanian *hora*)

Timbre: Lutes (plucked *tamburs* and *tamburitza* ensembles of Croatia and Serbia, Yugoslavia), *gaida* bagpipes (Bulgaria and Macedonia, Yugoslavia), accordions, *cimbaloms* (hammered dulcimers of Hungary), flutes, fiddles, and hand drums

126

■ OBJECTIVES:

Students will:
1. Sing a number of modes common to Irish songs.
2. Sing the song "Leaving Erin" first without and then with the characteristic melismas in the melody.
3. Accompany the song on guitar.
4. Identify the historical significance of the song's text.
5. Locate the British Isles and Ireland on a map.
6. Listen to examples of Irish jigs and tap the underlying pulse of the music.
7. Improvise jig rhythms, both vocally and on drums.
8. Identify traditional Irish instruments.

Materials:
1. Guitar
2. Hand drum
3. Recording:
   The Chieftains 8, Columbia 35726

■ PROCEDURES:

1. Sing each of the four common modes of Irish music: Ionian (the diatonic mode on C), Aeolian (on A), Dorian (on D), and Mixolydian (on G). Have the students imitate you—rote learning is the most efficient means of teaching these modes. Repeat the modes a number of times, changing the rhythm of the scale from quarter notes, to eighth notes, to eighth note triplets, to combined rhythm patterns in order to challenge the students while reinforcing the sound of the modes.

2. Sing the Irish-American song, "Leaving Erin" (see figure 1). Where there are triplets notated in the music, sing the circled pitch only (as a quarter note). Learn the additional verses:

Oh son, I loved my native land with energy and pride,
Until a blight came o'er my crops—my sheep, my cattle died,
My rent and taxes were too high, I could not them redeem,
And that's the cruel reason why I left old Skibberdeen [Ireland].

And you were only two years old and feeble was your frame,
I could not leave you with my friends, you bore your father's name,
I wrapped you in my woolen coat, and in the night unseen,
I heaved a sigh, and bade goodbye to dear old Skibberdeen.

Oh father dear, the day may come, when in answer to the call,
Each Irishman, with feeling stern, will rally one and all;
I'll be the man to lead the van beneath the flag so green,
When loud and high we'll raise the cry: "Remember Skibberdeen."

Figure 1.

3. Sing the song with the triplet figures added. Note the change from the rather syllabic setting of much of the melody to melismatic sections in which several pitches are sounded on one syllable. This is the typical Irish lyrical song style. The recording of "The Session," studied in this lesson, contains more florid melismas in an instrumental setting.
4. Discuss the meaning of the text. The song is popular in Ireland and in Irish-American communities. The harshness of the potato famine in Ireland and the dissatisfactions of the Irish with British rule brought about the migration of many Irish men and women to the United States and Canada in the mid-nineteenth century.
5. Locate Ireland on a map of Europe, and note its relationship to Britain. Point out the division of Ireland and Northern Ireland, which today is still ruled by the British.

6. Listen to "The Session" for the metric structure and for the use of traditional Celtic instruments. Define a session as an informal meeting of musicians to play traditional Celtic tunes, keeping the music alive by improvising on familiar melodies. Use the following outline as a listening guide:
   a. "Elizabeth Kelly's Delight"
      $\frac{9}{8}$ jig
      flute
   b. "Fraher's Jig"
      $\frac{12}{8}$ jig
      bagpipe, bodhran (large hand drum), fiddle
   c. "Elizabeth Kelly's Delight"
      $\frac{9}{8}$ jig
      bagpipe, flute
   d. "Dinny's Delight"
      $\frac{12}{8}$ jig
      fiddle, flute, bagpipe
   e. "Fraher's Jig"
      $\frac{12}{8}$ jig
      fiddle, flute, bagpipe
   f. "Dinny's Delight"
      $\frac{12}{8}$ jig
      bagpipe, flute
   g. "Elizabeth Kelly's Delight"
      $\frac{9}{8}$ jig
      fiddle, flute, bagpipe
7. Listen again, leading students in keeping the pulse of the music. Call attention to the heterophonic texture, in which the fiddle, flute, and bagpipe play slight variations of the same melody simultaneously.
8. Use the drum to keep a basic pulse. Lead students in performing subdivisions of the beat vocally on a neutral syllable such as "dee," "nah," or a combination of vocables. Ask students to imitate the following jig-like patterns immediately after you play them.

9. Encourage the vocal improvisation of jig rhythms. As a challenge, suggest a melodic improvisation in $\frac{9}{8}$ and $\frac{12}{8}$.
10. Listen again to "The Session" for the jig rhythms, and ask students to distinguish between $\frac{9}{8}$ and $\frac{12}{8}$ by patting the leg on the first pulse and clapping on the remaining two $\frac{9}{8}$ or three $\frac{12}{8}$ pulses.

129

2

L E S S O N   T W O

■ OBJECTIVES:

Students will:
1. Listen to the waltz tune "Vals from Orso" played by two fiddles.
2. Identify the arpeggiated melody as typical of Scandinavian folk music.
3. Clap the waltz pulse.
4. Dance a modified waltz step.
5. Play "Swedish Tune" on classroom instruments.
6. Locate Sweden and Scandinavia on a map.

Materials:
1. Recording: *Folk Fiddling from Sweden*, Nonesuch H-72033
2. Recorders
3. Autoharp

■ PROCEDURES:

1. Define waltz as a dance in triple meter that developed in the ballrooms and community halls of early nineteenth-century Europe, especially in Germany and the Scandinavian countries. The Swedes call it *vals*.
2. Have students listen to "Vals from Orso" as played by a pair of fiddles. Keep the triple meter pulse through pat-clap-clap movements; since the dance moves so quickly, try also a pat-clap-hold gesture. Note the melodic leaps in the arpeggios, the complimentary and interweaving melodies of the two fiddles, and the three themes (the third of which characteristically shifts between major and minor keys).
3. Learn a modified waltz step like the following: Form an inner circle and an outer circle with students in couples (not necessarily boy-girl) (see figure 2).

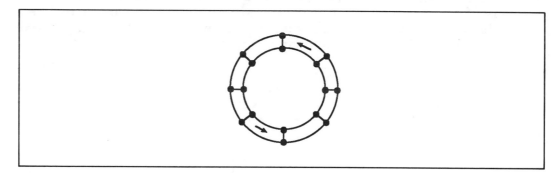

Figure 2. Formation of couples

Warm up by practicing a "limp step," moving right-left, left-right, around a circle in order to feel the rhythmic pattern:

(1)   (2–3)

Theme 1
Section A: Couple face each other, feet together, weight on left foot, step in place.

one box = one beat

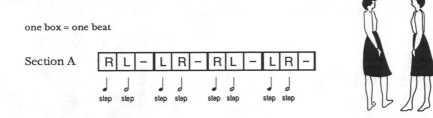

Section A

| R | L | – | | L | R | – | | R | L | – | | L | R | – |

step step   step step   step step   step step

Section B: Couple holds hands.

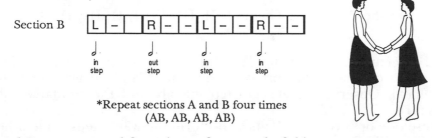

Section B

| L | – | | R | – | – | L | – | – | R | – | – |

in   out   in   in
step   step   step   step

*Repeat sections A and B four times
(AB, AB, AB, AB)

A and B are repeated four times, for a total of thirty-two measures: AB, AB, AB, AB.

Theme 2
Shoulder hold: Dancers extend their arms and hold partners' shoulders. Turn together in small circle with right-left, left-right steps; repeat eight times for sixteen measures.

| R | L | – | | L | R | – | *Repeat eight times

step step   step step

Theme 3
Couple promenades forward in skater's position with right-left, left-right steps; repeat eight times for sixteen measures.

| R | L | – | | L | R | – | *Repeat eight times

step step   step step

131

Theme 4

Couples separate, forming inner and outer circles. Inner circle moves forward, and back again; outer circle moves backward, away from the circle, and back in. Repeat four times for sixteen measures.

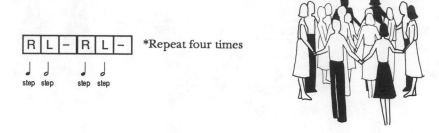

*Repeat four times

The form should follow: Theme I, II, III, IV; I, II, III, IV; I.

4. Lead the students in playing "Swedish Tune" on recorders (see figure 3). Add an accompaniment, or ask a student to add an accompaniment on Autoharp. Observe the arpeggiated melody and the fundamental chord structure.
5. Choose one or several students to perform the waltz steps while others play the "Swedish Tune."
6. Locate Sweden on a map of Europe. Note the countries that surround Sweden and name the Scandinavian countries. Locate Germany (to the south), where the language and culture, including the music components of melody and rhythm, bear a resemblance to expressions of Swedish culture.

Figure 3.

■ **OBJECTIVES:**

Students will:

1. Listen to songs that feature the yodel.
2. Identify instruments of Austria and the alpine countries.
3. Sing an Austrian folk song.
4. Accompany the folk song with guitar or Autoharp.
5. Locate Austria, Bavarian Germany, and Switzerland on a map of Europe.

Materials:

1. Recording: *Jodler und Schuhplattler*, Fiesta FLPS 1905
2. Guitar
3. Autoharp

■ **PROCEDURES:**

1. Play a recording from *jodlerer* (yodel songs) and *schuhplattler* (folk dances that feature the boot slapping of men). Call attention to the preponderance of triple meter and to the arpeggiated melodies in major keys. Many yodel songs are organized into a verse-refrain form, the refrain of which is usually the yodeling of syllables rather than words.
2. Sing "The Cuckoo's Song" in unison, adding the second part if appropriate for the age level (see figure 4). The first verse in Austrian German is "Wenn

Figure 4.

der Guggu schreit, aft is langiszeit" (pronounced *Vehn dehr googoo shraheet, ahft ess lahng-eest-aeet*)/ "Weard der Schnee vergehn, wearn die Wieslan grian" (pronounced *Veerd dehr shnee fehr-gaen, veern dee wees-lahn greeahn*).

3. While singing, add a step-pat-clap gesture to keep the triple meter feeling.
4. Accompany the song on guitar or Autoharp.
5. On a map of Europe, locate the Germanic countries of Austria, Switzerland, and the southern part of Germany known as Bavaria. Discuss the possible reasons for the development of the yodel. Could it be that the Alps motivated people to sing from one mountain to the next for the pure enjoyment of the echo (in which case words were not necessary and the pitched cries of the arpeggiated melody collided into chords as they were bounced back to the singer)?

4 L E S S O N F O U R

■ OBJECTIVES:
Students will:
1. Dance the *branle,* a French folk dance.
2. Recognize the division of dance music into musical themes and phrases.
3. Identify the sound of the concertina.
4. Locate France on a map of Europe.

Materials:
Recording: *Dances of the World's Peoples, European Folk Dances,* vol.2, Folkways FD 6502

■ PROCEDURES:
1. Play the recording of the *branle,* an old circle dance. The concertina (a small accordion) plays the melody, and a second, larger accordion plays the accompaniment. Keep the steady beat by patting or clapping softly with two fingers.
2. Teach students to dance the *branle.* The formation is a circle, with hands joined:

In the introduction students bend their knees and bounce in place for sixteen beats. Follow these patterns for the dance, and repeat until the music's end:

Part one
Move in the circle, eight running steps to the right, then eight running steps to the left, for sixteen beats.

Part two
Standing in place, step and kick for sixteen beats:

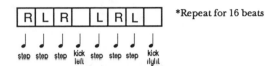

*Repeat for 16 beats

Part three
Step and kick, moving into the circle for eight beats and out of the circle for eight beats:

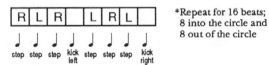

*Repeat for 16 beats;
8 into the circle and
8 out of the circle

Part four
Each dancer stands in place and alternately points the left foot over the right foot and the right foot over the left.

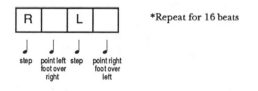

*Repeat for 16 beats

Repeat these steps as the dance music continues.

4. Locate France on a map of Europe. Cousins of the *branle* are found throughout France and in many parts of Europe. Along the Pyrenees in the south, the Basques dance a similar circle dance called the *sardana*, and throughout most of Europe, people enjoy the communal spirit of dancing in a circle.

135

L E S S O N   F I V E

■ OBJECTIVES:
Students will:
1. Listen to examples of Spanish dance songs.
2. Recognize the importance and extent of dance music in Spain, including the *fandango, seguidilla,* and *flamenco.*
3. Play the Andalusian cadence on the guitar.
4. Learn several Spanish rhythms on the castenets.
5. Sing "Tío Pep."
6. Locate Spain on a map of Europe.

Materials:
1. Guitar
2. Castanets
3. Recordings:

   Authentic Folk Music and Dances of the World, Murray Hill S-4195 ("Seguidillas Guitano")

   Spanish Folk Music, The Columbia World Library of Folk and Primitive Music: Spain, 91A-02001 ("Fandango de Comares")

■ PROCEDURES:
1. Listen to "Fandango de Comares," which features guitar, *bandurria* (large mandolin), castenets, and voice. Listen then to "Seguidillas Guitano" for the interplay of guitar and voice in a *seguidilla,* a *flamenco*-style dance song. Note the importance of guitar for both songs. Call attention to the melismatic melody of the *seguidilla* and to the shouts of joy and excitement.
2. Play the chords A minor, G major, F major, and E major in succession. This chord combination is known as the Andalusian cadence and is found in the music of southern Spain. Sing the root note as the cadence is played: A, G, F, and E. Listen again to "Seguidillas Guitano" for the cadence (see figure 5).
3. Listen for the castenets again on "Fandango de Comares." Ask several students to play the Andalusian cadence on guitars, while others first clap and later play castenets for these Spanish rhythms.

$$\text{X X} \quad \text{X} \quad \text{X} \quad \text{X}$$

4. Sing "Tío Pep" (see figure 6). Note the use of melisma in the refrain (on the vocable "ah"). If guitar accompaniment is added, transpose to the key of D major. The text is as follows: "Lo Tío Pep s'en va a Muro Tío Pep." (pronounced *Lo tee-oh Pehp sehn vah Moo-roh Tee-oh Pehp*)/ ¿"De Muro qué em portará? Tío Pep, Tío Pep" (pronounced *Day Moo-roh kaym pore-tah-rah Tee-oh Pehp, Tee-oh Pehp*)/ "Una tartana i un burro Tío Pep" (pronounced *Oo-na tahr-tah-nah ee oon boo-roh Tee-oh Pehp*)/ "Per'narse'n a passechar Tío Pep, Tío Pep." (pronounced *Payr-nahr-sayn ah pahs-say-chahr Tee-oh Pehp, Tee-oh Pehp*).

136

Figure 5. Andalusian cadence

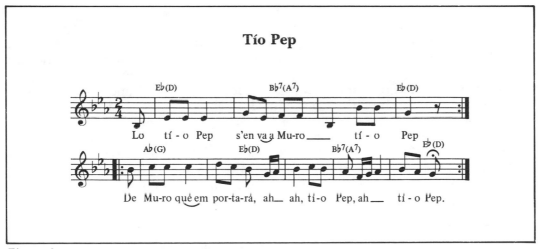

Figure 6.

Translation:
Old Uncle Joe's going to Muro, Uncle Joe.
What will he bring back from town? Uncle Joe, Uncle Joe.
A two-wheeled cart and a burro
So he can ride up and down, Uncle Joe, Uncle Joe.

5. Locate Spain on a map of Europe. Discuss the historical significance of Spain's proximity to North Africa across the narrow Strait of Gibralter. A report on the Moorish occupation of Spain over a five-hundred-year period can help students place the country and its culture in perspective. The North African–Middle Eastern influence on the music is found in the melismatic singing, the somewhat free and flexible rhythm, and the evolution of the guitar from its predecessor, the Egyptian ʻūd.

137

L E S S O N   S I X

6

■ **OBJECTIVES:**

Students will:

1. Listen to "Trugnal mi Yane Sandanski, lele," a Bulgarian work song in $\frac{7}{8}$ meter.
2. Sing a Bulgarian song in $\frac{7}{8}$ meter with drone.
3. Play a Bulgarian song on recorders.
4. Perform a Bulgarian dance.
5. Identify the sound of the *gaida* bagpipes.
6. Locate Bulgaria and Macedonia on the map.

Materials:

1. Recording:

   In the Shadow of the Mountain, Nonesuch H-72038 ("Trugnal mi Yane Sandanski, lele")
2. Recorders

■ **PROCEDURES:**

1. Listen to "Trugnal mi Yane Sandanski, lele" and tap the pulse of the $\frac{7}{8}$ meter. Listen for the sound of the *gaida* bagpipes, the flute, and the various fiddles and lutes.
2. The teacher should give the translation for the song: "Yane Sandanski sets off walking about the Pirin Mountains. He has a carbine over his shoulder, he has a double cartridge-belt. Yonder comes a young shepherd. Yane asks him: 'Didn't you see my people from my fighting band?' The young shepherd replies: 'Oh Yane, up in the mountain, at the high peak of the Pirin Mountains you will find them.' " Explain that Yane was fighting the Turks, who occupied Bulgaria, Albania, Romania, and the countries of Yugoslavia for about five hundred years.

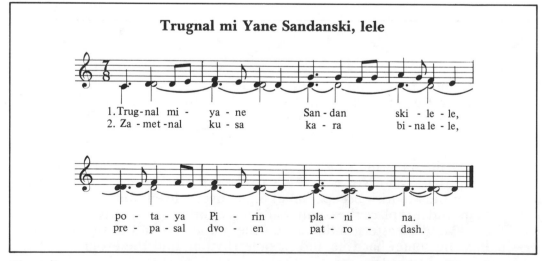

Figure 7.

138

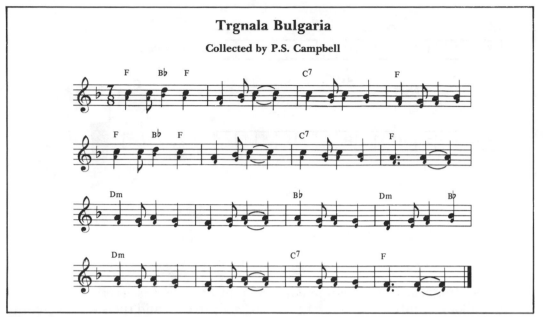

Trgnala Bulgaria

Collected by P.S. Campbell

Figure 8.

3. Sing "Trugnal mi Yane Sandanski, lele" (see figure 7) first in unison and later with the addition of the drone accompaniment. Note the only change that occurs: In measure seven, there is a shift from D to C and back to D again at measure eight. The text is as follows: "Trugnal mi Yane Sandanski lele" (pronounced *Troog-nahl mee Yah-neh Sahn-dahn-skee lay-lay*)/ "Potaya Pirin planina" (pronounced *Poh-tah-yah Pee-reen plah-nee-nah*)/ "Zametnal kusa karabina lele" (pronounced *Zah-meht-nahl koo-sah kah-rah-bee-nah lay-lay*)/ "Prepasal dvoen patrondash" (pronounced *Pray-pah-sahl dvoy-ehn pah-trohn-dahsh*).

4. Play the Bulgarian dance song "Trgnala mi Rumjana" on recorders (see figure 8). The teacher should point out that the drone of the previous song and the harmony in thirds found in this song are characteristic of different regions of Bulgaria. Add to the recorders a chordal accompaniment on guitar or piano and a rhythmic pattern on hand drum:

5. Learn the following dance to accompany either $\frac{7}{8}$ song:
Have the students form a line with arms in a "W" (holding hands with arms crooked at elbow). Each dancer then steps to the right with the right foot and places the left foot behind the right. Students step right again and then place the left foot in front of the right. For the third measure, they step right and then left, bringing the feet together; and in the fourth measure of the dance pattern, step left and then right, bringing the feet together again. This pattern is repeated to the end of the music (see figure 9 for a diagram of the dance steps).

139

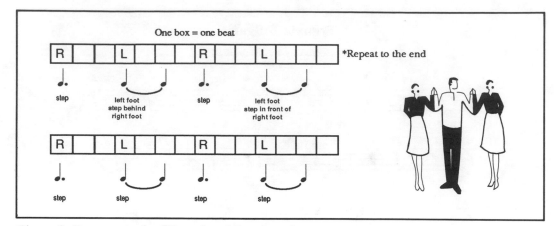

Figure 9. Dance steps for "Trgnala mi Rumjana."

6. Locate Bulgaria and Macedonia on a map of Europe. Discuss the isolation of the Balkan countries from the European mainstream and their close proximity to Turkey and Asia Minor.

7   L E S S O N   S E V E N

■ OBJECTIVES:
Students will:
1. Sing a Hungarian folk song.
2. Identify aspects of melody and rhythm that are typical of Hungarian folk music.
3. Dance the *czardas* national dance.
4. Listen to Kodály's *Hungarian Rondo.*
5. Locate Hungary on a map of Europe.

Materials:
Recording: Zoltan Kodály, *Hungarian Rondo*, Columbia MS 7034

■ PROCEDURES:
1. Sing the song "The Forest" (see figure 10). Note the way in which the melody seems to focus on C, the fifth of the key, especially at the beginnings and endings of phrases one, two, and four. Note also the dotted rhythms, especially in measures three, seven, and fifteen:

140

The Forest

Er - dö, Er - dö, Er - dö, All a - round Mar - os - szek grow - ing. Wing - ing through the green leaves, Birds of ev - 'ry co - lor show - ing. If I could I'd send a bird to tell you that you make me hap - py, warm and well, too. You, my friend I treas - ure. You are special be - yond mea - sure.

*Forest

Figure 10.

These are characteristic sounds of Hungarian folk music.
2. Dance the national folk dance of Hungary, the *czardas*.
   Students form a circle, either holding hands or with arms resting on neighbors' shoulders, and step, slide, and stomp, alternating motion to the right with motion to the left (see figure 11).
3. Through the efforts of Zoltan Kodály and Béla Bartók, Hungarian peasant music was collected and thus became the inspiration for their compositions. Kodály's *Hungarian Rondo* features "The Forest" as the A theme and four other folk songs in the contrasting sections. You can guide students in their listening by calling their attention to these items:
   A theme—"The Forest" theme played in a straightforward manner by strings, especially violins
   B theme—second folk song, played in conversation by clarinet and violins; stretched rubato tempo
   A theme—"The Forest" theme, third and fourth phrases only, played by violins
   C theme—third folk song, *czardas* style accompaniment with cellos representing the "oom-pah-pah" of the *cimbalom*; virtuosic, gypsy-sounding violin melody
   A theme—"The Forest" for violin solo, partly minor harmony, fragments of melody, and slowing rubato tempo

141

D theme—fourth folk song, strings sounding a syncopated accompaniment on the offbeats

E theme—fifth folk song starting with bassoon and double bass; increased tempo with clarinet and then high strings on melody, drone-like reference to tonic

A theme—"The Forest" theme, beginning with pulsing double bass drone; modulation of the theme and stretching of theme with slow tempo

E theme—return to the fifth folk song, a festive dance ending

6. Locate Hungary on a map of Europe. Discuss the early origins of the people deep within the Russian interior and their migration westward to Hungary. Consider other events of a historical nature such as the Austro-Hungarian Empire and the Hungarian Revolution of 1956.

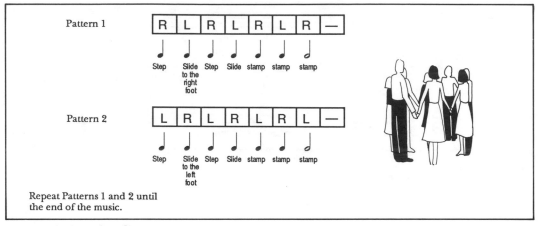

Figure 11. Czardas *diagram*

BIBLIOGRAPHY

Bartók, Béla and Albert Lord. *Serbo-Croatian Folk Songs.* New York: Columbia University Press, 1951. A technical study of South Slavic traditional songs collected by Slavist Millman Parry. Transcriptions and texts of 205 women's songs with analysis.

Bronson, Bertrand Harris. *The Traditional Tunes of the Child Ballads.* Vols. 1–4. Princeton, NJ: Princeton University Press, 1959. The musical counterpart to the Francis James Child collection of English and Scottish ballads from the thirteenth to the nineteenth centuries. Tunes and texts are arranged by period for the study of ballads in England, Scotland, Ireland, and America.

Karpeles, Maud. *Folk Songs of Europe.* London: Novello, 1956. A fine collection of texts and notations for European folk songs, transcribed by the author.

Kodály, Zoltan. *Folk Music of Hungary.* London: Barrie and Jenkins, 1971. Collected by Kodály, these songs represent the oral traditions of the Hungarian people. Several black-and-white photographs and illustrations of instruments are provided.

Lawson, Joan. *European Folk Dance.* London: Pitman Publishing, 1972. A description of folk dances from all of Europe, with instructions on specific movements. Melodies of dance songs are provided. The text also includes chapters on the development of the dances and costumes.

Lord, Albert. *The Singer of Tales.* Cambridge, MA: Harvard University Press, 1960. The author summarizes years of field work among the Yugoslav epic singers and discusses the nature of the oral tradition.

Nettl, Bruno. *Folk and Traditional Music of the Western Continents.* Englewood Cliffs, NJ: Prentice-Hall, 1973. Although quite brief, this publication is one of the most concise descriptions of European traditional music available. The author presents his thoughts on the character of European folk music and regional musics.

DISCOGRAPHY

Authentic Folk Music and Dances of the World. Murray Hill S-4195 ("Seguidillas Guitano").

Bavarian Yodeling Songs and Polkas. Olympic 6115C. This recording includes songs and instrumental music with emphasis on the *jodler*, clog dancing, and polkas.

The Chieftains 8. Columbia 35726. A collection of Irish instrumental music, featuring the *uillean* bagpipe, tin whistle, fiddle, harp, concertina, and the *bodhran* drum. The recording includes descriptive liner notes.

Dances of the World's Peoples, European Folk Dances. Vol. 2. Folkways FD 6502. Dance music for the Italian *tarantella*, French *branle*, Greek *horo*, Irish reel, and assorted Bulgarian dances. A pamphlet for learning the dance steps is included.

Folk Fiddling from Sweden. Nonesuch H-72033. Fiddle tunes from rural Sweden are performed on two fiddles, including dance music for *vals*, *polska*, and *langdans*.

Greece Is . . . Popular and Folk Dances. EMI 14C 062-70007. (Rashid Sales Company, 191 Atlantic Avenue, Brooklyn, NY 11201.) Twelve Greek dances performed on *bouzouki*, *santouri*, and *baglamas* are presented, along with an instructional pamphlet.

Hungarian Instrumental Music. Hungariton LPX 18045–47. The most complete collection of Hungarian instrumental music, this four-record set contains examples of every Hungarian instrument, from the *leaf* to the *cimbalom*. A descriptive pamphlet accompanies the recordings.

In Dublin's Fair City. Olympic 6169. The Guinness Choir sings favorite Irish tunes.

In the Shadow of the Mountain, Bulgarian Folk Music. Nonesuch H-72038. Songs and instrumental music of southwestern Bulgaria (Pirin-Macedonian) are presented. The recording includes the diaphonic song style and the *zurna*, *gaida*, and *gaydulka*.

Jodler und Schulplattler. Fiesta FLPS 1905. Yodelling songs and folk dances that feature the boot slapping of men.

Kodály, Zoltan. *Hungarian Rondo*. Columbia MS 7034.

The Long Harvest, Ewan Maccoll and Peggy Seeger. Records 1 and 2. Argo ZDA 67. (115 Fulham Road, London SW3.) Traditional children's ballads are presented in English, Scottish, and North American variants, including "The Elfin Knight," "The Daemon Lover," and "Riddles Wisely Expounded." A pamphlet gives the text and origin of songs.

Music and Song of Italy. Tradition 1030 (Everest Records, 10920 Wilshire Boulevard, Los Angeles 90024). This recording includes songs and instrumental music from various regions of Italy, with liner notes that describe the influences of Albania, the Moors, and the Germanic countries. The performance of an ancient polyphonic song of Sardinia is a jewel in itself.

Spain, World Library of Folk and Primitive Music. Columbia 91A-02001. This recording includes music from all regions of Spain, including Andalusia, the Pyrenees, Galicia, and the Mediterranean. The attached booklet provides a background for each recorded selection.

Spanish Folk Music. The Columbia World Library of Folk and Primitive Music: Spain, 91A-02001 ("Fandango de Comares").

Swiss Yodeling Songs. Olympic 6171. Ten Swiss yodelers perform these traditional songs.

FILMOGRAPHY

The following films can be ordered from Audio-Visual Library Services, 3300 University Southeast, Minneapolis 55414:

Danzas regionales españolas, 15 minutes, color. 1966. Appropriate for junior high school. This film covers the cultural background of various regional dances of Spain, which are performed by professional and folk troupes.

European Culture Region, 23 minutes, color. 1966. Appropriate for junior high school. This film provides a survey of the influences of the Greeks, Romans, Christians, feudal city states, and merchant traders in the development of Europe. It also gives a geographical and economic overview of the continent. Note the stress placed on the relationship of economy to geography.

Greece, the Land and the People, 11 minutes, color. 1977. For intermediate or junior high school. This film depicts the rich cultural background of Greece, which served as the trade center for southeast Europe, Africa, and Asia Minor. A Greek man and woman show the people, geography, industries, and agriculture in their homeland as well as the arts and sciences of its glorious past.

Singendes Deutschland, 16 minutes, black and white. 1952. For junior high school. Fifteen popular German songs are sung and illustrated with appropriate German scenes and dances.

143

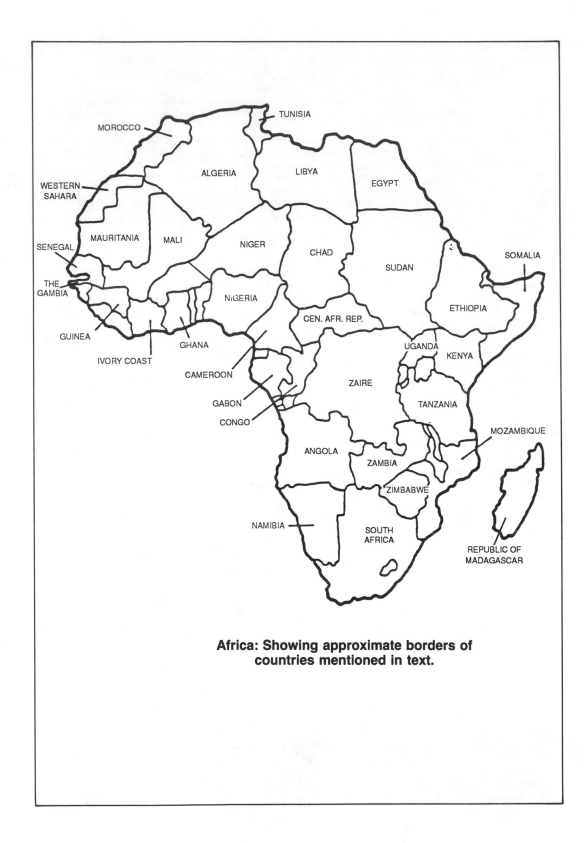

Africa: Showing approximate borders of countries mentioned in text.

CHAPTER FIVE

5

SUB-SAHARAN AFRICA

by Barbara Reeder Lundquist

A frica is the continent where human biological and cultural development began. Africans have always exchanged techniques, skills, goods, and raw materials within the continent and have been part of international trading systems from the earliest times. Africans have been enmeshed in many of the major events in the world's history: from the spread of Islam to the Crusades, from the making of America to World War II. The many languages and traditions of the diverse peoples of African ancestry provide such a rich record of human experience that it is difficult to discuss Africa in general terms. The ever-increasing rate of change adds to the difficulty of expressing any generally valid principles for the study of Africa, especially its many music cultures. To deal with this complexity, scholars normally make a distinction between Islamic North Africa and the culturally heterogeneous Sub-Saharan Africa, the focus of this chapter.

There are several dilemmas shared by Sub-Saharan Africans that, if understood, can help to structure perception of historical developments. First, the slave trade had a catastrophic effect on the entire continent. The violence, desensitization, and racism that accompanied the slave trade affected everyone involved, and its repercussions continue to affect both Africans and people of African, Arab, and European descent throughout the world. Second, the

145

experience of European domination, with its imposition of varied languages and colonial systems, led to a general disruption of social and cultural institutions throughout the continent. The intensity and duration of colonialism's disruption of African cultures interrupted the continuity in social interactions that permits gradual idiosyncratic change. Finally, the imposition of arbitrary national boundaries on a continent of thousands of indigenous Sub-Saharan African cultures, as well as the existence of Asian and European subcultures, has led to the breakdown of traditional power structures, socioeconomic systems, and cultural standards.

There are some pan-African continuities that seem to offer solutions to these three dilemmas. The first of these is education in the traditional schools of the indigenous cultures (in which the students are often grouped by age), formal educational institutions based on a Western model, and religious schools. In a second link with traditional culture, Sub-Saharan Africans are forming increasingly significant interrelationships with the modern, internationalized aspects of African life. For example, traditional healing practices are being used along with contemporary medical protocols to increase the effectiveness of health care. Third, religious systems present a unifying factor for the development and transmission of contemporary values for Africans. The need to work within foreign institutional frameworks to forge the integrating sociocultural structures necessary to support Sub-Saharan African aspirations, while reaffirming effective traditional values, is a challenge for contemporary Africans.

The continent of Africa is immense. The entire continental United States could fit three times into Africa's 11,506,000 square miles. About eight-tenths of the continent lies in the tropics, but only about 5 percent is tropical rain forest. About one-third of Africa is grassland with occasional deciduous trees, and more than one-half is semi-arid steppe and desert. Deserts are increasing because of changes in world climatic conditions, population growth, and problems caused by ineffective agricultural habits and overgrazing. In the past, the climate, with alternating wet and dry seasons, and the lack of geographical barriers in the massive savannah or grassland areas have encouraged seasonal migration of both animals and humans. The occasional mountain masses—including the highlands of Ethiopia and the rest of the awesome East African Rift System, with its high escarpments and sweeping valleys—serve as exceptions to the prevalence of savannah.

Africa has a shoreline with relatively few natural harbors. In many areas, there are plateaus that begin a short distance from the shore. Historically, these plateaus, drained by rapids and waterfalls, prevented easy inland navigation. The early great civilizations began in large inland basins beyond these plateaus. Other difficult terrain, such as the Sahara and Kalahari deserts and the rain forests of central and West Africa, increased the difficulty of contact and supported early European impressions of Sub-Saharan Africa's inaccessibility. Some of the world's great rivers can be found in Africa, and they have served as facilitators of communication rather than as barriers. The largest lakes, found in East Africa, function as inland seas for fishing, travel, and trade.

In contemporary Africa, where traditional, Islamic, and Western cultures exist side by side and where even the traditional culture can be divided into many different groups, it is difficult to discuss culture as a whole. Some statements are,

146

however, generally applicable to many traditional African cultures. One of these is the use of power-gathering emblems for clan or group membership found across the continent. In many places, musical instruments such as sets of drums have been used as emblems of power necessary to ratify political leadership. Among the Tutsi of Rwanda and Burundi, for example, sets of drums that belonged to the King and to the Queen Mother were played only upon their order. Historically, political power has been lost or gained with the loss or conquest of the royal drums as an emblem of power.

Language also serves as an important factor in transmitting and defining African culture. Living in a continent where seasonal migration rather than adherence to arbitrary political boundaries was a traditional way of life, some African people were connected more by language than by geography. There are many traditional, language-related African cultural practices, such as praise

147

singing, translating and interpreting the comments of political leaders, political commentary, telling stories, and maintaining personal and family history. Some of these practices are closely associated with music.

In most areas of Africa, traditional art is devoted to maintaining balance between nature and human beings, between people, and within individuals. The vitality of traditional African art is linked with its involvement in life. In Africa, movement is art, clothing oneself is art, carving is art, dreams are art, and music is art. Sub-Saharan African art forms are changing, and ceremonial occasions are being added or are falling out of use. The sculptor Chissano expresses the current tragedy of social disruption in Mozambique, while the painter Malangatana uses his personal style to celebrate traditional Mozambican design and cultural practices. The Tumbuka poets of Malawi reflect, in their language, on issues in contemporary life, and traditional Chewa songs are sung in that language at contemporary Malawian gatherings. National celebrations, however, are confirmed with the contemporary Malawian national anthem, sung in English.

In many areas, leading artists are teaching others. The *kora* playing of Amadou Bansang Jobarteh from The Gambia sustains the Mandinka musical tradition, carrying it to university settings in the United States, and King Sunny Ade travels the world performing in the contemporary Nigerian *juju* style. There are musicians, painters, sculptors, designers, weavers, potters, and metal workers as well as poets, playwrights, authors, and philosophers all over the continent. African art expresses the complexity of life in the contemporary world, and it is entering, with the arts of other areas of the world, a new era.

Melody

In many parts of Sub-Saharan Africa, traditional languages are tonal; that is, the meaning is conveyed by differences in the pitch of the speaking voice as the words are spoken. For example, in the language of the Kele people of Zaire, the

148

word *bosongo* can have three meanings. If it stays on the same vocal pitch it means copper or brass. If the first two syllables are low in pitch and the last syllable is higher, *bosongo* means a river's current. Finally, if the first syllable is lower than the last two syllables, *bosongo* refers to the wooden pestle that is used for pounding grain and spices.

The rising and falling of vocal pitch affect meaning in a tonal language, so the contour of the pitches of the spoken language has some similarities to the melodies of songs in other parts of the world. In such a language, it is not possible to convey the meaning of a song text clearly if the pitches selected for the melody are different in contour from those used in saying the words. Therefore, in much traditional African vocal music, the general contour of the melody is created just by the choice of words. This may be a reason why pitch-related characteristics of traditional music, such as melody, are not given the same analytic emphasis as are some other musical dimensions.

Sub-Saharan African speech and music are so interrelated that instrumental music is affected. Some instrumental works begin as songs; others may be based on word-related pitch and rhythmic patterns. When performing instrumental music, instrumentalists may "talk" to each other, as well as to the dancers and singers, by duplicating the commonly understood tonal relationships of a local language on their instruments.

Pitch resources may vary widely in different culture areas. In some areas the pitches form a pattern somewhat similar to a Western scale; in others they are totally different. The octave is found throughout the continent. Singers often use only those pitches that can be played on the instruments of particular areas. It is common to select starting pitches that are comfortable for the singer and to tune accompanying instruments, such as the *mbira* (a hand-held, metal-keyed instrument played with the thumbs and index fingers), to the pitches of that vocal range. Instruments may allow production of only a portion of the pitches that are theoretically available to them; musicians add pitches in the construction of their instruments as their musical ideas require an expanded range.

Although pitch may be determined partly by the convenience of the instrumentalist or singer and by the contour of the sung or implied text, there is a strongly tuneful, melodic quality in the musics of Sub-Saharan Africa. In most traditional musical forms, both vocal and instrumental musicians use short pitch sequences or melodic patterns that are repeated with variations. In some cases, musicians use longer, strophic melodic structures. In all melodic styles, singers and instrumentalists often interject shorter melodic fragments at points in a performance.

Rhythm

The music traditions of Africa emphasize temporal or rhythmic structures. Each musical part has its own independent rhythm, yet it interacts with the rhythms of the other parts. Interaction between the layers in a music selection is somewhat analagous to the mechanical workings of a clock. Just as the gears in a clock vary in size yet interact with precision, so the interacting rhythmic structures vary in length yet interact effectively and with precision.

Rhythm patterns can be generated in many ways. Some use the values of the duration of spoken words. Many are traditional: There are rhythmic motives

149

that underlie existing song styles and are used as sources for generating new works. There are also rhythm patterns that are created by performers as the basis of new music. Exemplary performers are sometimes credited with improvised patterns they create when the patterns are exceptionally effective. Some of these improvised patterns, as well as ceremonial or ritual rhythm motives, are very old and have the power that comes from their use in memorable musical performances for generations. All of them have a "feeling" that is brought to life in the combination of rhythmic structures, pitch patterns, music texture, timbres, and the movement of the musicians and dancers.

Rhythm patterns are expected to overlap, and the performers need a common sense of time so that the various rhythmic layers can accurately relate to each other in time. The resulting music can be viewed as the polyrhythmic interaction of overlapping layers: a timbre- and pitch-influenced temporal structure that moves through time, providing the structural stability necessary for improvisation.

The use of different timbres and pitch sequences provides for relationships among the polyrhythms in which different "tunes" or sound patterns emerge as interactions among the linear rhythmic figures change over time. These different tunes become a source of inspiration for the improviser, of new melodic motives for the singers, of new responding movements for the dancers, and of excitement and emotional response for all of the participants. African musicians are able to play "hot" rhythms, however, only to the extent that they remain "cool" or disciplined so that they can create, maintain, and develop music in performance.

There is usually a fundamental rhythm pattern that determines the temporal design of a musical work and often gives it a name. There are also multiple patterns that respond to the basic pattern. These responding patterns can begin before the basic pattern has finished, overlapping with it. These responses in the musical conversation overlap as statements in conversations among friends can overlap. Finally, there is always one improvised pattern that ornaments, expands, and comments on the new relationships that occur in the polyrhythmic interaction of the rhythmic layers.

Movement is an integral part of music making. The singers and instrumentalists move, and dancers communicate through posture, gestures, facial expressions, and costumes. The general character of the movements and posture differs from culture to culture. Sometimes the movements of the dancers are traditional and prescribed; sometimes they are improvised. Sometimes the dancers replicate orderly sequences of movements; at other times the instrumentalists signal the dancers with instructions to change movements. In some dances, the point is to demonstrate the expressive movement of the individual dancers; in other cases, it is to demonstrate the expressive power of the occasion. There is always, however, movement that is strongly linked to the feeling and expressiveness of the music. The musicians' movements may be perceived as a form of dance. Dance is so inextricably linked with rhythm that it becomes not only a way to experience the rhythm, but also its visual manifestation. The interaction of the temporal aspects of the music, along with the pitch, timbres, and movements of the dancers, provides a constantly shifting musical texture of varying levels of complexity.

150

Texture

In the musics of Sub-Saharan Africa, like those of other parts of the world, an instrumentalist or singer may perform an unaccompanied (monophonic) solo. Influenced by the social context of music performance in Africa, heterophony is often produced. Participants often use antiphonal or leader-chorus organization. The lead performer is joined by an overlapping response, usually performed by more than one musician. This chorus often remains much the same throughout the song, whereas the solo part is improvised. Textures often alternate from leader to chorus during a song. There are also songs in which solo singers alternate with each other or with instrumental sounds in an interlocking pattern of pitches and rhythms. Homophony can be found throughout the traditional music cultures of Sub-Saharan Africa. Some African musicians, such as the Yoruba of Nigeria, have developed homophonic texture that is formed from parallel melodies at the octave.

Polyphony is perhaps the most characteristic texture of the musics of Sub-Saharan Africa. This intricate texture involves cooperation between musicians to produce independent yet simultaneously sounding parts. This musical cooperation, analogous in perspective to the cooperation between individuals in African communities, is used all over the continent. For example, it is characteristic of the choral music of the Nguni, Zulu, Xhosa, Shangaan, and Swazi people of southern Africa. One polyphonic texture that is an excellent example of this musical cooperation is the hocket technique found in the music of the Ba-Benzele and Ganda people. Varied, gapped patterns are performed by each participant so that the sound of one pattern exactly fills the gaps, or silences, of another pattern. As all of these varied patterns are performed together, they combine to form a solid, continuous sound. Some culture groups use imitative or canonic techniques, although this is less common.

Timbre

Music in Sub-Saharan Africa encompasses the widest possible ranges and tone qualities of the human voice and of instruments constructed from a wide variety of natural and manufactured materials. Bottles can be used, for example, if the tone quality fits musical and acoustical requirements. The body is used as a percussion instrument to accompany singing and dancing and to create timbral effects, as is stamping on carefully prepared, resonant platforms of dried earth.

Some tone qualities are preferred over others. Africans generally prefer percussive sounds with sudden onsets and rather rapid decay, perhaps because this type of articulation allows a high degree of temporal precision. Africans seem to appreciate complex timbres. Musicians often attach devices (such as a flexible piece of perforated metal with metal rings or strips hung in the perforations) that add a complex tone quality to instruments that might otherwise have a clear timbre. This creates a buzzing sound as the instrument vibrates. On marimbas, the buzzing sound is created by covering a hole in the resonating gourds of the instrument with a thin membrane. Rattles also add a complex buzzing sound to an instrumental ensemble.

Timbral contrast is extremely important in African music. In vocal music, each singer is expected to retain an individual tone quality, even when his or her voice is combined with the voices of others. There is rarely a desire to blend toward a

151

Figure 1. Zanze (Mbira); Zaire

common, timbrally unified sound in vocal music. Traditional singing is open and natural, although in Islamic areas singers often use a narrower, more intensely focused vocal sound. The variety of timbres available to the human voice is explored in these music cultures. Male singers often use falsetto; the Ba-Benzele use yodeling vocal effects. Distinctive vocal techniques are found in all music cultures, such as the "whispering" vocal timbre of Burundi. Sub-Saharan Africans appreciate voices that are strong in personality, can be heard, are emotionally expressive, and are consistent in performance quality. Voices and instruments are closely related to each other in that timbral contrast is desired and the sound of individual instruments is valued.

Traditional Sub-Saharan African instruments exist in an enormous variety and commonly include idiophones, in which sound is produced by the vibration of the instruments themselves. These instruments vary from hollowed logs to the many different sizes of marimbas that are beautifully crafted from hardwood keys with gourd resonators. Other idiophones range from rattles, with beads hung from netting on the surface of dried gourds, to metal bells. *Mbira, sansa,* and *likembe* are three names for the well-known idiophone that is played by plucking metal keys with the thumbs and index fingers (see figure 1).

Membranophones are instruments in which the sound is produced by the vibration of a stretched skin. These are found in many sizes and shapes and have bodies made from pottery, gourds, metal, and wood. Some have two heads, others one. Some are played while held in the hand; others are on special racks. Some are held between the legs of the player or are carried on the head of a

152

marcher. Many are works of art; others are quite plain. Some have a deep tone; others are very high and sharp. In some cultures, membranophones are played with only the hands, in others they are struck with sticks, and in still others the players use both hands and sticks. Players of friction drums use sticks attached to the drumheads, which emit crying sounds when stroked.

Aerophones are instruments in which sound is produced by a vibrating column of air. Flutes of every size and description are found in Africa, as are horns and whistles. Many times, the music played on aerophones involves the hocket technique, in which musicians combine to perform one musical layer. Each performer plays one pitch, following a rhythmic pattern that interlocks with another player's pitch and rhythmic structure. These structures combine to form a single layer of music. Horns and whistles are also used for signaling during performances or ceremonial occasions. Bull-roarers, notched pieces of wood that are connected with cords and whirled through the air, produce a sound that is widely associated with supernatural power.

African chordophones, in which the sound is produced by a vibrating, stretched string, come in all sizes and shapes: from the musical bow, to the zither and guitar, to the twenty-one-stringed *kora* of West Africa. These instruments are identified by the way in which their strings are arranged. If the strings run parallel to the neck of the instrument, they are called lutes. Lutes can be found in many areas of Sub-Saharan Africa, including the area bounding the Sahara in West Africa. If the necks of the chordophones are arched and the strings enter the resonator at an angle, they are called harps, such as the *kora* found in the Senegambian region of West Africa. When the strings enter the resonator from a parallel frame, they are called lyres. Lyres are found mostly in East Africa.

Electrophones, instruments whose sound production requires electricity, are also found in most areas of Sub-Saharan Africa. The most common are electric guitars and keyboards.

Traditional instruments are played by both men and women, but the same instrument is usually not played by both within a specific music culture. Therefore, men and women may have different repertoires of music, which require specific instruments in addition to repertoires they share.

Listeners to African music can often identify the area of origin of a musical example by the sound of particular vocal or instrumental timbres, alone or in ensembles. The percussion ensembles of West Africa, with their timbrally varied layers of instruments, including drums, rattles, and metal bells, are examples of one such regionally recognizable ensemble timbre. The sound of a traditional *entenga*, or tuned-drum ensemble of Uganda, with its bubbling, interlocking texture, is another such timbre.

Dynamics

Variation in the loudness or softness of sounds is not as important an expressive characteristic as pitch, rhythm, or timbre in many traditional music cultures of Sub-Saharan Africa. There are instances in which sounds are louder and softer, but this may be the result of the tone quality of the instrument or the need to be heard rather than just the use of dynamic change. If dynamic accents are perceived, they may result from the coinciding sounds of several instruments rather than from the efforts of musicians to stress certain sounds by playing

153

them more loudly. The use of dynamics in the musics of different Sub-Saharan culture groups can be expected to vary, providing another example of the richly imaginative use of music elements among African cultures.

Form

Sub-Saharan African musics are most often orally transmitted and are integral to the context in which they appear. Even when written transcriptions are possible or desirable, most music repertoires of Africa cannot be analyzed out of context to determine form, for the form is connected directly with the context and interacts with it.

Every type of social occasion or subject calls for its own type of music. There are lullabies, songs that indicate how one should behave, songs that provide historical information, and those that tell stories or accompany storytelling. There are work songs, game songs, songs that educate people; songs that advertise businesses, that call people together, that announce the presence of important people; and religious songs. Funeral songs, love songs, and songs containing social and political commentary are also typical.

For all of these classifications, the form of the songs varies across music cultures. In some culture areas, songs are associated with their performers (for example, hunter's or herder's songs), by the instrument played (for example, *mbira*), or by the status of the musician (for example, the professional *griot* of West Africa) who performs them. Musical examples from these repertoires do not always demonstrate the same formal characteristics in or between music cultures. Nonetheless, the categorization of musical examples in these ways helps us to understand that there are culture-specific features that allow members of each music culture to group music into coherent units.

There are formal characteristics that can generally be applied to Sub-Saharan African music cultures. Songs are often built around comments on social occasions and responses to these comments, so song structure reflects this comment-response or leader-chorus alternation. People in many Sub-Saharan African cultures sing and play as they communicate verbally, with interruptions of encouragement, agreement or amplification, and alternation of voices. All of this can be observed in musical forms.

There is almost always a basic structure, with responding parts that overlap it, and an improvisational part. The improvisational part provides a link between the immediate musical interaction of the basic and responding parts and the social context of the performance. One can also find similarities between Sub-Saharan African musical forms and those of the West. These include the appearance of strophic songs in which the music for each verse consists of patterns that are repeated with occasional slight variations. Musicians may use ostinatos as a compositional device in both instrumental and vocal music.

There are also many different formal structures in specific culture areas of Africa, such as the Chopi *ngodo*, or dance-song-instrumental suites with many movements, of Mozambique. Local neotraditional and popular repertoires also include a variety of formal features, some of which are similar to those genres in the West.

Traditional musical forms in Sub-Saharan Africa are most often open forms. They lack clearly defined beginnings and endings and have variable structural

154

units that can be combined in different ways or transformed through improvisation. These open forms are of varying length and provide a structure for sociomusical interaction that reflects particular performance contexts. In such music, the nature of the event or occasion is crucial to the structural analysis of the music. These open forms also affect the expectations of musicians. Africans tend to identify exemplary musicians not only as charismatic, musically expressive, and technically consistent, but also as having the necessary creative power and kinesthetic endurance to perform during long-lasting ceremonial, ritual, or purely recreational occasions.

L E S S O N   O N E

■ OBJECTIVES:

Students will:
1. Perform the polyrhythmic patterns of two with three.
2. Improvise on an assigned pattern of pitches.
3. Listen to a marimba ensemble work, "Rufaro," after performing a study version of the piece.

Materials:
1. Five marimbas or wood-keyed classroom xylophones: one soprano, three altos or alto tenors, and one bass
2. Two rattles or maracas
3. Recording: *Rufaro! Dumi and the Minanzi Marimba Ensemble,* Northwest Folk Life Festival R5050

■ PROCEDURES:
1. Present the following pattern:

Have the students use both hands and play the pattern on their laps or desktops until it is firm and accurate. Then have the students play the pattern in the air above their desks. As they play, have them lower their right hands onto the desktops (but continue playing in the air with their left hands). This allows the students to hear the pattern of three played by their right hands. Students should then lower their left hands onto their desks

155

while their right hands continue to play the pattern in the air. This allows the students to hear the pattern of two played by their left hands.

Conclude by having students play the patterns on their desks with both hands, emphasizing first one hand and then the other. Students will gradually hear and experience (1) the triple rhythm, (2) the duple rhythm, and (3) both rhythms at once.

2. Have the whole class learn the order of the two-with-three pattern for the three alto or alto-tenor marimba parts in "Rufaro" without pitches but saying and playing the patterns:

   Both-right-left-right; both [move]-right-left-right
   [Repeat twice; then move back up as though playing higher pitches.]
   Both-right-left-right [Repeat twice; then move down.]
   Both-right-left-right [Repeat four times; move down.]
   Both-right-left-right [Repeat twice.]

3. Teach the pitches for the following patterns: A, B, and C. Use keyboards (paper keyboards if necessary) and marimbas to involve as many students as possible.

4. Teach everyone the bass marimba part. Note the use of a different ostinato from that used in A, B, or C:

5. Teach the class the lead soprano marimba part:

Note. Only one pattern is provided here: The lead is usually an improvised part. Have the class listen to the recording and note the variety of patterns played by the lead soprano marimba.

6. For a study version of this work, have some students use rattles (or maracas), playing the same pattern as the marimbas. Rattle:

7. Put the composition together gradually. Combine the parts in this order: three alto marimba parts, bass marimba, lead soprano marimba, and rattle. Have the rattle player play six even strokes as an introduction. All parts then enter except the lead soprano marimba. The lead part can be added after the other parts are secure and accurate.

8. The alto or alto-tenor marimba patterns on the opposite page can all be varied by occasionally playing a different pitch with the right hand, but the rhythm of the pattern must not be changed. Players must remember where they are in the pattern and be careful not to confuse anyone else. The rhythm of the bass ostinato must also be steady and constant.

9. The rattle (or maraca) players' part can also be varied. The following patterns are all possible:

10. The soprano marimba player can improvise more freely than any other instrumentalist, but must always be conscious of everyone else so that the improvisation does not confuse the other players.

11. Have students listen to the recording of "Rufaro" and compare their performance with the recording. (The tempo and timbre of the instruments will probably be the most noticeable differences.) Have students see if they can hear three different soprano marimbas, two tenor marimbas, one baritone marimba, one bass marimba, and a pair of rattles (called *hosho* by the Shona people). It is effective to have the students learn and play the study version of the work first and then listen to the recording.

Supplemental activities:

On another day, have the class learn part two of "Rufaro." On the recording, you will hear the lead soprano marimba play a repeated high pitch many times as a signal for the ensemble to change to part two. The same signal is used both to change back to part one again and to conclude the work. It is the same repeated high pitch. "Rufaro" is an example of a composition in a neotraditional style; that is, it is somewhat similar to traditional xylophone music but is composed by a contemporary African composer, Dumisani Maraire, and performed by contemporary musicians. The basic patterns for part two are shown in figure 2. The lead soprano marimba part is not given; listen to the recording for ideas of parts that can be performed.

Figure 2. Part two of "Rufaro"

158

L E S S O N   T W O

■ **OBJECTIVES:**

Students will:
Play a message on two-toned percussion instruments based on an African tonal language.

Materials:
Two-toned instrument of some kind, possibly a chair or desk that gives higher and lower sounds when struck in different places

■ **PROCEDURES:**

1. Have the students practice performing low and high sounds until the results are rhythmically accurate and clear.
2. Teach the class about tonal languages as introduced at the beginning of this chapter. Stress that meaning in tonal languages is attached to the pitch of the syllables of a word rather than only to the vowels and consonants or to the rhythm of the words (L = Low, H = High). For example, in the Kele language of Zaire, the following tonal patterns can give three distinct meanings to one word:
Bosongo: (LLL) Copper or brass
Bosongo: (LLH) River's current
Bosongo: (LHH) Pestle for pounding maize or other food

3. Teach the following message in the Kele language of the Lokele people of Central Africa:

Ito,   ito,   ito:
H L,   H L,   H L
(Pay attention!)

Wana
  L L
(The child . . .)
[Pause]

Asooinola   batindi mbisa,   asooinola bakolo mbisa
L HLL H H   L H H   H L   L HLL H H L L L   H L
(. . . has returned . . .)

As   li   batindi   bakolo se
L   H   L H H   L L L H
(. . . has arrived . . .)

Sokolaka   lik   ke   lya   botema
  L H H H   L   L   H   L H L
(. . . take away the knot of the heart . . .)

159

Yoruba dùndún (talking drum) drummers, Ibadan, Nigeria. Photograph courtesy of Christopher Waterman, University of Washington.

```
Likolo     ko     nda     use
 L L L      L      H      H H
( . . . up into the air . . . )
```

```
L L L L L L L L L L
(signal that message is concluded)
```

In any given language, many words have the same tone pattern, so there is a drum language in which longer phrases describe enough of the context of any given word so that people will understand. In normal conversation, the Lokele would say "*owangeke*," which means "don't be afraid," instead of the phrase meaning "take away the knot of the heart, up into the air."

160

LESSON THREE

■ **OBJECTIVES:**

Students will:
Perform and listen to musical examples that illustrate some general characteristics of Sub-Saharan African music.

Materials:
1. Recordings:
   Musiques du Cameroun, OCORA OCR-25
   Niger: La musique des griots, OCORA OCR-20
   African Mbira: Music of the Shona People of Rhodesia, Nonesuch Explorer Series H-72043
   Bantu Music from British East Africa, Columbia KL-213
   Mustapha Tettey Addy: Master Drummer from Ghana, Lyricord LLST 7250
   Music from Rwanda (UNESCO Collection), Barenreiter Musicaphone BM 30 L 230
2. Rattle or maracas
3. Double bell or two different-sized cow bells
4. Two drums of different pitches with two sticks

■ **PROCEDURES:**

1. Listen to short excerpts of Sub-Saharan African music. (Any of the recordings listed under "Materials" for this lesson will work.) Review any African music examples students have performed, and ask them to identify some of the following common characteristics:
   - the use of percussive timbres
   - the use of timbres with a prevalent buzzing quality
   - the use of a natural, open, personal singing style
   - the alternation of a leader with a chorus section or call-and-response
   - a texture of multiple, overlapping parts
   - a shared or common sense of time, or "rhythmic lock"
   - rhythmic or temporal precision
   - open forms using improvisation and variation
2. Have the students perform with the recordings of African music, listed under "Materials" for this lesson, in which these characteristics can be clearly perceived and understood. They should try to duplicate exactly one or more of the patterns played on the recordings. You should use the instructional method of oral transmission that would be used by a Sub-Saharan African musician. This can happen during one lesson or, more appropriately, in a series of lessons.
   a. The students can develop an appreciation for the percussive timbral ideal of Sub-Saharan music by imitating the prevailing patterns (including the two-with-three polyrhythm learned in lesson one). An example that is especially useful is the playing of long-necked lutes on *Niger: La musique des griots,* side two, band two ("Bako"). Have the students clap the rhythm

161

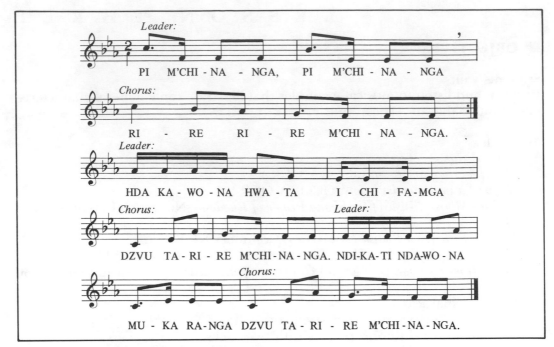

Figure 3. Transcription of "Pi M'chinanga"

    played by the long-necked lutes: (♩ ♩ ♫ ♫ ♩ ♪) and the rhythm of the rattles (♩ ♪), both alone and with the recording.

b. The class will better understand the African desire for sounds with prevalent buzzing by listening to the timbre of the xylophones or imitating the rattle patterns on any of the recordings listed under "Materials" for this lesson.

c. You can demonstrate the common African structural principle of alternation of a leader with a chorus by playing the recording of *Bantu Music from British East Africa*, side two, band two ("Pi M'chinanga"), transcribed in figure 3. This is a story song, or *nyaya*, about something that really happened. (If a story song is about something that did not really happen, the Shona of Zimbabwe call it *ngano*.)

The following is a translation of "Pi M'chinanga," supplied by Dumisani Maraire:

pi = in or at
m'chinanga = a spot or an area (for instance, a valley)
ndaka wona = I saw (*taka wona* = we saw)
hwata = a porcupine
ichifamba = walking
ndi kati = I thought
nda wona = I was seeing
m'karanga = a person (Karanga is a subgroup of the Shona)

162

rire (or *rure*) has no meaning; these are just syllables
dzvu = staring with one's eyes wide open in surprise; a look of surprise
tarire = looking, examining

d. Have students listen to and perform with a shared sense of time, or "rhythmic lock" or "feeling," by playing two rhythm patterns along with the recording of *Mustapha Tettey Addy: Master Drummer from Ghana*, side three, band three ("Ewe Atsimevu"). One rhythm pattern, in this case, is twelve pulses long, with low and high sounds distributed through the cycle, as shown in the following pattern. Have some members of the class play the bell pattern, using a two-toned bell or low and high sounds, while the others clap on pulses one, four, seven, and ten.

> 1–3–56–8–10–12 (double bell pattern)
> L H HH H H   H
> 1 – – 4 – –7 – – 10 – – (Clap)

e. Make certain that the students have a good understanding of the temporal precision of African music. Have the class perform steadily alternating left- and right-hand strokes in time with the two-tone tone block pattern on *Musiques du Cameroun*, side two, band seven ("Lali").

f. To gain an appreciation of open forms, improvisation, and variation, ask the class to perform the following patterns:
   (1) Right-left-right-left-right-left . . .
       (Right and left hands alternate evenly)
   (2) Right-right-left-right-right (rest)
       (a repeated six-pulse pattern)
       Combine these parts and increase the tempo.
   Have the class listen to the recording of musicians playing the royal drums of the Mwami, and notice what the improvised part does to the patterns on *Music from Rwanda*, side one, band one ("Rukina"). Pick additional patterns for the students to study from any of the recordings listed under "Materials" for this lesson. Have the students perform these patterns as they listen to the recordings. This participation will make it much easier for them to focus their attention on the music examples you have chosen.

L E S S O N   F O U R

4

■ **OBJECTIVES:**

Students will:
Learn a percussion ensemble selection from Zimbabwe in a rhythm called *shangara* and the song "Maiwe," which can be performed with it.

163

Materials:
1. High, medium, low, and very low conga drums
2. Tone block
3. Beater
4. Gourd rattle or maracas

■ PROCEDURES:

1. Teach the basic pattern of *shangara*, a rhythmic feeling that underlies a type of Shona song. The basic pattern or *kushaura* (what everyone relates to, the line that cuts through) is also sometimes called *dziro* (the foundation you put in before building your house). Have the students play the pattern until it is accurate, consistent, firm, and without accent. The pattern on the high-pitched drum is:

(12) R L R L R L R R L R R L

2. Teach the responsive patterns, or *kudaira* (sometimes called responding patterns, or *kudairana*), one at a time. Be sure that they are accurate and firm before moving on. Do not combine the patterns until they are steady and unaccented and can be repeated without errors.

    Key R = right hand
        L = left hand
        () = heel of the hand on the far edge of the drum

    ◯ = center of the drum with cupped hands

The rest of the patterns are open sounds, played with fingers near the rim, or edge of the drums.

(12) R L* ®--R L ® ®L ®- (medium drum)

(This *kudaira* or responding pattern begins on the second right-hand stroke of the basic pattern or *kushaura*.)

(12) R L R R L ®- R R L ®- (lower drum)

(This *kudaira* begins at the same time as the basic pattern or *kushaura*.)

(44) L R - (R L R -) R R L R L R R - (R L R - - R L R R L R -)

R R L R L R R -(R L R - - R L R R) (lowest drum)

164

(This improvisation pattern begins on the second stroke [left]of the first responding pattern, which is marked with an asterisk [*].)

While the parts are being played, the rest of the students can clap the basic pattern of *shangara* with the higher drum:

(12) Clap rest clap rest clap rest
Clap clap rest clap clap rest
The rattle or maraca part is:

(3)   Rest shake shake (This pattern begins on the first stroke (right) of the basic or *kushaura* pattern.)

3. The two-part song "Maiwe" can be sung along with *Shangara*. The words are: *Mai we, mai we nda neta (ku)kaiwa* (Mother, oh mother, I am tired and bothered). Singers can start on whatever pitch is best for their singing voices. "Maiwe" begins at the same time as the *kushaura* pattern:

Repeat all of the patterns as necessary until the song has been sung enough times to satisfy all of the students without boring them. It is better to leave students wanting more than to overextend the lesson.

4. During a future class period, students can dance to *shangara* by having individual dancers mark the *kushaura* pattern with their feet and then improvise and take turns making up movements, always using the *kushaura* of *shangara* as the basic pattern.

165

L E S S O N   F I V E

■ OBJECTIVES:

Students will:
Perform two *gome* songs from the Ga people in Ghana.

Materials:
1. Two sticks for each student
2. Recording: *Mustapha Tettey Addy: Master Drummer from Ghana*, Lyrichord LLST 7250

■ PROCEDURES:

1. Teach the sixteen-pulse clapping pattern called *gome*, making sure that it is consistent, fluent, and automatic:

    (16) Clap – – clap – – clap – – – clap – clap – – –

2. Teach the songs in figure 4 by rote, one at a time. When the students are able to sing each one accurately, add the clapping pattern. (Have the students clap one pattern per measure, based on a sixteenth-note pulse, beginning at the "X.") When the students can sing the songs while clapping the patterns, have them play the clapping pattern with the sticks held up and to the front of their left sides.

Figure 4.

166

Note: Shika (etc.) = rich man has friends.
        Ohiafo (etc.) = poor man has no friends.
        Maga = why?

WATEH EH

[Note: Harmonizing in thirds on the choruses of these two songs is expected..]

Figure 4. (continued)

3. Listen to the recording of "Gome Drum and Songs" from *Mustapha Tettey Addy: Master Drummer from Ghana.*

167

L E S S O N   S I X

■ OBJECTIVES:

Students will:
Perform with and listen to musical examples that illustrate the variety of music styles in different culture areas in Sub-Saharan Africa and learn to recognize musical examples from West Africa, East Africa (Uganda), Southern Africa, and Senegal.

Materials:
Recordings:
Music of the Dan, Barenreiter Musicaphone BM 30-L2301
The Naked Prey, Folkways FS 3854
Central Africa: Ba-Benzele Pygmies, Barenreiter Musicaphon BM 30-L2303
African Music: Uganda 1, Kaleidaphone KMA-10
African Journey, Vanguard Nomad SRV73014/5

■ PROCEDURES:

1. Have the students listen to the examples listed in "Materials" and try to identify, by listing and discussing, the musical characteristics of the regions. They should also listen for musical patterns that they can perform with the recordings:
    a. West Africa: "Rice Harvest," side two, band two, on *Music of the Dan*. Characteristics: layered, multipart music; different timbres; open form; work song; overlapping layers
    b. Southern Africa: "War Coward Song," side one, band ten, on *The Naked Prey*. Characteristics: multipart choral music; open, natural singing style; vocal sound effects; leader-chorus structure
    c. Central Africa: "Hindewhu," side one, band one, on *Ba-Benzele Pygmies*; East Africa: "Kalagala ebwembe," side one, band five, on *African Music: Uganda 1*. Characteristics: interlocking patterns, hocket. Notice, in the flute and voice example from the Ba-Benzele pygmies, that the flute part is almost completely steady. In the example from Uganda, there are five tuned *entamivu* drums and one *amadinda* xylophone, and the drum parts enter one at a time so that students can begin to hear the complexity of the musical texture.
    d. Senegambia: "Kelefa Ba," side one, band one, on *African Journey*. Characteristics: the *kora*, twenty-one-string chordophone of the Mandinka people of Senegal and The Gambia in West Africa, focused vocal sound of the Islamic area, song describing the oral history of a great Mandinka leader.

Additional experiences could be generated by selecting an area or instrument for further study or listening. Classes can study African music from different culture areas, using many of the instrumental records in the Discography, or they can study African Story-Songs, including the recordings by Hugh Tracey that are now available on African Music/Cassettes (see Discography).

168

Guitar players, Ibadan, Nigeria. Photograph courtesy of Christopher Waterman, University of Washington.

Integrating music with other studies

People interact with each other all the time. Learning from others by observation, people store visual or aural images mentally and reenact them either immediately or much later. This use of images as metaphors for social interactions is the basis of cultural transmission and growth. Music as a sociocultural metaphor provides a means by which social theories, philosophy, organization, politics, economics, symbols, and values can be examined.

Examples of acculturation in music can assist us in focusing on and understanding the nature of acculturation as a sociocultural process. Discuss some examples with the class, including the arrangement of "Watermelon Man" on Herbie Hancock's *Headhunters* album (see Discography). This is an example of use in the West of musical practices of the Ba-Benzele people of central Africa. A recording of Ba-Benzele music that may have influenced Hancock is "Hinde-whu," studied in lesson six. Africans also enjoy some Western music: For example, the music of Stevie Wonder is popular in many areas of Sub-Saharan Africa.

169

Classes can study musical instruments in terms of geography and its links to human culture. Large drums are used in the percussion ensembles of such people as the Akan of Ghana, where the coastal rain forests produce large trees. "Rukina," the example in lesson three, is performed on the drums that belong to the *mwami*, the ruler of the Tutsi people of Rwanda. Similarly, in areas near the forests of Zaire, political power has traditionally been linked with the possession of drums, whereas in southern Africa, an area with no rain forests, music relies heavily on vocal styles and body percussion.

Classes can also trace the appearance and migration of iron working by studying the musical evidence of bells and lamella (the thin metal plates used to produce sound) on *mbira*, the hand-held thumb instruments. Marimbas, *balaphons*, or xylophones may reflect early historical connections with Indonesian cultures. Xylophones can be found in East Africa and in much of central and West Africa. Further discussion on this topic appears in A. M. Jones's *Africa and Indonesia: The Evidence of the Xylophone and Other Musical and Cultural Factors* (Leiden: N.p. 1971). The introduction of the marimba or xylophone to Latin America from Africa is also an important subject; note the effective use of these instruments in Latin American music, especially in Guatemala and Mexico.

A class can also analyze the geographical and historical distribution of Sub-Saharan people and their music. The migration of people ahead of the Zulu wars in the opening years of the nineteenth century can be traced by the spread in stylistically characteristic choral music and stamping dances across the varied topography of southeastern and east central Africa. Increasing urbanization, bringing people of diverse cultural backgrounds together in complex urban settings, is currently resulting in the development of specifically urban African music styles. Some of these styles can be linked through instruments, forms, techniques, or compositional devices to traditional music of particular areas and used to demonstrate musically the geographical distribution of the music makers.

The effects of our African heritage on the music of the West can be easily followed. Since our African musical heritage has become a force in global music developments, the study of the geographical implications of this influence on contemporary music would make another interesting focus for study.

The desire to hold in memory, to reflect on, and to learn from the knowledge gained by the experiences of ancestors is one of the characteristics of the human species. Oral history is well illustrated in the recitations of the Mandinka of West Africa. You can use available recorded examples such as those listed in this chapter's Discography (especially *African Journey* and *Mandinka Kora par Jali Nyama Suso*) to observe and discuss differences and similarities in the maintenance of historical records in Africa as compared with other parts of the world.

In the traditional visual arts, as in music, artifacts are part of the occasions of everyday life and the ceremonies and rituals that are used to celebrate it. In many cases, African visual artifacts are made of materials that do not last beyond their use. In The Gambia, for example, there is a masking tradition in which the leaves of a tree are used to fashion a mask. Since the creators and users of traditional Sub-Saharan art objects and musical instruments were interested in using instruments to make music, not in collecting or maintaining them in museums, there was not a general need to create things that lasted through generations of use. When something no longer was usable, a new one was made. Many things have been made only to last for one use.

Some of the most famous products of African artistic endeavor are sculptures, including the masks of Africa. These are illustrated in the booklet by Furber and Kukuk, *An African Experience: Traditions in the African Arts* (see Bibliography). Study the masks of a specific area and have the students make them. The music of famous masking traditions can be found in the Discography of this chapter; see especially the recording *Masques Dan*. (Pictures of masks accompany the documentation of this recording).

Artists such as Pablo Picasso were affected by their exposure to the art of

Gambian kora *player Nyama Suso. Photograph courtesy of Roderic Knight.*

171

Africa, so it might be useful to examine the effects of African art on contemporary art in the West. You could also study the stylistic differences in artistic activity, using examples of decoration on musical instruments as well as cloth, weaving implements, cooking utensils, food containers, hunting and sports equipment, trucks, cars, boats, wagons, carts, combs and other personal artifacts, furniture, architectural features, game boards, toys, and religious items.

In your study of African art, pay particular attention to Robert Thompson's *African Art in Motion: Icon and Act* (see Bibliography). Lead a class discussion on how these characteristics compare and contrast with perspectives on art in the West.

There is a strong kinesthetic emphasis in the artistic attitude of many African culture areas. Elegance of movement, style of gesture, and characteristics of posture are evocative artistic components of African life. Have your class study the characteristics, meanings, and values attached to certain postures or styles of movement as a possible focus for the study of music and the performing arts in Africa. How are posture and movement different in African dance, generally, from other styles? What is the range of similarity and difference in posture and dance across Sub-Saharan Africa? How are characteristics of African dance similar to or different from those found in European, North American, Latin American, Native American, or Asian styles? Answers to these questions can be found by reading Thompson's perspective on motion and African art and by viewing the films listed for this chapter, contrasting them with films or videotapes listed in the filmographies for other chapters in this book.

There is a close relationship between Sub-Saharan dance and music. In fact, the motion involved in performing on instruments may itself be a form of dance. Seeing the movement of musicians as part of the art of movement in the culture is possible in any cultural context. How could this be applied in the United States?

In Sub-Saharan Africa, as in the West, storytelling and other forms of drama form an integral part of traditional African cultural transmission and socialization, and music plays an integral part in traditional African storytelling. Lesson three features a story-song. Some other stories and *ngano* (story-songs) are listed in the Discography and Bibliography in this chapter. *African Story-Songs, Let Your Voice Be Heard!*, and *Songs and Stories from Uganda* contain especially good examples.

The folk operas of the Yoruba of western Nigeria furnish a good example of African musical narrative (such as *Oba Koso*, listed in the Discography). The creators and directors of musical theater of the Yoruba are often so highly regarded that fans will attend their traveling performances even if they are in another town. What are the similarities between musical theater in Africa and the United States? Are there common themes? What are the differences? What role does musical theater play in different culture areas? (See the documentation to *Oba Koso* for information.)

Music in Africa is endlessly varied and always interesting, and its study is a route to understanding the similarity and diversity of the culture areas of Sub-Saharan Africa. The study of African music cultures is also critically important to our understanding of American music and the contributions of our African musical heritage to music in the United States.

172

BIBLIOGRAPHY

Adzinyah, Abraham Kobena, Dumisani Maraire, and Judith Cook Tucker. *Let Your Voice Be Heard! Songs from Ghana and Zimbabwe.* Danbury, CT: World Music Press, 1986. These songs are from the Akan people of Ghana and the Shona people of Zimbabwe. A one-hour companion audiotape is included.

Bebey, Francis. *African Music: A People's Art.* New York: Lawrence Hill, 1975. Written by an African musician and composer, this book provides an African's perspective on African music. It includes a discography and photographs.

Berliner, Paul. *The Soul of Mbira.* Berkeley: University of California Press, 1978. This classic discussion of the *mbira* (thumb instrument) emphasizes the Shona music culture of Zimbabwe.

Bowen, Elenore Smith [Laura Bohannan]. *Return to Laughter.* Garden City, NY: Doubleday, 1964. This book is a description of Laura Bohannan's personal reactions during her anthropological field work in West Africa.

Carrington, John F. *Talking Drums of Africa.* London: Carey Kingsgate Press, 1949. This definitive description of the message drumming of Africa includes illustrations about how it works and message phrases with English translations.

Chernoff, John Miller. *African Rhythm and African Sensibility.* Chicago: University of Chicago Press, 1981. This description of drumming in Ghana and the author's personal experiences with the music and culture includes comments by master musicians.

Courlander, Harold. *A Treasury of African Folklore.* New York: Crown Publishers, 1975. Some background is provided in stories of selected culture areas.

d'Azevedo, Warren L., ed. *The Traditional Artist in African Societies.* Bloomington: Indiana University Press, 1975. This collection includes essays on aspects of African culture by scholars describing arts, artists, and their social context.

Dietz, Betty Q., and M. A. Olatunji. *Musical Instruments of Africa.* New York: John Day, 1965. This book for students, especially for levels K–8, is about African musical instruments and includes pictures and descriptions.

Furber, Marthalie P., and Jack W. Kukuk. *An African Experience: Traditions in the African Arts.* Washington, DC: Educational Program of the John F. Kennedy Center for the Performing Arts, 1981. This publication is helpful for the study of the African visual arts. It is available from the Educational Program, JFK Center for the Performing Arts, Washington, DC 20566.

Jahn, Janheinz. *Through African Doors.* New York: Grove Press, 1969. This is an extremely readable description of the travels of a scholar in Africa.

Jessup, Lynne. *The Mandinka Balafon: An Introduction with Notation for Teaching.* New York: Magnum Music, 1985. The author includes transcriptions of Mandinka xylophone music and a practical teaching guide written after her field work in The Gambia.

Makeba, Miriam. *The World of African Song.* Chicago: Quadrangle Books, 1971. This collection of songs from South Africa includes urban musical examples.

Martin, Phyllis M., and Patrick O'Meara, eds. *Africa.* Bloomington: Indiana University Press, 1977. This collection of essays on African history, traditions, and contemporary concerns includes an extensive bibliography.

Mazrui, Ali A. *The Africans: A Triple Heritage.* Boston: Little, Brown, 1986. This commentary complements the television series of the same name. It covers history, culture, and contemporary issues; the arts are not an important focus of the discussion.

Mensah, A. A. *Folk Songs for Schools.* Accra-Tema, Ghana: Ghana Publishing, 1971. These songs are from different culture areas of Sub-Saharan Africa. Some cultural information and solfège syllables are included.

Musgrove, Margaret. *Ashanti to Zulu.* New York: Dial Press, 1976. This beautifully illustrated children's book contains pictures of people from different culture areas of Sub-Saharan Africa along with brief descriptions.

Nketia, J. H. Kwabena. *African Music in Ghana.* Evanston, IL: Northwestern University Press, 1963. This study of music in Ghana includes an appendix with eighteen songs.

Nketia, J. H. Kwabena. *The Music of Africa.* New York: Norton, 1974. This textbook provides information on the organization of musical groups as well as the tonal, timbral, rhythmic, and formal characteristics of the music and some information on its contextual use.

Roberts, John Storm. *Black Music of Two Worlds.* New York: Morrow, 1974. The author discusses the influence of African-American music on contemporary music in Africa.

173

Serwadda, W. Moses. *Songs and Stories from Uganda*. Danbury, CT: World Music Press, 1987. Beautifully illustrated and printed, this book provides traditional stories and songs from Uganda and includes an accompanying audiotape recorded by Serwadda and his daughter.

Standifer, James A., and Barbara Reeder. *Source Book of African and Afro-American Materials for Music Educators*. Washington, DC: Music Educators National Conference, 1972. This collection of resources for educators includes bibliographies, films, musicians, musical styles, and performance and listening experiences for students; it is being updated.

Thompson, Robert Farris. *African Art in Motion: Icon and Act*. Berkeley: University of California Press, 1974. The author discusses African art from a contextual perspective. The book contains not only pictures and discussions of art but ways that traditional art operates in the lives of Africans. It is available in paperback and is invaluable as an educational resource.

Titon, Jeff Todd, ed. *Worlds of Music*. New York: Schirmer Books, 1984. This is a survey of world music. The chapter on music in Ghana by James T. Koetting, which includes a look at contemporary music and taped examples, is appropriate for use in a teaching unit.

Turnbull, Colin. *The Forest People*. New York: Clarion Books, 1962. An anthropologist who lived with the pygmies describes their way of life in readable, interesting, and evocative language.

DISCOGRAPHY

African Journey. Vanguard Nomad SRV73014/5. This recording, produced and recorded by Samuel Charters, includes musical examples from the area of West Africa made famous by Alex Haley's *Roots*.

African Mbira: Music of the Shona People of Rhodesia. Dumisani Maraire, Nkosane Maraire, and Sukutai Chiora. Nonesuch Explorer Series H-72043. The *mbira* (thumb instrument) and the *hosho* (rattle) can be heard along with the three singers. The accompanying documentation is good.

African Music. Kaleidaphone KMA-1–10. These ten audiocassettes, recorded by Hugh Tracey and published originally by the International Library of African Music, are devoted to (1) strings, (2) reeds, (3) drums, (4) flutes and horns, (5) xylophones, (6 and 7) guitars, (8) music from Zimbabwe, (9) music from Tanzania, and (10) music from Uganda. They are very well recorded and useful. These recordings are available through Paul Tracey, 340 Las Casas, Pacific Palisades, California 90272.

African Story-Songs—Told and Sung by Abraham Dumisani Maraire. Seattle: University of Washington Press, 1969. This selection of stories and *ngano* (Shona story-songs from Zimbabwe) includes record notes by ethnomusicologist Robert Kauffman. Additional stories from Zimbabwe are available on cassette tapes from Paul Tracey, 340 Las Casas, Pacific Palisades, California 90272. These stories are accompanied by a book.

Bantu Music from British East Africa, Volume 10 of the *Columbia World Library of Folk and Primitive Music*. Columbia KL-213. The examples on this recording are from the area of East Africa south of the Equator. An accompanying map shows the areas where the selections originated. The selections are varied and have adequate documentation. This recording includes the example "Pi M'chinanga."

Central Africa: Ba-Benzele Pygmies (UNESCO Collection). Barenreiter Musicaphone BM 30-L2303. This well-documented variety of music from the Central African Republic includes the *hindewhu* whistle. See also *Music of the Rain Forest: Pygmies of the North-East Congo*.

Contemporary African Music Series. Original Music OMA 101. *Nairobi Sounds: Acoustic and Electric Guitar Music* was recorded in Kenya and compiled and produced by John Storm Roberts, author of *Black Music of Two Worlds* and *The Latin Tinge*.

Headhunters. Columbia KC 32731. This recording by jazz artist Herbie Hancock includes "Watermelon Man" (side one, band two), an example of an African-American musician's creative use of African music techniques.

Juju Roots: 1930s–1950s. Rounder Records 5017. Since recording conditions were difficult, the sound quality of this record is quite uneven. Nonetheless, for a historical perspective on contemporary popular music in Africa, especially Nigerian *juju*, this is an important recording.

Mandinka Kora par Jali Nyama Suso. OCORA OCR-70. This recording is of a well-known musician, or *jali*, of the Mandinka culture in The Gambia and Senegal. The documentation is by Roderic Knight, an authority on this music. His dissertation is very useful for developing an acquaintance with Mandinka music. Study of this recording might by aided by reference to the book by Lynne Jessup on teaching the *balofon* (xylophone) music of the Mandinka in music classrooms.

Masques Dan. OCORA OCR-52. The music on this recording is from the western mountains of the Ivory Coast and Liberia, from the Yacuba and Gio people, farmers and cattle raisers whose language is Dan. They are well known for their wooden masks, and this recording features music that accompanies the appearance of these masks. Documentation and photographs are by the ethnomusicologist Hugo Zemp.

Music from Rwanda (UNESCO Collection). Barenreiter Musicaphone BM 30 L 230. This recording includes useful examples of music from Rwanda (or Ruanda). Pictures and documentation accompany this excellent recording of music from the Tutsi culture and neighboring people.

Music of the Dan. Barenreiter Musicaphone, BM 30-L2301. This music from the western part of the Ivory Coast includes work songs, children's songs, hunters' songs, instrumental music, and festival music. This record presents a good cross-section of music from one culture area.

Music of the Rain Forest: Pygmies of the North-East Congo. Lyrichord LLST 7157. Recorded by Colin Turnbull, author of *The Forest People*, this recording is a useful adjunct to classroom study of Turnbull's book. The recording includes Pygmy music from the Ituri forest and music of their neighbors, the Lese. The recording also includes a prime example of acculturation: a Twa lady singing "My Darling Clementine."

Musiques Dahomeennes. OCORA OCR-17. This prize-winning recording provides samples of the music in different culture areas of Benin. It contains excellent documentation, usable selections, and a map.

Musique du Burundi. OCORA 558511. A wide variety of excellent, well-recorded, interesting music from this central African country; with documentation.

Musiques du Cameroun. OCORA OCR-25. Both instrumental and vocal examples representing the major culture areas of Cameroon can be found on this recording. It contains especially interesting examples such as a Bamileke-Bamoun secret society dance selection titled "Lali." The documentation is sketchy.

Mustapha Tettey Addy: Master Drummer from Ghana. Lyrichord LLST 7250. Addy is a Ga drummer who has studied in Ghana, the Ivory Coast, and Nigeria. The percussion parts on this recording are quite easy to hear.

The Naked Prey. Folkways FS 3854. Although this comes from a movie score, it contains excellent examples of traditional choral music from several culture areas in southern Africa.

Niger: La musique des griots. OCORA OCR-20. This contains an excellent recording, documentation, and selections from the Hausa and other cultures of Niger. The documentation is in French; photographs of performers are included.

Nigeria—Hausa Music I: An Anthology of African Music (UNESCO Collection). Barenreiter Musicaphone BM 30-L2306. This recording (and its companion, volume 2) provides a wide variety of examples from one culture area. The role of music in society is discussed briefly in the record's excellent documentation.

Oba Koso. The King Did Not Hang. Dance-Drama with Yoruba Festival Music. Kaleidophone KS 2201. From Nigeria, this two-record set is a play by Duro Ladipo, based on a great Yoruba legend and performed and accompanied by a traveling company of actors, singers, dancers, and drummers who regularly present such dance-dramas, especially in western Nigeria. The recording is accompanied by a synopsis of the plot in the form of a narrative text.

Rufaro! Dumi and the Minanzi Marimba Ensemble. Northwest Folk Life Festival R5050. Northwest Folk Life Festival (305 Harrison Street, Seattle 98019). This recording includes contemporary performances of traditional examples and some composed by Dumisani Maraire, a Shona musician from Zimbabwe.

Soul of Mbira. Nonesuch Explorer Series H-72054. Can be used with the book of the same title by Paul Berliner. It features Shona musicians from Zimbabwe.

Sound of Africa. Verve FTS 3021. Ranging from Nigeria to Botswana, the selections on this recording were recorded by ABC Television News for a four-hour special on Africa in June 1956. The documentation is useful, the variety is wide, and the recording quality is good.

Voices of Africa: High-Life and Other Popular Music. Saka Acquaye and his African Ensemble from Ghana. Nonesuch Explorer Series H-72026. This is an example of contemporary popular music from urban Africa. Other examples, such as King Sunny Ade performing juju music from Nigeria, are available from other recording companies. Check for current listings to keep up with developments in increasingly popular contemporary African music idioms.

FILMOGRAPHY

Atumpan. 16mm, 43 minutes, color. Institute of Ethnomusicology, The University of California at Los Angeles. This outstanding film deals with the geographical location, construction, performance, and social context of the *atumpan,* a Ghanaian drum.

Bitter Melons. 16mm, 32 minutes, color. Documentary Educational Resources. This is a well-known documentary film about the people who live in the Kalahari Desert. Filmed in Botswana, the sound track includes the singing of an old man, who accompanies himself on a musical bow. There are also some games with accompanying songs. It is a very realistic and impressive film. Preview the film before showing it in a class.

Black African Heritage. Four films, 60 minutes each, color. Distributed by Westinghouse Film Division and the University of California at Los Angeles. These four films are narrated by Julian Bond, Ossie Davis, Maya Angelou, and Gordon Parks. A great deal of Western and African music is included. Information is provided from many parts of the continent, although West Africa is emphasized, and connections are made with music in the West.

Discovering the Music of Africa. 16mm, 19 minutes, color. The Institute of Ethnomusicology, University of California at Los Angeles. This film shows UCLA students working with a Ghanaian master drummer. Drums are demonstrated, and the different patterns and parts of a percussion ensemble are played alone and together.

Jumpstreet: The West African Heritage. 30 minutes, color. Available from the New York State Education Department, Center for Learning Technologies, Media Distribution Network, Room C-7, Concourse Level, Cultural Education Center, Albany, New York 12230; 516-474-3168. This program is from a series of thirteen 30-minute television programs of the same name. It is useful in providing an African cultural perspective.

Repercussions: A Celebration of African-American Music. Seven videocassettes, 60 minutes each, color. Distributed by RM Arts Home vision, P.O. Box 800, Concord, Massachusetts 01742; 800-262-8600. Especially interesting are program one, "Born Musicians: Traditional Music from the Gambia," a 60-minute videotape available in VHS or Beta formats that focuses on the music of the *jali*s, the professional musicians of the Mandinka people; program five, "The Drums of Dagbon," a videocassette about the relationships between traditional music and popular dance music, or highlife, featuring drummers of northern Ghana; and program seven, "Africa Comeback—The Popular Music of West Africa," which focuses on juju performer King Sunny Ade with Fela Ankulapo-Kuti and Segun Adewale from the world of Ghanaian popular music.

176

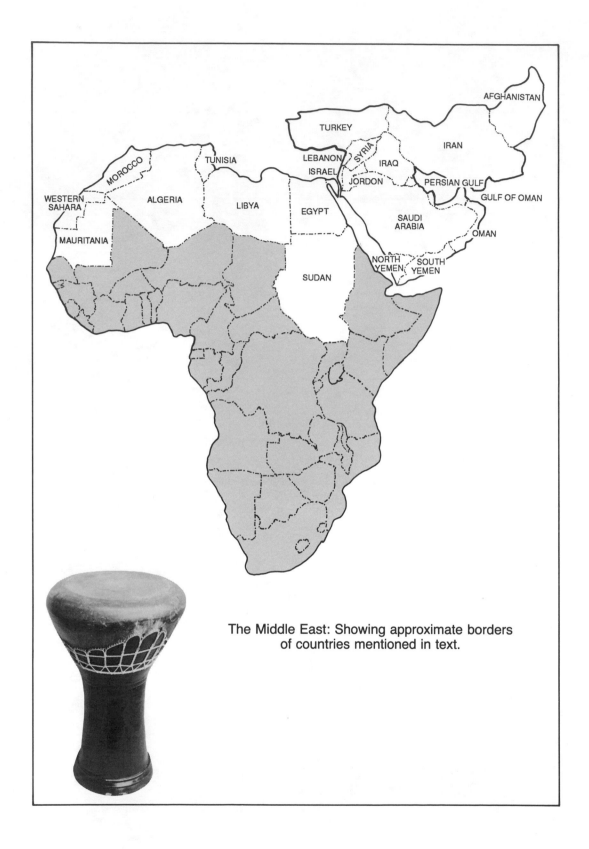

The Middle East: Showing approximate borders
of countries mentioned in text.

6

MIDDLE EASTERN

by George D. Sawa

The area known as the Middle East includes many cultures and varying geography. It is important to know the different parts that make up the whole to better understand the area. The Arabian Peninsula is surrounded by the Red Sea on the east, the Persian (or Arabian) Gulf and Gulf of Oman on the west, and the Arabian Sea to the south. Kuwait, Saudi Arabia, Bahrain, Qatar, and the United Arab Emirates are on the eastern side of the peninsula. Oman is on the southeast side, Yemen is on the southwest, and Saudi Arabia, the area's largest country, occupies most of the west coast, part of the east coast, and most of the center of the peninsula. The Levant is made up of Syria, Lebanon, Israel, and Jordan. The Nile Valley consists of Egypt and the Sudan. Considered by some Middle Eastern specialists to be part of the Middle East, North Africa includes Libya, Tunisia, Algeria, and Morocco, all of which are on the southern Mediterranean coast. Turkey, which is north of Syria, is surrounded by the Black Sea to the north, the Aegean Sea to the east, and the Mediterranean to the south. Iraq, which is east of Syria, includes the Tigris-Euphrates Valley. Afghanistan is the

179

easternmost country in the Middle East: It is landlocked and bordered by Iran, the Soviet Union, China, and Pakistan. Iran has the Caspian Sea on its north and the Persian Gulf and the Gulf of Oman on its south.

Taken as a whole, the topography and climate of the Middle East vary a great deal. There are coastal plains, oases, large fertile areas, arid deserts, plateaus, and mountainous regions. This wide variety has led, since ancient times, to a diversity in economic production and brought about a need for market centers, which explains the precocious growth of Middle Eastern cities.[1] Cities were also crucial because the Middle East occupies a unique geographical position: It serves as the land connection between the continents of Europe, Asia, and Africa. This geographical position has historically given Middle Easterners the role of an intermediary in trade, commerce, and culture.[2]

The outstanding Middle Eastern achievements in the sciences, arts, architecture, literature, philosophy, and religion are the reasons the area has been dubbed the "Cradle of Civilizations." Three of the great religions (Judaism, Christianity, and Islam) developed in the Middle East. King Hammurabi of Babylon (fl. 1792–1750 B.C.) produced one of the greatest ancient codes of law, and the area's temples, paintings, and engravings are testaments to Middle Eastern artistry.

Middle Easterners speak a variety of languages. Arabic is spoken from Morocco to the Arabian Peninsula. Turkish is spoken in Turkey, Cyprus, and parts of Iran. Persian is spoken in Iran, and variations of Persian are spoken in Afghanistan. Hebrew, Yiddish, and Arabic are spoken in Israel. In addition, there is a multitude of other languages currently in use including Aramaic (the language of Palestine during Jesus Christ's lifetime), Kurdish (a language related to Persian and spoken in many parts of the Middle East), Armenian (spoken in many parts of the Middle East), Greek (spoken in Cyprus), and Berber (spoken in parts of Morocco, Algeria, and Tunisia).

The Arabic-Islamic invasions, which started in the seventh century, resulted in the creation of an empire that extended from Spain, to North Africa, to the Middle East, to the borders of India and China. The empire was heir to the cultural legacies of the ancient Near East, Greece, Rome, Spain, India, and Persia. These legacies were received, developed, and expanded, and new ideas were brought in. The result is what Western scholars term Islamic civilization. Arabs, Persians, Turks, Berbers, and Europeans (peoples that practiced creeds including Islam, Christianity, Judaism, and Zoroastrianism) were among the contributors to this civilization.

This multicultural input is evident in the architecture of the Dome of the Rock in Jerusalem, the Alhambra Palace in Granada, and the Great Mosque at Yazd in Iran. Andalusian music (the music of *al-Andalus*, the Arabic word for Spain) thrived in the western part of the empire, in Granada and Cordoba; it was a product of cultural interchange between Arabs, Berbers, and Spaniards. Musicians of the eastern part of the empire flourished in cities such as Damascus, Baghdad, and al-Madina.

The Caliph al-Ma'mūn (d. 833) created an important center for music theory and many other fields of learning when he established the *Bayt al-Hikma* (House of Wisdom) in Baghdad. It served as a library, research facility, and center for the translation of Greek, Persian, and Hindu books. Translations of Persian

180

works inspired a great deal of historical and belles lettres writing. An important music example of this tradition is al-Isbahānī's *Grand Book of Songs*, which contains ten thousand pages that cover, in anecdotal form, musical and poetical life of Arabia, Syria, Persia, and Iraq from the sixth to the tenth centuries A.D.

Baghdad was also a center for the preservation of works on Greek music theory by translation into Syriac and Arabic, and scholars studied the Greek music concepts of the tetrachord as well as Greek theories about modes and rhythm. These ideas were then expanded and developed in Arabic writings and combined with new methods and ideas to evolve a theory that reflected the musical practices of the era. The greatest theorist of this period was al-Fārābī (d. 950): His writings have had, and continue to exert, a continuous influence on music theory.

After attaining its maximum military strength in the early eighth century, the empire began to disintegrate into petty dynasties. Art thrived in this period, because rulers competed with one another to attract the best talents to their courts. Successive invasions brought vitality and renewal to the arts and the rebuilding of a vast empire, the Ottoman Empire, which dominated the Middle East for the four centuries ending in 1917. Music at the Ottoman court was again the product of many cultures. The most serious impact on the music of the Middle East in this period was that of the West, starting with Napoleon's expedition into Egypt in 1798 and continuing to the present time with the importation of such stylistic traits as triadic harmonies and arpeggios.

The musical styles found in the Middle East vary greatly from country to country, and even from region to region. It is not possible to cover all these styles here. Rather, I will concentrate on the secular music of Egypt and parts of the Levant.

Characteristics

Middle Eastern music is essentially melodic in the sense that it does not use the harmonic and contrapuntal devices of Western music. Instrumental or vocal soloists or ensembles perform the highly ornamental melodies. Musical ornamentation, whether melodic, rhythmic, or timbral, embellishes and supports the melody. In ensemble music, melodies are performed in unison or in octaves. Each performer ornaments the melody according to his or her own taste and according to idiosyncratic capabilities of the instruments at hand. This approach results in a rich, heterophonic texture.

Melodies are built according to a complex modal system known in Iran as *dastgāh*, in Turkey as *makām*, and in the Arab world as *maqām*. This system includes the concepts of melodic mode—its motifs, cadences, ranges, and the concepts of *tetrachords*, tonics, and tonal centers. At their most basic level, modes are identified by scales of various intervallic structures using these approximate sizes: 1, ½, ¾, ⁵⁄₄, and 1½. Middle Eastern modes vary widely in the size of their intervals (for example, the "¾" tones of Egypt, Iran, and Turkey are all different), and their melodic movements, motifs, and cadences.

A tone system foreign to American students is sure to present a challenge. A study of the multitude of these Middle Eastern systems would surely frustrate and confuse students. This chapter, therefore, concentrates on only one system found in Egypt and the Levant. Once your students learn this system, they will

181

be equipped with the basics to study other Middle Eastern traditions.

Modes in scalar representations are made up of eight or more notes. Modes are usually built on tetrachords, less often trichords and pentachords. The following are the most important types:

Tetrachord rāst[4]

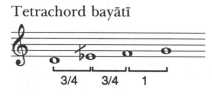

1   3/4   3/4

Tetrachord kurd

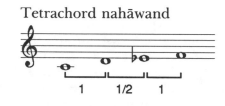

1/2   1   1

Tetrachord bayātī

3/4   3/4   1

Tetrachord nahāwand

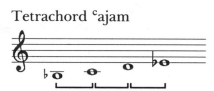

1   1/2   1

Trichord sīkāh

3/4   1

Tetrachord ᶜajam

1   1   1/2

Tetrachord hijāz

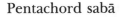

1/2   1-1/2   1/2

Pentachord sabā

3/4   3/4   1/2   1-1/2

When these tetrachords, trichords, or pentachords are strung together, they produce modal scales. It is the way in which they are strung together that determines the tonal centers and principles of modulation. Usually the *maqām* is named according to its lower tetrachord. The following is a list of some of the most important modes:

Maqām rāst

Maqām bayātī

Maqām sabā

Maqām hijāz

Maqām kurd

Maqām ᶜajam ᶜushayrān

Maqām nahāwand

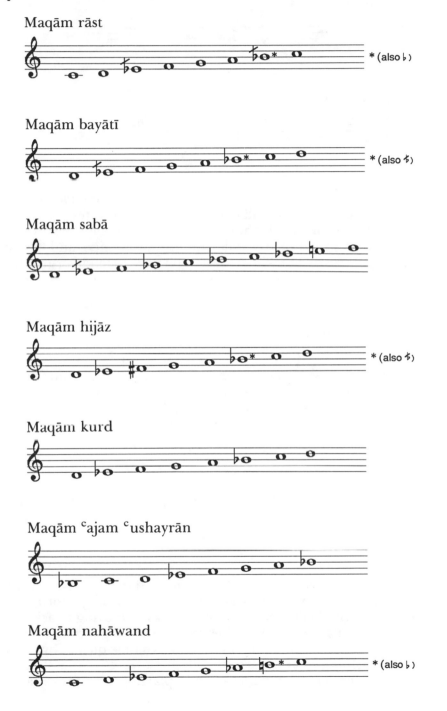

183

Maqām hijāzkār

Maqām sīkāh

Maqām huzām

The notated examples provided in the lessons that follow illustrate some of these modes. Some examples use all eight notes; some use fewer.

Īqāᶜ is the Arabic term for rhythm. Its definition includes the concepts of meter, rhythmic mode, rhythm, dynamics, timbre, and tempo, and it is especially used to denote a pattern of attacks performed on percussion instruments. These attacks are separated by rests of unequal durations, leading to a pattern such as the following:

Patterns could be as short as $\frac{2}{8}$ and as long as the Ottoman Turkish $\frac{176}{4}$. The attacks performed on percussion instruments carry both dynamic and timbral characteristics. In theory, there are two types of attacks: *dumm*, a low resounding sound represented by a note with a stem up,

and *takk*, a short crisp sound of a higher pitch, represented by a note with a stem down.

The basic rhythmic patterns are highly ornamented in performance (however, ornamentation should not obscure or alter the nature of the pattern). Rhythmic ornamentations consist of filling in rests with attacks, removing attacks (resulting in syncopation), altering the timbre (a low *dumm* replacing a crisp *takk*, and vice versa), and creatively expanding the timbre and dynamic quality by performing an infinite variety of *dumm*s and *takk*s.

The role of percussion instruments—beside playing solos for dancers—is to

184

control the tempo for a melody instrument or ensemble, to give punctuation and phrasing to a melody, and to support the rhythm by means of attacks with duration and accents (dynamics and timbre). The percussionist also acts as a conductor, tying together the members of the ensemble. Some $\bar{\imath}q\bar{a}^c$ patterns are notated in lesson one. Instructions on how to play the finger cymbals and the tambourines in order to obtain the dynamics and timbres are given in lessons two and three.

Most Middle Eastern music is performed mezzo forte with little change in dynamics (except for the percussion instruments). With the impact of Western music, dynamic contrasts have been used in some musical styles.

A kaleidoscopic effect of timbres is always present in Middle Eastern ensemble music. Each instrument has its own timbre, and a good instrumentalist has at his command a vast array of tone colors idiosyncratic to the instrument. Singers also have a variety of timbres at their disposal. (One often hears about vocal timbre as being pure, rough, smooth, soft, metallic, nasal, humid, or dry.) Some vocal timbres are specific to certain regions: The Iranians, for instance, are famous for their *tahrīr*, a vocal trill akin to sobbing.

Middle Eastern ensemble music has a rich, heterophonic texture that is caused by the interaction of percussion and melody instruments, a vocalist, and often a chorus. Melody instruments accompany a highly ornamented vocal melody in unison or in octaves; each instrumentalist then ornaments the melody according to his own taste and the capabilities of his instrument. Performers on melody instruments use rhythmic and timbral ornamentations as well as a rich array of ornaments consisting of notes added to the original melody, the removal of notes (resulting in syncopation), and the replacement of notes, turns, tremolo, and drones. The vocalist uses similar melodic and rhythmic ornamentation techniques.

One can often hear a thinner texture and a contrast when a dialogue occurs between instruments, between a vocalist and chorus, or between a vocalist and instruments. The heterophonic texture is most dense when the number of performers is large and when each performer ornaments the melody differently. Today the trend is toward large ensembles that maintain little heterophony.

The most important form in Middle Eastern urban music was a compound form similar to a suite. It contained instrumental and vocal composed and improvised pieces that lasted for at least one hour. Often more than one suite was performed in an evening: They were called *nawbah* in North Africa, *waslah* in Egypt, and *fāsil* in the Levant and in Turkey. The suite underwent changes in the twentieth century and is now extinct in Egypt, although long multisectioned songs still exhibit many features of the suite.

The component parts of a suite are fashioned in one melodic mode with occasional brief modulations, although a variety of meters and some free rhythm sections are found. Thus, an essential feature of the Middle Eastern suite is modal unity and rhythmic diversity.

The suite often starts with an instrumental prelude followed by improvisations. A series of precomposed songs (often featuring an improvised dialogue between vocalist and chorus and interspersed with improvisations) then follows. The suite ends with a lively vocal or instrumental postlude. Today, the component parts of the suites are often played outside the context of the traditional form as self-contained pieces. The following are some of the forms of a Middle Eastern suite's component parts:

1. *Strophic forms:* Instrumental strophic forms that include the *dūlāb* (prelude) and vocal strophic forms are found in *beste* (Turkish classic songs) and *muwashshah* (Arabic classic songs).

2. *ABA forms:* ABA forms abound in many music categories.

3. *Rondo forms:* Rondo forms also abound in many music categories with chorus or ensemble (or both) performing the refrain and the soloist performing the verses (ABABA).

4. *Reverse Rondo Forms:* These are the main forms of prelude and postludes in Ottoman Turkish and Arabic music. They have the form A (refrain) B (refrain) C (refrain) D (refrain).

5. *Multisection forms:* These are found in long songs and introductions to long songs.

The following are common Middle Eastern improvisatory musical genres:

1. *Taqsīm:* This is an unmeasured improvisation on a solo instrument in free rhythm with no regular pulse. This genre features the characteristics of a mode: tonal centers, cadential formulas, and melodic motives. Performers often modulate to neighboring modes. The *taqsīm*, usually unmeasured but occasionally measured, is often performed over an ostinato bass on a percussion or melody instrument.

2. *Mawwāl, gazel, avāz:* These are the Arabic, Turkish, and Persian vocal equivalents to instrumental improvisation. The vocalist improvises music to a poem and is accompanied by a melody instrument that closely follows the vocal melodic line. Between the vocal sections the instrumentalist improvises interludes based on the preceding vocal cadence.

3. *Layālī:* This is the Arabic equivalent to a *mawwāl* except that the vocalist improvises music to the simple words *Yā lēlī, yā ēnī* (O my night, O my eye).

L E S S O N   O N E

■ OBJECTIVES:

Students will:

1. Tap on a table or desk an assortment of rhythm patterns commonly heard in Middle Eastern music (a skill taught to classical singers to enable them to rhythmically guide their performance).
2. Produce particular timbres known as *dumm* (low) and *takk* (crisp).

Materials:
The student's hand and table (or his/her own thigh).

186

■ PROCEDURES:

1. Explain the concept of rhythmic patterns and the role of percussion instruments as outlined in the introduction to this chapter. The low *dumm* and the crisp *takk* sounds are produced by the hand in the following manner: The *dumm* (the low resounding sound represented by a note with its stem up) is performed by striking a table, desk, or thigh with the palm and fingers extended flat in one plane. The *takk* is performed with the hand closed into a fist and striking the table, desk, or thigh with the wrist, the first or second knuckles of the index, middle, ring, and little fingers, and all of the thumb. Students should follow the teacher, who may demonstrate the pattern first on his or her lap, then on a drum. The chanting of "dumm" and "takk" may enhance the learning and can later be said silently. Have the students try these rhythms:

   a. *Īqāᶜ* of Ayyūb el-Masrī— a pattern known as "Job the Egyptian," used in music to accompany therapeutic dances of women who are believed to be possessed

   b. *Īqāᶜ Saᶜīdī*—used in the folk songs and dances of Upper (southern) Egypt and in urban music

   c. *Īqāᶜ Wahdah w Noss*—a very popular rhythmic pattern used in rural and urban music, songs, and dances

   d. *Īqāᶜ Samāᶜī Thaqīl.* This is a rhythmic pattern used to accompany instrumental music known as *samāᶜī* and to accompany some *muwashshahāt* songs.

   Once students have maintained ease and facility in tapping these rhythms on desks, tables, or laps, they can transfer the rhythms to a drum.

187

L E S S O N   T W O

■ OBJECTIVES:

Students will:
Perform the finger cymbal techniques and sounds that are often used by Middle Eastern dancers, folk ensemble instrumentalists, and urban music groups. The three basic sounds are derivatives of the two basic *dumm* and *takk* sounds explained in the lesson one. They increase students' awareness of the concepts of timbre and dynamics.

Materials:
Provide two pairs of finger cymbals for each student. Use elastic to tie the cymbals to the thumb and middle fingers: Cut a piece 1½'' to 2'' long (depending on finger size and student's comfort). Let the middle of the elastic go through the lower cymbal hole, and tie the two ends of the elastic on the inside of the cymbal.

■ PROCEDURES:

1. Students should wear one finger cymbal on the left-hand thumb, one on the right-hand thumb, one on the left-hand middle finger, and one on the right-hand middle finger. Adjust these so that the bottom of the thumb cymbal faces the bottom of the middle finger cymbal. Practice the following sounds separately with each hand:
   a. *Dumm.* With the bottoms of the thumb and middle finger cymbals in a parallel position, hit the thumb and the middle finger cymbals together. Release the cymbals immediately after striking (see figure 1). The sound should be bright and resounding.
   b. *Takk.* With the bottoms of thumb and middle finger cymbals in a parallel position, hit the thumb and middle finger cymbals together and *do not* release cymbals after striking (see figure 2).

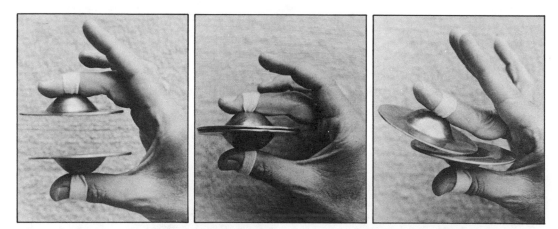

Figure 1. dumm   *Figure 2.* takk   *Figure 3.* sakkah

c. *Sakkah.* Two actions are required to obtain this sound: (1) placing the edge of the middle finger cymbals over the center of the thumb cymbal at a forty-five degree angle and (2) sliding the middle finger cymbal down over the thumb cymbal and towards the palm. Stop sliding when the two bottom flat surfaces meet, and do not release them (see figure 3). This sound is halfway between a *dumm* and a *takk* and is equivalent to the *sakkah* sound on a tambourine. It is represented by a note, stem down, and an arrow crossing through it:

2. After the students have practiced each sound and each hand separately, have the class play eighth- and sixteenth-note patterns, alternative left- right-hand strokes. Students should play each pattern, using only one type of sound—*dumm, takk,* or *sakkah.*
3. Using the finger cymbals, students perform the rhythms in lesson one and experiment with the *dumm, takk,* and *sakkah* sounds.

L E S S O N   T H R E E

3

■ **OBJECTIVES:**
Students will:
Hold the tambourine in a Middle Eastern fashion and produce particular sounds.

Materials:
Large and small tambourines (Avoid those with an inner wooden handle.)

Background:
Middle Eastern tambourines come in a large variety of sizes and are constructed of different materials. The *riqq,* the chief percussion instrument used in urban nineteenth- and twentieth-century music, has five sets of four brass jingles, and transparent Nile fish skin is used for its head. Its diameter is approximately eight inches. Large tambourines with jingles are made of goat or donkey skin and are known as *mazhar.* Without jingles they are called *duff* or *tār.* Some *tār* have two buzzing metallic wires that are attached to the frame and buzz over the skin. Some tambourines also have small bells attached to the inside of the instrument. Large tambourines are used in folk music and are now used increasingly in urban music. Conversely, the small tambourine is also used today in folk and urban music.

189

PROCEDURES:

1. Explain the role of percussion instruments in the Middle East. Stress that tambourine playing is a great art; in the case of the classical *riqq*, a bachelor's degree can be obtained in tambourine playing.
2. Divide the class into two groups; the first group plays the small tambourines, and the second group plays the large tambourines. After the techniques are well learned, switch the groups.
3. Using the following instructions, teach the following ways to play the tambourines:

Small tambourines:

Initial position. Rest tambourine frame on left-hand index finger. The index finger should be bent slightly inward toward the palm. Stabilize the tambourine by placing the thumb on the inner side of frame. The thumb should be at a ninety-degree angle with the head (see figures 4 and 5).

Dumm sound. With a brisk wrist motion, strike the head of the tambourine just above the rim with the first knuckle of the right-hand index finger. Release immediately (see figure 6).

Takk sound. Strike one set of jingles with the ring finger of the right hand. Experiment to find the method that produces the best sound (either remove the finger immediately or rest it on the jingle). For a left-hand *takk*, strike the jingles with the first knuckle of the ring finger (see figure 7).

Sakkah sound. Keep the left hand in its initial position and strike the center of the tambourine with the first knuckles of both the right-hand thumb and index finger in a brisk wrist motion. Rest the fingers on the head after striking it (see figure 8).

Tremolo sound: Keeping the left hand in its initial position, and place the middle and ring fingers of the right hand on the rim of the tambourine. With the left hand motionless, shake the tambourine with the right hand without removing it from its rim-resting position (see figure 9).

Figure 4. tambourine position

Figure 5. tambourine position

Figure 6. dumm

190

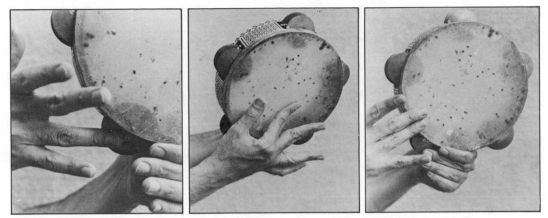

Figure 7. takk   *Figure 8.* sakkah   *Figure 9. tremolo*

Large tambourines:

Initial position. Rest the tambourine frame on the palm of the left hand, and rest the thumb inside the frame and pointing away from the body. The other four fingers should point out at a ninety-degree angle with the head, but not touching the head (see figures 10 and 11).

Dumm sound. Keeping the four fingers of the right hand close together, strike the rim of the tambourine and the head next to the rim with the first two or three knuckles. Release immediately. To prevent the tambourine from swinging in the direction of the attack, hold the tambourine at a sixty-degree angle from an imaginary horizontal plane (see figure 12).

Takk sound. Left-hand *takk:* Gently tap the head of the tambourine with the four protruding fingers of the left hand while keeping the fingers pressed on the head. The left-hand thumb is holding the instrument, so the *takk* sound will be faint. Right-hand *takk*: Hit the rim of the tambourine with the first

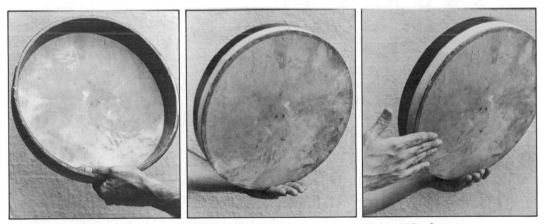

Figure 10. position for large tambourine   *Figure 11. position for large tambourine*   *Figure 12.* dumm

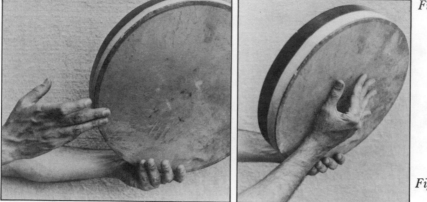

Figure 13. takk

Figure 14. sakkah

knuckles of the middle and ring fingers. Stay on the rim or release immediately, depending on the desired sound (see figure 13).

Sakkah sound. The wrist of the right hand should be positioned above the head, halfway between the center and the rim. First, hit the tambourine with the wrist of the right hand, and then snap the head with all five fingers outstretched. Rest the fingers on the head after striking it. The four fingers of the left hand can leave the head when it is struck, or, if a higher pitched *sakkah* sound is desired, the four fingers can rest tightly on the head (see figure 14).

4. Using the tambourines, have the class perform the rhythms of lesson one. Ask the students to experiment with the *dumm, takk,* and *sakkah* sounds and create their own rhythms.

L E S S O N   F O U R

■ OBJECTIVES:

Students will:

1. Sing or play two short instrumental preludes written in the basic modes (*nahāwand* and *hijāzkār*, discussed in the introduction) and become familiar with the ½ tone, whole tone, 1½ tone.
2. Tap the rhythmic pattern as they hum the prelude.
3. Listen to the heterophonic layers of sound.

Materials:

Any melody instrument can be used to perform the plain and ornamented melodies in this lesson. Students can use violins, recorders, piano, xylophones, or other available instruments, along with small tambourines, to mark the rhythmic pattern. Students may find singing on the vocable "ah" easier than playing on instruments, and they may internalize the sound more quickly.

■ PROCEDURES:

1. Two music selections, which function as preludes to be performed at the beginning of a concert, are transcribed in two versions: plain and ornamented. Performing the ornamented versions in figures 15 and 16 will depend on the students' ability to sing or to play the instruments and should be left to the discretion of the teacher. The ornamented version is only one of an infinite number of possible ornamentations, and it is given here to illustrate performance practice.

Figure 15. dūlāb *in mode* nahāwand

Figure 16. dūlāb *in mode* hijāzkār

2. After students feel comfortable performing the melodies on their respective instruments, the teacher should use what he or she thinks is the easier selection and have the students hum it as they tap the rhythm pattern. In older performances the pattern was:

(♩ ♫)

In more contemporary performances the pattern is:

(♪♪♪♪♪)

3. If time permits:
   a. The teacher can select a few students to perform either rhythmic pattern on small tambourines.
   b. Divide the class into three groups (only if the students are able to perform one prelude in its ornamented form): (1) one performing the melody plain; (2) one performing the melody ornamented; and (3) one performing the rhythmic pattern on tambourines. Thus, students will be able to experience the heterophonic effect that is so prevalent in Middle Eastern ensemble music.
   c. The teacher can explain that these preludes were performed and repeated many times before the beginning of the vocal or instrumental suite.
4. For another project, choose a Western folk song. Ornament and perform it in Middle Eastern style.

L E S S O N   F I V E

5

■ **OBJECTIVES:**

Students will:
1. Sing a Middle Eastern song containing a ¾-tone interval.
2. Tap the rhythm while singing the song. (The melodic rhythm of the song and the tapping pattern are the same.) Students can concentrate on trying to sing the ¾ tone.
3. Sing a Palestinian wedding song.

Materials:
1. Tambourines (any size)
2. An instrument of the violin family or a wind instrument (optional)

■ PROCEDURES:

Figure 17 is a humorous Palestinian wedding song, "Yā Nūr Yā Nūr." The guests surround and turn around the bride and groom in the circle; one by one they improvise words to the melody and sing the refrain together.

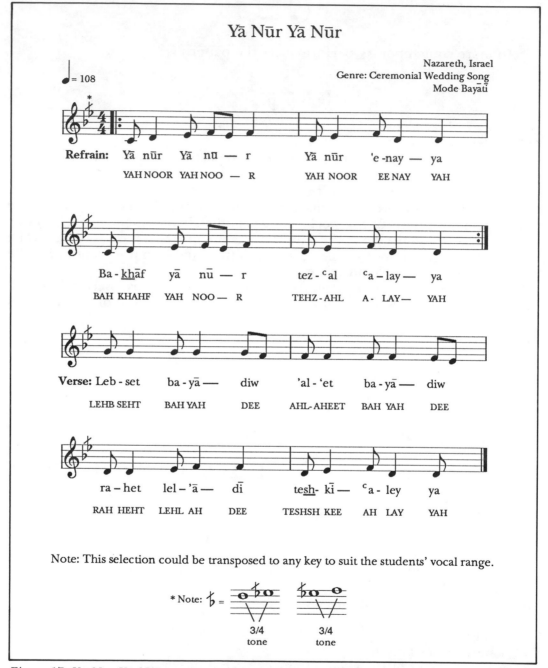

Figure 17. Yā Nūr Yā Nūr

1. Have the students read the translated text.
2. Have the students listen to the first eleven measures of "Samāʿī Bayātī" of Ibrāhīm al-ʿIryān, side one, band three of *Taqāsīm and Layālī*. Guide them in following the score, printed in lesson seven, to learn about the intonation of the mode *bayāti*.
3. Have them hum "Yā Nūr Yā Nūr," using the score printed in figure 17. Be careful that they remember and reproduce the mode's intonation as it is used on the record.
4. Tap the rhythm to the song.
5. Sing the song, adding the words.
6. Sing words and tap the rhythm at the same time.
7. Use the tambourines to play the rhythm.
   The following is a translation of the text of "Yā Nūr Yā Nūr" (O light, O light) [addressing the bride]:

Refrain
O light, O light, O light of my eyes
I am worried O light that you be angry with me

Verse 1
She put on a white dress
She took off the white dress
She went to the judge
To complain about me

LESSON SIX

6

■ **OBJECTIVES:**
Students will:
1. Become familiar with a song composed in an unusual meter.
2. Develop skill in singing and tapping a rhythm pattern at the same time.
3. Learn the flowery language of a classical love song.
4. Experience one of the *muwashashah* song forms.

Materials:
1. Any melody instrument, such as a flute, recorder, guitar, violin, or piano
2. Tambourine (preferably small) with jingles

■ **PROCEDURES:**
Figure 18 is a *muwashshah,* a love song that is part of a suite. The text is flowery, and it combines the ideas of nature and the singer's beloved; he compares the lady to the stem of a flower.
1. Students should read the Arabic text and the translation. Discuss the context

197

Figure 18. muwashshah

198

of the song (it is part of a suite), and emphasize the theme of love, the flowery language, and the comparison of nature and the singer's beloved.

2. Have the students hum the melody.
3. Hum the melody and tap the rhythmic pattern in figure 19 together.
4. Sing the song, adding the words and continuing to tap the rhythm.
5. Add the rhythmic pattern on tambourines and the melody (in unison or octaves, played by any students who have melody instruments and sung by the remainder of the class).

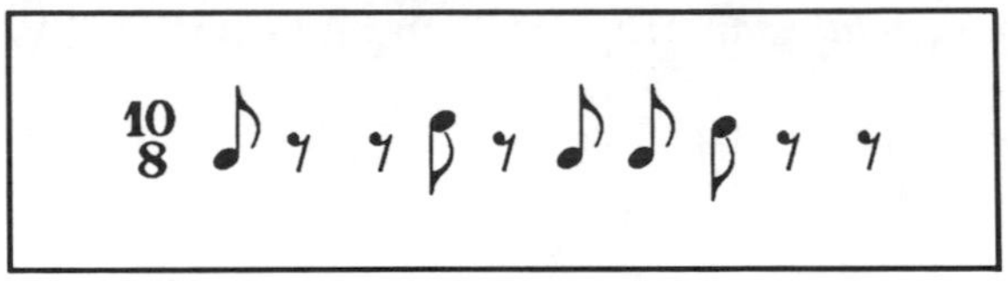

Figure 19. rhythm pattern

The following is a translation of "Lammā Badā Yatathannà" (When my love appeared walking with a swinging gait). The word *amān* in the text means safety or protection. It is often used in love songs by the lover to ask for mercy and protection from the torments of love. The word "stem" refers to the stem of a flower, or in this context to the beloved's body.

Verse 1
When my love appeared walking with a swinging gait
(*Amān*) Her beauty infatuated me (*Amān*).
Verse 2 [not sung]
Her look and glance made me prisoner of love (*Amān*) Her stem bent when she leaned during the walk (*Amān*).
Verse 3
I am bewildered at an unfulfilled promise
Who can respond to my complaints
About love and its torments
Except my beautiful queen (*Amān*).

L E S S O N   S E V E N

7

■ **OBJECTIVES:**
Students will:
1. Listen to the sounds of some Middle Eastern instruments.
2. Identify some Middle Eastern genres.

Materials:
1. Film: *Discovering the Music of the Middle East* (see filmography).
2. Articles: Refer to the articles by Pacholczyk, Racy, Feldman, and Zonis, along with Jenkins and Olsen's *Music and Music Instruments in the World of Islam*, for photographs and descriptions of the instruments studied in this lesson.

199

3. Recordings: (see bibliography).
Arab Music, Volume 1, Lyrichord LLST 7186
Arab Music, Volume 2, Lyrichord LLST 7198
Classical Music of Iran: Dastagh Systems, Volumes 1 and 2, Folkways FW 8831 and FW 8832
Music in the World of Islam, Tangent TGS 131–136
Taqāsīm and Layālī: Cairo Tradition. Modal Music and Improvisations, VI-5, Unesco Collection, Musical Sources, Philips 6586010
Taqāsīm: Improvisations in Arab Music, Lyrichord LLST 7374
Tunisia. Volume 1. The Classical Arab-Andalusian Music of Tunisia, Folkways FW 8861
Songs and Dances of Turkey, Folkways FW 8801

■ **PROCEDURES**

The instruments of Middle Eastern music are far too numerous to be covered in one class period. The teacher may choose to concentrate on one small geographical area and limit the instruments to one musical category (for example, urban or folk).

The following is an outline of such an approach, taking the *takht* ensemble as an example. The urban *takht* ensemble used in the nineteenth and early twentieth centuries consisted of a *qānūn*, *ᶜūd*, *nāy*, *riqq*, and *kamanjah* (a spike fiddle that has been replaced by the Western violin). The *takht* later developed into a larger ensemble, with violins, cellos, accordions, electric organs, and guitars added to the Middle Eastern instruments. The *takht* in its nineteenth-century format survives in some Arab countries such as Syria and in conservatory-type concerts in Egypt.

The *qānūn* is a trapezoidal zither with twenty-six sets of triple strings; the three strings in each set are tuned in unison. The strings are made of nylon, metal, and copper or silver-wound silk. On the right-hand side, a nonmovable bridge rests on five rectangular pieces of Nile fish skin, giving the instrument its characteristic brilliant sound. On the left hand side, six or more copper levers, built for each set of three strings, are raised or lowered to supply intervals ranging from a quarter tone to a full tone. The performer plucks each set of three strings simultaneously with water buffalo–horn picks attached to the two index fingers by means of silver or gold rings (see figure 20). The instrument has a range of three octaves plus a fifth. Play a recording of this instrument: Use any of the examples from *Arab Music, Volume 1, Arab Music, Volume 2*, or *Taqāsīm and Layālī*, and show the class figure 21.

The *ᶜūd* is a fretless lute that has five double strings tuned in fourths. The strings are made of gut, nylon, copper, or silver-wound silk. They are plucked with a water buffalo pick. Play examples from *Arab Music, Volumes 1 and 2, Taqāsīm and Layālī*, or *Taqāsīm. Improvisations in Arab Music*, and show figure 22 to the class.

The *nāy* is a reed flute with seven holes that is obliquely end-blown. It has a range of almost three octaves. Play one of the examples from *Arab Music, Volumes 1 and 2* or *Taqāsīm and Layālī*, and show figure 23 to the class.

The *riqq* is a fish-skin tambourine with brass jingles. Play one of the examples from *Arab Music, Volume 2* or *Taqāsīm and Layālī*.

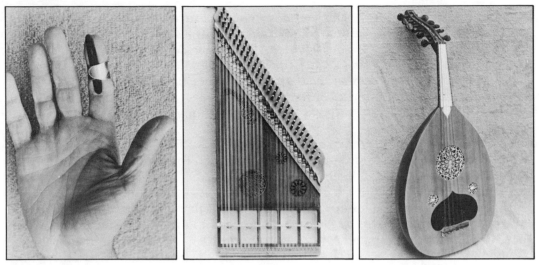

Figure 20. picks
for qānūn

Figure 21. qānūn

Figure 22. ᶜud

The *darabukkah,* not part of the *takht,* is occasionally used together with the *riqq.* It is a clay drum that has a Nile fish-skin head. Play the last selection on *Taqāsīm and Layālī,* and show figure 24.

Instruments of the *takht* are often used together with folk music instruments; for example, the ᶜ*ūd* and the violin are used with *duff* and *salamiyyah* (folk flute, shown in figure 25). Play an example from *Arab Music, Volume 1.*

Examples of several important genres of Middle Eastern music (*taqāsīm, layālī,* and *mawwāl*) can be found in *Taqāsīm and Layālī.* Descriptions of these forms are

Figure 23. nāy

Figure 24. darabukkah

Figure 25. salamiyyah

found in the first section of this chapter. The measured *taqsīm* can be found in *Arab Music, Volume 2* (side one, band three). Examples of a free rhythm *taqāsīm* can be found in *Taqāsīm: Improvisations in Arab Music*. Many *samāᶜis* are recorded on *Arab Music, Volumes 1 and 2* and *Taqāsīm and Layālī*.

Play the *samāᶜī* on *Taqāsīm and Layālī*, side one, band three, and have the students tap the $\frac{10}{8}$ rhythm while listening to the music and following the score in figure 26. Try to lead the students in humming along with the music.

Integrating music with other subjects

Musical events in the Middle East are not abstract, fossilized activities; they are vibrant and functional, and they are used in specific contexts. Music accompanies every step of the human life cycle: births, love, weddings, sickness, and death, to name a few. Each step of the life cycle has its repertoire of songs and often its own rhythmic pattern. A person not watching an event can immediately tell from the rhythmic pattern what is going on. Sacred chants and hymns are essential to the prayers, services, and festivals of Judaism, Christianity, and Islam. These chants and hymns vary according to ethnicity as well as denomination. Work songs accompany and facilitate the activities of fishermen, farmers, bricklayers, and other workers. Urban concert-type music functions as entertainment, and an aesthetic and emotional expression that often leads to a state of trance. Songs effectively function as vehicles for protest against social and political oppression. On the other hand, rulers often use songs to enhance their status and validate their institutions.

Middle Eastern music and the visual arts are intimately related. Al-Fārābī (d. 950), a philosopher and music theorist, related plain melody and ornaments in music to similar constituents in the arts of textiles and architecture:

> Every melody consists of two types of notes [those that form the main melody and ornamental tones]. The first plays the role of the warp and woof in a cloth, the mud, bricks, and wood in buildings. The second plays the role of the carving, the engraving, the facilities, and the exteriors in buildings, and the dyes, smoothing, ornaments and fringes in the cloth.[5]

Illustrate ornamentation techniques by studying and performing the examples in lesson four. There is a strong connection between the concept of ornamentation in music and that in Arabic, Persian, and Ottoman Turkish calligraphy and paintings; in rugs, furniture and objets d'art, and in jewelry and cosmetics (the word "mascara" is derived from Arabic).

Musical instruments are themselves works of art. They are ornamented with inlaid ivory, mother-of-pearl, as well as carved wood in floral, animal, and geometric designs not unlike the patterns used in Persian carpets and Islamic architecture.[6] The visual ornaments on instruments have an obvious aesthetic function—to make the instrument look beautiful. They also function as a visual counterpart to the musical ornamentation, satisfying both the aural and the visual senses.

Musical events, both sacred and secular, often include dancing. The type best known is what Westerners (not Easterners) have termed the "belly dance." This dance has been greatly popularized and grossly misrepresented (with coarse

202

Figure 26. samā^cī

203

Figure 26. samā[c]ī

Figure 26. (continued)

204

sexual connotations) in Hollywood movies, and is now extremely popular in North America, where schools have sprung up all over the continent. The music often borrows popular folk and urban melodies, adding to its own specific repertoire. In the Middle East the so-called belly dance is not confined to night clubs, but is performed by men and women, youngsters, adults, and the aged, in urban as well as rural settings. In the words of the famous Egyptian dancer Suhayr Zakī, "dancing is the body's way to smile."

BIBLIOGRAPHY

Browning, Robert H. *Maqām: Music of the Islamic World and its Influences.* New York: Athens Printing Company, 1984. This book contains concise articles on the music of the Arab world, Morocco, Iran, Turkey, Central Asia, Kashmir, and Judaic Spain. It also includes a useful bibliography and discography and a useful section on musical instruments.

Feldman, Walter Z. "Ottoman Turkish Music." In *Maqām: Music of the Islamic World and its Influences,* edited by R. H. Browning, 21–24. New York: Athens Printing Company, 1984. This article provides the cultural background of Ottoman Turkish music, its theory and practice, forms, and instruments.

Hayes, J. R., ed. *The Genius of Arab Civilization: Source of the Renaissance.* 2d ed. Cambridge, MA: MIT Press, 1983. This book contains an excellent collection of essays in which the authors describe the achievements of the Middle Eastern people in literature, philosophy and history, architecture and art, music, the exact sciences, the life sciences, mechanical technology, and trade and commerce. It is a useful introduction as well as a guide to the film *The Gift of Islam* (see Filmography).

Jenkins, Jean, and Poul Rovsing Olsen. *Music and Musical Instruments in the World of Islam.* London: World of Islam Festival Publishing, 1976. This book contains excellent drawings and photographs of instruments, as well as photographs of instrumentalists in the playing positions used in the world of Islam (Middle East and beyond to Islamic Africa and Southeast Asia). It also contains a section on Islamic influences on the music of the world. This is an excellent handbook that should be used in conjunction with its six albums (see Discography, *Music in the World of Islam*).

Pacholczyk, Josef M. "Secular Classical Music in the Arabic Near East." In *Musics of Many Cultures: An Introduction,* edited by Elizabeth May, 253–68. Berkeley: University of California Press, 1980. This article is a brief sketch of the history of the Middle East (as well as North Africa) from the rise of Islam. It provides a profile of current artistic music as a descendant of the court music traditions in the Islamic empire. The article also provides a discussion of the history of music theory (including the legacy of ancient Greek theory), musical forms, and instruments. It contains a glossary, a bibliography, a discography, and a filmography.

Racy, Ali Jihad. "Music." In *The Genius of Arab Civilization: Source of the Renaissance.* 2d ed., edited by J. R. Hayes, 121–45. Cambridge, MA: MIT Press, 1983. The author emphasizes both the unity and diversity of Arabic music, from the Atlas mountains in Morocco to the Arabian Gulf, and explains the five processes that have shaped Arabic music, from the rise of Islam in the seventh century until the modern era. The article includes a list of the most important modes (rhythmic and melodic), genres, and forms, as well as a useful section on musical instruments.

Sawa, George Dimitri. "The Survival of Some Aspects of Medieval Arabic Performance Practice." *Ethnomusicology* 25, no. 1, 1981, 73–86. The author traces some rhythmic and melodic ornamental techniques used in contemporary Arabic music (shown in transcriptions in this chapter) to a tenth-century source on musical practices in Middle Eastern courts.

Schwadron, Abraham A. "On Jewish Music." In *Musics of Many Cultures: An Introduction.* edited by Elizabeth May, 284–306. Berkeley: University of California Press, 1980. This article contains a useful, concise overview of the diversity of Jewish music in relation to Jewish history and religion. It also contains a glossary, a bibliography, a discography, and a filmography.

Zonis, Ella. "Classical Iranian Music." In *Musics of Many Cultures: An Introduction.* Edited by Elizabeth May, 269–283. Berkeley: University of California Press, 1980. This article includes a discussion of the context of performance of classical Iranian music, its theory, and its improvisation principles. The article contains excellent photographs that show instrumentalists in playing positions, a glossary, a bibliography, and a discography. There are minor inaccuracies in the medieval sections: Islamic medieval treatises are not solely modeled after the Greeks, and Islamic disapproval of the practice of music is in fact theoretical.

DISCOGRAPHY

Arab Music, Vol. 1. Lyrichord LLST 7186. Side one, bands one to four are Upper Egyptian folk songs sung by a female soloist and a chorus. The accompanying ensemble has folk instruments such as the *duff* and *salamiyyah* (folk flute) as well as urban instruments (ᶜ*ūd* and violins). These selections are interesting because they show the breakdown of the categories of folk instruments and urban instruments and illustrate the role of instrumental music. In addition, side one, band two illustrates an improvised dialogue between the vocalist and the ensemble. Side one, band five contains a *samāᶜī* in the major mode, played on the *qānūn*, and shows the Western influence of harmonies in thirds. Side two contains some important instrumental genres, namely one *samāᶜī* and improvisations. Side two, bands three and four contain superb *taqsīm* on the *nāy* (*maqām bayātī, sabā*) and ᶜ*ūd* (*maqām bayātī*). Side two, band two is a *taqsīm* on the *qānūn* in *maqām hijāzkār* that shows the Western influence of triads and arpeggios. The information on the record jacket is, however, unreliable.

Arab Music, Vol. 2. Lyrichord LLST 7198. Side one, bands one, two, and four are *samāᶜī*. Band one, an Ottoman selection played on the *qānūn*, is in the *maqām shadd-ᶜarabān* (a transposition of *hijāzkār*). Band two, played by a classical ensemble (ᶜ*ūd, qānūn, nāy, riqq*) is in *maqām bayātī* and is incomplete. Band four, played by the ᶜ*ūd*, is in *maqām nahāwand*; the last section before the refrain is in ⅜ meter. Band three is in an instrumental genre in which instruments perform measured improvisations on rhythmic patterns played by a *riqq*. Side two, bands one and two are Western-influenced examples of the *qānūn*, in the major and minor modes respectively. Side two, band three is in *maqām sabā*, played on the ᶜ*ud, nāy, qānūn*, and *riqq*, and contains a folk song and *nāy* improvisations. Side two, band four contains improvisations for *qānūn* (in a modern style) and *nāy*. The information on the record jacket is unreliable.

Classical Music of Iran: Dastagh Systems, Vols. 1 and 2. Folkways FW 8831 and FW 8832. This useful set illustrates the modal system of classical Persian music. Because of space limitations, the *dastgāhs* are short. The two records include classical instruments and vocal renditions of classical Persian poems.

Duo Mediterraneo. Gema LC 6768, MD+G G 1225, DG Musikproduktion Dabringhaus und Grimm. Issam el-Mallah and Jannis Kaimakis perform European music of the Medieval and Renaissance periods, using both Middle Eastern instruments and performing techniques. The result is musically and aesthetically pleasing.

Music in the World of Islam. Tangent Records TGS 131–136. This set of six records is a good representation of music from Morocco in the West to Indonesia in the East. The records are divided into six areas: the voice, lutes, strings, flutes and trumpets, reeds and bagpipes, and drums and rhythms. The set should be used with its accompanying handbook, *Music and Musical Instruments in the World of Islam.* The records and the handbook are an excellent pedagogical tool.

Songs and Dances of Turkey. Folkways FW 8801. The record includes a variety of folk instruments and folk styles from many regions of Turkey. There is also military music, and side two, bands one and two are excellent examples of the highly refined art of Turkish music.

Taqāsīm and Layālī, Cairo Tradition: Modal Music and Improvisations, VI-5. Unesco Collection. Musical Sources. Phillips 6586010. Side one, band one illustrates two widespread and related vocal genres, the *layālī* and *mawwāl*. The vocalist is closely followed by the *qānūn* accompanist and improvises in *maqām bayātī* and related modes. Side one, band two illustrates both free rhythm and measured *taqsīm* on the *nāy*, and side one, band three is an excellent example of a *samāᶜi* performed by a *takht* (an instrumental ensemble made up of *qānūn*, ᶜ*ud, nāy, riqq*; see transcription in lesson seven). Side two includes two *taqsīm* and an out-of-context though very useful *darabukkah* (drum) solo that demonstrates variations of the following meters: $\frac{10}{8}, \frac{3}{4}, \frac{7}{8}, \frac{9}{8}, \frac{13}{4}$, and $\frac{16}{8}$, as well as an improvisation.

Taqāsīm: Improvisation in Arab Music. Lyrichord LLST 7374. This record contains three *taqsīm*s in *kurd, nahāwand*, and *bayātī* with artful modulations to related *maqām*s. The record features Simon Shaheen on the ᶜ*ūd* and Ali Jihad Racy on the *buzuq*, both acknowledged virtuosos on their instruments. The record jacket notes are excellent.

206

Tunisia. Vol. 1, The Classical Arab-Andalusian Music of Tunisia. Folkways FW 8861. Side one contains instrumental genres known as *bashraf* and *taqsīm.* (The *nāy taqsīm* is recorded at the wrong speed; it should be slower.) Side two contains *taqsīm* as well as a very important (though short) example of a *nawba*, the North African type suite.

FILMOGRAPHY

Editor's note: The information about the films listed below is derived from data presented in *The World of Islam, Images and Echoes: A Critical Guide to Films and Recordings,* general editor, Ellen Fairbanks-Bodman. Islamic Teaching Materials Project, Unit #7. New York: American Council of Learned Societies, 1980. This book is highly recommended for follow-up and long-term activities requiring additional films and recordings. The publisher's address is American Council of Learned Societies, 228 East Forty-Fifth Street, Sixteenth Floor, New York 10017.

Afghanistan. 15 minutes. ACI Films, 1972. This film offers a panorama of daily life in the villages and in the capital (Kabul), for example, bazaars, cooking, weaving, farms, mosques, and monuments. There is also a musical performance. It can be obtained from AIMS, 626 Justin Street, Glendale, California 91201, 213-240-9300.

Arabesque. 7 minutes. John Whitney. 1976. In this film, a computer program uses the three notes C, D, and E to produce color image graphics that evolve from random arabesques to patterns reminiscent of formal Persian designs. Could be used to show the connection between music and Middle Eastern art and architecture. Contact Pyramid Films, P.O. Box 1048, Santa Monica, CA 90406, 213-828-7577.

Discovering the Music of the Middle East. 21 minutes. Bernard Wilets. In *Discovering Music Series,* 1968. Although the studio-produced demonstrations of traditional instruments and dances are out of context, this film is a useful tool to enable the student to watch the instruments being performed and to acquire further understanding of the concept of music ornamentation. Can be obtained from BFA Educational Media, 2211 Michigan Avenue, Department 7002-A, P.O. Box 1795, Santa Monica, California 90406, 213-829-2901.

An Egyptian Village—Gueziret Eldahab. 18 minutes. Goudsou Films, 1960. Stressing the theme of the unchanging nature of peasants in rural Egypt, this short film portrays aspects of life in an Egyptian village, for example, streets, mosques, irrigation, harvest, brickmaking, wedding rites, and rituals. Can be obtained from BFA Educational Media, 2211 Michigan Avenue, Dept. 7002-A, P.O. Box 1795, Santa Monica, California 90406, 213-829-2901.

The Gift of Islam. 28 minutes. Ray Graham, n.d. This cinematographic gem introduces the great cultural achievements of the Islamic world to the West in the fields of architecture, engineering, navigation, geography, mathematics, astronomy, medicine, horticulture, crafts, metallurgy, calligraphy, literature, music, and philosophy. This film can be used as a companion to *The Genius of Arab Civilization. Source of Renaissance,* edited by J. R. Hayes (see Bibliography). It can be obtained from Graham Associates, 1899 L Street NW, Washington, D.C. 20036, 202-833-9657.

In Arab Lands: An Age of Change. 28 minutes. Sunset Films, 1979. The theme is the challenge of and response to change in the traditionalist societies of the Arab Gulf States. With the coming of oil and modern technology, people now subjugate the land and plan their future. The film addresses modern problems such as the status of women as well as the role of television. Contact Bechtel Power Corporation, Public Relations, 50 Beale Street, San Francisco 94105, 415-768-4596.

Jerusalem: Center of Many Worlds. 29 minutes. Hagopian, 1969. The historical, economic, geographic, and religious significance of Jerusalem to three major religions—Judaism, Christianity, and Islam—are illustrated by contemporary scenes: shrines, the Wailing Wall, churches, and mosques. The film shows scenes of everyday life in the Arab and Jewish sectors, for example, markets, modern stores, and religious life (e.g., services of the three religions). It can be obtained from Atlantis Productions, 1252 La Granada Drive, Thousand Oaks, California 91360, 805-495-2790.

Journey to the West (Rihlah ila Gharb). 30 minutes. Don Dixon, Middle East Education Trust, 1978. This film is about Muslim and Christian Arabs, those who are newly arrived as well as those well established in the United States. It shows scenes of intercultural studies, maintenance of Arab cultural traditions, and the diversity of occupations and worship in localities such as Brooklyn,

Detroit, Houston, and Washington, D.C. It is an adequate production with an overall emphasis on Arab participation in the fulfillment of the American dream. It can be obtained from James D. Johnstone, Route 4, Box 169, Charlottesville, Virginia 22901, 703-973-5726.

Mideast: Land and the People. 20 minutes. Vocational and Industrial Films, 1977. The film emphasizes regional diversity. Arabs, Iranians, and Turks are presented as the three main peoples with a careful explanation of their linguistic, ethnic, and cultural differences. It juxtaposes the traditional and the modern in various settings—urban, villages, and nomad; barren mountain plateaus; lush farmlands; and arid deserts. The film, however, ignores the multitude of ethnic minorities. The film can be obtained from BFA Educational Media, 2211 Michigan Avenue, Department 7002-A., P.O. Box 1795, Santa Monica, California 90406, 213-829-2901.

Rivers of Time. 25 minutes. Contemporary Films, 1962. Artifacts, paintings, sculptures, and models of ancient cities from museums in Baghdad (and other cities) are used to illustrate aspects of Sumerian, Chaldean, and Babylonian life. Current use of ancient ways (for example, methods of irrigation) are shown in contemporary scenes. The film also focuses on ideas and techniques that were introduced by the Arabs and spread through the Mediterranean. The film is a good didactic mixture of artifacts and film footage of the Tigris and Euphrates valleys of Iraq. It can be obtained from McGraw-Hill Films, 1221 Avenue of the Americas, New York 10020, 212-997-1221, or from CRM, 110 Fifteenth Street, Del Mar, California 92014, 714-453-5000.

NOTES

1. W. B. Fisher, "The Middle East and North Africa: An Introduction," in *The Middle East and North Africa 1987*, 33d ed. (London: Europa Publications, 1986), 12.
2. Fisher, 12.
3. A useful book for this purpose is J. R. Hayes, ed., *The Genius of Arab Civilization. Source of the Renaissance*, 2d ed. (Cambridge, MA: MIT Press), 1983.
4. A flat sign with a slash through the stem indicates a note that is lowered by approximately ¼ tone. A sharp sign with only one vertical line is used to indicate a note that is raised by ¼ tone.
5. George D. Sawa, "The Survival of Some Aspects of Medieval Arabic Performance Practice," *Ethnomusicology* 25, no. 1, 1981, 80.
6. See Jean Jenkins and Poul Rovsing Olsen, *Music and Musical Instruments in the World of Islam* (London: World of Islam Festival Publishing, 1976), 34–35, 48, 81, and 84. Photographs are found on pages 84 and 85.

India, showing position of some
surrounding countries.

CHAPTER SEVEN

7

SOUTH ASIA: INDIA

by William M. Anderson

Sweeping southward from the world's highest peaks in the Himalayan mountains is the nation of India, the second largest country in Asia. India extends approximately two thousand miles south from central Asia to the tropical waters of the Indian ocean and approximately seventeen hundred miles eastward from the Arabian Sea to the eastern border with Burma.

Although it is positioned just north of the equator, India experiences great variety in climate and weather. The snow-capped peaks in the north provide a welcome cool in contrast to the warmth of much of the subcontinent; they also function as the source of the three great rivers, the Indus, the Ganges, and the Brahmaputra, which sustain much of the country. As one follows these rivers into the Indo-Gangetic plain of northern India, a huge, fertile river valley emerges. The rich soil and the warm, humid climate of the lower elevation support some of India's best agriculture. To the west of this region, in stark contrast, lie the parched desert areas of Rajasthan. Moving south and toward the center of the country, one finds a large and relatively high plateau region known as the Deccan, where the weather is integrally related to the prevailing winds, the monsoons. Stretching south from the Deccan is a temperate coastal plain and tropical beaches.

211

More than 70 percent of the people living in the subcontinent make their living from agriculture, so the weather is an important factor in the economy. Because India is so close to the equator, it does not have the four seasons of Europe or North America; its seasonal changes are caused by the monsoons. In April, May, and June, extremely hot weather grips most of the country until the west winds bring quenching rains to many parched areas from late June through September. In the winter, the winds reverse, providing a cool easterly flow of air that produces more comfortable temperatures.

India has often been described as a dozen countries in one, a democratic republic that exemplifies the doctrine of "unity through diversity." Its twenty-two states and nine territories form a mosaic of different ethnic groups. Millions of negrito tribal peoples, ethnically related to the aboriginals of Malaysia, the Philippines, and Australia, live in remote jungle areas. Dark-skinned peoples who descend from the Dravidians (the most ancient people on the subcontinent) inhabit the southern regions of the country. Farther north, innumerable incursions of peoples from central Asia, the Near East, and Europe have made the majority of present-day Indians primarily of Caucasian stock. India today has a burgeoning population of nearly 833 million inhabitants, the second largest in the world (exceeded only by China). The large and ethnically diverse population has made it one of the most fascinating countries in Asia.

The linguistic diversity of the subcontinent is almost beyond comprehension. In an area only half the size of the United States, 845 languages and dialects are used; 14 of these languages and dialects are each spoken by millions of people. The news on All-India Radio, for example, is broadcast in Hindi, English, Bengali, Oriya, Tamil, Telugu, Kannada, Malayalam, Punjabi, Marathi, Gujarati, Assamese, Urdu, and Kasmiri. Hindi is the official language of the country, but English remains the language of educated persons and government officials. Although the British promoted the English language in this area of the world, many Indian words have been adopted by Westerners including such familiar ones as bungalow, dungarees, punch, shampoo, and pajamas.

Religion is the strongest binding force in this enormously diverse population. At least 85 percent of the population is Hindu, with the remaining populace dispersed among Moslems, Jains, Buddhists, Sikhs, Parsis, and Christians. The sanctions and mores of Hinduism affect the lives of millions of people; a host of Hindu gods and goddesses oversees almost every facet of existence and provides a common basis for uniting the lives of millions of people. Hinduism has also inspired the work of numerous sculptors, painters, writers, and musicians (see the bibliography for good sources for pictures of architecture, sculpture, and painting). Two common symbols of music's close relationship with this religion are Saraswati, the goddess of learning and music, who is usually depicted holding the *vina* (a stringed instrument), and Krishna, playing the flute.

In addition to Hinduism, the religious and cultural traditions of India have been enormously influenced by Islam, which was brought to India more than one thousand years ago. Great Muslim courts were established throughout northern India, and spectacular buildings, such as the Taj Mahal in the city of Agra, are vivid examples of Indo-Islamic art.

At about the same time that Columbus was sailing to the New World, the Portuguese explorer Vasco da Gama came to India, hoping to establish trading posts. Since India was rich in silk, gems, indigo, and spices, which were in great demand in the West, Dutch, Danish, French, and British traders soon followed the Portuguese to this eastern paradise. The British gradually took control of the country, bringing about great changes by developing cities, industries, and transportation.

In 1947 India became an independent nation and the world's largest democracy. Growing nationalism has led to many outstanding achievements in all areas of human endeavor including the sciences, humanities, and arts. Music has become part of the curriculum of many primary and secondary schools and universities, and distinguished Indian musicians such as Ravi Shankar and Ali Akbar Khan have traveled to Europe and the United States to make Westerners aware of the sophistication and brilliance of the Indian musical tradition. Both Shankar and Khan have now established schools of music in California in which many Americans study Indian vocal and instrumental music.

Characteristics

India has one of the world's oldest and most sophisticated musical traditions. Its history stretches back at least thirty-five hundred years and involves the development of a great variety of vocal and instrumental music. There are two principal stylistic traditions in Indian music: the *Hindustani* system of north India and the *Carnatic* system of south India. There are many similarities between the two traditions, but they differ from each other in a number of nuances of melody, rhythm, timbre, and form. This chapter focuses on music in north India.

Indian melodies are derived from a prescribed series of notes known as *raga*s (see figure 1). There are hundreds of *raga*s, and each has a particular name and a distinctive structure.

*Raga*s differ from Western scales in that they often indicate the contours or shapes of melodies. Thus, the notes of *raga*s frequently do not move straight up and down but in "crooked" melodic fashion. The structure of a *raga* often calls for its pitches to be ornamented with subtle "slides" and "shakes." This ornamentation includes microtonal intervals (intervals that are smaller than a half step). *Raga*s also express emotions or feelings and have designated performance times throughout the day or night or at given times of the year.

Figure 1. raga bhupali

Rhythm in Indian music is highly developed. It may either be free and flexible or strictly organized. Strict rhythm is organized in cycles of beats known as *tala*s. *Tala*s have names and distinctive characteristics, such as overall length and division into subsections. For example, *tintala* is a rhythmic cycle of sixteen beats that is divided into four sections, each with four beats (4 + 4 + 4 + 4), and *jhaptal* is a rhythmic cycle of ten beats, divided into four sections: a group of two beats, followed by a group of three beats, followed by a group of two beats, followed by a group of three beats (2 + 3 + 2 + 3).

Some Indian music is monophonic; that is, it uses only one melodic line. Most Indian music, however, makes use of drone harmony, in which a constantly sounding pitch or group of pitches supports the singing or playing of other melodic lines. The melodic lines themselves often imitate one another.

A great variety of timbres or tone colors are present in Indian music. In general, singers tend to produce a more nasalized tone color with less vibrato than do Western classical singers. Many instruments produce rich and distinctive tone colors through sympathetic vibrating strings (small strings that vibrate in "sympathy" when the main melody strings are plucked or bowed).

Typical Indian musical compositions are multisectional. Many compositions begin with the *alap*, an improvised section in free and flexible rhythm. The *alap* is followed by a composed (but generally not written) section known in vocal music as *chiz* and in instrumental music as *gat*. The *chiz* or *gat* is cast in the strict rhythm of a particular *tala*. Following the composed section is improvisation, which continues the rhythm of the *tala*.

Sometimes the form is enlarged to include several composed and improvised sections, the first in a slow tempo followed by one or more in faster tempos.

L E S S O N   O N E

1

■ OBJECTIVES:

Students will:
1. Sing the short Indian composition "Namane Kare Chature" in *raga bhupali*.
2. Add a *tambura* drone accompaniment to "Namane Kare Chature."
3. Keep track of the *tala* rhythmic cycle in "Namane Kare Chature."

Materials:
1. Indian *tambura* or makeshift "drone" played either on a guitar or a piano (You may wish to purchase a tambura;[1] alternately, since a large number of Asian Indians now reside in the United States, you may wish to try to find

---

1. Indian musical instruments can be purchased from Ali Akbar College Store, 215 West End Avenue, San Rafael, California 94901. House of Musical Traditions, 7040 Carroll Avenue, Takoma Park, Maryland 20912 sells a wide variety of musical instruments from all over the world. Write for a catalog from either of these two companies.

some families in the community that have instruments they would be willing to loan to your school).
2. Sixteen-beat *tala* cycle shown on board or on a transparency

■ PROCEDURES:
1. Have the students design a bulletin board with information about the music of India. Organize the chart with categories of melody, rhythm, texture, timbre, dynamics, and form.
2. Sing the Indian composition "Namane Kare Chature" (see figure 2). First, pronounce the Hindi words with the class. The text is as follows: Namane kare chature shiri guru charana (pronounced *nah-mah-nuh kah-ruh cha-too-ruh shee-ree goo-roo chah-rah-nah*)/ tane mane niremale kare bhave tarana (pronounced *tah-nuh mah-nuh nee-ruh-mah-luh kah-ruh bhah-vuh tah-rah-nah*).

Translation:
Respect your teachers and
keep a clean body and mind.

Some students will probably know the word *guru* (teacher). Comment on the text, which focuses on one's guru. You may wish to read and paraphrase for the class some of the remarks about the importance of the guru from pages 11–13 of Ravi Shankar's book *My Music, My Life* (see Bibliography). Second, sing the song for the class. Call attention to the repeated phrases (the first line repeats, and the last line is the same as the first). Teach the song phrase by phrase, singing slowly with the students so they can grasp the pitches and the pronunciation of the words. Third, tell the students that singing in India is often accompanied by a stringed instrument known as the *tambura*, and show the class the picture of a *tambura* (see figure 3).
Explain that the instrument has a large base made either from wood or a hollowed-out gourd. Extending from this base is a long neck with pegs at the top. Four strings run across the base of the instrument and along the neck to

Figure 2.

the pegs. The player holds the instrument upright and plucks the strings from left to right with the middle and index fingers of the right hand.

The strings of the *tambura* are normally tuned to the pitches G_3, C_4, C_4, and C_3 and are plucked over and over in a flexible rhythmic style to produce a steady drone. The distinctive tone color of this instrument is produced by small threadlike strings inserted between the main strings and the flat bridge (see figure 4). The main strings are thus raised slightly above the slightly sloping, flat bridge. When the strings are plucked, they vibrate against the bridge, producing a distinctive buzzing timbre.

Try to obtain an actual *tambura* for the students to use. If you are unable to find the instrument, you may wish to use a makeshift *tambura* by tuning the four highest pitched strings of a guitar to the pitches used for a *tambura*. Position the guitar with the base on the floor and the neck pointing upward.

Figure 3.
Woman playing
the tambura.
Photograph by
Graeme
Vanderstoel

216

Figure 4. *Base of* tambura

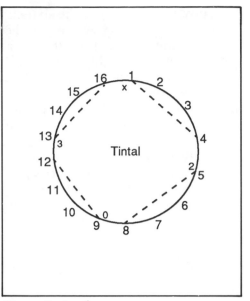

Figure 5. tintal

Have a student pluck the strings one at a time in a repetitive cycle to produce the drone sound. If a guitar is not available, have a student play the *tambura* pitches over and over on a piano with the damper pedal depressed; this will also produce the continuous drone effect.

3. Have the students sing "Namane Kare Chature" with *tambura* accompaniment. For a follow-up discussion, ask the students if they can think of other types of music that make use of drone harmony. You might start the discussion by using examples such as bagpipe or Kentucky mountain dulcimer music.

4. Introduce students to rhythmic cycles called *tala*s. Explain that *tala*s are cycles of beats that repeat in a musical composition. There are many *tala*s, and each has a particular name and structure. One of the most common north Indian *tala*s is known as *tintala*. It has sixteen beats, divided into four sections (see figure 5). Indians have devised a number of ways to count the beats in *tala*s. A common way to follow *tintala* is to clap lightly on the strong beats (one, five, and thirteen), wave the right hand outward on the weak beat (nine), and count the intervening beats by touching the right-hand fingers against the thumb, beginning with the little finger and moving toward the middle finger. Count, emphasizing the first beat of the cycle, as follows:

1	2	3	4	5	6	7	8
clap	(Count 2, 3, and 4 by placing right thumb on little, fourth, and middle fingers.)			clap	(Count 6, 7, and 8 by placing right thumb on little, fourth, and middle fingers.)		
9	10	11	12	13	14	15	16
wave	(Count as 2, 3, and 4 above)			clap	(Count at 6, 7, and 8 above)		

217

Have the class count the sixteen beats of the *tala* over and over and follow the beats by clapping, waving, and counting the intervening beats on the fingers. Start the cycle on another beat, such as nine (the cycle will, in this case, continue through sixteen to finish with counts one to eight. Continue practicing with the class until keeping track of the cycle of beats becomes fairly easy.

5. Divide the class, having one-half sing the song "Namane Kare Chature" (with *tambura* accompaniment by a student) as the other half keeps track of the sixteen-beat *tala*, known as *tintala* (see figure 5). Note that "Namane Kare Chature" begins on beat nine of the *tala*. After the students have learned to sing the song and keep track of the *tala* easily, switch the groups so that all members of the class have a chance to follow the *tala*.

6. Summarize the lesson by having the students place comments on the board (under the appropriate categories) about what they have learned in this lesson: rhythm (cycles of beats known as the *tala*); texture (drone harmony played by the *tambura*); timbre ("buzzing" tone color on the *tambura* achieved by the use of small threads placed between the main strings and the flat bridge).

2 L E S S O N   T W O

■ OBJECTIVES:
Students will:
1. Use rhythmic syllables to perform on either *tabla* drums or a substitute such as bongo drums.
2. Play the rhythmic syllables for *tintala* on either *tabla* or bongos.
3. Add a *tabla* accompaniment to "Namane Kare Chature."

Materials:
1. *Tabla* or substitutes such as bongo drums
2. The composition "Namane Kare Chature," shown on a transparency

■ PROCEDURES:
Explain that the *tabla* (see figure 6) are the most important drums of north India. *Tabla* actually consist of two drums: a large, somewhat low pitched drum made from metal and a higher pitched drum usually constructed from wood. Both drums have black, circular patches made from a paste of iron filings, flour, and water applied to their heads. *Tabla* are played by striking various parts of the drum heads with the fingers and hands while in a sitting position. Percussionists use mnemonic syllables known as *bol*s to facilitate the playing of rhythms on the drums. For example, striking the left drum with the third and fourth fingers is identified with the *bol* "dhe"; striking the right drum on the edge with the index finger produces the *bol* "na" or near the center the *bol* "tin" (see figure 7). If "dhe" and "na" are combined in a single stroke (both left- and right-hand fingers striking at the same time), the *bol* is known as "dha." If "dhe" and "tin" are combined into a single stroke, the *bol* "dhin" is produced.

218

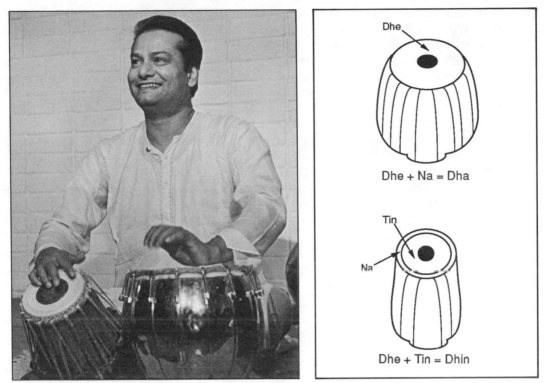

Figure 6. Man playing tabla.
Photograph by Graeme Vanderstoel

Figure 7. Striking areas on tabla.

1. Have the students try to produce the *bol*s "dhe," "na," "tin," "dha," and "dhin" either on *tabla* or a bongo drums. Those without drums can practice on desk tops or laps.
2. Have the students play (maintaining a steady pulse) the following rhythmic patterns on the drums after reciting the syllables in each line from memory:

   Dhe Na/Dhe Na/Dhe Dhe Na   (repeat)
   Dhe Tin/Dhe Tin/Dhe Dhe Tin   (repeat)
   Dha Dha Na/Dha Dha Na   (repeat)
   Dhin Dhin Na/Dhin Dhin Na   (repeat)
   Dha Dhin Dhin Na/Dha Dhin Dhin Na   (repeat)
   Tin Tin Na/Tin Na/Tin Na   (repeat)

Explain that for each *tala* there is a standard rhythmic pattern played on the drums. For example, the rhythmic pattern for *tintala* is as follows:

Dha	Dhin	Dhin	Dha	Dha	Dhin	Dhin	Dha
1	2	3	4	5	6	7	8

Dha	Tin	Tin	Na	Na	Dhin	Dhin	Dha
9	10	11	12	13	14	15	16

219

3. Have the class learn to pronounce the syllables from memory. Note that there are four groups, each with four syllables; call attention to the similarity of groups one, two, and four.
4. Have one or two students play the rhythmic syllables on a *tabla* or bongo drum while the rest of the class recites the syllables. Practice until the rhythmic syllables can be played on the drums with ease.
5. Divide the class into three groups: (1) one or two students who play the *tabla* or bongos, (2) a large group that recites the drum syllables (*Dha, Dhin, Dhin, Dha,* and so on), and (3) a large group that keeps track of the sixteen-beat *tintala* through hand claps, waving the right hand outward, and counting the intervening beats on the fingers as outlined in lesson one.
6. Divide the class into three groups with the first singing the song "Namane Kare Chature," the second group keeping track of the *tala* (*tintala,* beginning on beat nine), and the third group (composed of several students) playing the rhythm on the *tabla* or bongos.
7. Summarize the lesson by having the students discuss and add comments to the music section of their Indian bulletin board: Indian drums known as *tabla,* rhythmic syllables known as *bol*s, and the specific *bol*s for *tintala.*

3   L E S S O N   T H R E E

■ OBJECTIVES:
Students will:
1. Explore Indian *raga*s by singing the Western major scale and two *raga*s on a neutral syllable. Students will identify differences in whole- and half-step patterns between an Indian *raga* and the Western scale. They will learn that *raga*s have distinctive names and structures.
2. Sing the song "America": first in the Western major scale and then in the *raga*s *bhairavi* and *purvi.*
3. Create a short, improvised composition on the *jaltarang* in *raga bhupali.*

Materials:
1. Transcriptions of two *raga*s, (*bhairavi* and *purvi*) and the C major scale on a transparency or on the chalkboard
2. A transcription of "America" on transparency—first in a major scale and then in the *raga*s *bhairavi* and *purvi.*
3. Seven glass bowls (cereal or soup bowls are fine)

■ PROCEDURES:
1. Explain to the class that one of the major reasons why melodies in Indian music sound so different to us is that they are developed from *raga*s. *Raga*s

are organized series of pitches from which musical composition are developed. There are hundreds of *raga*s, and each has a particular name and structure.

2. Place the following *raga*s on the board or on a transparency. Ask the class to sing each *raga*, using a neutral syllable such as "ah" or "loo." Then sing the Western major scale on a neutral syllable. What difference do you hear and see? (The students should be able to respond that there are different patterns of intervals [whole and half steps].)

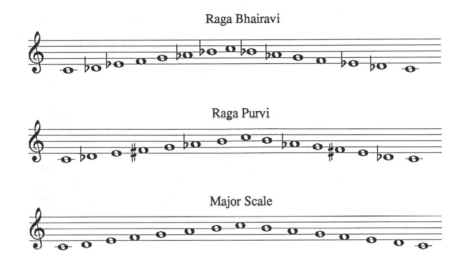

3. Write or project transcriptions of "America" as sung in the Western major scale system and the Indian *raga*s, *bhairavi* and *purvi*. Have the class sing and compare the sound of each example.

221

America
Raga Bhairavi

My coun - try, 'tis of thee, Sweet land of lib - er - ty, of thee I sing. Land where my fath - ers died, Land of the pil - grims' pride. From ev - 'ry moun - tain side Let free-dom ring.

America
Raga Purvi

My coun - try, 'tis of thee, Sweet land of lib - er - ty, of thee I sing. Land where my fath - ers died, Land of the pil - grims' pride. From ev - 'ry__ moun - tain side Let_ free - dom ring.

4. Improvise short compositions in the *raga*s *bhairavi* and *purvi* on an Indian instrument known as the *jaltarang* (see figure 8).
   a. The *jaltarang* is a very interesting musical instrument that consists of a series of tuned bowls arranged in a semicircle around the performer. The bowls are of different sizes and are tuned precisely to the pitches of

222

various *ragas* by adding appropriate amounts of water. The instrument is played by striking the inside edge of the bowls with two small wooden sticks, one held in each hand.

    b. Collect seven glass bowls and devise a *jaltarang*. Tune the various bowls to the pitches in *raga purvi* by filling them with appropriate amounts of water. (Depending on the size of bowls you choose, you may have to transcribe the *raga* to a different pitch level.) Using a pair of chopsticks as mallets, create an improvised composition in flexible or free rhythm.

        (1) Change the pitches of the bowls to *raga bhairavi* and create another improvised piece of music in flexible rhythm.

        (2) Compare the sounds produced by *raga*s *purvi* and *bhairavi* and the Western scale by creating an improvised composition on the *jaltarang* in the C major scale.

5. Add to the bulletin board chart things that you have learned in this lesson: the *raga*s *purvi* and *bhairavi* and the *jaltarang*.

Figure 8. Student playing jaltarang

4 L E S S O N   F O U R

■ OBJECTIVES:

Students will:

1. Follow the seven-beat *tala* know as *rupak* with handclaps, waves, and counting on the fingers. Learn about the asymmetrical subdivisions of the *tala* (3 + 2 + 2) and draw parallels to Western compositions.
2. Learn to speak the drum (*tabla*) syllables for *rupak*: tin-tin-na, dhin-na, and dhin-na. Keep track of the *tala* while speaking the syllables.
3. Play the pattern indicated by the drum syllables on a *tabla* or a pair of bongo drums.
4. Learn the composition "Ha-Nan-De," which is cast in the seven-beat *rupak tala*; keep track of the *tala* and add a *tabla* accompaniment.

■ PROCEDURES:

1. Review the rhythmic cycle known as *tintala*, introduced in lesson one. Have the students follow the beats by clapping and waving their hands on the principal beats and counting the intervening beats on their fingers. Draw particular attention to the fact that the cycle is composed of four even sections.
2. Explain that in some *talas* the internal sections are not equally divided. Have the students follow the unequal grouping of beats found in the seven-beat *rupak tala*. The children should speak the numbers and clap lightly on the beginning of each subdivision (*1—2—3, 4—5, 6—7*) (see figure 9). Notice the asymmetrical rhythmic feeling of the group of three beats followed by the two groups of two beats (3 + 2 + 2). You may wish to draw parallels to other Western compositions such as Paul Desmond's "Take Five" in which the meter comprises asymmetrical groups of beats (*1—2—3, 4—5*). (The song "Take Five" is recorded on *Time Out: The Dave Brubeck Quartet*, Columbia CL 1397.)

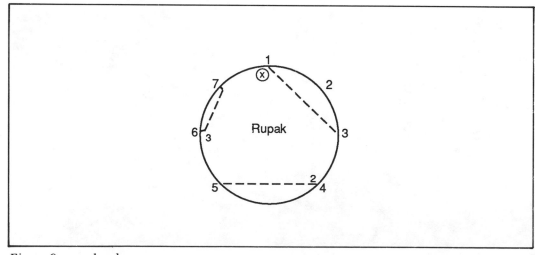

Figure 9. rupak tala

224

Ha-Nan-De

Ha Nan-de La - le A - ti Hi - ra Sa - le

Ni - re - tet - te Sun - ge Goo - pi

Gwa - le Ha Nan - de La - le

Figure 10.

3. Have the students recite the *tabla* rhythmic syllables or *bols* for *rupak tala:* tin-tin-na, dhin-na, dhin-na. Then have half of the class recite the syllables over and over while the other half counts the numbers.
4. Have several students play the rhythms dictated by the syllables on *tabla* or bongo drums. Refer to figure 7 for the locations on the drum heads at which the students should produce these sounds.
5. Sing the song "Ha-Nan-De" (see figure 10).
   Pronounce the words with the students, explaining that this song is about the Hindu god Krishna. The text is as follows: Ha nande lale ati hira sale (pronounced *hah nahn-duh lah-luh ah-tee hee-ray sah-luh*)/ niretette sunge goopi gwale (pronounced *nee-ruh-teht-tuh soon-guh goo-pee gwah-luh*).

   Translation:
   The Son of God [Krishna]
   is very happy

   Show a picture of Krishna (this illustration may be found in the books by Bussagli and Sivaramamurti and by Munro listed in the Bibliography).
   Point out that the first line of the song is sung twice, the second line once, and that a short portion of line one returns at the end of the song.
   Assist the students with a *tambura* accompaniment, either with an Indian instrument or one of the substitutes suggested in lesson one.

225

6. Divide the class and have some students sing "Ha-Nan-De" while other students keep track of the *tala*. Note that this composition begins on beat four of *rupak tala*, so that the pattern from the beginning is 4 5 / 6 7 / 1 2 3, which is usually kept track of as follows (the wave outward, used to show a relatively weak beat on beat one, is an idiosyncrasy of this *tala*):

4	5	6	7	1	2	3
clap	right-hand thumb placed on little finger	clap	right-hand thumb placed on little finger	wave	right-hand thumb placed on little finger	right-hand thumb placed on fourth finger

7. Divide the class with some singing "Ha-Nan-De," others keeping track of the *tala*, and still others providing a *tabla* accompaniment.
8. Summarize on the board what you have learned in this lesson: *rupak tala* with its unequal subdivisions, drum syllables (*bols*) for *rupak*, and the composition "Ha-Nan-De" in *rupak tala*.

LESSON FIVE

■ OBJECTIVES:
Students will:
1. Sing the *raga bhupali* and study some characteristics of *ragas*.
2. Identify the form in a north Indian vocal composition accompanied by *tambura* and *tabla* in *raga bhupali* by performing (1) a short, improvised introduction (*alap*) in flexible rhythm, (2) a composed segment (*chiz*) in the sixteen-beat cycle *tintala*, and (3) improvised phrases.
3. Follow the form in an Indian instrumental composition (featuring *sitar* with accompaniment by *tabla* and *tambura*) in *raga maru bihag* by listening to an improvised introduction or *alap* followed by a precomposed piece (*gat*) in the ten-beat *jhaptal tala* and improvised phrases.
4. Listen to the rock composition "Love You To" by the Beatles (see Discography), which features both Indian instruments (*sitar* and *tabla*) and Western instruments; follow the "Indian form" of the song.

Materials:
1. Transparency with transcriptions of *raga bhupali,* an *alap,* a *chiz,* and improvised phrases
2. *Tambura* and *tabla* or appropriate substitutes
3. Pictures of a *sitar, tabla,* and *tambura*
4. Recordings:
   The Beatles, *Revolver,* Capitol Records ST2576
   Ravi Shankar, *The Sounds of India,* Columbia CL9296

■ PROCEDURES:

1. Indian musical compositions are created from prescribed series of notes known as *ragas.* Have the students study the *raga* known as *bhupali* as follows: First sing the *raga* using the Indian note names: sa (sah), re (ray), ga (gah), pa (pah), and dha (dhah) (see figure 11). Explain that *ragas* have many characteristics. Discuss some of these characteristics and compare them to Western music:
   a. Each *raga* has a particular name, such as *bhupali.*
   b. *Ragas* provide pitches (notes) that are used in creating musical compositions.
   c. *Ragas* often have a "crooked" movement with different ascending and descending forms. Point out to the students that the notes that make up *raga bhupali* are not arranged in a strictly scalar fashion, but in a form that indicates the distinctive melodic movement characteristic to the *raga.*
   d. *Ragas* often have specific ornamentation such as the "slide" in pitch from pa (G) to ga (E) shown by a straight line in figures 11 and 12.
   e. *Ragas* convey specific moods or feelings; *bhupali,* for example, conveys the mood of majesty or grandeur.
   f. *Ragas* are assigned specific performance times (day or night) when the mood of the *raga* can best be achieved. *Bhupali,* for example, is an evening *raga.*
2. Give the students some background information on the practical use of *ragas* by explaining that most Indian musical compositions begin with an improvised section of music known as the *alap,* and the performer uses the notes of a selected *raga* to create a segment of music that has a free, flexible rhythmic style.

SA RE GA PA GA DHA PA GA SA DHA PA GA GA RE SA DHA SA

Figure 11. raga bhupali

Figure 12. Ornamental "slide"

3. Figure 13 provides a transcription of a short *alap* in *raga bhupali*. Normally the music is improvised rather than written down, but Western notation is used here so that the students can easily follow the example.

   a. Have the students sing the *alap* in a free, flexible rhythmic style, using either the Indian scale degree syllables or a neutral syllable such as "ah." Assist the class by singing or playing the notes on the piano or melody bells as they sing.

   b. The *alap* is generally accompanied by the *tambura*. Try performing the *alap* with accompaniment by a *tambura* or a substitute drone instrument such as guitar or piano.

4. The *alap* is followed by a segment of composed music (not necessarily written down, but conceived beforehand rather than improvised) known in vocal

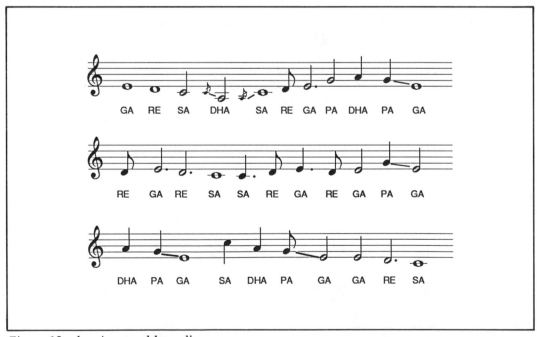

Figure 13. alap *in* raga bhupali

228

music as the *chiz*. The *chiz* is played in a *tala* rhythmic cycle with *tabla* joining the *tambura* accompaniment.

Have the class perform the *chiz* (see figure 14). Divide the class so that one group sings while another group keeps track of the *tala* (*tintala*) through hand claps, hand waving, and counting on the fingers. Add a drum accompaniment either on *tabla* or bongos (see lessons one and two).

Figure 14. Chiz *in* raga bhupali

5. After the composed section, the performer begins to improvise again. This improvisation is often created by taking a portion of the composed music (for example, "Namane Kare Chature") and adding improvised phrases. Encourage students to try singing, with a neutral syllable such as "ah," the following improvised phrases:

"Namane Kara Chature" with improvisation

229

Have the students make up some short, improvised phrases by using the first section of "Namane Kare Chature" to create several eight-beat improvised phrases. The students should alternate the song's beginning with improvised passages in a continuous cycle.

6. Follow the form in an Indian instrumental composition in *raga maru-bihag*, on *The Sounds of India*, side one, band three, featuring Ravi Shankar playing the *sitar* accompanied by *tabla* and *tambura*.

   a. Show the pictures of the *sitar* (see figure 15), and explain that the *sitar* is one of the principal stringed instruments of India. It has a large base fashioned from a hollowed-out gourd. A long neck, supporting a number of curved, movable frets, extends from the base. Seven strings run over the top of these frets and are attached to pegs at the upper end of the neck. Some of these strings are used to play melodies and are plucked by a wire plectrum attached to the right-hand index finger. To produce different pitches, the performer presses the strings against the frets at various points. Several of the strings running over the frets are not used to play melodies but rather are tuned to the drone and are plucked by the performer to provide rhythmic accentuation. An additional group of small metal strings, known as the sympathetic vibrators, are stretched along the neck of the instrument under the frets. As their name suggests,

Figure 15. Students playing the sitar

230

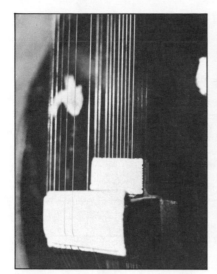

Figure 16. Sympathetic vibrating strings on sitar

Figure 17. North Indiana ensemble; from left: tabla, sitar, *and* tambura

these strings are not plucked but rather oscillate in sympathy when the strings running over the frets are activated (see figure 16).

b. Show a picture of the *sitar, tabla*, and *tambura*, a very common instrumental ensemble of North India (see figure 17).

c. On *The Sounds of India*, Ravi Shankar illustrates the ascending and descending forms of the *raga maru-bihag* (pronounced mah-roo—bee-hahg). Listen to the *raga* and discuss its distinctive ascending and descending patterns of notes with "crooked" melodic movement, its ornamentation of particular notes (shown in figure 18 with a wavy line), and the fact that it is evening *raga* conveying a feeling of melancholy or loneliness.

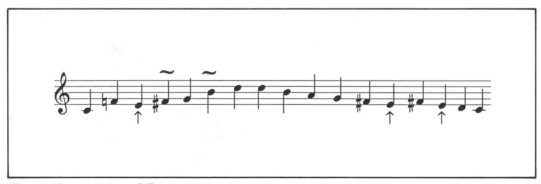

Figure 18. raga maru-bihag

231

d. Place the following diagram on the board for the students to follow as they listen to the music:

Alap section	*Gat* section	Improvisation
Sitar plays melody ———————————————————————————→		
Tambura plays drone accompaniment ——————————————————→		
Flexible, free rhythm ——→	Change to steady beat of *tala jhaptal* ————————————→	
	Tabla enters ——————————————————→	

(1) In the opening section of the *alap*, the *sitar* improvises in the *raga*. Notice the flexible, free rhythmic style. The *sitar* is accompanied by the *tambura*, which provides a soft drone background.

(2) The *alap* is followed by a composed section of music known in instrumental music as the *gat* (comparable to the *chiz* of vocal music). The *gat* in this example is in the strict rhythm of *tala jhaptal*. *Jhaptal* has ten beats that are divided into four subsections (2 + 3 + 2 + 3). Make sure that the class understands the asymmetrical quality of this *tala* (see figure 19). Have the class follow the *tala* by speaking the numbers and clapping lightly on beats one, three, and eight; waving

Jhaptal									
1	2	3	4	5	6	7	8	9	10
Clap	Place	Clap	Place	Place	Wave	Place	Clap	Place	Place
	thumb on right little finger		thumb on right little finger	thumb on right fourth finger		thumb on right little finger		thumb on right little finger	thumb on right fourth finger

Figure 19. tala jhaptal

232

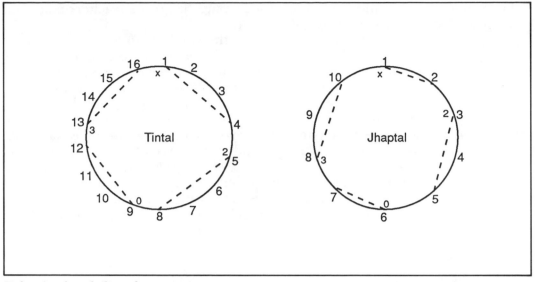

Talas tintal and *jhaptal*

     the right hand outward on beat six; and counting the intervening beats on the fingers.

    (3)   The *sitar* player begins to improvise again. Listen for the increasingly elaborate melodic phrases and the accelerando to a faster tempo.

7. Listen to the Beatles perform George Harrison's "Love You To" from the album *Revolver*, side one, band four. Listen for the combination of Indian and Western instruments and the "Indian" form: starting with a slow introduction in free, flexible rhythm with the main melody played on the *sitar* and then moving to a medium tempo main segment in strict rhythm with singers, *sitar*, *tabla*, and the Western addition of guitars.

8. Summarize on the board what you have learned in this lesson: some characteristics of *ragas*, including distinctive ascending and descending forms ornamentation, moods, and performance times; the formal sections of Indian compositions called *alap*, followed by *chiz* (in vocal music) or *gat* (in instrumental music), in turn followed by increasingly elaborate, improvised phrases; *jhaptal* with ten beats subdivided into unequal groups (2 + 3 + 2 + 3); and Western popular music, combining Indian and Western musical traits.

Integrating music with other subjects

    Helping students attain an understanding of the cultural context is an important part of any program devoted to teaching Indian music. Students enjoy learning about other peoples, their customs and crafts, their architecture, sculpture, painting, literature, dance, and music. Through the interrelated study of many aspects of a culture, they develop new understandings of other people. They also begin to realize the integral place of the arts in many aspects of a society.

233

The following are some suggestions for helping classroom teachers place the study of music in a broader cultural context:

1. Plan a study of Indian geography. Ask the students to locate India on a globe. Compare its size to that of the United States. Develop a bulletin board with a map of India in the center. Have the students draw or trace the map and include the various states of the country. Identify some of the most important cities with stick-pin flags. Study the various kinds of terrain found throughout the country: the gigantic mountains in the north (Himalayas), the fertile river valleys such as the Ganges, the parched deserts such as those in Rajasthan, and the balmy seacoasts areas found in Kerala and other areas. Look for pictures that illustrate different geographical areas. *National Geographic* magazine provides good sources for pictures (see the Bibliography for specific examples).

2. Look for pictures of Indian architecture, sculpture, and painting. (One source is the journal *Asian Art*, listed in the Bibliography.) These should include Hindu and Muslim temples and the Taj Mahal, sculptures of Hindu gods and goddesses, and numerous intricately designed, multi colored "miniature" paintings. Place these on the bulletin board.

3. Encourage students to visit the library, find books about India, and read about the many different cultural groups. Encyclopedia articles, such as those found in the *World Book Encyclopedia*, are good sources of information.

4. Invite Indians living in the community to come and speak to your students. The students will enjoy seeing the native costumes.

5. Discuss the most important religions of India, Hinduism and Islam, pointing out some of their central beliefs. Children are particularly fascinated to learn why certain animals, such as cows, are held in such high regard. Veronica Ions's *Indian Mythology* (see Bibliography) provides a good introduction to the subject for teachers. Since Hindu temples and Muslim mosques are now located in the United States, it may be possible to arrange a visit to one of these centers.

6. A number of Indians now living in the United States have had excellent training in traditional dance. Search your Indian community for someone who could perform for your students. Also view some of the videotapes on dance listed at the end of this chapter.

7. Show films on India (see the annotated list of films in the Filmography). India also has one of the largest movie industies in the world, and many Indian films are now shown in many areas of the United States, particularly in metropolitan areas. Students may enjoy attending one of these.

BIBLIOGRAPHY

Asian Art. This journal is a publication of the Smithsonian Institution and is available from the Journals Department, Oxford University Press, 16–00 Pollitt Drive, Fair Lawn, NJ 07410. It is a good source for pictures of Indian architecture, sculpture, and painting.

Barnett, Elise B., ed. *Ravi Shankar: Learning Indian Music.* Los Angeles: Ravi Shankar Music Circle (7911 Willoughby Avenue, Los Angeles, CA 90046), n.d. This book, with three audiocassettes, presents the fundamentals of Indian music.

Bussagli, Mario, and Calembus Sivaramurti. *Five Thousand Years of the Art of India.* New York: Harry N. Abrams, n.d. This book includes pictures and information about India.

Deneck, Marguerite-Maria. *Indian Art.* London: Paul Hamlyn, 1967. This book is a good source of reproductions of Indian art.

Edwards, Mike, and Roland Michaud. "Paradise on Earth: When the Moguls Ruled India," *National Geographic* 167, no. 4, April 1985, 463–93. This article contains photographs and information about India.

Feldman, Jeffrey M., comp. *Learning Tabla with Alla Rakha.* Los Angeles: Ravi Shankar Music Circle, n.d. This book includes a manual and an audiocassette and presents a systematic approach to rhythmic solfège and principles of improvisation and composition. It also includes an appendix on adapting lessons to Western percussion instruments.

Hodgson, Bryan, and Steve Raymer. "Mirror of India: New Delhi," *National Geographic* 167, no. 4, April 1985, 506–33. This article contains photographs and information about present-day India.

Holroyde, Peggy. *The Music of India.* New York: Praeger, 1972. This interesting book, about many facets of Indian music, is written for the general reader.

Ions, Veronica. *Indian Mythology.* London: Paul Hamlyn, 1967. This is a good introduction to Indian religions: Hinduism, Buddhism, and Jainism.

Jairazbhoy, N. A. *The Rags of North Indian Music.* Middletown, CT: Wesleyan University Press, 1971. This book contains a detailed discussion of *rags* [*ragas*] in north India; chapter one on present-day classical music is particularly recommended. A record is included with Vilayat Khan playing *sitar*; he illustrates the characteristics of eight *rags*.

Kaufmann, Walter. *The Ragas of North India.* Bloomington: Indiana University Press, 1968. This paperback contains a detailed discussion of the *ragas* of north Indian music. It is useful for the teacher who is looking for information on the characteristics of various *ragas*.

Lee, Sherman E. *Far Eastern Art.* Englewood Cliffs, NJ: Prentice-Hall, and New York: Harry N. Abrams, n.d. This book contains information about Indian art.

Munro, Eleanor C. *The Encyclopedia of Art.* New York: Golden Press, 1961. This book contains photographs of Indian architecture, sculpture, and painting.

Neuman, Daniel M. *The Life of Music in North India.* Detroit: Wayne State University Press, 1980. This is a well-written study of music in the culture of north India.

Putman, John J. "Focus on India: Festivals across U.S. Celebrate a Diverse Culture," *National Geographic* 167, no. 4, April 1985, 460–61. This article contains photographs and information about India.

Sadie, Stanley, ed. *The New Grove Dictionary of Music and Musicians.* London: Macmillan, 1980. An outstanding section on the music of India is included in volume 9, pp. 69–166.

Satow, Michael G. "India's Railway Lifeline," *National Geographic* 165, no. 6, June 1984, 744–49. This article contains both information and photographs.

Scofield, John, and Raghubir Singh. "Bombay, the Other India," *National Geographic* 160, no. 1, July 1981, 105–29. This article contains information and pictures about the metropolis of Bombay.

Shankar, Ravi. *My Music, My Life.* New York: Simon and Schuster, 1968. This paperback contains one of the best short descriptions of north Indian music. Pictures of musical instruments are provided as well as a section on learning to play the *sitar*.

Sivaramurti, Calembus. *5000 Years of the Art of India.* New York: Harry N. Abrams, n.d. This is a good source of art reproductions.

Theroux, Paul, and Steve McCurry. "By Rail across the Indian Subcontinent," *National Geographic* 165, no. 6, June 1984, 696–749. This is a source of pictures and information about India.

Titon, Jeff, ed. *Worlds of Music.* New York: Schirmer, 1984. This book includes chapters on Indian music, instrument building, and performance.

Wade, Bonnie C. *Music in India: The Classical Traditions.* Englewood Cliffs, NJ: Prentice-Hall, 1979. This book provides a concise introduction to both the north Indian (Hindustani) and south Indian (Carnatic) musical traditions. It includes an annotated bibliography, discography, filmography, and glossary.

Wade, Bonnie C. "Some Principles of Indian Classical Music." In *Musics of Many Cultures*, edited by Elizabeth May. Berkeley: University of California Press, 1980, 83–110. This article serves as an excellent introduction to Indian music. It includes a selected bibliography, discography, and filmography.

Welch, Stuart C. *India: Art and Culture, 1300–1900.* New York: Metropolitan Museum of Art and Holt, Rinehart and Winston, 1985. This book contains good photographs of Indian architecture, sculpture, and painting.

235

FILMOGRAPHY

Bismillah Khan. 29 minutes, black-and-white. Available from Indiana University Audiovisual Center, Bloomington 47401. This is an excellent film featuring India's foremost *shahnai* (double-reed aerophone) performer, Bismillah Khan.

Classical Music of North India. 35 minutes, color. Available from University of Washington, Instructional Media Services, 23 Kane Hall, DG-10, Seattle 98195. This film features the distinguished *sarod* performer Ali Akbar Khan.

Discovering the Music of India. 22 minutes, color, BFA Educational Media, 2211 Michigan Avenue, Santa Monica, CA 90404. This film contains excellent examples of both north and south Indian music. South Indian examples include music played on the flute (*venu*), the drum (*mridangam*), violin, and *tambura.* It features north Indian music played on the *sitar* and *tabla.* A short example of Indian dance is also included.

God with a Green Face. 25 minutes, color. Available from University of Missouri Academic Support Center, 505 East Steward Road, Columbia, 65211. This film is about *Kathakali,* the brilliant dance-drama from the southwestern state of Kerala.

Kathak: North Indian Dance. Available from The Asia Society, Performing Arts Department, 725 Park Avenue, New York 10021. Birju Maharaj and Company appear in this presentation, which includes *vandana* (prayer dance), a *kathak* solo demonstration of pure dance movement and intricate rhythms, and *Geetopadesh,* the gambling scene between the Pandava and the Kaurava princes in a story from the Mahabharata.

Kathakali: South Indian Dance-Drama from the Kerala Kalamandalam. Videocassette. Available from The Asia Society, Performing Arts Department, 725 Park Avenue, New York 10021. Dating from the sixteenth century, the *Kathakali* dance-drama is India's most dynamic epic theater form. *Kathakali* performance technique stems in part from a vigorous martial arts tradition. The form is a fascinating combination of music, a sung text, mime, and dance with rich costumes and elaborate makeup.

Music of North India: Vijay Raghav Rao (Flute). 29 minutes, color. Beveridge James, 1974. Available from Bureau of Audiovisual Instruction, University of Wisconsin, Madison 53701. This film shows how a flutist of India relates to other musicians as he plays and gives some background on the performer and Indian culture. Rao is seen in concert and with his family.

Musical Tradition in Benares. 40 minutes, color. R. Hartman, 1974. Available from Bureau of Audiovisual Instruction, University of Wisconsin, Madison 53701. This film provides a view of how some people in India practice traditional classical music in their homes and depicts family involvement and children's early musical training. It features singing and instrumental music.

Percussion Sounds. 18 minutes, color. Churchill Films, 662 North Robertson Boulevard, Los Angeles 90069. This film contains a short example of a *tabla* composition.

Sitara. Videocassette. Available from The Asia Society, Performing Arts Department, 725 Park Avenue, New York 10021. India's most celebrated *kathak* dancer, Sitara, performs an invocation to the elephant god Ganesha, as well as *Tora Tukra,* a pure dance form that emphasizes time measure and different rhythmic patters; *Mayur Nritya,* the dance of the peacock; and *Tatkar,* in which the intricate footwork displays *kathak*'s complicated and varied rhythms.

String Sounds. 18 minutes, color. Churchill Films, 662 North Robertson Boulevard, Los Angeles 90069. This film is about stringed instruments throughout the world and contains a short performance on the *sitar* accompanied by *tabla* and *tambura.*

Yamini Krishnamurti: South Indian Dance. Videocassette. Available from The Asia Society, Performing Arts Department, 725 Park Avenue, New York 10021. A virtuoso of south Indian dance, Yamini Krishnamurti performs in two classical styles. In the *bharata natyam* style, she presents "Navarasa Slokam" (The Nine Classical Sentiments), and in the romantic, ebullient style of *kuchipudi,* she dances "Manduka Sabdam" (The Frog Who Became a Queen). The program ends with "Tillana," a pure, abstract *bharata natyam* dance.

DISCOGRAPHY

Editor's note: Recordings of Indian music can be obtained from Ali Akbar College Store, 215 West End Avenue, San Rafael, California 94901. This company offers an excellent selection of records, audiocassettes, and compact discs of Indian vocal and instrumental music. Write for a catalog. Ravi Shankar Music Circle (7911 Willoughby Avenue, Los Angeles 90046) also offers a large selection of records and audiocassettes, and has a catalog available. Schwann Record and

Tape Catalogs (535 Boylston Street, Boston 02116) prints a list of commercial records of Indian music that are commercially available.

The Beatles. *Revolver.* Capitol ST-2576. Features Indian instruments and Indian musical form on the selection "Love You To."

Hariprasad Chaurasia, Flute Concert. RSD-22. Available from Ravi Shankar Music Circle, 7911 Willoughby Avenue, Los Angeles 90046. This recording features two of Indias most outstanding contemporary performers: Hariprasad Chaurasia, flute, accompanied by Zakir Hussain, *tabla,* Performing in *raga madhuvanti.*

Improvisations. RSD-6. Available from Ravi Shankar Music Circle, 7911 Willoughby Avenue, Los Angeles 90046. This recording features Ravi Shankar on *sitar* and Paul Horn and Bud Shank on flutes. Combines Indian melodic and rhythmic modes with jazz to produce an exciting contemporary musical ensemble.

Improvisations—West Meets East: Yehudi Menuhin, Ravi Shankar, and Jean-Pierre Rampal. Angel SFO-37200. This is an interesting intercultural recording containing four compositions by Ravi Shankar, who is joined by Yehudi Menuhin on violin, Jean-Pierre Rampal on flute, Martine Geliot on harp, and Alla Rakha on *tabla.*

Indian Street Music: The Bauls of Bengal. Nonesuch 72035. This recording contains Indian folk music, vocal and instrumental, by one of India's most interesting ethnic groups, the "Bauls of Bengal."

Ustad Ali Akbar Khan—Soul of the Sarod. Oriental BGRP 1041. Also available from the Ali Akbar College Store, 215 West End Avenue, San Rafael, California 94901. One of India's greatest *sarod* players is accompanied on *tabla* by Swapan Chaudri on this recording.

Ravi Shankar's Festival of India. RSMC-33. Available from Ravi Shankar Music Circle, 7911 Willoughby Avenue, Los Angeles 90046. This two-album set contains vocal selections, including a Vedic hymn, a *khyal,* a *thumri,* and instrumental selections featuring the *shahnai, sarod, sitar, santur, sarangi, rebab,* and flute.

Ravi Shankar's Introduction to Indian Classical Music. RSMC-4. Available from Ravi Shankar Music Circle, 7911 Willoughby Avenue, Los Angeles, 90046. This audiocassette features Ravi Shankar introducing Indian classical music with actual musical examples.

Sarangi, the Voice of a Hundred Colors. Nonesuch II-72030. Ram Narayan gives masterful performances on the *sarangi,* a north Indian bowed stringed instrument.

The Sounds of India: Ravi Shankar. Columbia CL 9296. This record contains four north Indian instrumental compositions performed by Ravi Shankar; an explanation of the *raga* and *tala* used is given before each performance.

China and Japan
Note: Map is not to scale.

CHAPTER EIGHT

8

EAST ASIA

by Han Kuo-Huang, Ricardo D. Trimillos, and William M. Anderson

The term East Asia (used interchangeably with "the Far East" and "the Orient") can be defined in three ways: geographically, racially, and culturally. Geographically, this chapter will include the area from the Mongolian Plateau in the north to the monsoon coastline of southeastern China and the western Tibetan mountains to the eastern volcanic Japanese islands. Before the modern industrial age, geographical barriers kept this vast area fairly independent from the rest of the world, resulting in a unique culture.

The majority of East Asian people belong to the Mongoloid race, one of the three major racial classifications of humanity. Mongoloidan people are characterized by yellowish skin, brown eyes, and straight, black hair. Numerous subgroups of different languages, dialects, customs, and habits exist throughout this region. The largest linguistic division is the Sino-Tibetan family of languages: Tibetan, Mandarin, and many Chinese dialects belong to this family. The second largest group is the Altaic languages: The Mongolian, Korean, and Japanese languages belong to this classification.[1] The majority of people who speak these languages practice various forms of Buddhism, while a minority practice Islam and Christianity.

East Asia was ruled for hundreds of years by the highly developed civilization of China and was sometimes referred to as the "Chinese culture area." Despite the close association with China, each country or region also developed its own

239

unique culture. The major cultural divisions of East Asia are China (mainland China and Taiwan), Japan, Korea, Mongolia, and Tibet (an autonomous region of China). In a sense, Vietnam, though a country in Southeast Asia, is also culturally related to East Asia (see Chapter 9). This chapter focuses on China and Japan.

CHINA

The immense land mass of China, which stretches across more than three million square miles, is slightly smaller than continental Europe and larger than the continental United States. Only the Soviet Union and Canada exceed China in size. The country is enclosed by high plateaus or towering mountains on three sides and is sheltered by the Pacific Ocean on the east and southeast. The country can be broadly divided into five principal regions: Northeast (Manchuria), North (Yellow River area), South (Yangzi River area and southeastern coast), Tibet, and Northwest.[2]

Since about four-fifths of the land is composed of mountains and plateaus, the eastern plains are heavily cultivated and densely populated. The majority of Chinese people who live in the plains are farmers. This eastern portion (with the exception of the northeast) has served as the heartland of Chinese culture. Two great rivers, the Yellow and the Yangzi, pass from west to east and play key roles in the lives of Chinese people. Each river also represents one of the two conventional north-south divisions of Chinese culture: The Yellow River is the cradle of Chinese civilization, and the Yangzi River is the Chinese equivalent of the Mississippi.

China's population is close to one billion—the largest in the world. One of every four persons on earth is Chinese. The majority of the Chinese people belong to the Han people, who were named for the great Han Dynasty. They make up 94 percent of the total population, so the Chinese culture we know is essentially the Han culture. The remaining 6 percent of the population is composed of fifty-five national minorities scattered over 50 to 60 percent of the country. They live mostly in mountainous hinterlands or border areas. Their languages and customs may be totally assimilated in the dominant culture or completely foreign. For instance, the Manchu in the Northeast are highly Sinicized, but the Uygur in Xinjiang (northwest region) are Turkic people whose religion is Islam and whose culture is Central Asian.

The Han Chinese are further divided into various subgroups, each of which has its own dialect and customs. A northerner would not understand a southern dialect and vice versa. For thousands of years, the unifying element of the people has been a common written language. The language is based on single characters; many characters have been formed from a representative picture of the word.

Since the early twentieth century, the Beijing dialect (Mandarin) has been adopted as the national language. Like many African languages, Mandarin is a tonal language with four levels of intonation for each phoneme. This means that a phonetic can have four meanings depending on the tonal level at which it is

240

pronounced, and the written character for each one of the four is different. For instance, "ma" can mean "mother" (with *ping*, or even intonation), "hemp" (with *shang*, or rising intonation), "horse" (with *qu*, or falling intonation), or "to curse" (with *ru*, or entering intonation, an abrupt downward pitch glide) Its monosyllabic nature and changing tones distinguish Mandarin from Western languages, which are written with combinations of letters in an alphabet.

Many Westerners believe that Chinese people subscribe to three major religions: Confucianism (native), Daoism (native), and Buddhism (imported from India). To the Chinese, however, Confucianism is a code of ethics rather than a religion. Its philosophical principles permeate many aspects of their lives and merge with Daoism, Buddhism, and Christianity. The Chinese are able to embrace two or more philosophical and religious beliefs without contradiction. The following anecdote reflects this: "When a man is in a position of authority he is a Confucianist, because that doctrine supports the status quo. Out of power or office, a man becomes a Taoist, because Taoism deprecates both worldly authority and individual responsibility. As death approaches, a man turns to Buddhism, because that faith offers hope of salvation."[3] No matter what religion a Chinese person embraces, the most fundamental principle in his or her life is the filial piety that is realized in the practice of ancestor worship.

The Chinese refer to their country as *Zhongguo*, which is literally translated as "The Middle Country": In ancient times, the Chinese considered their locality to be the center of the world and their culture far superior to those of surrounding peoples. In a historical and cultural sense, *Zhongguo* is more appropriately translated by Western authors as "The Middle Kingdom." The Han Chinese have lived and worked in this Middle Kingdom for more than four thousand years.

The legendary history of China begins with the Five Emperors Period (2250–2140 B.C.). The Zhou Dynasty succeeded the Five Emperors Period and set up a system of feudal lords. By the end of the Zhou Dynasty, the feudal lords were in constant battle, and a powerful lord was needed to unite the country. Qin Shi Huang became the First Emperor of China in 221 B.C. (the Qin Dynasty). Under his rule, the Chinese built the famous Great Wall and created thousands of terracotta warriors and horses. Imperial China lasted for two thousand years, and in 1912, the last emperor was dethroned and a republic was founded. Some of the important dynasties include the Zhou (1122–221 B.C.), Han (206 B.C.–220 A.D.), Tang (618–907), Sung (960–1127), Yuan or Mongolian (1278–1368), Ming (1368–1644), and Qing, the Manchu (1644–1912).

Unlike many ancient civilizations that have risen and fallen, Chinese culture has continued uninterrupted for thousands of years. The numerous contributions the Chinese offer to the world are not limited to philosophy and applied science, but include the arts. Chinese bronze casting, jade carving, ceramic making, sculpture, painting, calligraphy, and music are highly valued throughout the world.

Chinese music

When discussing Han Chinese music, it is common to distinguish two major styles: northern and southern. The styles correspond to the two major geographical and cultural areas where most Han people live. Although both styles

241

emanate from the general Han Chinese culture, they differ in detail because of environmental conditions. The north is cold, dry, and windy. The hardships of life are reflected in the high-pitched, tense, and agitated style of folk song. The south, on the other hand, has mild weather and much rain. Life seems to be easier, and the folk songs of the south are generally lyrical and gentle in nature. Chinese music today is also influenced by Western musical concepts, which is an inevitable consequence of historical and social change.

The common belief that the Chinese scale is a pentatonic scale (without half steps, as on the black keys of the piano) is only partly correct. The Han Chinese have at least three forms of a seven-tone scale (see figure 1). They also use various forms of a five-tone pentatonic scale (see figure 2).

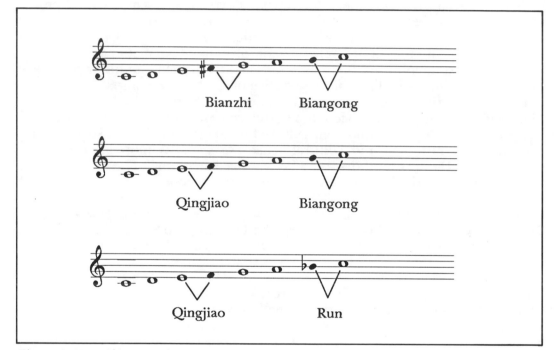

Figure 1. Han Chinese and seven-tone scales

Southern Chinese folk songs tend to progress in more conjunct motion and smoother lines and emphasize the intervals of thirds and fifths. Northern melodies tend to progress in more disjunct, angular motion, and emphasize intervals of a fourth. These tendencies in the use of melodies are related to the tonal characteristics of the contrasting dialects of the two areas.

Except in special cases (such as free-rhythm introductions), most Chinese music is in duple rhythm. This fondness for duple rhythm (the Western equivalent of $\frac{2}{4}$ and $\frac{4}{4}$) can be attributed to the belief in the principle of natural duality (such as the female-male or yin-yang relationship). Chinese rhythm patterns may also reflect the Confucian *Zhongyong* concept: a "doctrine of the

242

Figure 2. Han Chinese pentatonic scales

mean" that stresses moderation and balance. However, the weak beat to strong beat stresses in Western music are not necessarily used. Triple meter is rare, even in modern folk compositions. Syncopation, on the other hand, is the norm rather than the exception.

Chinese instrumental music is traditionally heterophonic if it is performed on more than one instrument or for an instrument and voice. Although Chinese music does not use the triadic, four-part harmonic progressions of Western music, harmony may occur occasionally. In fact, the *sheng* mouth organ produces fourths and fifths when played in the traditional manner, and some *qin* and *zheng* zither passages have two or more pitches sounding together when the musicians pluck two or more strings simultaneously. The Chinese people's fondness for clarity may have prevented them from developing a heavy musical texture.

Perhaps the most intricate aspect of traditional Chinese music, and of much East Asian music, is the use of nuance in instrumental and vocal timbre. Even when playing one instrument, there are minute differences in timbre production of a single tone. Much attention is placed on the production and control of single

243

tones; each tone is regarded as a musical entity. The best example of this is heard in *qin* zither music.

Vocal music is also complicated because of complex tonal inflections and the intricacies of the Chinese language. For example, even though Chinese words are monosyllabic, a singer takes great care in enunciating the "head" (beginning), "belly" (middle), or "tail" (end) of each word in Kun opera and Nanguan music. Therefore, timbre in Chinese music has a deeper meaning than simply tone color as an end in itself.

Chinese vocal quality is often described as being high-pitched and nasal. This is generally true, but again, there are regional differences. The northern style of singing (such as Peking opera) tends to be higher and more shrill than the southern style of singing (such as Kun opera or Nanguan). This north-south contrast in vocal quality can even be heard in the local Baiguan (northern-style theater) and Nanquan (southern-style theater or lyric song) on the island of Taiwan.

Thousands of indigenous and Sinicized musical instruments exist in China, but the Chinese seem to favor chordphones and aerophones. The famous term "silk and bamboo" refers to the ancient use of stringed instruments with silk strings and wind instruments made of bamboo. Of all the chordphones, the *qin* zither is by far the most venerated. It is depicted in many paintings and mentioned in classic literature. Next in importance to the *qin* zither is the *zheng* zither. In the past, solos and small ensembles were more characteristic of traditional Chinese music making; the large Chinese orchestra with a baton-waving conductor is a product of the twentieth century.

The *pipa* lute originated in Central Asia and is an instrument of great virtuosic possibilities. It is the subject of many paintings and poems and has held a societal position similar to that of the guitar in Western culture. Currently, the *erhu*, or two-stringed fiddle, is the most popular instrument in China. It originated in the northern tribes and is available in many sizes and variations. This fiddle is the "violin" of the modern Chinese orchestra. The *sanxian* lute is a banjo-like instrument that is used to accompany narrative singing. The *yangqin* is a many-stringed hammered dulcimer that originated in Persia. Its function is somewhat like that of the piano: It serves as either a solo instrument or an accompanying instrument.

In the aerophone category, *di* or *dizi* side-blown flutes are the most numerous. The *xiao* end-blown flute is also a popular instrument. Perhaps the most exotic wind instrument is the *sheng*, a mouth organ that can produce many notes simultaneously. A popular folk wind instrument is the *suona*, a double-reed instrument that evolved from the Middle Eastern *zurna*. Because of recent archaeological discoveries, Chinese musicians have had a revived interest in the ancient *bianzhong* (bronze bell chimes) and *bianqing* (stone chimes). Variations of many Chinese musical instruments can be found in Japan, Korea, Vietnam, Tibet, and Mongolia.

Westerners sometimes describe Chinese music as "loud." The Chinese themselves consider the northern style more dynamic and energetic and the southern style softer and more graceful. All of these characterizations are oversimplified: The dynamics in Chinese music actually vary according to the nature of the musical genres and instruments. The classical music of Confucian scholars, such

244

as *qin* zither music and lyric songs, are naturally soft. Players of *pipa* lute music are capable of expressing a full range of dynamics. Music for the *suona* is loud and piercing because of the instrument's construction and its function as an outdoor instrument. Theater orchestra music is loud because it was originally played outdoors in a festive atmosphere. Because of the many factors affecting dynamics in Chinese music, there is no one concept that can adequately describe them.

With the exception of work songs and *shange* (mountain songs) most Han Chinese folk songs, like most songs in Western folk music, are constructed in strophic form. Chinese folk music, however, uses fewer refrains. Typically, a folk song consists of two or four phrases of equal length; each phrase contains a new musical idea. Two-phrase songs are called "question-answer" songs, and four-phrase songs "open" (*qi*), "inheriting" (*cheng*), "turned" (*zhuan*), and "closed" (*he*) songs, all of which are terms borrowed from literary writing techniques. Much of Chinese opera music is based on a more complex melodic and rhythmic motivic system called *Banqian*.[4]

Of all the instrumental forms of Chinese music, the most popular are suites and variations. These forms are not, however, entirely equivalent to their Western counterparts. A Chinese suite is a series of musical movements that are loosely connected. These movements may be independent selections that do not have an apparent melodic or rhythmic relationship, or they may be related for programmatic reasons.

A major characteristic of Chinese instrumental variations is the use of identification motives called the *hetou* (refrain head) or *hewei* (refrain tail) that appear in the beginning and end of each movement. Again, except for these refrain motives, there might be no other relationship between the variations and the refrains or among the variations themselves. Sometimes, a movement appears several times among the other movements in a suite; this is considered a variation technique. Due to Western influence, ABA form has become extremely popular in modern instrumental folk music.

The Chinese have traditionally shown a fondness for extramusical connotations, so program music, poetic titles, and descriptions of compositions are popular. The existence of a sophisticated literary class is responsible for shaping this tradition, which is found not only in old music but also in modern socialist and so-called revolutionary works.

L E S S O N   O N E

1

■ **OBJECTIVES:**
Students will:
1. Sing the songs "The Eldest Daughter of the Jiang Family" and "Jasmine Flowers of the Sixth Moon."
2. Identify the pentatonic scales in each song.

245

3. Identify the use of duple (quadruple) meter and syncopation.
4. Identify strophic form.

Materials:
Pictures of the Great Wall of China (See Kenneth C. Danforth, editor, *Journey into China*, Washington, DC: National Geographic Society, 1982)

■ PROCEDURES:
1. Sing "The Eldest Daughter of the Jiang Family" (see figure 3) and "Jasmine Flowers of the Sixth Moon" (see figure 4). The first song is about a woman

2. The lotus trembles in the summer heat,
   Flying insects fill the evening air,
   Let them feast on my limbs tender and frail,
   lest they should torment my love Xi Liang.

3. Autumn flowers gild the Ninth Moon,
   Wine cups pass round where the asters bloom,
   My cup untouched, brimming like by tears,
   Since my love is away, I cannot drink wine.

4. Winter ushers in ice and snow,
   Meng Jiang Nü toils a thousand miles through,
   I trudge alone, for I hear the call
   Of my love dying by the Great Wall.

Figure 3.

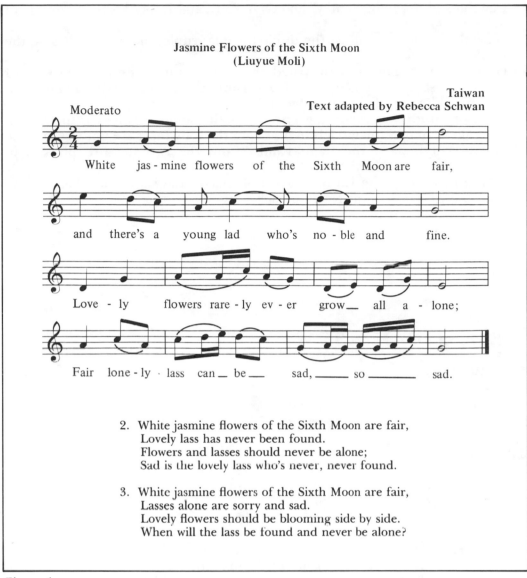

Figure 4.

who thinks of her husband, who has gone off to build the Great Wall. Students should look for good pictures of the Great Wall to place on the bulletin board. The second song, "Jasmine Flowers of the Sixth Moon," is from southern China and is about a girl who compares herself to jasmine flowers. "Sixth moon" means the sixth month of the lunar calendar, which is in the spring.

2. Have the students write the five pitches of the pentatonic melodies for each song on the board. These pitches are G, A, B, D, and E for "The Eldest

Daughter of the Jiang Family" and G, A, C, D, and E for "Jasmine Flowers of the Sixth Moon."

3. Have the students conduct the duple (or quadruple) meter as they sing the songs.
4. Have the class clap the syncopated rhythms found in the first measure of "The Eldest Daughter of the Jiang Family" and the sixth measure of "Jasmine Flowers of the Sixth Moon."
5. Have the students outline the phrases of the songs by moving their right arms alternately right and left in time with the four-measure phrases in "The Eldest Daughter of the Jiang Family" and the two-measure phrases in "Jasmine Flowers of the Sixth Moon."
6. As the class sings the various verses of text to the same melodies, calling attention to the strophic form of each song.

L E S S O N T W O

■ OBJECTIVES:
Students will:
1. Play in a Chinese percussion ensemble.
2. Perform several compositions with percussion instruments.

Materials:
1. Cymbals
2. Small gongs played with a thin wooden mallet
3. Large gongs played with a padded mallet
4. Large drums played with two thick sticks

■ PROCEDURES:
1. Give the students this background information:
The Chinese call their percussion ensemble *Luogu*, which means "gongs and drums" (see figure 13). It may range in size from two to several players. Percussion ensembles are used in a variety of settings, in theaters, parades, and folk music groups. The four major instruments used in Chinese percussion music are *bo* cymbals, the *xiaoluo* (small gong), the *daluo* (large gong), and the *dagu* (large "skinned" drum). If Chinese instruments are not available, use Western substitutes such as drums, tam-tam, and small cymbals.
2. Perform the Lion Dance Number 1, Lion Dance Number 2 (see figure 5), and Dragon Dance (see figure 6). Read the following performance instructions before proceeding.
   a. The drummer is the leader of the ensemble and sets the tempo (approximately ♩ = 100–112) by striking the drum twice on the rim before each

Figure 5.

Figure 6.

249

selection (indicated in the score by the x-shaped note heads). Each composition repeats in ostinato fashion. To end the performance the drummer should play the ending signal, which is a drum roll followed by two eighth notes, shown just below the appropriate measure of the score. This signal leads the group to the conclusion.

  b. Perform each composition alone. When composition is mastered, play all of them together as a suite, repeating the individual segments as many times as you wish. When played as a suite, only the introductory signal for the first piece is used; the ending measures of the first and second pieces are omitted. The "ending signals" in the first and second pieces become "changing signals" for the next section.

LESSON THREE

■ OBJECTIVES:

Students will:

1. Sing the song "Fuhng Yang Wa Gu" (Feng Yang Hua Gu: Flower drum song) and identify the pentatonic scale and the quadruple meter.
2. Accompany the song with percussion instruments.

Materials:

1. Cymbals
2. Small gongs played with a thin wooden mallet
3. Large gongs played with a padded mallet
4. Large drums played with two thick sticks

■ PROCEDURES:

1. Have the class sing "Fuhng Yang Wa Gu" (Flower drum song) (see figure 7).[5] Explain that this is one of the most famous Chinese folk songs. It even became the title of a Broadway musical. Traditionally, the song is sung by a girl who dances and plays a small, flower-decorated drum attached to her waist. Another person, usually a man, plays an accompaniment on a small gong. The words *Drr ling dang piao e piao* mimic the sounds produced by the drum. The students can imitate the drum rolls by rolling their tongues on the syllable *drr*. Notice the pentatonic scale and the quadruple meter.

2. Add a percussion accompaniment as a prelude to the song. As accompaniment to the refrain, use *bo* (cymbals), *xialuo* (small gong), *daluo* (large gong), and *dagu* (large skin-headed drum) (see figure 8). You may substitute Western drums, tam-tam, and small cymbals.

Fuhng Yang Wha Gu

Moderately ♩=92

Tso_ shou_lo,   yu_shou_gu   Shou na___ to gu_

lai_ chang_guh,   Bieh de___ guh er,___   wo yeh be huei chang;

Jih huei_ chang guh _ fuhng_yang_guh,   Fuhng fuhng_ yang_guh_

refrain Fast ♩=144

c _ ao _ ya.   Drrr ling dang piao c piao, Drrr ling dang piao c piao,

Drrr piao, drrr piao, Drrr piao, drrr piao piao yu drrr, Ling dang piao e piao.

Left hand gong, right hand drum—
With drum and gong in hand
I come to sing;
Other tunes I do not know
But *Fung Yang* song . . .

Figure 7. From John M. Kelly, Folk Music in Hawaii *(Boston: Boston Music Co., 1965). Used by permission.*

Cymbals

Small gong

Large gong

Drum

Figure 8.

L E S S O N F O U R

4

■ **OBJECTIVES:**
Students will:
1. Listen to the *zheng* and *xiao* in the composition, "Winter Birds (Ravens) Flying Over the Water." Students should be able to identify the duple meter, heterophonic texture, and the programmatic character of the music.
2. Listen to the last two minutes of the programmatic composition, "The Hero's Defeat." This work is played on the *pipa*, a plucked, stringed instrument.
3. Listen to the composition, "Old Monk Sweeping the Buddhist Temple," played on the *sheng*.

Materials:
Recordings:
China's Instrumental Heritage, Lyrichord LLST 7921
Chinese Classical Masterpieces, Lyrichord LLST 7182

■ **PROCEDURES:**
1. Place a picture of the *zheng* on the bulletin board (see figure 9). Explain that the *zheng* is a zither with strings that run parallel across the instrument (an Autoharp is also a zither.) The number of strings on the *zheng* varies from sixteen to twenty-one. Originally, the strings were made of silk, but today they are brass. The instrument is tuned by moving the small bridges under each string, and the instrument is often tuned pentatonically. The *zheng* is traditionally played by plucking the strings with the right hand; in modern playing, performers also use the left hand. A great variety of subtle ornamentations are possible on this instrument.
2. Place a picture of a *xiao* on the bulletin board (see figure 10). The *xiao* is a vertically played flute constructed from bamboo. A notch is fashioned at the upper end of the instrument, and air is directed across it to produce sounds. The air moving across the notched area produces a distinctive, somewhat breathy tone. Different pitches are made possible by the six tone holes, five on top and one on the underside of the instrument.
3. Listen to the composition "Winter Birds (Ravens) Flying Over the Water" (on *China's Instrumental Heritage*, side two, band three), and point out how the title is depicted programmatically in the music (particularly in the sweeping, decorative quality of the melodic lines that captures the sense of birds flying over the water). Also note the distinctive heterophonic texture created by the use of two instruments that are basically playing the same melody with simultaneous variations. (Heterophonic texture is sometimes present in such Western musical genres as Dixieland.)
4. Write the following list on the board and circle the appropriate items as you listen to the music:

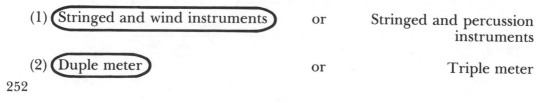

(1) (Stringed and wind instruments)   or   Stringed and percussion
                                                                    instruments

(2) (Duple meter)   or   Triple meter

252

(3) Major scale   or   (Pentatonic scale)

(4) (Soft dynamic level)   or   Loud dynamic level

(5) Chordal harmony   or   (Heterophony)

5. Place a picture of the *pipa* on the bulletin board (see figure 11). Explain that the *pipa* is a plucked stringed instrument similar to the Western guitar. Unlike our guitar, however, the *pipa* is held with the base end of the instrument resting on the lap with the neck standing more or less straight up. Sounds are produced by plucking the four strings of the instrument. Since the sounds of the vibrating strings die away quickly, *pipa* players pluck the

Figure 9. Professor Liang Tsai-Ping playing the zheng.

253

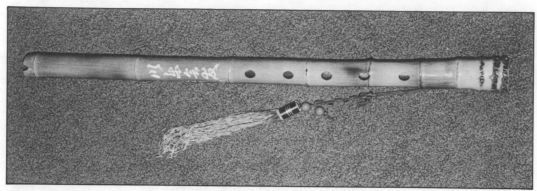

Figure 10. xiao

strings repetitively; rolling the fingers in a tremolo technique like that used on the flamenco guitar so that a nearly continuous sound is produced.

6. Explain that many of the compositions for the *pipa* are programmatic; that is, a program or story is depicted through music. In "Hero's Defeat," the *pipa* is used to depict a battle between the kingdoms of Han and Chu. The marching of the armies and the clashing of swords are vividly portrayed in the music.

7. As you listen to the last two minutes of the "Hero's Defeat" (on *Chinese Classical Masterpieces*, circle the items below:

   (1) Bowed stringed instrument   or   (Plucked stringed instrument)

   (2) Very slow tempo   or   (Moderate tempo)

   (3) (Duple meter)   or   Triple meter

   (4) (Program music)   or   ABA form

8. Listen to the composition "Old Monk Sweeping the Buddhist Temple" (on *China's Instrumental Heritage*, side one, band two) played on the *sheng* (see figure 12). Explain that the Chinese *sheng* is one of the most unusual wind instruments in the world. It is constructed with a rounded, bowl-shaped base from which extend many vertical bamboo pipes of different lengths. Each of these contains a small, "free" reed that is activated when air passes through the pipe. A mouthpiece is joined to the base of the instrument and the performer both exhales and inhales air into the instrument. To produce different pitches, the performer covers small holes located at the bottom of each bamboo pipe, making the air move through the pipe and activate a reed. One of the distinctive features of *sheng* music is produced by uninterrupted exhaling and inhaling, making a continuous sound on the instrument. Another feature is that a *sheng* player can play several notes at once—a kind of harmony—by covering the holes in several bamboo pipes at the same time.

9. The harmonica is a distant relative of the *sheng*. Bring a harmonica to class and demonstrate how "continuous" sound is produced by exhaling and

254

inhaling air through the instrument. Demonstrate how harmony is created by several different reeds being activated at the same time. Carefully remove the outer covering of the instrument and show the students the "free" reeds that are activated to produce the sound.

10. Have the students listen to "Old Monk Sweeping the Buddhist Temple" again, this time circling the appropriate items in the following list as they listen:

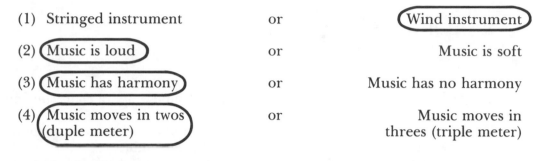

(1) Stringed instrument   or   (Wind instrument)

(2) (Music is loud)   or   Music is soft

(3) (Music has harmony)   or   Music has no harmony

(4) (Music moves in twos (duple meter))   or   Music moves in threes (triple meter)

Figure 11. A pipa *player*

Figure 12. sheng

255

11. Summarize the lesson by having the students discuss similarities and differences between Chinese instruments and instruments with which they are more familiar.

L E S S O N   F I V E

■ OBJECTIVES:

Students will:

1. Study Chinese opera by sketching pictures of Chinese opera characters and musical instruments.
2. Watch the film *A Night at the Peking Opera*, noting the elaborate costuming, the sparse staging, and the highly developed use of mime.
3. Listen to a brief segment of spoken dialogue and an aria from Peking opera, particularly noticing the tense, nasalized vocal quality.

Materials:

1. Illustrations of Chinese opera characters and instruments. One source is *Peking Opera: A Short Guide* by Elizabeth Halson (see Bibliography)
2. Film: *A Night at the Peking Opera* (see Filmography)
3. Recording: *The Chinese Opera*, Lyrichord, LLST 7212, side two, band three

■ PROCEDURES:

1. Explain that Chinese opera is a brilliant art form in which musical dramas are executed by elaborately attired actors who speak the dialogue and sing songs (arias). Among the interesting visual features of the opera are the beautiful costumes and the ornate make-up used by the characters. Each character is dressed in a distinctive costume to highlight his or her position in the drama.
2. Have the students sketch pictures of Chinese opera characters and musical instruments (using models from *Peking Opera: A Short Guide*), and place them on a bulletin board.
3. Watch the film *A Night at the Peking Opera*. This film contains several segments from different operas. Notice the elaborate costuming of the characters, the great attention placed on mime (specifically how the characters are able to create powerful effects through imaginative suggestion), and the distinctive spoken dialogue and singing style.
4. Listen to an aria from *The Chinese Opera*. This aria contains brief segments of dialogue and is sung by two characters who are accompanied by *huqin* and *erhu* (bowed stringed instruments), *dizi* (a flute), and percussion (see figure 13).

   Have the students pay particular attention to the singers' nasalized tone quality and lack of wide vibrato, the elongated speech patterns of the dialogue, the heterophonic nature of the accompanying stringed and wind instruments, and the punctuating and concluding percussion sounds.

256

As the students listen, have them circle the appropriate items:

(1) Voices only   or   (Voices and instruments)

(2) (Loud dynamic level)   or   Soft dynamic level

(3) (Nasalized tone colors)   or   Open, full sounds

(4) Brass instruments   or   (Percussion instruments)

(5) Chordal harmony   or   (Heterophony)

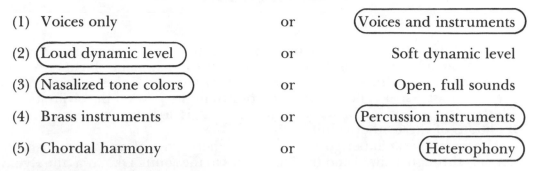

Figure 13A. An Erhu *player*

Figure 13C. A dizi *player*

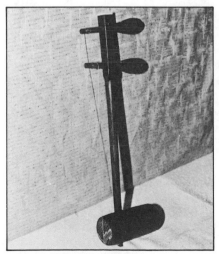

Figure 13B. hugin

Figure 13D. Students playing in a Chinese luogu *ensemble*

257

JAPAN

Japan forms the eastern boundary of northeast Asia and the Chinese culture area (the area in which Chinese cultural influence is dominant). Japanese culture is the East Asian culture most familiar to Americans, and serves as a summary of the northeast Asian experience: It has drawn in the past on the civilizations of China, Korea, and Okinawa. In one sense it is a living museum of some traditions of these other cultures.

The Japanese archipelago forms the northern part of an island chain that extends through Taiwan and the Philippines to the south. Okinawa (the Ryukyu Islands) was formerly an independent kingdom situated between Japan and the Philippines. It is now politically part of Japan but maintains a distinct culture. The central island of Honshu, where the capital city of Tokyo and the historical capitals of Kyoto and Nara are located, is the focal point for traditional Japanese culture as well as for many economic, religious, and political developments important to present-day Japan.

The islands are volcanic in origin, with dramatic, mountainous landscapes. The topography, climate, and geography of the islands have helped shape a cultural attitude of great respect and closeness to nature. The Japanese have survived in a harsh natural environment, featuring limited arable land, typhoons, earthquakes, and tidal waves. An aesthetic counterpoint is, however, provided to this harshness by hot springs, mountains, whirlpools, and lakes. The changes in the seasons are extreme. Most of Japan experiences seasons similar to the northeastern United States: cold, snowy winters and hot, humid summers. Spring and fall are transitions between these two extremes, times for celebrations such as cherry blossom viewing in the spring and rice festivals in the fall. Southern Japan is semitropical, which contrasts with the rest of the country. In Okinawa, tropical fruit such as pineapple and papaya can be found.

As an island nation, Japan's relation to the sea is a very special one. Rather than functioning as a barrier, the ocean serves as an important means for international contact and trade. Japanese merchant and military fleets have traveled throughout Asia and the Pacific. The Japanese have used this seagoing mobility to enrich their own culture as well as to influence other cultures. The sea is also the basis for such disparate industries as growing cultured pearls and oil supertanker construction. Finally, the sea is the source of the fish, shellfish, and seaweed that form a major part of Japanese cuisine. The staple food, rice, dominates the Japanese diet so much that the word for rice (*gohan*) also means meal. The important cycle of planting, growing, and harvesting rice is marked by a number of folk and court ceremonies. Rice is also the source of *sake*, the distinctive wine used for rituals such as marriages or the dedication of a shrine, as well as for general celebrations.

The ritual life of traditional Japan is greatly enriched by the presence of two belief systems: Shinto, an indigenous veneration of ancestors, and Buddhism, a religion introduced from China. Many Japanese families observe both Shinto and Buddhist rites, exhibiting a talent for accommodation that has served the Japanese well in both the cultural and economic spheres. Shinto has a rich

258

repertoire of music and dance used for its rituals and observances. Buddhism has had far-reaching effects on philosophy, aesthetics, and literature, and has also had a profound impact on the secular performing arts, particularly theater and music. Japan today is a fairly homogeneous society and is one of the few modern Asian nations that has had a single language throughout most of its history. The elite or "artistic" cultural traditions, in particular, encapsulate the Japanese cultural identity. It is therefore these formal traditions, rather than the regionally distinct folk traditions, that are discussed here.

History

In its first historical phase (Nara Period, 553–794 A.D.), Japan was greatly influenced by Chinese civilization and subsequently absorbed cultural streams from Korea and India as well. Buddhism was introduced from India via China, and court life borrowed much from the Qin and Tang courts. Buddhist chant and the ritual music of Shinto developed in this early era. The first Golden Age followed (Heian Period, 794–1185), in which foreign elements were assimilated, forming the basis for many Japanese traditions. The emperor unified political power, his divine right rule reinforced by Shinto principles. During this period, traditions of Buddhist music and *gagaku* court music were prevalent. In the fourteenth century, political unity disintegrated, the emperors lost their power, and a rising merchant class led to the development of popular theater and other entertainment traditions.

In the seventeenth century, Japan enjoyed a second Golden Age, politically unified by the military rule of the shogunate with its *samurai* warrior class. During this remarkable two centuries of conscious isolation from the rest of the world (Tokugawa Period, 1615–1868), the traditional arts as we know them reached their zenith: *kabuki* theater, lyric and narrative song traditions, the chamber music of *koto*, *shakuhachi* and *shamisen*, and the renewed sixth century *gagaku* court music, to name a few. In the last few decades of the nineteenth century (Meiji Restoration), Japan opened itself to the rest of the world, accepting and actively importing Western products and culture, including technology, public education systems, and music. This was a second era of internationalism, this time absorbing European and American sources rather than Chinese and Korean ones. Western-influenced folk song, such as "Sakura" (Cherry Blossoms), was a creation of this time (see lesson five).

The mercantile economy of the second Golden Age was joined by industrialization and colonial adventurism, a combination that led to World War II. At the conclusion of this war in 1946, familiarity with and interest in things Japanese increased, especially in the United States. The musical traditions of eighteenth- and nineteenth-century Tokugawa Japan were particularly appealing. At the same time, post-war Japan developed a cultural pluralism in which traditional music, European concert music, and a variety of international commercial musics all thrived.

Throughout its history, Japanese culture can be characterized as innovative rather than inventive. It is successful in borrowing items from other cultures and then changing, improving, and incorporating them into the cultural mainstream. This process of innovation is found in many parts of Japanese society. For example, it can be seen in musical instruments (the three-stringed *shamisen*

259

was developed from the Chinese *sanxian*), cuisine (*tonkatsu* is a Japanese version of the Austrian Wiener schnitzel), and manufacturing (lenses and cameras were originally made by German industries).

A grasp of Japanese values is helpful in understanding cultural attitudes toward music and the arts. First, great value is placed on preservation. Old artifacts, including musical instruments, are highly regarded and often revered. A particularly old musical instrument might be given a proper name. Second, there is a focus on form or design. For example, in music an often-used compositional form is *danmono*, a set of strict variations. Similarly, the triangle is popular in design; it provides the basic structure for *ikebana* (flower arrangement). Finally, the Japanese give great attention to formalism, the way in which tasks are accomplished. This attention is reflected by the prescribed order of brush strokes in writing *kanji* (Chinese ideographs), in the steps for folding a square piece of paper to produce an *origami* (folded paper) crane, and through the codified gestures and movements of *cha-no-yu* (the tea ceremony).

Music

Pentatonic melodies are quite common in Japanese music. However, the generalization that all Japanese music is pentatonic is not entirely true. There are often five main pitches in Japanese melodies (and therefore pentatonic orientation), but secondary pitches are also used, raising the total number of pitches to seven or ten. Indigenous folk melodies often use a pentatonic scale with two half-steps, as illustrated in the folksong "Kuroda-bushi" (see figure 14). There are also pentatonic melodies without half steps, as illustrated by the opening lines of the *gagaku* piece, "Etenraku" (in the tuning *hyojo*) (see figure 15). These melodies are based on scales that are derived from Chinese models.

Although there is some music that is in free meter, such as Buddhist chant or solo *shakuhachi* flute music, the majority of Japanese music is set in duple meter, usually in groups of four beats or multiples of four. The metric pulse may be reinforced by instrumental or body percussion (drums, gongs, or hand clapping).

Characteristics of rhythm include offbeat (or more accurately, between beat) syncopations, common in singing with the *koto* (thirteen-stringed zither) and rhythmic ostinatos such as the percussion patterns in *gagaku*. Another characteristic is a composite rhythm formed by two interlocking parts superimposed on one another. Such composite rhythm phrasing results from the interlocking *otsuzumi* hip drum and the *kotsuzumi* shoulder drum in *noh* and *kabuki* theater.

The most notable texture in Japanese music is heterophony, in which a single melody is sung or played and simultaneously varied in one or more independent lines. In Japanese heterophony, each line is rhythmically displaced from the others (this may be done in a number of ways), although the lines (as a sequence of pitches) are essentially the same. For example, in *koto*-accompanied song the melody line of the *koto* and that of the voice are heterophonic. In addition, monophony occurs, such as the chorus in *noh* theater or in *kagura* Shinto dance-song.

Polyphony also exists, although it is not as common. A second part, called *kaede* in the *koto* repertoire and *uwajoshi* in *nagauta shamisen* tradition, may be added (often by another composer) to composed pieces. Finally, there are instances in

260

kabuki theater in which a number of unrelated pieces are played at the same time to musically represent different aspects of the scene, yielding a texture that William P. Malm terms "multiphony."[6]

The timbres of Japanese music are generally heterogeneous rather than homogeneous; that is, each instrument has a unique tone color or timbre. Even the two indigenous bamboo flutes, the *shakuhachi* and the *nohkan,* have very different timbres within the constraints of the hollow sound produced by all flutes. Ensemble music makes use of the distinctive timbre of each instrument; the *sankyoku* chamber ensemble consists of *koto* (a zither), *shamisen* (a plucked lute), *shakuhachi* (an end-blown flute), and voice. The *shakuhachi* (see figure 16) itself illustrates how a number of different tone colors are produced by one instrument—its tone quality runs the gamut from a breathy, airy sound to a tightly focused one that sounds almost electronic.

Vocal performance also exploits a number of tone qualities. In theater traditions like *kabuki* and *bunraku,* there is a wide range of vocal sound that includes speech-like and shouted sounds as well as those more similar to our concept of singing. Most Japanese vocal production centers in the throat with little head resonance or vibrato. The quality, therefore, is direct and penetrating, closer to rock than to opera.

Attention to form is characteristic of Japanese tradition in general, and music is no exception. Music structure often follows an overall design of three parts, called *jo ha kyu.* The *jo* is the introduction, the *ha* presents the principal material, and the *kyu* is the drive toward the conclusion. In a single *gagaku* work, for example, the *jo ha kyu* design is expressed through tempo—the first part of the work (*jo*) is in flexible meter, the bulk of the piece (*ha*) maintains a slow and steady tempo, and the final part (*kyu*) increases both the tempo and the rhythmic density as it drives toward conclusion. This tripartite form is hierarchical. It governs multi-movement works; for example, the piece "Goshoraku" has three movements, called *jo, ha,* and *kyu,* respectively. On an even broader level it guides the arrangement of items in a program. For example, dance pieces (*bugaku*) constitute the *kyu* of a *gagaku* presentation and are placed at the end. The *jo ha kyu* design is also applied to *noh* drama and *shamisen* song traditions.

There are also specific composition forms. In *koto* music, there are two principal forms—one for *koto* compositions with song and one for purely instrumental compositions. The form for *koto* with song is *tegotomono.* It consists of three principal sections: the opening song (*maeuta*), the instrumental interlude (*tegoto*), and the closing song (*atouta*). The melodies of the opening and closing songs are not necessarily related so the form (in terms of melodic material) can be described as ABC, or progressive. However, the form still has the flavor of an ABA or closed form, since both the first and third sections are *koto* with song, while the second section is purely instrumental, a strong contrast in performing medium.

The second form is a set of variations, called *danmono.* Each variation must be 104 beats long, a limitation similar to the syllable count of *haiku* poetry. The best known *danmono* include one with six sections ("Rokudan") and one with eight sections ("Hachidan"). Interestingly, for these instrumental pieces the tempo increases toward the end, similar to the *jo ha kyu* treatment in *gagaku.*

LESSON ONE

■ **OBJECTIVES:**
Students will:
1. View and identify instruments of the Japanese *gagaku* orchestra.
2. Listen to the composition "Etenraku" played by a *gagaku* ensemble.
3. Identify the sound of the instruments.

Materials:
1. Pictures of *gagaku* instruments from William P. Malm's *Japanese Music and Musical Instruments*, Masataro Togi's *Performing Arts of Japan: V, Gagaku— Court Music and Dance*, and Shigeo Kishibe's *The Traditional Music of Japan* (see Bibliography)
2. Recording: *Gagaku, the Imperial Court Music of Japan*, Lyrichord LLST 7126 ("Etenraku")

■ **PROCEDURES:**
1. Show pictures of the Japanese *gagaku* court orchestra. Explain that the *gagaku* ensemble consists of three types of melody instruments (*ryuteki* flute, *hichiriki* oboe, and *sho* mouth organ); two instruments that play set melodic formulas that relate to structural aspects of a specific piece (*koto* zither and *biwa* lute); and three percussion instruments (*kakko* small drum, *taiko* big drum, and *shoko* gong). You may wish to have your audiovisual department place pictures of the instruments onto slides. As part of the class presentation, you can lead the students in a discussion of the designs and shapes of the instruments and their animal symbology as discussed in *Japanese Music and Musical Instruments*.
2. Listen to "Etenraku." Explain that the melody is played by the *ryuteki*, a transverse bamboo flute. Ask them to pick out the flute melody (it begins the selection). Play the recording several times asking the students to hum along. Point out that the piece begins very slowly and then speeds up toward the end. Have the students keep the beat. They will notice that the duration between beat four and beat one of the next measure is slightly elongated, a technique that is referred to as "breath rhythm." The elongation is particularly noticeable in the first two phrases. This breath rhythm is a style characteristic of *gagaku* performance that provides some of its suspense. The listener must wait for the first beat.
   Follow the form of the selection by phrase: AABBCCAABB, which can be simplified to a larger ABA design.
3. Review the pictures and names of the *gagaku* instruments. In what ways is the *gagaku* orchestra like the Western orchestra? (Both have wind, stringed, and percussion instruments.) In what ways does it differ from the Western orchestra? (There is no conductor in the *gagaku* orchestra; the *gagaku* orchestra does not have brass instruments; and the dynamic level of *gagaku* music is softer and slower than much Western orchestral music.)

■ OBJECTIVES:

Students will:
1. Sing the folksong "Kuroda-bushi."
2. Accompany the song with an alto recorder.
3. Perform the melodies of two compositions, "Etenraku Imayo" and "Kuroda-bushi" on recorders and notice the similarities and differences of the melodies.

Kuroda-Bushi
Song of Kuroda

Is it a mountain storm?	Meenuh no arahshee kah?
The wind in the pines?	Mahtsou-kahzuh kah?
Or is it the sound of the *koto*	Tahzoonooroo heetoh noh
Of the lady whom I seek?	Kohtoh no nuh kah?
Reining up my horse,	Kohmah heekee tohmehteh.
I approach and hear	Tahchee youruhbah
The distinct strains of the piece.	Tsuhmah-ohtoh tahkahkee, Koorohdah booshee.

Figure 14. From John M. Kelly, Folk Music in Hawaii *(Boston: Boston Music Co., 1965). Used by permission.*

263

At the dawn of Spring in March
If you look out over the four cardinal directions from the mountaintop
You might see flowers blossoming and—indeed—
Mountain peaks free of white cloud cover

When it becomes Autumn
Half this year has already gone
My evening is passing
So beautiful and melancholy to watch the shadow of the crescent moon

Figure 15.

4. Listen to "Kuroda-bushi" accompanied by bamboo flute, *shamisen,* and drum, identifying the heterophonic texture between the voice and flute melodies.

Materials:
1. Alto recorders
2. Recording: *Traditional Folk Songs of Japan,* Folkways FE 4534

■ **PROCEDURES:**
1. The folksong "Kuroda-bushi" (see figure 14), whose melody is derived from the *gagaku* composition "Etenraku" (see figure 15), describes a lady of the court playing the *koto.* Notice the references to nature (for example, mountain storm, wind, pines), a common occurrence in Japanese arts.
2. Accompany the singing by playing along on the melody with alto recorders. Students may also play the melody on alto recorders.
3. Explain that some songs are based on the same melody. Notice how the Shinto song "Etenraku Imayo" is related to the melody of the folk song "Kuroda-bushi." A translation, by Elizabeth Yamaguchi, of "Etenraku Imayo" appears in figure 15. The text is pronounced as follows:

Ha-ru no ya-yo-i no a-ke-bo-no ni
Yo-mo no ya-ma-be o mi-wa-ta-se ba
Ha-na za-ka-ri-ka mo shi-ra-ku mo no————
Ka-ka-ra-nu mi-ne-ko-so na-ka-ri-ke-re

A-ki no ha-ji-me ni na-ri-nu-re ba
Ko-to-shi no na-ka-ba wa su-gi ni ke-ri
Wa ga yo fu-ke yu-ku tsu-ki ka-ge no ————
Ka-ta-bu-ku mi-ru-ko-so a-wa-re-na-re

   a. Divide the class into two segments, having one half play the melody of "Etenraku Imayo" on recorders (or some play and others hum) while the other half of the class plays or hums the melody of "Kuroda-bushi." Notice that many notes of the two melodies are the same. However, also notice that there are differences in the two melodies.
   b. Listen to "Kuroda-bushi" accompanied by bamboo flute, *shamisen,* and drum. Particularly notice the heterophonic texture between the voice and flute melodies.

L E S S O N   T H R E E

3

■ **OBJECTIVES:**
Students will:
1. Look at pictures of the *noh* theater.
2. Perform a short segment of *noh* music.
3. Listen to a segment of *noh* theater.
4. Watch the film *Noh Drama.*

Materials:
1. *Japanese Music and Musical Instruments* by William P. Malm and *Performing Arts of Japan: IV, Noh—The Classical Theatre* by Yusuo Nakamura (see Bibliography)
2. Recording: *UNESCO Collection—A Musical Anthology of the Orient: Japan III.* Bärenreiter Musicaphon BM L 2014
3. Film: *Noh Drama* (see Filmography)

■ **PROCEDURES:**
1. Prepare a bulletin board of pictures from *noh* theater, including musical instruments. (The books listed above are good sources, as is the accompanying explanatory material for the record listed.)
2. Explain that *noh* is one of the oldest forms of theater drama in Japan. It began approximately six hundred years ago but is still a popular form of theater in modern Japan; it is said to have at least one million enthusiastic followers. *Noh* drama features a story that is told by actors who sing their parts. A small chorus sometimes performs in the plays. There is also dancing in the plays. The instruments of *noh* drama include:
   ● *Taiko*—a round, floor drum; played with sticks
   ● *Otsuzumi*—an hour-glass shaped drum held at the left side and played by striking it with the right hand.
   ● *Kotsuzumi*—an hour-glass drum held on the right shoulder and played by striking it with the right hand
   ● *Nokan*—a horizontally played flute

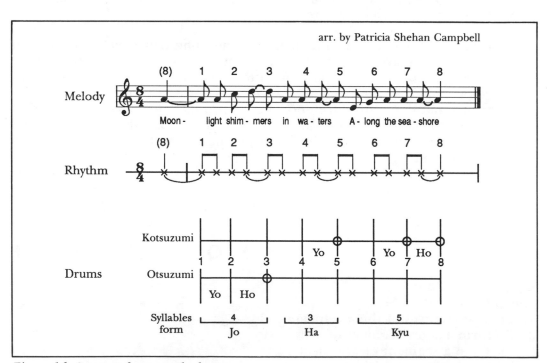

Figure 16. Segment from a noh *drama*

266

3. Perform a short segment of music from a *noh* drama (see figure 16).
   a. Sing the melody.
   b. Clap the rhythm of the voice line.
   c. Explain that in order for instruments, such as the *otsuzumi* and *kotsuzumi*, to play in correct rhythm, the Japanese use *kakegoe* (calls; for example, "Yo" and "Ho") to coordinate the drumming. Following the diagram in figure 17, have half of the class count the beats in the selection (one through eight) while the other half of the class gives the calls "Yo" and "Ho." Have the students play drums at the appropriate times to simulate the *otsuzumi* and the *kotsuzumi*. Repeat the example several times.
   d. Have some students sing the melody while others speak the "Yo" and "Ho" syllables and others perform on the drums. Repeat the example several times.
   e. Call attention to the *jo-ha-kyu* (*jo*, introduction; *ha*, principal material; and *kyu*, drive toward the end) form of the selection.
4. Listen to an example of music from the *noh* drama *Hagoromo* ("The Robe of Feathers," the first two minutes of side one on the *UNESCO Collection—A Musical Anthology of the Orient: Japan III*). As the students are listening, have them circle the appropriate items:

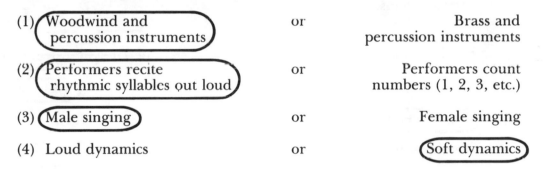

(1) Woodwind and percussion instruments	or	Brass and percussion instruments
(2) Performers recite rhythmic syllables out loud	or	Performers count numbers (1, 2, 3, etc.)
(3) Male singing	or	Female singing
(4) Loud dynamics	or	Soft dynamics

5. Watch the film *Noh Drama*. Observe the staging, costumes, placement of musicians, the extremely sustained movement of the actors, and the singing style. Discuss the concept of "less is more" as it is reflected in the musical and dramatic elements of this art form.

LESSON FOUR

4

■ **OBJECTIVES:**
Students will:
1. Look at pictures of *kabuki* drama.
2. Listen to a segment of music from the *kabuki* theater.
3. Watch a film about *kabuki*.

Materials:

1. *Japanese Music and Musical Instruments* by William P. Malm and *Performing Arts of Japan: II—Kabuki, The Popular Theater* by Yasuji Toita (see Bibliography). (These are suggested books for finding pictures of *kabuki* theater.)
2. Recording: *Japan: Kabuki and Other Traditional Music*, Nonesuch H-72084 (the last two minutes of side one)
3. Film: *Kabuki: Classic Theater of Japan* (see Filmography)

■ PROCEDURES:

1. Look for pictures of *kabuki* theater in the books listed in Materials or in other sources and place them on the bulletin board. Explain that *kabuki* is perhaps the most flamboyant of the musical dramas of Japan. Established approximately four hundred years ago, it involves elaborate scenery, costuming, acting, dance, and music.
2. Both singing and instrumental music are found in *kabuki*. Some of the most prominent instruments include the *nokan* (flute), the *otsuzumi* and *kotsuzumi* (hour-glass shaped drums), the *taiko* (floor drum), and the *shamisen*, a three-stringed plucked lute.
3. Listen to a short selection of music from the *kabuki* theater while circling the appropriate items:

   (1) Brass and   or   **(Strings, flute, and percussion instruments)**
          percussion instruments

   (2) Slow tempo   or   **(Fast tempo)**

   (3) **(Duple meter)**   or   Triple meter

   (4) Female singing   or   **(Male singing)**

4. Watch the film *Kabuki: Classic Theater of Japan*. Call attention to the on-stage instruments and the extremely flamboyant costuming of the actors. Compare *kabuki* to the more subtle *noh*.

5

L E S S O N   F I V E

■ OBJECTIVES:

Students will:

1. Listen to the *shakuhachi* composition "Deer Calling to Each Other in the Distance."
2. Identify the programmatic nature of the music (use of imitation to indicate the calling of two deer). They will discover that the composition exemplifies

the Japanese ideal of "less is more" through free rhythm (the absence of a steady beat), a slow pace, a soft dynamic level, and a thin texture created by only two instruments.
3. Compare the music to Japanese visual and literary art.
4. Sing the Japanese song "Sakura." Identify the pentatonic scale and the duple meter of the song.
5. Listen to the composition "Variations on 'Sakura'" played on the *koto* and identify the use of the variation form.
6. View the *koto* and *shakuhachi* on the film *Discovering the Music of Japan* (see Filmography).

Materials:
1. Recordings:
   UNESCO Collection—A Musical Anthology of the Orient: Japan III, Bärenreiter Musicaphon BM 30 L 2014
   Art of the Koto: The Music of Japan Played by Kimio Eto, Elektra EKL234
2. Film: *Discovering the Music of Japan*, 22 minutes, color (see Filmography)
3. *Cricket Songs* by Harry Behn (Haiku poetry) (see Bibliography)
4. *A History of Far Eastern Art* by Sherman E. Lee (Japanese painting) (see Bibliography)
5. Pictures of *shakuhachi* and *koto* in *Japanese Music and Musical Instruments*, by William P. Malm and the October 1972 issue of the *Music Educators Journal*

▪ PROCEDURES:
1. Place a picture of the *shakuhachi* on the bulletin board. Explain that the instrument is made from bamboo, which is plentiful in Japan. Bring a small piece of bamboo to class and let the students see and feel the material. Notice the "joints" between the segments. To make a *shakuhachi*, a notch is cut at the upper end of the bamboo. (The sound is produced by blowing across the notch as you would on a soda bottle.) Five holes are cut along the bamboo: one on the back and four on the front. The back hole is covered by the thumb of the left hand; the other four holes are covered by the second and fourth fingers of both hands. The *shakuhachi* was derived from the Chinese *xiao*.
2. Listen to the composition "Deer Calling to Each Other in the Distance," which is played on two *shakuhachi*s. This composition, like much Japanese music, is programmatic; that is, the music depicts a theme or story. In this composition the two *shakuhachi*s answer each other in imitation, thus portraying two deer calling to each other.

As you listen to the music, circle the appropriate items:

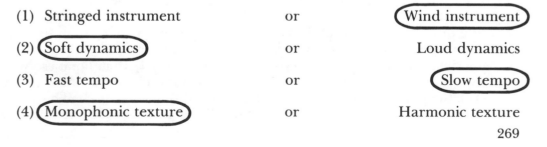

(1) Stringed instrument   or   Wind instrument

(2) Soft dynamics   or   Loud dynamics

(3) Fast tempo   or   Slow tempo

(4) Monophonic texture   or   Harmonic texture

Figure 17. A shakuhachi *player*

3. You will notice that this piece seems understated (this is achieved primarily through the soft dynamics, slow tempo, and monophonic texture). Much Japanese art seems to be understated. Read selections of haiku poetry, which is based on minimal materials (three lines, seventeen syllables, organized into groups of five, seven, and five syllables). Look at traditional Japanese paintings that are delicately executed with just a few lines and the use of muted colors.

4. Look for pictures of Japanese cherry trees in blossom, perhaps those surrounding the Jefferson Memorial in Washington, D.C., which were given to the United States by Japan. (You can find pictures of these trees in the Spring 1984 issue of *National Geographic Traveler*.) Have the students include these pictures on a bulletin board devoted to Japan. Also, look for examples of Japanese art and haiku poetry that focus on nature.

5. Sing the song "Sakura" (Sah-koo-rah) (see figure 18), both in Japanese and in English. Notice the references to nature (cherry blossoms, mist, clouds). Write the pentatonic scale of the song (E, F, A, B, C) on the chalkboard and have the students sing it on a neutral syllable such as "loo" or play it on

Sakura
(Cherry Blossoms)

Sa-ku - ra! Sa-ku - ra! Ya-yo - i no so-ra_ wa,
Sa-ku - ra! Sa-ku - ra! Cher-ry blos-soms, mist and_ clouds,

Mi - wa - ta - su Ka-gi - ri Ka-su-mi ka ku-mo_ ka,
Gent-ly float-ing in the_ sky, As_ far as one can_ see,

Ni - o - i zo i - zu_ ru. I - za - ya,
The_ fra - grance is ev-'ry - where. Come,_____

i - za - ya, Mi_____ ni yu_ ka - n.
come, _____ Let_____ us go_ and see!

Figure 18. From John M. Kelly, Folk Music in Hawaii *(Boston: Boston Music Co., 1965). Used by permission.*

classroom instruments. Have the students conduct the duple meter as they sing the song.

6. Listen to the composition "Variations on 'Sakura'," side one, band one of *Art of the Koto*. Place a picture of the *koto* (see figure 19) on the bulletin board, and explain that the instrument is made of paulownia wood, a soft wood of the acacia family that grows only in Japan and Korea. The koto is approximately six feet long and ten inches wide. There are thirteen silk strings that are stretched parallel across the body of the instrument. Bridges hold the strings above the body of the instrument. These bridges are movable to allow the player to adjust the tuning of the instrument, which is commonly tuned to any one of several pentatonic scales. The *koto* is played by plucking the strings with three plectra attached to the thumb, index, and middle fingers of the right hand. As the class listens to the selection, have them circle the appropriate items:

Theme

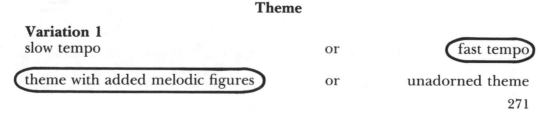

Variation 1

slow tempo · · · · · · · · · · · · · · · · · · or · · · · · · · · · · · · · · · · · fast tempo

theme with added melodic figures · · · · · · · or · · · · · · · · · · · unadorned theme

271

Figure 19. Student playing a koto

Variation 2

fast tempo	or	(slow tempo)
(soft dynamics)	or	loud dynamics

Variation 3

slow tempo	or	(fast tempo)
unadorned theme	or	(decorated theme)

7. Watch the *shakuhachi* being played in the film *Discovering the Music of Japan*. Make sure that the class notices the emphasis on nature and the Japanese ideal of "less is more."

Integrating music with other studies

The following are some suggestions for integrating the study of Chinese and Japanese music with other classroom learning experiences:

1. Make a bulletin board composed of pictures from many different aspects of Chinese and Japanese culture, such as architecture, music, painting, sculpture, and other forms.

2. Invite Chinese and Japanese guests to speak to your students. Encourage the visitors to bring authentic items such as textiles.

3. Show films of Chinese and Japanese cultures. Excellent film rental catalogs are available from university film libraries (for example, the Universities of Michigan, Washington, and Wisconsin).

4. Combine songs with social studies. For example, along with singing the Chinese song, "The Eldest Daughter of the Jiang Family" (see figure 3), plan a geography and history lesson based on the Great Wall of China.

5. Have your class plan a Chinese New Year celebration (it falls sometime in February on the Western calendar). Lion and dragon dances are often performed. Collaborate with art and physical education teachers in designing costumes and performing lion or dragon dances. The percussion pieces given in figures 5 and 6 can be used as accompaniment.

6. Study the relationships between music and other arts; for example, the texture of heterophony can be related to the Japanese aesthetic of clarity for all aspects of an art expression. Just as all the elements of a formal Japanese garden are clearly presented (for example, the rocks and the pine tree), each musical part is made clear through heterophony and by the difference in timbres of each instrument ensemble.

Note: China Books and Periodicals has a large stock of English books (including children's books) related to Chinese culture. Catalogs are available. Their addresses and telephone numbers are 136 West Eighteenth Street, New York 10011, 212-627-4044; 2929 Twenty-fourth Street, San Francisco 94110, 415-282-2994; and Suite 600, 37 South Wabash, Chicago 60603, 312-782-6004.

Records and audiocassettes produced in Mainland China, Hong Kong, and Taiwan can be obtained through World Music Enterprises, 717 Avondale Street, Kent, Ohio 44240.

General articles on Chinese and Japanese music and musical instruments can be found in standard dictionaries such as *The New Grove Dictionary of Music and Musicians*, edited by Stanley Sadie (New York: Macmillan, 1980), *The New Grove Dictionary of Musical Instruments*, edited by Stanley Sadie (New York: Macmillan, 1984), and the *New Harvard Dictionary of Music*, edited by Don Michael Randel (Cambridge, MA: Belknap, 1986). The following list is compiled for books and articles in English that are essential in the field, easily available, and cited in this chapter.

Chinese musical instruments are available from Exelsis Music, 816 Sacramento Street, San Francisco 94018, 415-986-7038.

Other resources are The Asia Society, 725 Park Avenue, New York 10021, 212-288-6400; and the Chinese Music Society of North America, 2329 Charmingfare, Woodridge, Illinois 60517.

CHINA

BIBLIOGRAPHY

Blunder, Caroline, and Mark Elvin. *Cultural Atlas of China*. New York: Facts on File, 1983. This is a very useful book for quick reference. In addition to maps for many purposes and fine photographs, there are also short articles on all aspects of Chinese culture (including the arts).

Chen, Chin-hsin, and Shin-hsing Chen. *The Flower Drum and Other Chinese Songs*. New York: John Day, 1942. Seventeen songs arranged with piano parts and grouped by geographical divisions and subjects; texts in Chinese and English.

273

Chen, Lan-ku. *Development of a Chinese Music Listening Program.* Ann Arbor, MI: University Microfilms, 1983. (University Microfilms number DA 8322188). Using multiple media, the author outlines and develops a listening program for teaching Chinese music in elementary school in this Ed.D. dissertation from Columbia University Teachers College.

Craig, Dale A. *The Chinese Orchestra: An Alternative Instrumental Group for School.* Queensland, Australia: Global Music, 1984. A practical pamphlet for teachers who wish to organize a Chinese orchestra.

Danforth, Kenneth C., ed. *Journey into China.* Washington, DC: National Geographic Society, 1982. This is a good source for photographs of the Great Wall of China.

Eberhard, Wolfram, ed. *Folktales of China.* Chicago: University of Chicago Press, 1965.

Halson, Elizabeth. *Peking Opera: A Short Guide.* Hong Kong: Oxford University Press, 1966. Based on the author's personal observations, this book explores all aspects of Peking opera in nontechnical language. The illustrations are hand drawings; no photographs. Fourteen stories of famous operas are given. A handy book for the subject.

Han, Kuo-huang. "The Modern Chinese Orchestra." *Asian Music* 9, no. 1, 1979, 1–40. The article traces the rise of the type of orchestra that is currently popular in all Chinese communities.

Han, Kuo-huang. "Titles and Program Notes in Chinese Musical Repertoires." *The World of Music*, no. 1, 1985, 68–78. An exploration of the nature of the Chinese people and their fondness of program music.

Liang, Minguye. *Music of the Billion: An Introduction to Chinese Music Culture.* New York: Heinrichshofen Edition, 1985. This is the best and only comprehensive book on Chinese music in a Western language. Though it is labeled as an introduction, it covers all aspects of Chinese music. There is a useful general description of musical instruments for quick reference. A discography, classified by musical genre and instrument, is given along with many music examples.

Lieberman, Frederic. *Chinese Music: An Annotated Bibliography.* 2d ed. This is the standard research tool for anyone working with Chinese music in Western languages. Included are more than two thousand items ranging from popular concert reviews to scholarly research.

Mai, Ding. *Chinese Folk Songs: An Anthology of 25 Favorites with Piano Accompaniment.* Beijing: New World Press, 1984. This anthology includes some newer folk songs and songs of national minorities.

Perris, Arnold. *Music as Propaganda: Art to Pursue, Art to Control.* Westport, CT: Greenwood Press, 1985. Chapter five gives information on the control of the arts in China, a practice partly learned from the Russians and partly inherited from ancient Chinese ideas.

Scott, Adolphe Clarence. *The Classical Theatre of China.* London: Allen and Unwin, 1957. Still a classic for the general reader, this book investigates all aspects of Peking opera. It includes a glossary of technical terms.

Thrasher, Alan R. "The Role of Music in Chinese Culture." *The World of Music*, no. 1, 1985, 3–17. Much Western writing on Chinese music has been concerned with ancient music and historical documents. This article explores music in a modern social setting.

Thrasher, Alan R. "The Sociology of Chinese Music: An Introduction." *Asian Music* 12, no. 2, 1981, 17–53.

Wiant, Bliss. *Chinese Lyrics.* New York: J. Fischer and Brothers, 1947. A collection of twenty-seven songs arranged with piano accompaniment.

DISCOGRAPHY

China I. Anthology AST 4000. A collection of fine performances by masters on *qin, zheng, yangqin,* and *sanxian.* Good annotation by Frederic Lieberman.

China: Music from the People's Republic of China. Rounder Records 4008, 1976. Taped live in Hubei, this is an interesting album containing short examples of instrumental and vocal performances by professionals and children. Instruments featured are *suona, zheng, erhu, pipa,* and *sheng.*

China: Shantung Folk Music and Traditional Instrumental Pieces. Nonesuch H72051. The Lu-Sheng Ensemble gives a fine performance of a repertoire of Shantung (northern Chinese) music.

China's Instrumental Heritage. Lyrichord LLST 7921. Performed by the *zheng* master, Liang Tsai-ping and his group, this album features *zheng, xiao, sheng, erhu* (called *nanhu*), and a rare example of the *xun* ocarina.

Chine Populaire: Musique classique. Ocora 558519. Reproduced from Chinese recordings, this album features good examples of *qin, zheng, erhu, di,* and *pipa.* The annotation is not very complete.

Chinese Classical Masterpieces. Everest 3212. The two works featured in this album are not classical, but contemporary. They represent a fusion of Western and Chinese musical idioms.

Chinese Classical Masterpieces, Lyrichord LLST 7182. This album consists of standard solo compositions for the *pipa* lute and *qin* zither. The *pipa* piece, "The Hero's Defeat," is included. The master who performs these two instruments, Lui Tsun-yuen, teaches at UCLA.

Chinese Masterpieces for the Er-hu. Lyrichord LLST 7231. Performed by Lui Man-sing and his group, this album features the *erhu* and small ensemble pieces in heterophonic style.

The Chinese Opera. Lyrichord LLST 7212. Children trained in the Fu Hsin Opera School in Taiwan perform works; their vocal quality is not typical of the genre.

Chinese Opera: Songs and Music. Folkways FW8880. Includes excerpts from Cantonese (*Guangdong*) local opera. Included are good examples of instrumental works performed in heterophonic style.

Exotic Music of Ancient China. Lyrichord LLST 7122. The album includes the famous *pipa* piece, "Ambush from Ten Sides" (The Great Ambush).

Floating Petals, Wild Geese, The Moon on High: Music of the Chinese Pipa. Nonesuch H72085. This album contains seven masterpieces for *pipa,* and the modern work "Dance of the Yi Tribe" is included.

Hong Kong. UNESCO/EMI C 064 17068. (Musical Atlas.) The instruments featured are the *qin, zheng, pipa, yangqin, sheng, erhu,* and *xiao.*

Musik für Ch'in–China. Museum Collection Berlin MC 7. *Qin* master Liang Mingyue provides commentary. Fine photos showing the finger and hand positions for playing the instrument.

Nan-Kouan, Vol. I: Musique et chant courtois de la Chine du Sud. Ocora 558612. The first good recording in the West of this refined and courtly genre (Nanguan). The singer (Cai Xiaoyue) and the instrumentalists are the very best in Taiwan.

Orchestral Music of China. Orion PGM 6903. Side A contains works written in the 1950s and 1960s for the modern Chinese orchestra. The famous composition "Dance of the Yao" is included.

Peking Opera. Seraphim 60201. Only three compositions are actual Peking opera excerpts. The rest are works for the *pipa, zheng,* and *gaohu.*

Phases of the Moon: Traditional Chinese Music. CBS M 36705. Recordings produced by the China Record Company for the CBS Masterworks Album. A fine album of works performed by the modern Chinese orchestra.

Shantung: Music of Confucian Homeland. Lyrichord LLST 7112. This album features *sheng, di, erhu* (*nanhu*), and the special effect of *suona* (imitating human voice).

The Song of the Phoenix: Sheng Music from China. Lyrichord LLST 7369. Ten traditional and modern compositions for the *sheng.*

Vocal Music of Contemporary China. Vol. I: The Han People. Folkways FE4091. The album contains folk songs and contemporary songs; some are accompanied by traditional ensemble and others by piano.

FILMOGRAPHY

Chinese Music and Musical Instruments, 16mm, 24 minutes, color. Chinese Information Service (Taiwan). This film can be obtained from Audio-Visual Services, Northern Illinois University, DeKalb 60115, or the Chinese Coordination Council for North American Affairs Office in the United States, 5061 River Road, Washington, DC 20016. It depicts the social and educational aspects of Chinese music and introduces all types of musical instruments. Scenes of Confucian ceremony and imaginary court dance are included. It concludes with a performance of a modern Chinese orchestra. The lengthy and somewhat monotonous section in which each instrument is shown but not played is a drawback. (Filmed in Taiwan)

Chinese Musical Instruments: An Introduction, VHS videocassette, 30 minutes, color. The Yale-China Association. Available from Erlham College, East Asian Studies Program, Richmond, IN 47374. This film features four Chinese musicians performing six compositions. The instruments used are the *zheng, pipa, erhu, sanxian, yangqin, sheng, di,* and *xiao.*

Chinese Shadow Plays, Wango Wen, 16mm, 11 minutes, color. China Film Enterprise of America, 1947. Available from Erlham College, East Asian studies program, Richmond, IN 47374. After

275

a brief introduction, this film presents episodes from the famous story, "White Snake Lady." The backstage is shown at the end.

Chinese Shadow Plays, VHS videocassette, 30 minutes, black-and-white. The Asia Society, 725 Park Avenue, New York 10021. This film, directed by Wen Wago, features the shadow puppet troupe from Taiwan performing scenes from the famous story, "The Monkey King." A demonstration is included.

The Fujan Hand Puppets from the People's Republic of China, VHS videocassette, 30 minutes, color. The Asia Society. This film features the three-dimensional hand puppets performing a story that has a slight socialist overtone. A short demonstration is included at the end of this skillful performance.

The Heritage of Chinese Opera, 16mm, 32 minutes, color. Chinese Information Service (Taiwan). This film can be obtained from the Chinese Coordination Council for North American Affairs Office in the United States of America, 5061 River Road, Washington, DC 20016. It introduces the various aspects (pantomime, acrobatics, singing, and dancing) of Peking opera and shows the training of an opera school (Fu Hsin Opera School). The excerpts that follow are "The Jade Bracelet," "The Monkey King," "The Cross Road," "Two Loyal Officials," and "Yueh Fei."

Hu Hung-yen: Aspects of Peking Opera, Videocassette, 30 minutes, color. The Asia Society. Hu, a famous actress of Peking Opera, demonstrates the make-up and performs two excerpts.

An Introduction to Traditional Chinese Music: Instrumental Music, VHS videocassette, 60 minutes, color. Ministry of Education and the National Taiwan Normal University. This videotape was made in Taiwan at the request of MENC. Most of the performers are high school or college students. It includes an explanation of the classification of instruments, demonstrations of six solo instruments and percussion instruments, and five ensemble compositions performed by a high school Chinese orchestra and a primary school chorus.

A Night at the Peking Opera, 16mm, 20 minutes, color. Film Images. This resource can be obtained from Audio-Visual Services, University of Michigan, Ann Arbor 48015; or Northern Illinois University, DeKalb 60115. It is a classic film that shows excellent performances of four excerpts performed at the Paris International Festival of Dramatic Art in 1955. The excerpts are "The White Snake Lady," "The Monkey King," "The Cross Road," and "The Autumn River."

Shantung: Traditional Music, Videocassette, 30 minutes, black and white. The Asia Society. Performances by the Lu-Sheng Ensemble from Taiwan. The *suona*, the *di*, and the *sheng* are the instruments featured.

Tai Ai-lien in Chinese Folk Dance, 16mm, 12 minutes, color. Fictura Films, 1972. This film can be obtained from Audio-Visual Services, University of Illinois, Urbana 61801. Tai, the leading dancer and dance teacher in China for forty years, performs a drum dance and a southwest Chinese folk tale allowing her to play both parts simultaneously.

Asian Dance and Drama, Vol. 3: East Asia, The Asia Society. Three hundred slides with an illustrated annotated guide. The cultures represented in this volume include Korea, Japan, and China.

JAPAN

Araki, Nancy, and Jane M. Mori. *Matsuri: Festival; Japanese American Celebrations and Activities*. San Francisco: Heian International, 1978. This is an informative manual of specific activities that can be done in the classroom, including recipes, paper folding, and one Bon dance, "Tankobushi."

Behn, Harry. *Cricket Songs*. New York: Harry N. Abrams, n.d. This is a collection of *haiku* poetry.

Kelly, John M. Jr. *Folk Music Festival in Hawaii*. Rutland, VT: Charles E. Tuttle, 1963. This is a compendium of songs from Hawaii, the Pacific, and Asia, most with piano accompaniment. Translations are included for all songs. Japanese songs include "Sakura," "On-koto," "Kisobu-shi," "Hiraita," and "Kutsu ga naru."

Kishibe, Shigeo. *The Traditional Music of Japan*, 2nd ed. Tokyo: Ongaku no Tomo sha, 1984. This book contains a detailed introduction to the major genres of Japanese art music, including history, description of instrument tuning systems, and musical features. Many black and white illustrations of instruments and performers are included.

Lee, Sherman E. *A History of Far Eastern Art*. New York: Harry N. Abrams, n.d. This is an excellent general survey of Asian art.

276

Malm, William P. *Japanese Music and Musical Instruments*. Rutland, VT: Charles E. Tuttle, 1959. An informative and thorough account of music in Japan, this text is very readable, with many illustrations in both color and black and white. The most comprehensive treatment of Japanese music by a non-Japanese.

Nakamura, Yusuo. *Performing Arts of Japan: IV, Noh—The Classical Theatre*. New York: Walker/ Weatherhill, 1971. This is an excellent introduction, with good illustrations, to *Noh* drama.

Togi, Masatoro. *Performing Arts of Japan: V. Gagaku: Court Music and Dance*. New York: Weatherhill, 1971. This book gives an engaging description of *gagaku* by a court musician in his own words. There are many pictures of actual court performances and some good plates of instrument construction.

Toita, Yasuji. *Performing Arts of Japan: II—Kabuki, The Popular Theater*. New York: Walker-Weatherhill, 1970. This is a good, well-illustrated introduction to *kabuki* theater.

Yamaguchi, Osamu. "Musics of Northeast Asia." *Music Educators Journal*, 59 no. 2, Oct. 1972, 31–34. An overview of Northeast Asia with other pictures useful for instruction. This special issue of *MEJ* is useful for the teacher interested in world music; it contains a useful bibliography and discography.

DISCOGRAPHY

Art of the Koto: The Music of Japan Played by Kimia Eto. Elektra Records EKL 234. This record includes an example of *tegotomono* ("Yachiojishi"), *danmono* ("Hachidan"), and an arrangement of "Sakura" (Cherry Blossoms).

Gagaku, the Imperial Court Music of Japan. Lyrichord LLST 7126. This is a recording of a shortened version of "Etenraku" performed by the Kyoto Imperial Court Music Orchestra.

Japanese Traditional Music for Two Shakuhachi. Lyrichord LLST 7386. This record includes solos and duets for *shakuhachi* by two American performers with detailed liner notes. It illustrates the different timbres of *shakuhachi* and the concept of free meter.

Japan: Kabuki and Other Traditional Music. Nonesuch H-72084. This is a collection of traditional music, performed by the famed Ensemble Nipponia.

Kyomono Series Vol. 1: Works of Matsuura Kengyo. Hogaku Society HS-101. This is a recording of performances of *sankyoku* (*koto, shamisen, shakuhachi*, and voice) by American and Japanese performers with translations and notes. It illustrates the *tegotomono* genre of *koto* music and heterophony.

UNESCO Collection—A Musical Anthology of the Orient: Japan III. Bärenreiter Musicaphon BM 30 L 2014. This is an anthology (part of a six-volume set of traditional Japanese music) that includes the *shamisen*-song traditions, *danmono* form ("Rokudan"), and *shakuhachi* duets ("Shika no tone").

Traditional Folk Songs of Japan. Ryutaro Hattori, collector. Folkways FE 4534. "Kuroda-bushi" is sung, accompanied by *shamisen*, bamboo flute, and drum. Also includes "Tanko Bushi" ("Coal Miner's Song" in Kyushu).

FILMOGRAPHY

Note: The address of The Asia Society, a supplier for many of the films listed here, is The Asia Society, Performing Arts Department, 725 Park Avenue, New York, NY 10021.

The Awaji Puppet Theater of Japan, 16mm, 20 minutes, color. Available from The Asia Society. Scenes from classic Japanese tales: Keisei Awa Naruto, The Miracle of Tsubosaka Temple, and Ebisu-Mai, as well as a demonstration of how the puppets are manipulated.

Bugaku: The Traditional Court, Temple and Shrine Dances from Japan, ¾″ videocassette, 30 minutes. Available from The Asia Society. For more than a thousand years, Bugaku has been the ceremonial dance of the Japanese Imperial household, temples, and shrines. The ancient music of drums, flutes, strings, and gongs accompany the elegant and austere movements of the dance.

Discovering the Music of Japan, 16 mm, 22 minutes, color, Bernard Wilets, Film Associates, 1967. Introduction to three Japanese instruments—*shakuhachi, koto*, and *shamisen*.

Edo Festival Music and Pantomime, 16mm, 50 minutes, color. Available from The Asia Society. This three-part film recreates the Lincoln Center performance of the famed Taneo Wakayama troupe. The film consists of three dance-pantomimes: "Destroying the Giant Serpent" (Orochi Taiji), "Homage to the Gods and Love for the Homeland" (Keishin Aikoku), and "The Felicitous Lion" (Kotobuki Jishi). All three features are available on separate reels.

Kabuki: Classic Theater of Japan, 16mm, 30 minutes. Available from Japan Information Service, Consulate General of Japan, Water Tower Place, Suite 950 E, 845 North Michigan Avenue, Chicago 60611.

Martial Arts of Kabuki from the National Theater Institute of Japan, ¾″ videocassette, 30 minutes. Available from The Asia Society. Dancers from the National Theater Institute of Japan demonstrate stage fighting based on the martial arts and perform two excerpts from the kabuki repertory: "Hama Matsukaze" (a major battle between a man and a woman using makeshift weapons including an oar and a piece of rope) and "Kujira no Danmari" (in which a samurai is swallowed by a whale and eventually fights off a swarm of reptilian creatures).

Noh Drama, 16mm, 29 minutes. Available from Japan Information Service, Consulate General of Japan, Water Tower Place, Suite 950 E, 845 North Michigan Avenue, Chicago 60611.

The Soloists of the Ensemble Nipponia, ¾″ videocassette, 30 minutes. Available from The Asia Society. This is a performance by the soloists of the Ensemble Nipponia of Tsuru no Sugomori (the Tenderness of the Crane on the *shakuhachi*, a bamboo flute, Makuai Sanju (Kabuki interlude) on the *shamisen*, Oji-no-Nato (the Folding Fan as a target) on the *biwa*, and Tatsuta no Kyoku (the Venus in Autumn) on the *koto*, as well as Wa (a composition for ensemble).

NOTES

1. John K. Fairbank, Edwin O. Reischauer, and Albert M. Craig, *East Asia: Tradition and Transformation* (Boston: Houghton Mifflin, 1973), 6–8.
2. Philip A. True, "Geography," in *The People's Republic of China: A Handbook*, ed. Harold C. Hinton (Boulder, CO: Westview Press, 1979), 9–10.
3. Loren Fessler, *China* (New York: Time–Life International, 1968), 78.
4. For more information see Mingyue Liang, *Music of the Billion: An Introduction to Chinese Music Culture* (New York: Heinrichshofen Edition, 1985), 143–254.
5. "Fuhng Yang Wa Gu" is the title of this song in the older (Wade-Giles) System of romanization. It may also be spelled "Feng Yang Hua Gu."
6. William P. Malm; "Ethnomusicology: The World of Music Cultures," in *Research News* (Ann Arbor: University of Michigan, 1970), 11.

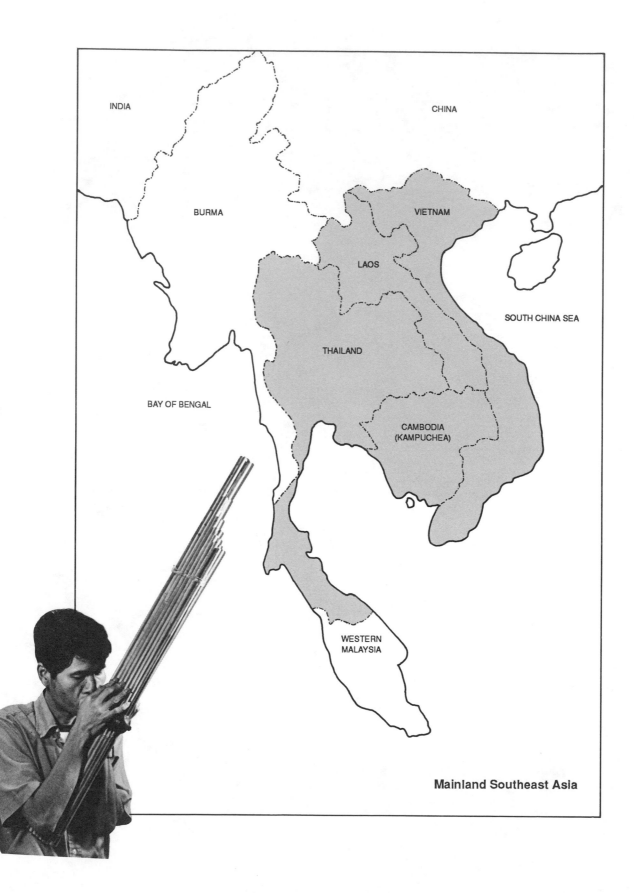

INDIA

CHINA

BURMA

VIETNAM

LAOS

BAY OF BENGAL

THAILAND

SOUTH CHINA SEA

CAMBODIA
(KAMPUCHEA)

WESTERN
MALAYSIA

Mainland Southeast Asia

SOUTHEAST ASIA

by Patricia Shehan Campbell and William M. Anderson

CAMBODIA (KAMPUCHEA), LAOS, THAILAND, AND VIETNAM

Mainland Southeast Asia is located south of China and east of India and includes the countries of Vietnam, Laos, Kampuchea (Cambodia), Thailand, Burma, and Malaysia. Its geographical setting between powerful neighbors has always been of prime importance in the development of its philosophy, architecture, legends, dance, drama, and music.

The influence of Indian and Chinese cultures has been considerable, despite the partial isolation imposed on the region by mountains and flooding river valleys. Many Indian artists and scholars enjoyed high status in the courts of Southeast Asia as they introduced aspects of Hindu and Buddhist traditions. Young men frequently traveled to India for training in literature, art, and culture. China annexed Vietnam in the first century B.C., and during this period Vietnamese culture was strongly influenced by its northern neighbor.

Ethnic groups from southern China, including the Mons, Lao, Shan, Siamese, Karen, and Khmer, followed the Mekong and Irrawaddy rivers to settlements in

281

Southeast Asia. The Hmong people migrated from China as recently as two thousand years ago. The growth of nationalism led to the adoption of an official language by each country, but the large number of languages still in use today is evidence of the mainland's multicultural society.

With the arrival of missionaries in the sixteenth century and merchants and statesmen in the seventeenth, Southeast Asia was introduced to Western culture. From the late nineteenth century through World War II, France was the area's principal colonial power, but the unique, millennium-old cultural identities of Vietnam, Laos, and Cambodia were maintained throughout this period. The kingdom of Siam remained independent during the colonial period, and in 1939 it took the name of Thailand ("land of the free") to reflect its status. Compared to other Southeast Asian countries, Thailand today is relatively prosperous. The capital city of Bangkok seems Western in its fashion, media, music, and even cuisine, whereas the ethnic minorities in rural areas of the north and northeast retain traditional customs from the past.

While the French whittled away at Indochina, the British annexed portions of Burma and slowly built a political state during the nineteenth century. The states at the southern end of the Malay Peninsula became British protectorates in the late nineteenth century. Burma gained its independence in 1948, and Malaysia attained independence fifteen years later, in 1963.

In the mid-1970s, the condition of the war-torn countries of Vietnam, Laos, and Cambodia brought about a massive influx of refugees to the United States. As their governments disintegrated, the South Vietnamese, Cambodians, Lao, and ethnic groups such as the Hmong were transported to camps in Thailand, Hong Kong, Guam, and Indonesia before they finally settled not only in America, but throughout the world. Life in the New World held promise for these Southeast Asians, but the memory of their homeland remained an important influence in their lives.

The traditional sounds of ancient civilizations can be heard in Southeast Asian communities in cities such as Los Angeles, San Francisco, Seattle, and Dallas. Refugees brought folk and classical instruments and a repertoire of songs and melodies that had been transmitted through many generations. These musical traditions also survive in those areas of the old world where the governments give permission and support.

This guide to Vietnamese, Thai, Lao, and Cambodian traditional music styles is organized by elements of melody, rhythm, texture, form and genre, and timbre. Unfortunately, there is little information available on the music of Burma and Malaysia, but students can learn that Burmese music shows strong Indian characteristics and that Malaysian music resembles the Islamic-influenced styles of the two populous Indonesian islands of Java and Sumatra.

Vietnamese music

Pentatonic melodies, with the addition of two auxiliary pitches, used primarily for ornamentation, are common in Vietnamese music. These melodies are seldom plain; they are distinguished by the use of decorative techniques similar to tremolos and trills. Almost all metered Vietnamese music is in duple meter. Except for the recitative-style music of certain religious chants and opera, rhythmic cycles of eight or sixteen beats are standard. Vietnamese vocal and

282

instrumental music frequently uses unaccompanied solos and simultaneous melodic variations called heterophony.

The most common formal device is strophic form, in which the melody repeats as the verses change. Some traditional pieces have an introductory section called a *rao*, similar to the Indian *alap* (see chapter 7). Theme and variation, as well as programmatic devices, such as the portrayal of bird calls and falling water, are typical in instrumental works, and opera is particularly prominent in the south.

In folk and classical music, vocal quality may be strident and rather nasal. Among the traditional instruments are the indigenous *dan bau* (monochord) and several Chinese-influenced stringed instruments: the *dan tranh* (a sixteen-stringed zither), the *dan co* (a two-stringed fiddle), and the *dan ty ba* (a four-stringed, long-necked lute). Folk instruments include flutes, oboes, mouth organs, bells, gongs, coin clappers, and barrel drums.

Thai, Lao, and Cambodian music

Folk music in these countries is derived from pentatonic scales, and art music is based on seven-tone scales. The pitches of these heptatonic scales are each separated from the next by an equal interval slightly larger than the Western semitone (100 cents) yet slightly smaller, at about 171 cents, than the whole step (200 cents). Duple meter is the standard, with most music set in two-beat groupings. In classical forms, a rhythmic cycle of beats can be heard, throughout which various drums, gongs, and hand cymbals punctuate phrases.

Students playing in a Thai classical orchestra at Kent State University

Student playing a
kong wong

Student learning to play the ranat

284

Heterophonic texture is common in the classical orchestras, with instruments providing impetus to the music by playing individual lines rather than using a unified, harmonic approach. Certain folk instruments, including the free-reed mouth organ (*kaen*), produce drone-like harmonic accompaniments.

Strophic form is found in many vocal pieces. Orchestral music is frequently organized in a three-part form, in which the melody is reduced by half or enlarged to twice its original length by adding or subtracting melodic detail. In the reduced melody, the ornamentation is removed and only the chief structural pitches are retained; the expanded version features greater ornamentation than in the original melody. Improvisational styles exist in Lao folk music in the *mawlum* form for voice and *kaen*.

Singers typically use a nasal quality. The instruments of the *pi phat* (also called the *pin peat*) orchestra include the *ranat* (wooden xylophones), the *kong wong* (a circle of knobbed gongs), the *pi nai* (oboe), several percussion instruments, and drums. There are also string ensembles that feature two-stringed fiddles, lutes, and zithers. The *ching* (finger cymbals) serve as the beat keepers for all classical ensembles. Mouth organs of the Lao (*kaen*) and Hmong (*gaeng*) produce an open timbre and tuning that is Western-sounding and immediately pleasing, even to the uninitiated.

L E S S O N   O N E

1

■ **OBJECTIVES:**
Students will:
1. Watch films that show the land, the people, and their costumes and customs.
2. Discuss recent political events and their effects on arts and life-styles.
3. List instruments and musical elements evident in a first hearing of brief selections.
4. Locate Southeast Asia on a map.

Materials:
1. Films:
   "Mekong," 25 minutes, color (see filmography)
   "Boy of Southeast Asia," 17 minutes, color (see filmography)
2. Articles:
   "Leading a Charmed Life in Thailand," *Asia* 3, no. 1, May/June 1980, 22–28
   "Cambodian Civilization at the Razor's Edge," *Asia* 3, no. 3, September/October 1980, 6–11
3. Recordings:
   "Laos (vol. 2), "Cambodge" (vol. 1), "Thailande" (vol. 8), and "Vietnam" (vol. 10) from *Musiques de l'Asie traditionnelle*. (International Book and Record

Distributors, 40–11 Twenty-Fourth Street, Long Island City, New York 11101)
4. Map of Asia

■ **PROCEDURES:**

1. Show one or both of the films listed under "Materials" as an introduction to the region. Note the effect of climate on costume and the effect of religion and philosophy on family relationships. Discuss the similarities and differences between the life-style in Southeast Asia and that in the United States. If you have presented previous units on China or India, observe the influences of those countries on the physical traits of Southeast Asian people, their dress, economy, philosophy, and religion.

2. Find photographs from *National Geographic* articles or use the selected articles about Asia listed under Materials. Discuss the traditional arts that have been preserved and the changes that have occurred as a result of political upheaval in Indochina in the last two decades. Draw the students' attention to the architecture (some of which has been destroyed recently) and the traditional silk costumes of dancers and actors in Vietnam, Laos, or Cambodia, which are seldom worn today.

3. Have the students listen to selections (lasting about two minutes) of the folk and classical musics in the Materials list. Point out (1) the instruments and vocal quality, (2) the melody, and (3) the rhythm. Listening to the same brief excerpt three times will allow students to assimilate the style and to focus on one musical element at a time. Use class discussion or a work sheet to provide students with an opportunity for comparative listening and analysis. If possible, prepare a listening guide for these examples, and focus on the instruments and on familiar musical elements that are treated in less familiar ways. For example, sing an Anglo-American song that is based on a pentatonic scale and written in duple meter (such as "Mister Froggie Went A-Courtin' "). Play the scale and tap or conduct the meter while singing. Then ask the class to listen to the Asian examples again, and tap out the duple meter while you identify the scale pitches by singing them or playing them on the piano or xylophone.

4. Refer to a map that includes Southeast Asia, and note its position relative to India, China, and the islands of Indonesia to the south.

2

L E S S O N   T W O

■ **OBJECTIVES:**

Students will:
1. Listen and identify instruments of the *pi phat* orchestra.
2. Discover aspects of rhythm, melody, and texture by performing "Courtly Evening."

Materials:
1. Wooden xylophones, kazoos, finger and hand cymbals, drums
2. "Lao." In *Sounds of the World: Music of Southeast Asia*. Reston, VA: Music Educators National Conference, 1986

■ **PROCEDURES:**
1. Have the students listen to the recording of a classical court orchestra from *Sounds of the World*, tape 1, example 1. The orchestra in the recording is composed of Lao refugees and is playing in a style that is derived from the Thai *pi phat* ensemble that is also found in Cambodian culture. Describe the instrumentation: It includes melody instruments such as the *ranat* (wooden xylophone), the *kong wong* (circle of knobbed gongs with a characteristic mellow timbre), and the *pi nai* (oboe); and the rhythm instruments *chap* (hand cymbals), *ching* (finger cymbals), and *taphon* (double-headed drum).
2. Direct the students' attention to the steady duple meter, and lead them in patting the first beat of each measure (listen to the *chap* hand cymbals as a guide). Note the incessant melodies of xylophones and knobbed gongs, which are derived from a pentatonic scale. Emphasize the heterophonic texture, in which many layers of melodies occur simultaneously. Have the students tap the rhythmic ostinato of the *taphon* drum:

3. Play a traditional *pi phat* orchestra composition, "Courtly Evening" (see figure 1), using classroom instruments:

Melody 1   *ranat* (or wooden xylophone)
Melody 2   *pi nai* (or kazoo)
Rhythm:
ching (or finger cymbals). The notation used in the score is as follows:
    o = "chop": Strike cymbals flat and hold together to prevent ringing.
    + = "ching": Let cymbals ring.
    (Play the finger cymbals every measure, alternating between "ching" and "chop.")
chap (hand cymbals)
    Play one stroke every four measures, letting the hand cymbals ring.
taphon (drum)
    Play a four-measure ostinato:

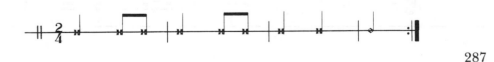

Courtly Evening

 Figure 1.

288

a. Begin by asking the entire class to sing "Courtly Evening." The text printed in the example is a liberal translation of the nineteenth-century romantic song. Students may wish to clap lightly on the first beat of each measure.

b. Demonstrate the role of the "ching" finger cymbals, the true conductor of the court orchestra, by dividing the class into singers and "chingers." The second group will chant "chop" as they muffle a clap with the cupped hands and "ching" as they brush their fingers together in a quick clap. Switch groups; select a student to play the *ching* while the others chant.

c. Double the melody on the xylophone. Add the second melody on kazoo or on a second xylophone, calling attention to the independent lines that converge on the same pitch every four measures. If enough instruments are available, divide the class into groups and have everyone play a part.

d. Add the drum ostinato and the hand cymbal part.

L E S S O N   T H R E E

3

■ OBJECTIVES:
Students will:
1. Listen to examples of *kaen* music.
2. Demonstrate an understanding of texture by singing several versions of "Frère Jacques": in unison, in canon, and as a melody with chordal accompaniment on piano or Autoharp.
3. Discover the principle of free-reed performance on the harmonica.
4. Play a *kaen* piece arranged for classroom instruments.

Materials:
1. *Thailand: Lao Music of the Northeast,* Lyrichord LLST 7357
   "Lao." In *Sounds of the World: Music of Southeast Asia.* Reston, VA: Music Educators National Conference, 1986
2. Piano
3. Xylophones

■ PROCEDURES:
1. Listen to the national instrument of Laos, the *kaen,* a free-reed mouth organ (both recordings listed under "Materials" have appropriate excerpts). The *kaen* is shaped like a raft and is made from sixteen bamboo tubes and a wooden central wind chest (see figure 2). There are holes in the bamboo tubes just above the wind chest. Players select pitches by stopping the holes with their fingers or produce drones by blocking the holes with beeswax. *Kaen* music is highly virtuosic and improvisatory.

Figure 2. Kaen

2. Listen to the continual sound of the *kaen*. Explain that the player produces
   sound on the instrument both by inhaling and exhaling. Demonstrate this
   principle on the harmonica.
3. Note the homophonic texture with the use of cluster chords (chords built
   with a combination of intervals such as seconds and thirds, such as D-E-G-B)
   and drones in the solo *kaen* selections. Contrast the homophony of the *kaen*

290

with the heterophony of the classical *pi phat* orchestra. Demonstrate these textures vocally by singing "Frère Jacques" as a single melody (monophonic texture), a melody with chordal accompaniment (homophonic texture), and simultaneous melodies (heterophonic texture). Demonstrate heterophonic texture by asking the class to sing "Frère Jacques" while you sing a simultaneous variation on the melody (see figure 3).

Figure 3. Heterophonic version of "Frère Jacques"

4. Play the following example of *kaen* music on the piano, divide it among students on xylophones, or divide the class into sections and ask them to sing it.

L E S S O N   F O U R

4

■ OBJECTIVES:

Students will:

1. Sing the song "Phleng Wan Koet" in Thai and in English.
2. Keep the duple meter by clapping and waving.
3. Listen to the Lao ensemble's instrumental version of the song "Lao Duang Duan" and play the melody on classroom instruments.

Materials:

1. "Lao." In *Sounds of the World: Music of Southeast Asia*. Reston, VA: Music Educators National Conference, 1986
2. Recorders, xylophones, finger cymbals, and drums

■ PROCEDURES:

1. Introduce the birthday song "Phleng Wan Koet" (see figure 4) by singing it once through in Thai and once in English. Instruct students to tap the beats on their laps or desks in accompaniment to your singing. The words are pronounced: Wahn nee pehn wan koh-et, mee sook toh-eht tahng chah-ee kah-ee. Wahng dah-ee dah-ee som-mah-ee ah yoo mahnkwahn yoon nahn.

2. Pronounce the Thai words in short phrases, in rhythm, with students echoing each phrase. Chant the words together while waving one hand gently outward on the accents and clapping on the second beat of each measure. This timekeeping technique is traditional in Thai music.
3. Teach the melody by rote, phrase by phrase, using your hand to indicate the level of the pitches. Sing the entire song with the class as the students continue to wave and clap the beats. Add finger cymbals (the Thai *ching*) to keep the beat. Finally, sing the English words.
4. Ask the students to listen to "Lao Duang Duan," example three on *Sounds of the World: Southeast Asia*, "Lao." Note that the instrumental piece is related to the birthday song "Phleng Wan Koet." Identify the sound of the flute, xylophones, gongs, drums, and accordion. Play the melody with a classroom ensemble of recorders and xylophones. Add finger cymbals and drums to improvise an ostinato pattern of the player's choice.

Integrating music with other studies

On a map of Southeast Asia, color code the areas whose artistic traditions have been influenced by Chinese, Indian, and Islamic cultures. Emphasize, however, that although some regions are influenced by other cultures, there are indigenous elements that produce unique interpretations of musics from beyond the borders. In mainland Southeast Asia these unique elements include instruments such as the wooden xylophones; the knobbed gongs (in particular the circle of gongs); the *ching* (finger cymbals) of the Thai, Lao, and Cambodian cultures; and the Vietnamese monochord. Copy illustrations of these native musical instruments from the illustrations in this chapter, and attach them to the map.

Ask the students to imagine that they are French missionaries in 1700, traveling by boat up the Mekong River, which runs through Cambodia, Laos, and Thailand. What would be their impressions of the people and their music on first hearing it? Teach the class a French folk song (for example, "Sur le pont

Figure 4.

d'Avignon"). How might the Southeast Asian peoples react to it? What are the similarities and differences between a French folk song and "Courtly Evening"? List the students' responses on the board.

Tell the Thai story of "Why the Parrot Repeats Man's Words," the Lao tale of "Mister Lazybones," or the Vietnamese fable of "The Little Lizard's Sorrow" in *Best-Loved Folk Tales* (see bibliography). Guide the students to an understanding of the moral of each story as it might be applied to American life. Point out that these morals are easily grasped in any culture. Images such as the parrot, the lizard, and jungle flowers, on the other hand, are not easily transferable to life in North America, but are characteristic of Southeast Asia.

Invite a Southeast Asian person to visit the class and share his or her stories, arts and crafts, songs, and descriptions of life-styles there. A university community or international center may be able to suggest people who represent Mainland Southeast Asian countries, or your students may have friends or family members who would be willing to help.

Discuss contemporary films that illustrate the American experience in Southeast Asia from the 1950s to the present: *Apocalypse Now, The Deer Hunter, Platoon, Good Morning, Vietnam, The Killing Fields,* and *Vietnam: A Television History.* Which parts of these films can be interpreted as strictly Hollywood interpretations and which parts are authentic renderings of the historical situations? Assign readings from newspapers and magazines of that period as a comparison.

INDONESIA

Indonesia, the largest country in Southeast Asia, is composed of more than fourteen thousand islands stretching between mainland Southeast Asia and Australia. The islands that form Indonesia stretch nearly three thousand miles (the approximate distance from San Francisco to Boston) but contain only twice the total land area of Texas. The principal islands or island groups include Java, Sumatra, Kalimantan (the Indonesian section of Borneo), Sulawesi (Celebes), the Moluccas, Nusa Tenggara (The Lesser Sundas), and Irian Jaya (West New Guinea).

In the relatively small land area of Indonesia live approximately 175 million people, making it the fifth largest population of the world. More than two-thirds of the inhabitants reside on the island of Java, which contains the capital of the republic, Jakarta.

The people of Indonesia are generally short and slender with light brown skin and straight, black hair. Ethnic diversity abounds in the islands, however, and several million Chinese constitute an important minority in the society. Most Indonesians are Moslems, but their beliefs often consist of a mixture of Islam, Hinduism, and animism. The people of the island of Bali, just off the east coast of Java, are predominantly Hindu.

Large numbers of Indonesians earn their living from farming and fishing. The islands of Indonesia are intersected by the equator, making the climate warm and humid except in the cooler regions of the volcanic mountains. The warm temperatures, combined with the rich, volcanic soil, allow growth of

294

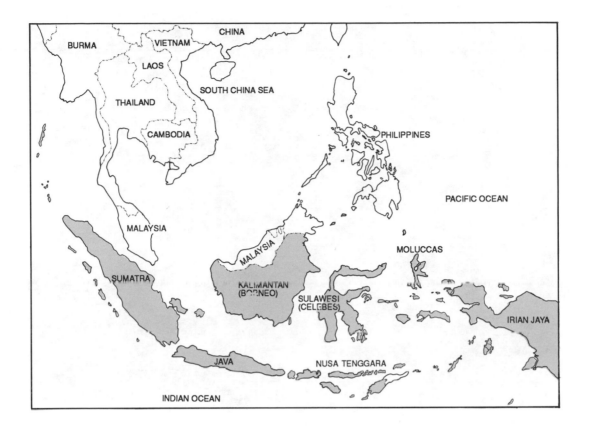

various agricultural crops including rice, tobacco, rubber, spices, and tea. Early explorers called Indonesia the Spice Islands, and it was a western route to these islands that Christopher Columbus sought when he discovered America.

Many diverse influences have shaped Indonesian culture. As early as 2500 B.C., people from southern China were migrating to the islands. At the time of the Roman empire in the West, Indian traders traveled to Indonesia, bringing with them the Hindu and Buddhist religions. The many Hindu and Buddhist monuments found throughout the islands attest to their brilliant artistic accomplishments. In the fourteenth and fifteenth centuries, Muslim traders brought Islam to the islands, particularly to Java. The nearby island of Bali, however, became a haven for Hindus, who nurtured one of the most brilliant artistic traditions in the islands. Beginning in the sixteenth century, European traders arrived. The Dutch exerted the greatest influence on the islands, which they called the Netherlands East Indies. Growing nationalism in the twentieth century eventually led to the establishment of the independent Republic of Indonesia in 1949.

Despite considerable outside influence, the traditional arts of dance, puppet theater, and music have continued to flourish throughout Indonesian history.

295

Figure 5. Javanese gamelan

General characteristics

One of the most sophisticated types of music found in Indonesia is played by *gamelan* orchestras (see figure 5). A Javanese *gamelan* is composed primarily of xylophone-like instruments and knobbed gongs. The orchestra also contains a flute, several stringed instruments, and drums. Vocalists are also important members of the orchestra.

For many centuries *gamelan* music has been an integral part of Indonesian life, accompanying puppet plays and dance-dramas and being featured at temple festivals, weddings, birthdays, visits of guests and heads of state, and numerous other occasions. Hundreds of *gamelan*s are present throughout the islands today and their performances are an important artistic and recreational activity for many people. Performances by the most distinguished ensembles are often broadcast on the radio; Conservatories of music have also been established where students can study this orchestral tradition.

There are several styles of *gamelan* music in Indonesia. Although there are similarities between the styles of different localities, this segment deals primarily with the characteristics of Javanese music.

Melodies use two principal scale or tuning systems: the five-toned *slendro* and the seven-toned *pelog*.

296

Slendro

Pelog

The scale intervals used in Java are quite different from those used in Western music, so Western notation can give only an approximation of the actual pitches. Indonesian musicians often use numbered notation like that printed above the notes in the *slendro* and *pelog* scales. Melodies often use considerable stepwise motion in ascending, descending, and undulating contours. Hocket or resultant melodies (those made when several different players add notes at appropriate times) are sometimes used.

Javanese music commonly uses duple meter with beats grouped into cycles that are marked off by the sounding of various sizes of gongs. The musical texture is polyphonic with melodies organized in strata or levels. Musicians often play simultaneous variations of a melodic line (heterophony).

Various dynamic levels occur in *gamelan* compositions, including both loud and soft sections as well as the use of crescendo and decrescendo. The timbre of Javanese music is quite different from that of Western music: Voices often have a somewhat nasal or pinched quality, and although percussion, wind, and stringed instruments are used in the *gamelan*, percussion instruments predominate. Musical forms in *gamelan* music often involve the repetition of melodies and rhythms.

The lessons in this section are designed to introduce students to some of the principal characteristics of Indonesian *gamelan* music through performance on instruments that are commonly found in most schools. The lessons include instructions for fashioning a makeshift *gamelan* using xylophones, melody bells, glockenspiels, and so on. Students will learn the principal characteristics of Indonesian music more quickly through a hands-on approach than through lectures alone.

Along with performing in an "American *gamelan*," have students listen to several examples of *gamelan* music from Indonesia. It is especially important for students to listen to these authentic examples carefully since they are the actual musical sounds of the Indonesian *gamelan*.

297

Figure 6. American children playing gamelan *music*

LESSON ONE

■ OBJECTIVES:

Students will:

Perform a Javanese *gamelan* composition titled "Ritjik-Ritjik" (Sound of Flowing Water).

Materials:
1. Xylophones, glockenspiels, and melody bells of different sizes
2. Gongs of different sizes: These can be fashioned from pie pans or other kitchen utensils
3. A small, barrel-shaped drum (a drum of any size may be used)

■ PROCEDURES:

1. At its simplest, Javanese *gamelan* music is based on a fixed melody that is played over and over in ostinato fashion.

298

In "Ritjik-Ritjik," the melody is in the *pelog* scale system. The numbers under the notes in this example refer to specific pitches. Write the numbers on the melody bells (ensuring that the numbers do not leave permanent marks) so the students can easily see and play the pitches. Make certain that the students notice the repetition in the melody.

2. Traditionally, the fixed melody is generally played on the *saron barung, saron demung,* and *slentum* (see figure 7). In the classroom you can use glockenspiels, melody bells, or xylophones. Have several students play the melody while the rest of the class sings on a neutral syllable such as "loo."

3. In a *gamelan* composition, the fixed melody is punctuated at various points by a series of gongs (see figure 9). The largest gong, called the *gong ageng*

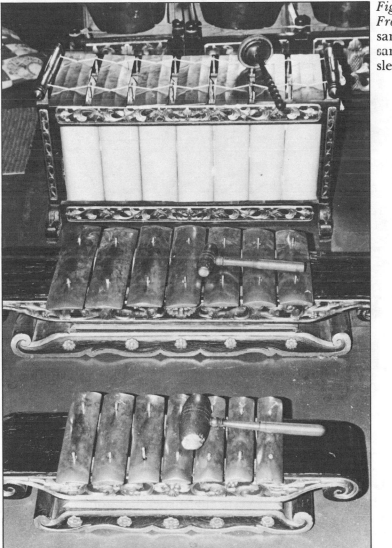

Figure 7.
Front to back:
saron barung,
saron demung,
slentum

299

Figure 8. Students playing a melody on saron

(marked "G" in the score), is sounded at the ends of the longest melodic phrases; in "Ritjik-Ritjik" this occurs at every eighth beat. The *kempul* (marked as "P" in the score), smaller, vertically suspended gongs, sound on beats three, five, and seven of each melodic phrase. The *kenong* (marked as "N" in the score), pot gongs placed horizontally on wooden-frame supports, are played on beats two, four, six, and eight. The *ketuk* (marked as "T" in the

Figure 9. Background: gong ageng *(right) and* kempul *(left); foreground:* ketuk *(right) and* kenong *(left)*

Students playing a gamelan *melody on Orff instruments*

301

Student playing the kenong

score), a set of small horizontally-placed gongs, is played on the off-beats (the eighth note following each beat: counted "1 *and* 2 *and*"). In effect, the sounding of the gongs at various points in the melody forms a cycle of beats:

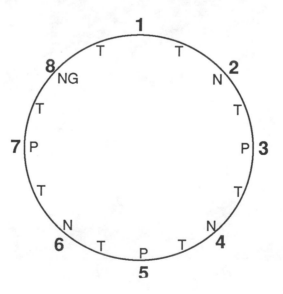

4. Have the students devise some gong-like instruments analogous to the Indonesian gongs and play them at the appropriate places in the fixed melody. (Create gongs by using pots and pans. Select some that produce a pleasant sound when struck in the middle with a soft-headed mallet made from a stick that is covered with heavy cloth on one end.)
Play the fixed melody and add the *gong ageng* ("G") on beat eight.

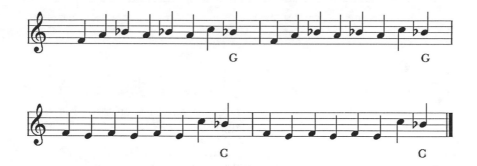

Play the fixed melody and *gong ageng* and add the *kenong* ("N") on beats two, four, six, and eight.

Play fixed melody, *gong ageng*, and *kenong*, and add the *kempul* ("P") on beats three, five, and seven.

Play fixed melody and *gong ageng*, *kenong*, and *kempul*, and add the *ketuk* ("T") on the offbeats.

5. The fixed melody, with its underlying framework of gongs, is embellished or elaborated on by a variety of percussion, wind, and stringed instruments (see figures 11 and 12). The embellishing parts in a *gamelan* composition may be simple or highly complex, and some require years to learn. One of the simplest embellishing techniques consists of repeating each tone of the fixed melody.

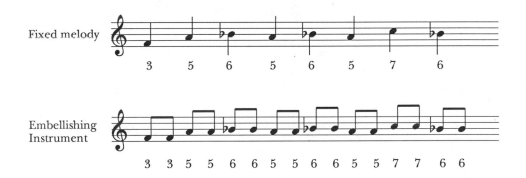

   Have several students play the fixed melody while other students embellish it, doubling on xylophones, glockenspiels, or melody bells.
6. Perform the entire piece. Divide the class so that some students are playing the fixed melody, others are playing the gongs, and still others are playing embellishing parts. Play the piece through several times at a moderate tempo (♩ = 88).
7. In *gamelan* compositions, there are two basic styles of playing: a loud style in a moderately fast tempo and a soft, slower style, played at approximately one-

304

half the tempo of the fast section. Have the class rehearse the composition by playing it through six times; two times loud and in a moderately fast tempo, two times soft and in a slow tempo, and two times loud and in a moderately fast tempo. The teacher or a student should keep the beat on a drum (*kendang*) and should lead the group in making changes in tempo.

Loud/fast	Soft/slow	Loud/Fast
3 5 6 5 6 5 7 6	3 5 6 5 6 5 7 6	3 5 6 5 6 5 7 6
3 5 6 5 6 5 7 6	3 5 6 5 6 5 7 6	3 5 6 5 6 5 7 6
3 2 3 2 3 2 7 6	3 2 3 2 3 2 7 6	3 2 3 2 3 2 7 6
3 2 3 2 3 2 7 6 :‖	3 2 3 2 3 2 7 6 :‖	3 2 3 2 3 2 7 6 :‖

8. Have the students summarize on the board some of the things they have studied in this lesson: the *pelog* scale, ostinato, duple meter with the cycle of beats outlined by the playing of gongs, loud and soft sections, and the *gamelan*'s focus on percussion instruments and timbres.

Figure 11. Embellishing instruments: peking, gender, gambang, *and* bonang *(foreground to background)*

305

Figure 12.
Embellishing
instruments: celempung
suling, *and*
rebab *(from*
left to right)

Student playing the kendang

■ OBJECTIVES:

Students will:

1. Perform the Javanese *gamelan* composition titled "Udan Angin" (The Monsoon).
2. Identify the use of ostinato, duple meter, and cycle of beats outlined by the sounding of gongs, embellishing the fixed melody, and the timbre of percussion instruments.
3. Listen to a selection of Javanese *gamelan* music, and correctly identify musical events.
4. Watch a segment of the film *Percussion Sounds*, which shows elementary school students in California playing the *gamelan* composition "Udan Mas."

Materials:

1. Several Orff metallophones to simulate the *saron barung, saron demung*, and *slentum* and embellishing instruments (see figure 7)
2. Four sizes of gongs made from pots and pans. Select those that produce a pleasant sound when struck in the middle with a soft-headed mallet made from a stick that is covered with heavy cloth on one end.
3. Film: *Percussion Sounds*, 18 minutes, color (see filmography)
4. Recording: *Javanese Court Gamelan*, Nonesuch H-72044, side one, band one

■ PROCEDURE:

1. Play the following Javanese *gamelan* composition "Udan Angin" on the Orff metallophones. (It is in the *slendro* scale system.) Make sure that the students know that phrases one and two are identical and phrases three and four are identical. As selected students play the melody, have the rest of the class sing along on a neutral syllable such as "loo." Repeat the melody until every one has learned it, having the students take turns playing the melody.

2. Add the gong parts to the melody.
   a. As the students play and sing the fixed melody, strike a large gong (*gong ageng*), sounding on the last beat of each phrase, as follows:

   b. Have the class play "kenongs" on beats two, four, six, and eight of each phrase of the fixed melody. The "kenongs" should be selected so that their approximate pitches blend with the melody notes that are played at the same time as they sound.

   c. Have the class play the *kempul* on beats three, five, and seven of each phrase of the fixed melody. Again, the sounds should be consonant with the pitches on which they sound.

308

d. Have a student play the *ketuk* on the offbeats.

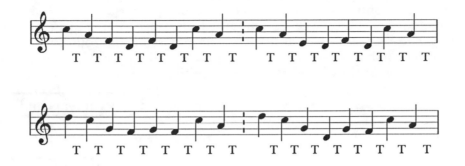

3. Practice "Udan Angin" with some members of the class playing and singing the fixed melody and other members of the class playing the gong parts. Repeat the complete composition over and over in ostinato fashion.
4. Add a simple, embellishing part to the fixed melody and gongs. Using small metallophones, have several students double the fixed melody by repeating its notes:

5. Once the students feel comfortable doubling the melody, have several of them double and anticipate the fixed melody, adding their part to the rest of the ensemble.

Have the students practice "Udan Angin" by playing the fixed melody (and including the gongs and the embellishment parts) over and over as many times as they wish. Have one student keep the tempo by beating a drum

($\downarrow$ = 88). When the students wish to end the composition, the drummer should guide an increase in tempo through several cycles of the melody, closing on the final note of the fixed melody.

6. Have the students listen to the selection from *Javanese Court Gamelan*, side one, band one. This piece accompanied entrance of the prince into the *pendopo*, the reception hall at a royal palace. Create the following chart on either the chalkboard or a handout and have students circle the appropriate musical events as they listen to the composition:

(1) Instruments only	or	(Instruments and voices)
(2) (Tempo moderate)	or	Tempo very fast
(3) One line of music	or	(Many lines of music)
(4) Rapid changes in dynamic levels	or	(Dynamic levels stay at about the same level)
(5) (Orchestra composed mainly of percussion instruments)	or	Orchestra composed mainly of wind instruments
(6) (Music generally reserved or restrained)	or	Music generally active or spirited

7. Show film *Percussion Sounds*, which includes a short *gamelan* composition titled "Udan Mas." This selection is particularly attractive because it is played by a group of fifth-grade students performing in a *gamelan* at the University of California at Los Angeles.
   a. Listen for the slow-moving melody played on some of the metallophones.
   b. Notice the gongs that sound at various points in the melody.
   c. Listen to the doubled embellishing part played on some of the metallophones.
   d. Notice how the entire ensemble is kept together by the drummer.

3

L E S S O N   T H R E E

■ OBJECTIVES:
Students will:
1. Listen to a Balinese *gamelan* composition as they follow a listening chart and identify the characteristic elements of strong beat, fast tempo, ornamented melody, predominant timbre of percussion instruments, and duple meter.
2. Perform the Javanese *gamelan* composition "Bendri" and identify the principal musical characteristics of the selection.

3. Sing (on "loo") the *gamelan* composition "Bendri" and include the fixed melody, gongs sounding at various points in melody, and elaborating parts.
4. Listen to "Ketjak," the monkey chant from the *Ramayana*, and identify some of the salient characteristics of the music.
5. Listen to the rock composition "Monkey Chant" by Jade Warrior and identify the use of the Balinese "Ketjak."

Materials:
Recordings:
"Hudjan Mas." *Gamelan Music of Bali*, Lyrichord LLST 7179, side two, band four
"Ramayana Monkey Chant," *Golden Rain*, Nonesuch H-72028, side two
"Monkey Chant," *The Floating World*, Jade Warrior, Island Records, ILSP 9290

■ PROCEDURES:

1. There are several styles of *gamelan* music in Indonesia. One of the most brilliant is found on the island of Bali. Have the students listen to an example of Balinese *gamelan* music, "Hudjan Mas" (Golden Rain). This selection normally accompanies a dance. Place the following items on either the chalkboard or a handout, and have the students circle the appropriate musical events as they listen to the composition:

(1) Slow tempo   or   (Fast tempo)

(2) (Strong feeling for the beat)   or   Weak feeling for the beat

(3) Melody unornamented   or   (Melody heavily ornamented)

(4) (Orchestra composed mostly of   or   Orchestra composed
      percussion instruments)   mostly of stringed instruments

(5) (Duple meter)   or   Triple meter

(6) Music generally   or   (Music generally active,
      reserved, restrained   spirited)

2. Use the *gamelan* instruments and instructional techniques of lessons one and two to teach the class to play the Javanese *gamelan* composition "Bendri" (Wedding Processional), which is in the *slendro* scale system.
   a. Using several sizes of Orff metallophones (that simulate the *saron barung*, *saron demung*, and *slentum* seen in figure 7), have several students play the following melody. As these students play the melody, have other members of the class sing the melody on a neutral syllable ("loo"). Repeat the melody over and over until every one has learned it, taking turns with other class members playing the melody.

```
6   5   2   1   2   1   6   5
```

311

b. Have the students fashion three sizes of gongs, ranging from large to small, simulating *gong ageng, kempul,* and *kenong* (see lesson one for details). In the *gamelan* composition "Bendri," gongs are sounded at various points in the fixed melody.

(1) A large, vertical gong called *gong ageng* (abbreviated as "G" in the score) is struck on the last note of the fixed melody of "Bendri." Have the students play and sing the fixed melody with the large *gong ageng* (or its substitute) sounding on the last beat.

(2) Somewhat smaller, horizontally struck gongs (called *kenong,* abbreviated as "N" in the score) sound on beats two, four, six, and eight. Have the class fashion *kenong* and play them on beats two, four, six, and eight of the fixed melody. (The sounds of the *kenong* should blend with the pitches on which they sound.)

(3) Medium-sized vertically struck gongs (called *kempul,* abbreviated as "P" in the score) sound on beats three, five, and seven. Have the class fashion *kempul* and play them on beats three, five, and seven of the fixed melody.

c. Practice "Bendri" with some members of the class playing and singing the fixed melody while other members of the class play the gong parts. Repeat the fixed melody and gongs over and over in ostinato fashion.

d. Add simple embellishing parts to the fixed melody and gongs. Choose several small metallophones and have students double the fixed melody in the following fashion:

e. Once the students feel comfortable just doubling the melody, ask several students to also double and anticipate the fixed melody in the following fashion:

f. Have the students practice "Bendri" by playing the fixed melody, with gongs and embellishing parts, over and over, for as many times as they wish. Have one student keep the steady beat on a drum (♩ = 88). When the students wish to end the composition, the drummer should gradually slow the tempo to a close on the final note of the fixed melody.

3. Produce a vocal *gamelan* in your classroom.
   a. Return to the *gamelan* composition "Bendri" but this time sing the parts rather than playing them.
      (1) Sing the fixed melody using the syllable "loo." Have about one-quarter of the class repeat the melody over and over in ostinato fashion.
      (2) Divide the rest of the class into thirds and sing the gong parts:
         (a) *Gong ageng* with the sound of a low "gung" being sung by one group of students on beat eight
         (b) *Kenong* with the sound "nong" being sung by another group of students on beats two, four, six, and eight
         (c) *Kempul* with the sound "pool" being sung by the last group of students on beats three, five, and seven

313

    (3) Add the embellishing technique of doubling the fixed melody. Choose several members of the class to double the melody by singing the syllable "lah." Several members of the class double and anticipate the notes of the fixed melody, again using the syllable "lah."

    (4) Perform the entire composition vocally by repeating the fixed melody, gong parts, and embellishing parts over and over in ostinato fashion.

4. Have the class listen to a selection of "Ketjak," the monkey chant from the *Ramayana*. This music is traditionally performed in a temple courtyard in Bali, where several hundred men sit in circular fashion around a central space. In this central area, actors/dancers tell the story of the *Ramayana* epic, in which Prince Rama's wife Sita is captured by the evil King Ravana, and the monkeys assist Prince Rama in his battle with the King. The several hundred men in the circle around the dance drama imitate the monkeys as they chant the syllable "tjak." The music produced by this group gives the effect of a large vocal *gamelan*.

5. Place the following items on either the chalkboard or handouts for the students, and have them circle the appropriate items as they listen to the composition:

    (1) Instruments   or   **(Voices)**

    (2) Tempo slow   or   **(Tempo fast)**

    (3) **(Strong beat)**   or   Weak beat

    (4) **(Much repetition)**   or   Little repetition

    (5) Triple meter   or   **(Duple meter)**

    (6) **("Vocal" *gamelan*)**   or   "Instrumental" *gamelan*

6. Listen to "Monkey Chant" from the rock album *The Floating World* by Jade Warrior. Ask the students if they can identify the use of "Ketjak" in this rock music.

Integrating music with other studies

Whenever possible, you will want to integrate the study of Indonesian music with other subject areas to help students develop a broader cultural context for their musical study. Consider the following suggestions:

Develop a bulletin board, focusing on Southeast Asia and particularly Indonesia. Have the students look for maps and good pictures of the people and their arts and crafts. (*National Geographic* magazines are a good source of both information and pictures; see also Eric Oey's *Indonesia*, Frits A. Wagner's *Indonesia: The Art of an Island Group*, and Sherman Lee's *Far Eastern Art* (see the bibliography).

If possible, invite Southeast Asians to visit your class and speak about their

314

cultures. Encourage the visitors to wear native dress and to bring artifacts that can illustrate cultural values or practices.

Show general introductory cultural films on Indonesia (see filmography). If you live near a college, university, or an Indonesian consulate that has a *gamelan*, plan a field trip to see and perhaps play on the real instruments of the ensemble.

MAINLAND SOUTHEAST ASIA

BIBLIOGRAPHY

Campbell, Patricia Shehan. *Sounds of the World: Music of Southeast Asia: Lao, Hmong, and Vietnamese.* Reston, VA: Music Educators National Conference, 1986. The three tapes include performances of refugee musicians residing in the United States and interviews. A teaching guide is included with transcriptions of some of the recorded music.

Cole, Joanna. *Best-Loved Folk Tales.* Garden City, NY: Doubleday, Anchor Press, 1983. This book contains some Southeast Asian folk tales.

De Roin, N. *Jataka Tales.* New York: Dell Yearling, 1975. This book includes stories about the virtues and adventures of Buddha in his former lives. An important source of Southeast Asian education and folklore.

Grabt, B. *The Boat People: An "Age" Investigation.* New York: Penguin, 1979. An important study of the causes for and the events of the exodus from Vietnam. Includes information from correspondents' reports.

Jairazbhoy, N., and S. De Vale. *Selected Reports in Ethnomusicology.* Vol. 6, *Asian Music in North America.* Los Angeles: Regents of the University of California, 1985. Includes reports on the music of Lao and Hmong refugees.

Newman, T. *Contemporary Southeast Asian Arts and Crafts.* New York: Crown Publishers, 1977. An illustrated study of craftsmen and their work.

Sadie, Stanley, ed. *New Grove Dictionary of Music and Musicians.* London: Macmillan, 1980. Includes articles on the traditional musics of Thailand, Burma, Laos, Kampuchea, Vietnam, and Malaysia. Some photographs are included.

Shaker, P., and B. Holmes. *Indochina is People.* Philadelphia: United Church Press, 1973. A historical account of the Indochinese and ethnic minorities of the area.

DISCOGRAPHY

Hi Neighbor! CMS UNICEF, 8 vols. Vol. 3: *pi phat* orchestra from Thailand, music accompaniment for a classical play, and folk dance music. Vol. 8: *pi phat* orchestra from Cambodia, music accompaniment to the classical ballet, and Buddhist chant-song.

Music of Southeast Asia. Folkways FE 4428. Selections from Burma, Malaya, Thailand, Laos, and Vietnam.

Musiques de l'Asie traditionnelle. 17 vols. Available from International Book and Record distributors, 40–11 Twenty-fourth Street, Long Island City, NY 11101. Examples of folk and classical styles are included, with representative vocal and instrumental selections from urban and rural areas. Four of the volumes deal with Southeast Asia: Volume 1, Cambodge. PS 33501; Volume 2, Laos. PS 33502; Volume 10, Vietnam. PS 33514; Volume 8, Thailand. PS 33512.

Music of Vietnam. Lyrichord LLST 7337. Includes music for classical zither and lute, monochord, and such folk instruments as coin clappers.

Thailand, Its Music and Its People. Desto D-502. Songs, stories, description of the people, instruments.

Thailand: Lao Music of the Northeast. Lyrichord LLST 7357. Features the *kaen* mouth organ and the oil-can fiddle.

Vietnamese Dan Tranh. Available from World Music Enterprises, 707 Avondale Drive, Kent, Ohio 44242. This record includes seven improvisations, representing six modes, played on the seventeen-stringed zither by Dr. Phong Nguyen.

FILMOGRAPHY

Boy of Southeast Asia. 17 minutes, color. Ann Arbor: University of Michigan, 1967. Appropriate for primary through junior high school levels. Includes fishing, farming, education, health, and the family life of a Thai boy.

City Streets and Silk Sarongs. 29 minutes, color. St. Louis: St. Louis International Center, 1986. Appropriate for junior high school. A day in the life of a young Lao refugee girl who adjusts to American life but learns the traditional dance of her ancestors.

Mekong. 25 minutes, color. 1970. Produced by Shell Oil; available from AVLS, 3300 University Southeast, Minneapolis, MN 55414. Appropriate for grades 4–9. A study of the powerful Mekong River, which runs through Thailand, Cambodia, Laos, and Vietnam, and the problems of surplus, shortage, drought, and flood.

INDONESIA

BIBLIOGRAPHY

Balungan. A publication of the American Gamelan Institute for Music and Education, a nonprofit organization that sponsors courses, workshops, and concerts in the United States. *Balungan* is published three times a year and contains a variety of articles and sources of materials on *gamelan.* Write to the American Gamelan Institute for Music and Education, Box 9911, Oakland, CA 94613.

Beach, Milo Cleveland. *The Adventures of Rama.* Washington, DC: Smithsonian Institution, Freer Gallery of Art, 1983. A translation of the Hindu Epic, the *Ramayana.*

Becker, Judith. *Traditional Music in Modern Java.* Honolulu: The University Press of Hawaii, 1980. An outstanding book on music in present-day Java.

Lee, Sherman. *Far Eastern Art.* Engelwood Cliffs, NJ: Prentice-Hall, n.d.

May, Elizabeth, ed. *Musics of Many Cultures.* Berkeley: University of California Press, 1980. An excellent compilation of individual articles on nearly twenty musical traditions of the world, including Indonesia. It is well illustrated, and each article contains a glossary, a select bibliography, a discography, and a filmography. The book also includes a recording of selected examples.

McPhee, Colin. *Music in Bali.* New Haven, CT: Yale University Press, 1966. An outstanding survey of Balinese music. Many good black-and-white pictures.

Oey, Eric, ed. *Indonesia.* Singapore: Singapore National Printers, 1986 (available from Prentice-Hall, Gulf and Western Building, One Gulf and Western Plaza, New York 10023). A 418-page travel introduction to Indonesia. It contains good articles that summarize many phases of Indonesian culture and include outstanding color photographs.

Sadie, Stanley, ed. *The New Grove Dictionary of Music and Musicians.* London: Macmillan, 1980. There is an outstanding section on the music of Indonesia (vol. 9, 167–220).

Sprague, Sean. *Bali: Island of Light.* Palo Alto, CA: Kodansha International, 1970. A beautiful pictorial introduction to Bali. Many outstanding color pictures, including several of Balinese dances, are included in this paperback.

Wagner, Frits. *Indonesia: The Art of an Island Group.* New York: Greystone Press, 1967. Contains examples of Indonesian artworks.

DISCOGRAPHY

Gamelan Music of Bali. Lyrichord LL7179. An outstanding recording of seven Balinese *gamelan* selections.

Gamelan Semar Pegulingan (Gamelan of the Love God). Nonesuch H-72046. Six *gamelan* selections from Bali played on the *gamelan* Semar Pegulingan, said by Colin McPhee to be "the most exquisitely beautiful of all the thousands of *gamelans* in existence on the island."

Golden Rain. Nonesuch 72028. Contains three selections of Balinese music: "Hudjan Mas" (Golden Rain), "Tunililingan" (Bumblebee), and "Ketjak," the monkey chant from the *Ramayana.*

Javanese Court Gamelan. Vols. 1, 2, and 3. Nonesuch H-72044, H-72074, and H-72083. Three outstanding recordings of central Javanese music.

Music from the Morning of the World. Nonesuch H-72015. Eight selections of music from Bali. Includes a great variety of music: a lullaby sung by a young girl, a *gender* quartet (quartet of metallophones, used here to accompany puppet play), *ketjak* (monkey chant), and several types of *gamelan* music.

FILMOGRAPHY

Bali: Isle of Temples. 27 minutes, color, 1973. Chatsworth Film Distributors. Available from Audiovisual Services, Kent State University, Kent, Ohio 44242. Against a background of traditional Balinese music, this film shows boat building, communal rice farming, sculpting, shadow play, painting, wood carving, and religious ceremonies. It also contains segments of *barong* and *ketjak* dance.

Bali Today. 18 minutes, color, 1969. Hartley Productions, Cat Rock Road, Cos Cob, Connecticut 06807. Written and narrated by Margaret Mead, this documentary shows how art permeates the daily life of the Balinese as demonstrated in the most simple acts to the elaborate ceremonies held for weddings and cremations. Includes background music by *gamelan* orchestras and temple singers.

Indonesia: A Time to Grow. 20 minutes, color, 1970. CRM/McGraw-Hill, 2233 Faraday Avenue, Carlsbad, California 92008. Portrays Indonesia as a country emerging into the modern world. Centering around a trip to the market by an Indonesian farmer and his ten-year-old son, the film presents sharp contrasts between farm and village life.

Miracle of Bali: Music and Dance. 45 minutes, color, n.d. Distributed by Xerox Educational Publications, 245 Long Hill Road, Middletown, Connecticut 06457. An excellent introduction to several styles of Balinese *gamelan* music and dance.

Percussion Sounds. 18 minutes, color, 1969. Distributed by Churchill Films, 662 North Robertson Boulevard, Los Angeles 90069. Contains a short performance of Javanese *gamelan* music ("Udan Mas") played by fifth-grade students.

Wayang Kulit: Shadow Puppet Theater of Java. 22 minutes, color. Baylis Glascock Films, 1017 North La Cienega Boulevard, Los Angeles 90069. An excellent film showing selections of Javanese puppet theater. Includes many interesting segments of puppets and accompanying *gamelan*.

GLOSSARY

Note: The phonetic transcriptions in this glossary use the symbols listed in Webster's New Collegiate Dictionary *(Springfield, MA: G. & C. Merriam, 1977). The transcriptions are meant as a guide only; they do not accurately reflect every nuance of pronunciation for every term. For example, native speakers of some of the languages included here do not use accents, but elongate certain vowels.*

acculturation: culture change that results from contact and interaction between two cultural traditions; an equivalent term is transculturation

aerophone: the category of instruments in which the sound is produced by activating a moving, vibrating column of air

alap \à-làp\: the first segment of many Indian compositions; characterized by improvisation and flexible rhythm

alphorn \'alp-hōrn\: a long, wooden wind instrument used by herdsmen in the Alps for signalling and playing simple melodies

amadinda \'àm-à-'din-d\: a wooden-keyed xylophone of the Ganda people of Uganda; with twelve keys resting on rails made from banana-tree trunks and held in place by small, upright sticks

anacrusis \à-nà-'krü-sis\: upbeat

andalusian cadence: a type of ending for music that shows Spanish influence; consists of the chord progression A minor, G, F, and E (when the music is in A minor); may reflect ancient Moorish roots of Spanish music

arka \'àr-kə\: one half (the follower) of an Amayra Indian panpipe or *siku* (the *ira* half is the leader); usually has seven tubes

arullo \ə-'rrü-yü\: literally "cooing"; a song form that can be a lullaby or a song sung by women to honor a saint on a special saint's day in Colombia

atouta \ä-tō-ü-ta\: the closing song of a Japanese *tegotomono* composition

avāz \a-'va-z\: Persian vocal and instrumental improvisations

bajo \'bə-hō\: Spanish word for bass, meaning the string bass in a salsa orchestra

balafon \'bal-à-fōn\: this word is formed from *Bala* (a general name for West African xylophones) and *fōn* (to play or to sound); refers to the act of playing a xylophone as well as the instrument itself

ballad: a narrative song, usually handed down orally, that tells a story

bandurria \han-'dü-rē-à\: Spanish lute, like a guitar but with six double courses of strings

banqian \ban-chīn\: the melo-rhythmic motivic type of vocal composition used in Peking opera and other Chinese operas

baquiné \bə-kē-nā\: a word used in Puerto Rico to refer to a funeral wake

Bayt al-Hikma \Bīt al-'Hik-ma\: the "house of wisdom," a combination library, research facility, and center for the translation of Greek, Persian, and Hindu books; founded in Baghdad by the caliph al-Ma'-mün

bear's roar: a friction drum that, when played, imitates the growl of a bear

bhupali \bhü-pà-lì\: an evening *raga*

bianqing \byan-chiŋ\: series of tuned stone chimes used in Chinese music

bianzhong \byan-zhōŋ\: series of tuned bronze bells used in Chinese music

binary structure: a two-part structure such as a verse-chorus or A-B structure

bitonic: a musical scale that has only two notes

bluegrass music: a type of country music that is performed by singers with acoustic stringed instruments including the guitar, fiddle, banjo, mandolin, Hawaiian steel guitar (Dobro), and double bass

blue notes: notes used in African-American music and derived from an altered version of the major scale; this blues scale contains third, fifth, and seventh steps lowered by an interval that approximates a quarter tone and cannot be played on the piano keyboard

blues: a type of early African-American folksong, characterized by frequent use of blue notes

bodhran \'bō-drȧn\: a large Irish hand drum, played with a small, thick mallet

bo \bō\: Chinese cymbals

bols \bōls\: mnemonic syllables that facilitate the learning and playing of rhythms on Indian drums

318

bombo \\'bōm-bō\\: a Spanish term for the large double-headed drum of Latin America, particularly the Andes

bongos \\bōŋ-'gōs\\: the Spanish name (perhaps African in origin) for two small single-headed drums used in salsa and other forms of Caribbean music

bouzouki \\bə-'zü-kē\\: a Greek long-necked lute, popular in dance ensembles

branco \\'brə-kō\\: the Portuguese term for "white," in this case a person with white skin; or in Brazil, a person who has been socially accepted as being economically "white" regardless of skin color

branle \\'brȧn-əl\\: a traditional French dance in duple meter, dating from the fifteenth century

bullroarer: a musical instrument, made from a slat of wood with holes cut into it, that is tied to a string and swung through the air to produce whistle-like sounds; used by Native Americans and other cultures

bunraku \\bün-rä-kü\\: a Japanese theater tradition

call-and-response: a musical form that features a lead singer who sings a short phrase that is answered by a chorus or small group of singers; also applies to instrumental music when one instrument is answered by several

calypso: the predominant musical form in Trinidad and Tobago; sung by a solo singer, a calypso is a song form that often makes comments on people, events, and social situations

candomble \\kȧn-dōm-'blä\\: a religious form, type of music, and place of worship among the blacks and other inhabitants of Bahia, Brazil; a syncretic blend of African and Catholic religious elements

canonic technique: a compositional device in which a single melody or musical layer is repeated, starting at different times, to create a layered musical work

cante jondo \\'kȧn-tä 'hōn-dō\\: literally "deep song," this was the predominant vocal musical form of the Spanish gypsies and others in Andalusia, Spain; developed into the Spanish *flamenco*

Cariban: the language of the Carib Native Americans who inhabit parts of northern South America, and who were the predominant cultural group of Native Americans in the Caribbean when Columbus arrived

Carnatic system of music \\kȧr-na-tic\\: the music system of South India

castanets \\kas-tə-'nets\\: a Spanish clapper instrument consisting of two wooden pieces tied together with a string that passes over the player's thumb and first finger; played by *flamenco* dancers

celtic harp \\'kel-tik harp\\: the national instrument of Ireland; smaller than the orchestral harp

ceremonial song: song to accompany certain ancient rituals of birth, adolescence, marriage, and death

charango \\chə-'rən-gō\\: a small guitar-type instrument found in the Andean highlands of Peru, Bolivia, northern Chile, and northern Argentina; many *charangos* are constructed from armadillo shells

cheng \\chəŋ\\: "inheriting": the second idea or phrase of a four-line Chinese composition

ching \\chiŋ\\: Thai finger cymbals that keep the pulse in that country's classical (and some folk) music

chiz \\chiz\\: a composed segment in a North Indian vocal composition; cast in a particular *tala*

chordophone: the category of instruments in which sound is produced by a vibrating string or strings

cimbalum \\'sim-bu-lùm\\: the hammered dulcimer of Hungary

claves \\'klə-vās\\: two hardwood dowels or sticks that are used to play rhythmic patterns (the *clave* rhythm) in *salsa*

clog: a heavy shoe that has a thick sole; clog dancing, a dance step traditionally used in the Southern Appalachians, is a flat-footed walk with embellishments

colonial rhythm: the predominant rhythm of Spanish-derived Latin America; consists of $\frac{6}{8}$ and $\frac{3}{4}$ meters, played simultaneously

concertina: a small accordion popular in Britain and France

congas \\'kōn-gəs\\: the Spanish name (perhaps African in origin, from the Bantu *Congo*) for a large single-headed, barrel-shaped drum; two are used together in *salsa* and other Caribbean musics

conjunct motion: melodic motion by step

coyote tales: Native American stories with a moral, used for entertainment and for teaching right and wrong

cueca \kü-ʹwā-kə\: the African-influenced national dance of Chile, featuring colonial rhythm and rapid dancing by a man and a woman; originated from the *zamacueca* of colonial Afro-Peru

currulao \kü-rrü-ʹlaù\: a rhythmic music and dance form of the blacks of the Pacific coast of Colombia and Ecuador: features the dancing of couples to the music of a marimba, drums, and a rattle

czardas \ʹchȧr-dȧs\: Hungarian national dance in duple meter, performed in circles and by partners

dagu \dä-gü\: a large, skinned, Chinese drum, usually played with two sticks

daluo \dä-lō\: a large Chinese gong, usually played with a padded mallet

dan bau \dȧn baù\: a monochord; an indigenous instrument of Vietnam

dan ko \dȧn kō\: Vietnamese two-stringed fiddle

danmono \dä-n-mō-nō\: a Japanese music form; a strict set of variations

dan tranh \dȧn trȧn\: Vietnamese sixteen-stringed zither

dan ty ba \dȧn tē bə\: Vietnamese four-stringed, long-necked lute

darabukkah \da-ra-ʹbuk-ka\: a cylindrical- and conical-shaped clay drum with a head made from the Nile fish skin

dastgāh \dast-ʹga\: the Persian equivalent of the Arabic *maqām*

desafío \de-sə-ʹfē-yō\: the Brazilian term for a challenge song or musical duel; this term was also found in Renaissance Spain and Portugal

diatonic: not chromatic; diatonic modes use a fixed pattern (traditional in Western music) of intervals

disjunct motion: melodic movement in skips

dizi: \di-z\: a Chinese transverse flute, usually made of bamboo

drone: long sustained notes, usually in the lower-pitched parts of a composition; in Indian music, often played on the *tambura*

Dr. Watts style: a hymm-singing procedure among African Americans consisting of one individual chanting one or two lines of a tune at a time, ending on a definite pitch, and a group responding to that pattern with the same line or an elaboration of that line

dulcimer \ʹdùl-si-mər\: a plucked zither that consists of an elongated sound box with three or four strings that sound a melody and drone; traditional in the Southern Appalachian Mountains

dumm \dùm\: a low, resounding sound produced on Middle Eastern percussion instruments; represented in notation by a note with the stem up

dziro \ʹdzē-rō\: a term for the basic rhythm pattern of a Shona (Zimbabwe) work; it means "foundation you put in before building your house"

electrophones: the category of instruments in which the sound is produced and transmitted or modified by electric or electronic circuitry

entamivu \en-tȧ-ʹmē-vü\: a xylophone and drum ensemble of the Ganda people of Uganda

entenga \en-ʹten-gȧ\: a set of fifteen tuned drums of the *Kabaka*, or traditional ruler of the Ganda people of Uganda

epic: a long, narrative song

erhu \ər-hü\: a two-stringed Chinese fiddle

fandango \fȧn-ʹdan-gō\: a Spanish dance for couples, in moderate to quick triple time, accompanied by guitar and castanets

flamenco \flȧ-ʹmen-kō\: a southern Spanish (Andalusian) dance, with accompanying music that includes guitar and singer and uses ornamented melodies

flauta \flə-ʹü-tə\: the Spanish term for flute, one of the featured solo instruments in *salsa*

flipper-dinger: a folk toy, made of a hollow reed with a cup attached at one end, that has a lightweight ball in it; when air is blown into the reed, the ball in the cup rises into the air

friction drum: a membranophone in which the sound is produced by rubbing the stretched drum with the fingers or other material or by stroking a stick or string that has been fixed to the drumhead, causing it to vibrate

gaeng \gäŋ\: a Hmong mouth organ, a free-reed bamboo instrument with several pipes, each generating a separate pitch

gagaku \gä-gä-kü, gä-ŋä-kü\: the traditional court music of Japan

gaida \ʹgī-də\: Bulgarian and Macedonian (Yugoslavian) bagpipes

gamelan \gȧ-me-län\ The Indonesian word for a musical ensemble

320

gat \gát\: a composed segment in a North Indian instrumental composition; cast in a particular tala

gauchos \gə-'ü-chōs\: the cowboys of Argentina

gazel \ga-'zel\: Turkish vocal improvisations

gee-haw-whimmy diddle: a folk toy, similar to a top, that can spin clockwise or counterclockwise

gong ageng \gong à-gung\: the largest gong used in *gamelan* music

gospel: a style of folksong originally associated with evangelistic revival meetings

griot \'grē-ō\: a generic term for musicians of professional status in West Africa who are hired to sing in praise of important persons and orally recount history

guiro \'wē-rō\: a scraper used in the Caribbean and made from either a gourd (the term originally means "gourd") or metal. It is an important instrument in *salsa* and other Caribbean musics, and is perhaps derived from a Native American instrument

guitarrón \gē-tə-'rrōn\: literally a "large guitar"; often resembles an oversized guitar in Peru; characterized by a very fat resonating body in Mexico

hambo \'màm-bō\: a dance for couples, in triple meter, from Sweden

he \hə\: "closed": the final idea or phrase of a four-line Chinese composition

heterophony: simultaneous use of slightly different versions of the same melody by two or more performers

hetou \hə-tò\: "refrain head": a musical motive that appears at the beginning of each section of a Chinese suite

hewei \hə-wā\. "refrain tail": a motive that appears at the end of each section of a Chinese suite

Hindustani system of music \hin-dü-stan-ì\: the music system of North India

hocket technique: a compositional device in which each musical layer consists of a single sound or a sound pattern that alternates with sounds or sound patterns of other layers—each layer resting while the other is sounded

holler: a type of work song, sung in a shouting style and originated by the African-American field worker

homophony: the multi-voiced music texture in which one voice acts as the principal melody and the other voices move in the same or in a similar rhythm

hora \hō-rə\: an Israeli circle dance

hornpipe: a duple-metered dance of the British Isles, consisting of two groups of four eighth notes

hosho \'hō-shō\: a Shona (Zimbabwe) term for a rattle made from a gourd; a network of string with beads or shells attached hangs around the head of the gourd

huasos \'wə-sōs\: the term for cowboys in Chile

hurdy-gurdy: a medieval stringed instrument whose strings are sounded by a rotating wheel that is operated by a crank at the lower end of the body of the instrument, producing melody and drone simultaneously

hyojo \hyō-jō\: a Japanese pentatonic scale without half steps

idiophone: the category of instruments in which the sound is produced by the vibration of the primary material from which the instrument is made (e.g., the struck key of a marimba)

interlocking parts: music that is made up of several melodic parts that alternate or interlock to form a single melody; a technique used by handbell ringers in America and *siku* players in Peru and Bolivia

īqāᶜ \i-'ka\: the Arabic term for rhythm, also used for the concepts of meter, rhythmic mode, dynamics, timbre, and tempo; used especially to denote a pattern of attacks performed on a percussion instrument

ira \'ē-rə\: one half (the leader) of an Aymara Indian panpipe or *siku*; usually with six tubes

jaltarang \jàl-tà-rang\: an Indian idiophone consisting of a series of bowls that are graduated in size

jazz: a type of music, originally improvised but now also arranged, that is characterized by syncopation, rubato, heavily accented rhythms, dissonance, individualized melodic variation, and unusual tonal effects

jhaptal \jhàp-tàl\: a *tala* consisting of ten beats, divided 2–3–2–3

jig: a dance form of the British Isles, particularly Ireland, in compound duple or triple meter

jo-ha-kyu \jō–hä–kyü\: a tripartite design in traditional Japanese music. *Jo* is the introductory section; *ha* is the central section, containing the principal material; and *kyu* is the last section or drive toward the end

jodlers \'yōd-lùrz\: an Alpine song style that features frequent and rapid passing from a low chest voice to a high falsetto

321

joropo \hō-'rō-pō\: an important song and dance form in Venezuela, characterized by fast colonial rhythm, and often played on the harp

jota \'hō-tə\: a common song and dance form in Spain that features colonial rhythm

juju \'jü-jü\: a style of Nigerian urban popular music, of which King Sunny Ade is a well-known performer

kabuki \kä-bū-kē\: a type of Japanese music theater

kaede \kī-de\: a melodic part added in counterpoint to the principal line in *koto* music

kaen \kān\: a mouth organ, the national instrument of Laos; played soloistically and to accompany singers

kagura \kä-gü-rä, kä-ŋü-rä\: Shinto (Japanese) dance-song

kamanjah \ka-'man-ja\: the Arabic name for the violin

kanji \kä-n-jē\: the Japanese word for Chinese ideographs

kantele \'kán-tel\: a small Finnish zither, similar to the psaltery, shaped like a bird's wing and strung with twenty to thirty strings

katsima \ka-'tchē-mə\ the ancestral spirits of the Hopi or Zuni Indians of the southwestern United States; the masks or dolls made to personify or represent those spirits

kempul \kem-pül\: the vertically positioned, knobbed gongs used in *gamelan* music

kena \'kä-nə\: an Aymara Indian term for flute. It refers to the Andean instrument that has a notch in its end to function as a mouthpiece

kendang \ken-dȧng\: drums used in *gamelan* music

kenong \ke-nȯng\: the horizontally positioned knobbed gongs used in *gamelan* music

ketuk \ke-thuk\: the small, horizontally positioned gongs used in *gamelan* music

kong wong \kȯŋ wȯŋ\: a circle of knobbed gongs, one of the principal melody instruments in the Thai *pi phat* orchestra

kora \'kō-rȧ\: a twenty-one-stringed harp-lute of the Mandinka and Wolof people of Senegal and The Gambia in West Africa

koto \kō-tō\: a Japanese thirteen-stringed zither

kotsuzumi \kō-tsü-zü-mē\: a Japanese shoulder drum, used in *noh* and *kabuki* theater

kudaira \kü-dȧ-'ē-rə\: rhythm patterns that respond to the basic pattern of a Shona music example from Zimbabwe

kudairana \kü-dȧ-ē-'rȧ-nȧ\: responsive rhythm patterns in music of the Shona people of Zimbabwe

kushaura \kü-shȧü-r\: the basic rhythm pattern in Shona music from Zimbabwe; the word can be translated, "what everyone relates to, the line that cuts through"

langeliek \'lang-e-līk\: a Norwegian plucked dulcimer

lavway \'ləv-wä\: an early form of *calypso* in Trinidad and Tobago; uses the call-and-response form

layālī \la-'ya-lē\: Arabic vocal improvisation on the words yā lēlī yā ᶜēnī

likembe \lē-'kem-be\: one of many names for the hand-held, keyed idiophone, played with the thumbs and index fingers, that is found in most areas of Sub-Saharan Africa

limberjack: a rhythm instrument native to the Southern Appalachian Mountains

luogu \lō-gü\ "gongs and drums": a Chinese percussion ensemble

maeuta \mī-ü-tä\: the opening song in a Japanese *tegotomono* composition for the *koto*

maqām \ma-'kam\: the complex modal system governing Arabic music; includes the concepts of melodic modes, motifs, cadences, tonics, and tonal centers

marimba \mȧ-'rēm-bȧ, mȧ-'rim-bȧ\: **1.** a xylophone, found in various sizes and shapes in music cultures across the upper two-thirds of Sub-Saharan Africa **2.** \mə-'rēm-bə\: derived from the African term; refers to a xylophone in Colombia, Ecuador, Guatemala, and elsewhere in Latin America

marinera \ʐmə-rē-'nä-r\: the national dance of Peru; a song and dance form of the coastal region that is very similar to the Chilean *cueca* named for the navy men killed in the War of the Pacific, which Chile lost to Peru that conflict

maru-bihag \mȧ-rü–bi-hȧg\: an evening *raga*

mawlum \maù-lam\: a song style of Laos and northeast Thailand, accompanied by the *kaen*

mawwāl \maw-'wal\: an Arabic poem set to improvised music

mazhar \maz-har\: a large tambourine with a donkey- or goat-skin head and jingles

mbira \m-'bē-rȧ\: one of many names for the hand-held keyed idiophone, played with the thumbs and index fingers, found in most areas of Sub-Saharan Africa. *See also* likembe; sansa

322

membranophone: the category of instruments in which the sound is produced by the vibration of a stretched membrane which is struck, rubbed, or otherwise activated

mestizo \mā-'stē-sō\: literally "mixed," used in the Andes and Pacific coastal region of Latin America to refer to people whose racial background includes Spanish and Indian ancestors

metallophone: the category of instruments in which sound is produced by the vibration of tuned metal bars or slabs

microtonal: music that is based on a system in which the pitches are spaced more closely than the Western semitone

mode: on its most abstract level, a series of notes arranged in scalar fashion, with an idiosyncratic intervallic structure

monody: the music texture in which only one melody is sounded at a time

montuno \mōn-'tü-nō\: the improvisational section in a *salsa* composition; the singer makes up a melody and words, and the musicians often play solos

mordent: a short trill downward from the principal note

mulato \mü-'lə-tō\: in Latin America, a person of mixed black and white ancestry

muwashshah mù-'wash-sha\: Arabic classic song

narrative song: a song that tells a story, such as the ballad or epic

nāy \nay, nī\: a Middle Eastern, obliquely end-blown reed flute

nawbah \'nī-ba\: a North African suite-like form

ngano \n-'gà-nō\: a story-song about something that did not really happen; sung as part of storytelling occasions among the Shona people of Zimbabwe

ngodo \n-'gō-dō\: traditional dance suites, usually in nine to eleven movements, of the Chopi people of Mozambique; accompanied by a large ensemble including xylophones, drums, rattles, and the sound of shields striking the earth

noh \nō\: a six-hundred-year-old Japanese genre of drama; it is still an active form of theater

nohkan \nō-kä-n\: a transverse flute used in Japanese *noh* drama

noter: a narrow piece of dowel, approximately four inches long, that is placed on the melody string of a dulcimer (to the left of a selected fret) and used to change the pitch

nyaya \'nyà-yà\: a story-song about something that really happened; sung as part of storytelling occasions among the Shona people in Zimbabwe

nykelharpa \'nik-àl-harp-ə\: a keyed Scandinavian fiddle that was used for popular dance and festive music; often boat-shaped, with drone strings, one or two melody strings, and up to twelve wooden keys

ostinato: a musical phrase or pattern that is repeated many times. Its use in *salsa* is derived from African music practices

otsuzumi \ō-tsü-zü-mē\: a Japanese hip drum, used in *noh* and *kabuki* theater

oud \üd\: the Greek name for the 'ud

pampas \'pəm-pəs\: the vast grasslands of central Argentina

pelog \pe-lòg\: a seven-toned Indonesian scale or tuning system

pentatonic: any five-note scale

pi nai \bē nī\: a quadruple-reed instrument of the Thai orchestra that produces a sound similar to the oboe

pi phat \bē pàt\: the Thai classical ensemble of xylophones (*ranat*), gong circles, drums, oboe (*pi nai*) and cymbals

pipa \pi-pä\: a four-stringed, short-necked Chinese lute

play-party games: children's songs that combined music with prescribed movement; because selection of partners was the primary function of the songs, they often provided recreational and social activities for young, rural adults

polka: a Bohemian dance in a fast duple meter

polska \'pōls-ka\: a Swedish dance in triple meter, probably of Polish origin, similar to the *mazurka*

polymeter: the simultaneous performance of musical passages in two or more meters

polyphony: the music texture in which two or more rhythmically independent melodies are combined

polyrhythm: simultaneously sounded combinations of different rhythms that form a more or less complex rhythmic texture

power-gathering emblem: an object or symbol that represents or influences the political power of a ruler or ruling group

323

pueblo \\'püäb-lō\\: Native American housing complex built of adobe (sun-dried mud brick), for up to several hundred people

punteado \\pün-tä-'yə-dō\\: in playing guitar or guitar-type instruments, the style of performance in which the musician picks the individual notes of a melody or bass line

purvi \\pür-vì\\: a late afternoon *raga*

qānūn \\ka-'nün\\: an Arabic trapezoidal zither

qi \\chì\\ "open": the first idea or phrase of a four-line Chinese composition

qin \\chin\\: a seven-stringed Chinese board zither

rachenitsa \\rà-chen-'ēt-sà\\: the Bulgarian national dance in ⅞ meter with three beats: ♩ ♩ ♩.

raga \\rà-gà\\: a prescribed series of pitches from which an Indian musical composition is created

ragtime\\ a type of American music, largely composed, that was popular from about 1890 to 1915 and was characterized by strong syncopation in fast, even time, and the use of a regular phrase structure

ranat \\rà-nàt\\: a Thai wooden xylophone

rao \\ràu\\: the unmeasured, improvisatory introduction to traditional Vietnamese music

rap: a type of musical declamation in a strong set meter and rhythm; a kind of rhythmic and rhyming talking

rasqueado \\rəs-kā-'yə-dō\\: in playing guitar or guitar-type instruments, when the musician strums the strings to produce chords

reel: a dance form of northern Europe for lines of couples, with music in duple meter

reverse rondo form: a form akin to the rondo except that the refrain comes after the first verse: A–Refrain–B–Refrain–C–Refrain–D–Refrain

rhythm and blues: a form of popular African-American music, influenced by the blues and gospel music; characterized by a strong, frequently syncopated, beat

rhythmic density: the number of rhythmic pulses per second; often refers to music played with African-derived drumming

rhythmic feeling: in Sub-Saharan African music, the perceptual effect of a rhythmic pattern, which includes the timbres and the movements of musicians and dancers associated with it

rhythmic layering: in African and African-derived music, when several drums of different sizes and tone colors (or other percussion instruments) play individual patterns, the resultant sound consists of layers of rhythms

riqq \\rikk\\: a small Middle Eastern tambourine with a Nile fish-skin head and jingles

rommel pot \\'ròm-məl pòt\\: a friction drum of the Netherlands, played by pulling a rope through a small hole in a pot

runes \\rünz\\: a Finnish narrative song in $\frac{5}{4}$; a collection of them was gathered in the Finnish national epic, the *Kalevala*

rupak \\rü-pàk\\: a *tala* characterized by seven beats divided 3–2–2

sakkah \\'sak-ka\\: a percussive sound half way between the timbre of the *dumm* and that of the *takk*

salsa \\'səl-sə\\: literally "hot sauce," this is Afro-Cuban music from New York, Miami, Havana, San Juan, and other centers of Afro-Cuban population

samāᶜī \\sa-'ma-ì\\: a rhythm in $\frac{10}{8}$; a prelude in reverse rondo form in $\frac{10}{8}$

sankyoku \\sän-kyō-kü\\: a Japanese chamber ensemble, usually consisting of *koto, shamisen, shakuhachi*, and voice

sansa \\'sàn-sà\\: one of many names for the hand-held, keyed idiophone, played with the thumbs and index fingers, that is found in most areas of Sub-Saharan Africa. *See also* likembe; mbira

sanxian \\sän-shan\\: a three-stringed, fretless Chinese banjo

sardana \\sàr-'dà-na\\: a Basque circle dance in duple meter; found in southern France and the Spanish Catalan region

saron barung \\sa-ròn bà-rùng\\: a metallophone used in *gamelan* music

saron demung \\sa-ròn de-mùng\\: a metallophone, sounding one octave lower than the *saron barung*, that is used in *gamelan* music

scat: a way of singing in some African-American music, in which the singer improvises using meaningless syllables in imitation of the sounds of a musical instrument

schuplattler \\'shü-plàt-lər\\: an Austrian boot-slapping dance in triple meter

seguidilla \\se-gē-'dē-yà\\: a dance of southern Spain in triple meter, with a text based on four-line poems and guitar accompaniment

sesquiáltera \\sàs-kē-'əl-tā-rə\\: an alternation of $\frac{3}{4}$ and $\frac{6}{8}$ meters in Latin American music

324

shakuhachi \shä-kü-hä-chē\: an end-blown Japanese bamboo flute with five finger holes; the player blows across a notch in the upper end of the instrument

shamisen \shä-mē-se^n\: a three-stringed Japanese plucked lute

sheng \shəŋ\: a Chinese mouth organ

Shinto \shi-n-tō\: a Japanese belief system involving the veneration of ancestors

siku \'sē-kü\: an Aymara Indian term for panpipe; the instrument consists of two halves (*ira*, or leader, and *arka*, or follower) played by two musicians who interlock their parts

silk and bamboo: the Chinese phrase that designates stringed and wind instruments

sitar \si-tår\: one of the most important plucked chordophones of India

slendro \slen-drō\: a five-tone Indonesian scale or tuning system

slentum \slen-thùm\: a *gamelan* metallophone, constructed with thin metal plates placed over resonating tubes

soca \'sō-kə\: a modern form of calypso from Trinidad and Tobago, performed on electronic instruments and featuring singers. The term is a shortened form of "soul calypso"

strophic melodic structure: a melodic structure in which the same music or melodic material is used despite changes in the text

suona \sò-nä\ a double-reed Chinese shawm or oboe

sympathetic vibrating strings: thin metal strings that lie below the main strings of many Indian chordophones and vibrate in sympathy when the main melodic strings are activated

syncopation: a displacement of the normal metric accent; the accentuation of normally unaccented beats

tabla \tà-blà\: the most important drums of North India

tahrīr \tah-rēr\: a Persian vocal trill, akin to sobbing

taiko \tī-kō\: a round floor drum used in Japanese *Noh* and *Kabuki* music

takk \takk\: a short, crisp sound produced on percussion instruments and represented in transcriptions of Middle Eastern music by a note with the stem down

tala \tà-là\: a cycle of beats in Indian music

tambur \'tàm-bùr\: a long-necked, plucked lute of the Middle East and Yugoslavia

tambura \tam-bü-rà\: a plucked chordophone that produces the drone in Indian music

tamburitza \tàm-bùr-'it-zà\: an ensemble of *tambur*s of different sizes and pitch ranges

taphon \tà-fōn\: the large, double-headed drum used in Thai ensembles

taqsīm \tak-sēm\: Arabic and Turkish instrumental improvisations, mainly unmeasured

tarantella \tà-ràn-'te- là\: Italian (Neopolitan) dance in a quick ⁶⁄₈ meter, named for the tarantula spider whose poisonous bite the dance was supposed to cure

tegoto \te-gō-tō\: an instrumental interlude in Japanese *tegotomono* compositions

tegotomono \te-gō-tō-mō-nō\: the Japanese genre of songs accompanied by *koto*

tetrachord: a series of four notes with an idiosyncratic interval structure; used in Middle Eastern music to construct modes

tetratonic: a four-toned scale

timbales \tēm 'bə läs\: a Spanish term for two single-headed, shallow-bodied drums in Caribbean *salsa*. They are placed on stands and played by one musician

time-line: in African and African-derived music, the basic rhythmic line that is played by the *claves* in *salsa* and by a bell or bottle in other African-American forms of music

tintala \tin-tà-là\: a *tala* consisting of sixteen beats divided 4–4–4–4

tonal language: a language in which meaning is determined by the difference in the pitches of spoken syllables

tres \'trās\: a Caribbean guitar-type instrument that has three courses of double strings and is often used in Cuban *salsa*

tritonic: a three-toned scale

tsamiko \sà-mē-kō\: a Greek line dance in slow ⁶⁄₈ meter (here grouped in steps alternating slow-quick, slow-quick)

TUBS notation: a form of notation designed by James Koetting for African drumming. The term refers to "time unit box system": Individual beats of a percussion instrument are indicated by an individual box in a series of boxes

ᶜud \üd\: **1:** an Arabic short-necked, plucked lute. **2.** a lute, brought by the Moors to Spain; ancestor of the Spanish guitar

vals \vàls\: a Scandinavian waltz, or triple-meter dance

vaquero \bə-'kā-rō\: the term for a cowboy in Venezuela and Colombia; derived from *vaca* (cow)

vina \vi-nȧ\: one of the oldest plucked chordophones of India

vocable\ syllables with extra-linguistic meaning, such as *he, ne, yo,* or *heyo,* used by Native Americans to communicate special messages in their songs

waslah \'was-la\: a suite-like form from nineteenth- and early twentieth-century Egypt

wayno \'wəy-nō\: an Andean Native American dance and song form (also spelled *huayno*)

work song: any type of song that accompanies work or that may be used to make work easier or more efficient; often using rhythms that imitate the type of work being done

xiao \siaů\: an end-blown Chinese bamboo flute

xiaoluo \siaů-lō\: a small Chinese gong, usually played with a thin, wooden mallet

zamba \'səm-bə\: a song and dance form from Argentina

zambo \'səm-bō\: Latin American, especially Peruvian, term for an individual of mixed black and native American descent

zheng \zheŋ\ a Chinese board zither with an individual, adjustable bridge for each string

zhuan \zhwän\: "turned": the third idea or phrase of a four-line Chinese composition

INDEX

Accordion, 38, 123, 124, 126, 134, 293
Aerophones. *See* Instruments
Africa
  culture of, 145–48, 170–72
  geography of, 144, 146, 147, 170
  history of, 145–46, 170
  language of, 145, 147–49
African Americans, 48–67. *See also* North America, ethnic groups of
Alap, 214, 226, 227–28, 232, 233, 283
Alphorn, 123, 124
Amadinda, 168
America. *See* Latin America; North America
Anacrusis, 126
Andalusian cadence, 83
Andes. *See* Latin America
Anglo-Americans. *See* North America, culture of
Antiphony. *See* Texture, antiphonal
Appalachia, 10–32 (*see also* North America)
Arab countries. *See* Middle East
Argentina. *See* Latin America
Arpeggios. *See* Melody, characteristics of
Arka, 85, 87, 88
Arrullo, 93, 94
Arts, visual. *See* Interdisciplinary education
Asia, culture of, 211–12, 225, 234, 239–42, 258–60, 282, 293, 294–96
  ethnic groups of, 239–40
  geography of, 210–11, 234, 238–40, 242, 258, 280–81, 294–95
  history of, 212–13, 239–41, 281–82, 295
  languages of, 211, 239–41, 259
Asymmetrical rhythm, 126, 224, 232
Atouta, 261
Audiovisual aids, use of, 6, 43, 61, 172, 234, 256, 262, 267, 268, 272, 273, 286, 294, 310, 315. *See also Discography and Filmography sections at end of each chapter*
Autoharp, 132, 133, 134, 252
Avāz, 186

Bagpipes, 123, 125, 126, 129, 138, 217
Bajo, 112
Balafon, 170
Ballads. *See* Songs
Bandurria, 136
Banjo, 15, 16–17
Banqian, 245
Bartók, Béla, 141
"Bear's roar" instrument, 22
Bells, 6, 35, 297, 298–99, 304. *See also* Melodic instruments

"Belly dance," 202, 205
Bianqing, 244
Bianzhong, 244
Binary structure. *See* Form, musical
Bitonic. *See* Scales
Biwa, 262
Bluegrass music, 12, 27
"Blue notes," 52
Blues, 51, 52, 55, 58–60, 61, 63
Bo, 248, 250
Bodhran, 123, 129
Bolivia. *See* Latin America
Bols, 218–20, 224–26
Bombo, 104, 105, 109
Bonang, 305
Bongos, 111, 112, 218–20, 224–25, 229
Bouzouki, 126
Branle, 134–35
Brass band, 124
Brazil. *See* Latin America
Breath rhythm, 262
British Isles. *See* Europe
Bugaku, 261
Bulgaria. *See* Europe
"Bullroarer," 36

Call-and-response, 53, 59–60, 67, 83, 93, 94, 95, 97, 99, 111, 113, 161
Calypso, 96–97, 98, 99, 114
Cambodia. *See* Asia
Canto jondo, 81
Carnatic system, 213
Carribean. *See* Latin America
Castanets, 126, 136
Celempung, 306
Celtic harp, 123
Central America. *See* Latin America
Ceremonial song. *See* Songs
Chamber music. *See* Instruments, ensembles of
Chanting. *See* Rhythmic activities
Chants, 125, 202, 259, 260, 282
Chap, 287
Charango, 104, 105, 106, 107, 109, 110, 114
Cheng, 245
Child, Francis James, 13
Chile. *See* Latin America
Chimes, 244
China, 238–257 (*see also* Asia)
Ching, 285
Chiz, 214, 226, 228–29, 232, 233
Chordophones. *See* Instruments
Cimbalom, 126, 141

327

variation, 161, 163, 245, 260, 262, 271–72, 283
verse-refrain, 133

Gaeng, 285
Gagaku, 259, 260, 261, 262, 265
Gaida bagpipes, 126, 138
Gambang, 305
Gambia, The. See Africa
Gamelan, 296–314
Gankogui, 6
Gat, 214, 226, 232, 233
Gazel, 186
Gender, 305
Geography. See Interdisciplinary education, social studies
Germanic countries. See Europe
Ghana. See Africa
Glissando, 105
Glockenspiel, 297, 298–99, 304
Gome songs, 166–67
Gongs, 248–51, 283, 293, 296, 297, 298–305, 308–9, 312–14
  daluo, 248
  gong ageng, 299–300, 301, 303–4, 308, 312, 313
  kempul, 300, 301, 303–4, 308, 312, 313
  ketuk, 300, 301, 304, 309
  kong wong, 284, 285, 287
  xiaoluo, 284, 250
Gospel songs. See Songs, religious
Griot, 154
Güiro, 112
Guitar, 15, 42, 58, 59, 100, 104, 105, 106, 109, 112, 126, 127, 133, 134, 136, 137, 139, 153, 169, 197, 214, 216–27, 228, 233
Guitarrón, 106
Gypsy scale, 126

Hambo, 124
Hardanger fiddle, 123, 124
Harmonica. See Mouth organ
Harmony, 51, 59, 83, 99, 106, 112, 123, 132, 136, 139, 141, 243, 254–55
Harp, 105, 123, 153
He, 245
Heterophony. See Texture, heterophonic
Hetou, 245
Hewei, 245
Hichiriki, 262
Hindustani system, 213
History. See Interdisciplinary education, social studies
Hocket technique, 151, 153, 297
"Hollers," 55, 59
Homophony. See Texture, homophonic

Hora, 126
Hornpipe, 123
Hosho, 158
"Hot" rhythms, 48
Hungary. See Europe
Hurdy-gurdy, 125
Hymns. See Songs, religious
Hyojo, 260

Idiophones. See Instruments
Immigration to U.S. See North America, immigration to
Improvisation, 4, 48, 51, 52, 54, 83, 214, 222–23, 228, 229–30, 285
  in movement, 150
  instrumental, 67, 111, 158, 161, 163, 185, 186, 226, 227, 233, 293
  melodic, 154, 155
  rhythmic 89, 92, 93, 150, 164–65
  textual, 99
  vocal, 41, 50, 54, 63–64, 186
India. See Asia
Indonesia, 294–315 (see also Asia)
Instruments, 80. See also Classroom instruments; Melodic instruments; Orff instruments; names of individual instruments
  aerophones (wind), 80, 153, 244
  African, 6
  brass, 113
  chordophones (strings), 153, 168, 244, 296
  construction of, 6, 21, 22, 25, 40, 43–46, 86–88, 96, 99–100, 107–8, 223, 269, 303, 312
  double-reed, 123, 126, 244
  electrophones, 153
  ensembles of, 80, 83, 89, 90, 92, 93, 96, 97–98, 105, 106, 109, 111–13, 124, 125, 170, 185, 188, 244, 262. See also Gagaku; Gamelan; Luogo; Pi phat; Steel bands
  idiophones (percussion), 83, 89–92, 94, 99–100, 126, 151, 152, 153, 159, 161, 184–85, 283, 298
  keyboard, 153
  membranophones (drums), 35, 36, 38, 40, 41, 80, 82, 83, 85, 89–94, 96–98, 104, 105, 109, 111, 112, 113, 123, 126, 129, 147, 148, 152–53, 160, 161, 170, 186–87, 248–51, 265, 283, 285, 287, 289, 293, 296, 298, 309–10, 313
  metallophones, 96, 307, 309, 310, 311, 313
  "pan-European," 123
  playing of (see Performing activities)
Interdisciplinary education, 1–2, 7, 113, 233. See also Bibliography sections at end of each chapter; individual geographical areas
  arts, visual, 1, 4, 5, 7, 30, 32, 46, 47, 67, 114–

Membranophones. *See* Instruments
Metallophones. *See* Instruments
Meter. *See* Rhythm, meter of
Microtonal. *See* Scales
Middle East
   culture of, 179–81
   geography of, 178–80
   history of, 180–81
   language of, 180
Modes. *See* Scales
Monochord, 283, 293
Montuno, 111, 113
Mordents, 105
Mouth organs, 243, 244, 254–55, 262, 283,
   285
Movement, 4, 6, 14, 48–49, 54, 150, 172. *See*
   also Dance activities
Multicultural music education, importance of,
   3–4
Multiphony, 261
Multisection form. *See* Form, musical; Songs
Music Educators National Conference, 3
Muwashshah, 186, 187, 197–99

Nagauta shamisen, 260
Native Americans, 33–47. *See also* Latin Amer-
   ica, ethnic groups of; North America,
   ethnic groups of
Nawbah, 185
Nāy, 200, 201
Ngano, 162, 172
Ngodo, 154
Nigeria. *See* Africa
Noh, 260, 266–67
Nohkan, 261, 266, 268
North America
   culture of, 9–10, 11, 12, 33–35, 48–51
   ethnic groups of, 2, 9–10, 11, 16, 33–35, 38,
      47, 48–51, 67
   geography of, 8–10, 11, 12, 33–34, 67
   history of, 10, 11–12, 33–34, 48–51
   immigration to, 2, 5, 9–12, 16
   languages of, 34
Nyaya, 162
Nyckelharpa, 123, 124

Oboe, 262, 283, 285, 287
Olsen notation, 110
Opera, 172, 244, 245, 256–57, 282, 283
Oral transmission of songs, 12, 18, 32, 36–37,
   40, 58, 61, 161
Orff, Carl, pedagogy of, 6
Orff instruments, 21, 94, 96, 301, 307, 311. *See*
   also Melodic instruments; *names of individ-*
   ual instruments
Organum, 123
Ornamentation, 50, 53, 54, 55, 63, 105, 123,
   181, 185, 193, 195, 202, 213, 227, 231,
   233, 252, 282, 285, 304, 307, 309, 310,
   311
Ostinatos. *See* Melodic ostinatos; Rhythmic
   patterns
Otsuzumi, 260, 266, 267, 268
Oud, 126

Panpipe. See *Siku*
Peking, 305
Pelog, 296–97, 299, 305
Pentachord, 182
Pentatonic. *See* Scales
Performing activities, 4, 5–6, 18, 21, 22, 24–
   25, 27, 38, 43, 45, 93, 99, 104, 107–9, 132,
   139, 156–65, 190–95, 216–17, 219–20,
   222–23, 228–29, 248–51, 265, 287–89,
   292, 298–313 passim. *See also* Dance; In-
   struments, ensembles of; Movement;
   Singing
Peru. *See* Latin America
Piano, 42, 112, 113, 139, 192, 197, 214, 217,
   228, 286
Pi nai, 285, 287
Pipa, 244, 245, 253–55
Pipe and drum, 125
Pi phat, 283, 285, 286, 287, 291
Play-party games. *See* Songs, game and party
Polkas, 126
Polska, 124
Polymeter. *See* Rhythm, meter of
Polyphony. *See* Texture, polyphonic
Polyrhythm. *See* Rhythmic patterns
Program music, 245, 252, 254, 269, 283
Puntaeado, 84
Puppets, use of, 18, 22, 25

Qānūn, 200, 201
Qi, 245
Qin, 243, 244, 245

Rachenitsa, 126
Ragas, 213
   bhairavi, 220–23
   bhupali, 213, 214, 226–29
   maru-bihag, 226, 230–31
   purvi, 220–23
Ragtime, 51, 61–63
Ranat, 284, 285, 287
Rao, 283
"Rap," 51
Rasqueado, 84
Rattles, 6, 35, 36, 40, 41, 43–46, 82, 93, 94,
   151, 155, 157, 158, 161, 162, 164
Rebab, 306
Recitative style, 282

Recorder, 100, 104, 132, 138, 139, 192, 197, 265, 293
Reels, 123
Reverse rondo. *See* Form, musical
Rhythm, 4, 5, 6, 82, 121, 184, 213, 215, 286. *See also* Movement
  meter of, 254, 314
  additive, 82
  alternating, 83
  asymmetrical, 126, 224, 232
  duple, 15, 36, 41, 67, 82, 83, 122–26 passim, 242, 248, 252, 260, 271, 282, 283, 286, 287, 292, 297, 305, 307, 311, 312
  free, 55, 59, 126, 137, 214, 260, 261
  overlapping, 124
  polymetric, 48
  quadruple, 250
  triple, 15, 122–26 passim, 130, 133, 134
Rhythm and Blues, 51, 59
Rhythmic activities, 36, 61–62, 65, 89–93, 99, 101–2, 127, 129, 130, 134, 136, 155–57, 161–62, 164–65, 166, 186–92, 195, 197, 199, 217–20, 224–26, 228–29, 232, 248, 262, 267, 292–93
Rhythmic density, 83, 261
Rhythmic layering. *See* Rhythmic patterns, layered
Rhythmic patterns, 97, 99, 149–50, 187. *See* *Īqāᶜ*; *Talas*
  "colonial," 83, 100, 101, 102
  composite or combined, 90, 92, 93, 127, 260
  cross rhythms, 83, 90
  dotted, 140
  free, 82, 185, 202, 216, 226–28, 232
  improvised, 150, 164–65
  interlocking, 89, 91, 153, 168, 260
  isometric, 126
  layered, 52, 53, 83, 89, 90, 91, 92, 149, 168
  ornamented, 184
  ostinatos, 53, 83, 90, 91, 92, 93, 94, 111, 113, 154, 156, 157, 186, 250, 260, 289, 293, 298, 305, 307, 312, 314
  overlapping, 150, 168
  polyrhythmic, 52, 150, 155
  Spanish, 136
  subdivided beat, 129
  syncopated, 52, 53, 59, 61, 65, 83, 84, 86, 90, 97, 142, 184, 185, 243, 248, 260
  time-line, 90, 91
  waltz-time, 100, 101, 102, 130
Riddle songs. *See* Songs
Riqq, 189–90, 200, 201
Ritmo coloniál. See Rhythmic patterns, "colonial"
Rommel pot, 124
Round dance, 39
Rounds, 125

Rwanda. *See* Africa
Ryuteki, 262

Sakkah, 188, 189, 190–92
Salamiyyah, 201
Salsa, 111–13, 114
Samāᶜī, 187, 202, 203–4
Sankyoku, 261
Sansa, 152
Sanxian, 244
Sardana, 135
Saron barung, 299, 311
Saron demung, 299, 311
Scales, 51, 52, 88. See also *Ragas*
  bitonic, 82
  gapped, 52
  gypsy, 126
  heptatonic, 242, 283, 296
  hexatonic, 52
  major, 83, 105, 123–26 passim, 133
  microtonal, 82, 181–84, 213
  minor, 83, 105, 123, 124, 126
  modal, 14–15, 16, 18, 27, 51, 83, 123, 126, 127
  pentachord-based, 182
  pentatonic, 14, 20, 52, 82, 83, 105, 125, 126, 242–43, 247–48, 250, 253, 260, 270, 271, 282, 283, 286, 287, 296, 311
  tetrachord-based, 181–84
  tetratonic, 40, 41, 82
  titronic, 82
  trichord-based, 182
Scandinavia. *See* Europe
"Scat," 52
Schuhplattler, 133
Seguidilla, 136
Senegal. *See* Africa
Sesquiáltera, 83
Shakuhachi, 259, 260, 261, 269–70, 272
Shamisen, 259, 261, 265, 268
Shangara, 163–65
Shange, 245
Sharp, Cecil, 12, 14
Shekere, 6
Sheng, 243, 244, 254, 255
Siku, 84, 85, 86–88, 104, 105, 109, 110
"Silk and bamboo," 244
Singing activities, 6, 18–23 passim, 25, 27–28, 30–31, 36–39, 48, 54, 57–58, 63–67, 93, 95, 101–3, 111, 127–28, 133–34, 136–39, 140–41, 165–67, 196–99, 215, 217–18, 220, 221–22, 225–26, 228–30, 246–48, 250–51, 263–67, 270–71, 289, 291–93, 313–14
Sitar, 226, 230–33
Slendro, 296–97
Slentum, 299, 311

1500-10-3M-7/89